The Foreign Policy Disconnect

AMERICAN POLITICS AND POLITICAL ECONOMY

A series edited by Benjamin I. Page

The Foreign Policy Disconnect

What Americans Want from Our Leaders but Don't Get

Benjamin I. Page *with* Marshall M. Bouton

The University of Chicago Press   Chicago and London

1/10/11
Lan
 # 22.50

BENJAMIN I. PAGE is the Gordon Scott Fulcher Professor of Decision
Making in the department of political science at Northwestern
University. He is the author or coauthor of, among other books,
The Rational Public, Who Deliberates?, and *What Government Can Do,*
all published by the University of Chicago Press.

MARSHALL M. BOUTON has been president of the Chicago Council
on Foreign Relations since 2001. He is the author of *Agrarian
Radicalism and South India* and *Korea at the Crossroads.*

The University of Chicago Press, Chicago 60637
The University of Chicago Press, Ltd., London
© 2006 by The University of Chicago
All rights reserved. Published 2006
Printed in the United States of America

15 14 13 12 11 10 09 08 07 06   1 2 3 4 5

ISBN-10: 0-226-64461-8 (cloth)
ISBN-13: 978-0-226-64461-5 (cloth)
ISBN-10: 0-226-64462-6 (paper)
ISBN-13: 978-0-226-64462-2 (paper)

Library of Congress Cataloging-in-Publication Data

Page, Benjamin I.
    The foreign policy disconnect : what Americans want from our
leaders but don't get / Benjamin I. Page ; with Marshall M. Bouton.
        v.   cm.
    Includes bibliographical references and index.
    Contents: Introduction : what sort of foreign policy? — Taking
public opinion seriously — The goals of security and justice —
Friends and foes in the world — Military strength and the use
of force — Political cooperation — Economic well-being and
economic justice — A disconnect between policy makers and the
public? — Conclusion : foreign policy and democracy.
    ISBN 0-226-64461-8 (cloth : alk. paper) — ISBN 0-226-64462-6 (pbk. :
alk. paper)
    1. United States—Foreign relations—2001—Public opinion.
    2. United States—Foreign relations—2001—Decision making.
    3. Public opinion—United States. I. Bouton, Marshall M., 1942–
II. Title.

E902.P34 2006
327.73009'0511—dc22   2006010699

Contents

Illustrations

Preface

In a world of terrorist threats, geopolitical shifts, economic pressures, environmental dangers, extreme poverty, and threats to human rights, what should be the most important goals of U.S. foreign policy? What means should be used to pursue those goals? Military, diplomatic, or economic? Unilateral or cooperative? In what combinations, under what circumstances?

For answers to these questions we will turn to a surprising source: the American people. We will describe in detail the collective policy preferences of the American public—or, if you wish, "public opinion" about foreign policy. It turns out that most Americans want a foreign policy that places a high priority on economic and social security at home and justice abroad, not just security from attack. Moreover, most Americans favor cooperative, multilateral foreign policies—peaceful, when possible—rather than unilateral military ones. We will see that actual U.S. foreign policy has often diverged markedly from what the public wants. There have been frequent gaps, perhaps even a "disconnect," between citizens and decision makers. We argue that this is troubling for a democracy, and that U.S. foreign policy would be better and more sustainable if decision makers paid more attention to what ordinary citizens want.

Our argument flies in the face of claims that public opinion about foreign policy is ignorant, emotional, vacillating, and perhaps downright dangerous to coherent policy making. In order to sustain our argument, therefore, we need to look closely at the structure and dynamics of public opinion as well as its substantive content. Using extensive survey data collected over a thirty-year period, with a particular focus on recent years, we show that collective opinion is not in fact flimsy, disorganized, or vacillating; it is generally coherent and consistent and, allowing for reasonable adjustments to world events, tends to stay steady over time. Collective opinion about foreign policy reflects a great deal of information and knowledge about the world—more knowledge than most individuals can muster on their own—but it is built upon a solid foundation of individual behavior. Contrary to a good deal of conventional wisdom, individual citizens' expressed foreign policy attitudes and opinions are not random or haphazard: they tend to be structured in logical ways, with policy preferences following from the foreign policy goals that individuals seek, the threats they perceive, and other relevant attitudes and perceptions. While making this last point, which we sum up by saying that Americans tend to have "purposive belief systems" about foreign policy, we offer some new contributions to the understanding of individual political psychology and political behavior.

In the course of arguing that U.S. foreign policy decision makers should pay more attention to public opinion, therefore, we bring together several topics that are often treated in isolation from one another: the pros and cons of alternative military, economic, and diplomatic foreign policies; democratic responsiveness—or lack of responsiveness—by policy makers to ordinary citizens; the nature of public opinion (or Americans' collective policy preferences) about foreign policy; and the structure and determinants of individuals' opinions. Thus the book has something to say to several quite different audiences. We hope it will be of interest to anyone who cares about U.S. foreign policy and the role of the United States in the world: practitioners, experts, and observers of U.S. foreign policy, including general readers. It is also intended for citizens and scholars who care about democratic theory and about connections or nonconnections between political leaders and their constituents; for specialists in public opinion or individual political behavior; and for students and teachers involved in courses in American politics or foreign policy, empirical democratic theory, or international relations.

To gain the fullest benefit from the book, members of these different audiences may want to pursue somewhat different reading strategies. General readers who are chiefly interested in U.S. foreign policy, for example, might skim over the material on public opinion theory in chapter 1 in order to focus on chapters 2 through 6, which tell what the American public thinks about many different foreign policy issues, and chapter 7, which describes the divergence between citizens and decision makers. Skipping past fancy statistics, skimming digressions about population subgroups, and ignoring the detailed (sometimes *very* detailed) endnotes should not present a problem; one can get the gist from the main text, which is—we hope—written in a simple, clear style. The most relevant material should not require much statistical skill beyond a comprehension of percentages.

Scholars who specialize in public opinion or individual political behavior, on the other hand, may prefer a very different tack. They may even want to *start* with the multiple regression tables, in order to learn about the distinctive opinions of demographic subgroups (women, evangelicals, African Americans, and so forth) and to get a quick look at the evidence behind our arguments about "purposive belief systems" in the mass public. Political behavior specialists will probably also want to read carefully through chapter 1 and examine the book's endnotes, which present many quantitative findings not given in the text, including some opinion trends over time, and discuss certain tricky methodological issues. The notes to each chapter (located at the end of the book) are designed to be readable as a block on their own, independent of the chapter they refer to, in order to spare readers from having to shuffle back and forth.

Readers in a hurry could go straight to the conclusion (chapter 8), in order to get an overview of our main arguments and our most important findings, and then go back to examine the evidence for those of greatest interest.

Our main advice to all readers is not to get bogged down. Feel free to read only those parts of the book that interest you, with perhaps a quick glance at the rest, and to skim or skip past material that seems unduly difficult, keeping hold of the thread of the argument.

*   *   *

For help with this project we are grateful to many individuals and institutions. First and foremost, for conceiving, funding, carrying out, and analyzing the seven Chicago Council on Foreign Relations (CCFR) studies conducted between 1974 and 1998, we are indebted to John E. Rielly, the chief entrepreneur and director of the studies; to his teams of CCFR employees and consultants (notably Arthur Cyr, Nora Dell, Bernard Cohen, Robert Hunter, William Schneider, Catherine Hug, Bernard Roscho, Richard Sobel, Stephen Del Rosso, and April Donnellan); to the Gallup and Harris survey organizations; and to the Ford Foundation, the Lilly Endowment, the Board of the Chicago Council on Foreign Relations, the U.S.–Japan Foundation, and especially the John D. and Catherine T. MacArthur Foundation.

For help in funding, designing, and analyzing the 2002 and 2004 studies directed by Marshall Bouton, we are grateful to the MacArthur Foundation, the McCormick–Tribune Foundation, the German Marshall Fund (especially Craig Kennedy), the U.S.–Japan Foundation, members of the CCFR Board (particularly Lester Crown, John Manley, and Richard Behrenhausen), the Ford Foundation, and James Denny; to Harris Interactive (particularly Harold Quinley, Beverly Romanowski, David Krane, and Shawn Wade), Knowledge Networks (especially Mike Dennis and Stefan Subias), and CCI; and to the study teams, which included Steven Kull, Larry Jacobs, Richard Longworth, Robert Y. Shapiro, Christopher Whitney (executive study director), and Catherine Hug. Those teams, along with the present authors, were largely responsible for designing the questionnaires and for coming up with interpretations and analyses—and in some cases sentences or paragraphs—that have carried over into this book.

For very helpful research assistance we are grateful to Dukhong Kim, Julia Rabinovich, Jenny Taylor, David Tully, and (on chapter 7) Martin Kifer. The work of research assistants for past CCFR studies (Robert Pearson, Glenn Dempsey, Bruce Peterson, Donald (Pete) Jordan, Trevor Thompson, and Jason Barabas) has also contributed significantly to our analyses.

Too many people have generously commented on drafts of individual chapters to list them all here; we have attempted to do so at the beginning of the endnotes for each chapter. We apologize to anyone we have inadvertently omitted. For comments on multiple chapters (including some very rough early drafts), we are especially grateful to Ed Greenberg, Tom Ferguson, Larry Jacobs, Steve Kull, Art Cyr, Ole Holsti, and Bob Shapiro. Of course responsibility for the final product rests with us, not our helpers or reviewers, particularly since we did not always follow their advice.

Finally, we thank our institutions, Northwestern University and the Chicago Council on Foreign Relations, for providing stimulating and rewarding work environments; and we thank our wives, Mary and Barbara, for providing the most important kind of support. Mary deserves special thanks for tolerating all-consuming writing blitzes and for offering shrewd suggestions about research sources, arguments, and style.

Benjamin I. Page
Marshall M. Bouton
Chicago, September 2005

Introduction:
What Sort of Foreign Policy?

What sort of foreign policy should the United States pursue? What should our general goals and objectives be? What types of policies should we use to achieve those goals? This book aims to contribute to foreign policy decision making by adding a new voice to ongoing debates: the voice of the American public.

The country faces daunting challenges. The September 11, 2001, terrorist attacks against the World Trade Center and the Pentagon brought international conflict to our own cities. How can we best defend ourselves against future attackers from abroad, attackers who might use plastic explosives, "dirty" radioactive bombs, chemical or biological weapons, or even nuclear weapons? Economically, onrushing globalization is bringing cheap consumer goods to the United States and creating lucrative investment opportunities abroad, but it may also be undercutting Americans' wages and job security. Moreover, our huge trade deficit may be unsustainable. What should we do about it?

What, if anything, should U.S. foreign policy do to deal with extreme poverty and AIDS in Africa? With genocide in Sudan? With human rights violations, ethnic strife, and the collapse of government authority in many places around the globe? How about potential threats from nuclear programs in North Korea, Iran, and elsewhere? Possible conflicts between nuclear-armed states like India and Pakistan? Threats to U.S. supplies of oil and natural gas? Climate change and global warming? The rise of China as an economic and military power? Continued turmoil and bloodshed in Iraq? Instability in the Middle East and much of the Islamic world?

Much of this book is devoted to describing how majorities of American citizens would answer such questions. In this chapter we briefly sketch the context into which the public's voice might fruitfully be inserted: debates among officials, experts, and pundits about the proper course of U.S. foreign policy. We also discuss how the debates have unfolded over time and the lessons that Americans—ordinary citizens as well as elites—have learned from history.

CONTENDING APPROACHES TO U.S. FOREIGN POLICY

The administration of President George W. Bush took clear—and sometimes controversial—stands on many of these issues.

In terms of national security, President Bush put the "war on terror" at the top of the agenda. In his January 2002 State of the Union address, Bush declared, "Our war against terror is only beginning. . . . Tens of thousands of trained terrorists are still at large. These enemies view the entire world as a battlefield, and we must pursue them wherever they are." Hinting at unilateral action, he said, "Some governments will be timid in the face of terror. And make no mistake about it: if they do not act, America will." He set forth two major objectives: first, to shut down terrorist camps, disrupt terrorist plans, and bring terrorists to justice; second, to "prevent regimes that sponsor terror from threatening America or our friends and allies with weapons of mass destruction." He warned against an "axis of evil" that included North Korea, Iran, and Saddam Hussein's Iraq.[1]

Speaking to West Point graduates in June 2002, President Bush argued that the world has changed. The spread of chemical and biological and nuclear weapons means that "even weak states and small groups could attain a catastrophic power to strike great nations." The old doctrines of deterrence and containment of nations mean nothing against "shadowy terrorist networks." Pointing toward preemptive action, he declared, "If we wait for threats to fully materialize, we will have waited too long. . . . We must take the battle to the enemy, disrupt his plans, and confront the worst threats before they emerge." Suggesting worldwide action, he stated that "we must uncover terrorist cells in 60 or more countries."[2]

Some administration members and supporters have maintained that the overwhelming military and economic might of the United States makes it possible to deal with terrorism and other international threats unilaterally. Our traditional allies, they suggest, are too weak and too pacific to be helpful; better to act swiftly and powerfully on our own than to get entangled and bogged down with formal alliances or international organizations. To the extent that we need help, ad hoc "coalitions of the willing" will generally suffice.

Certain "neoconservatives," including Paul Wolfowitz (U.S. deputy secretary of defense during Bush's first term and now president of the World Bank), have long argued that the best way to reduce terrorist and other threats is to spread democracy, free markets, and individual liberty to other countries, especially to repressive Arab or Islamic nations in the Middle East, and that if necessary we should overthrow dangerous tyrants by military force. A 1998 letter to President Bill Clinton from Wolfowitz and other neoconservatives (as well as nationalist Donald Rumsfeld, soon to be Bush's secretary of defense) urged the president to aim at "the removal of Saddam Hussein's regime from power.... This means a willingness to undertake military action." President Bush eventually came to endorse the neoconservative program: in November 2003 he declared, "The United States has adopted a new policy, a forward strategy of freedom in the Middle East. . . . The establishment of a free Iraq at the heart of the Middle East will be a watershed event in the global democratic revolution." At the 2004 Republican National Convention Bush asserted, "In our world, and here at home, we will extend the frontiers of freedom. . . . I believe in the transformational power of liberty: The wisest use of American strength is to advance freedom."[3]

But American political leaders, policy experts, scholars, and pundits hold a variety of opinions on these and other matters. Many disagree sharply with the Bush administration. Often they disagree with each other as well. We will briefly outline some of the issues, beginning with fundamental questions about what U.S. foreign policy goals or objectives should be, then proceeding to specific policies. Finally we will discuss what Americans have learned from history.

Security from attack. Practically everyone agrees that security from physical attack must be the first priority for any nation's foreign policy. "Realist" theorists of international relations, in particular—whether "classical" realists, who attribute a "limitless lust for power" to human nature, or "structural" realists, who see international anarchy (the absence of any overriding authority over nation-states) as forcing great powers to compete for survival—have long emphasized the primacy of defense against foreign threats. Political scientist John Mearsheimer, who proposes a theory of "offensive" realism, argues that uncertainty drives all major nations, including the United States, relentlessly to maximize their relative power. He says that major states are "destined to compete for power" for the foreseeable future and warns of "trouble ahead," especially if China's rapid economic growth continues and it seeks to become a regional hegemon in northeast Asia.[4] The focus of U.S. foreign policy, then, should be on building U.S. power and defending against attack by other states.

Since the advent of international terrorist attacks by elusive, nonstate actors, however, others—including President Bush—have argued that the threat of terrorism now exceeds any potential danger from nation-states (except, perhaps, "rogue states" that might share nuclear or biological weapons with terrorists); hence the top priority for U.S. foreign policy should be to prevent terrorist attacks through a "war on terror." Is this emphasis appropriate, or is it a distraction from core security concerns involving other great powers? How should a "war on terror" or "struggle against violent extremism" be carried out?

Clearly, security from attack—whether by terrorist groups or by nation-states—may require other means in addition to or instead of military might: economic strength, for example, which in the long run is a prerequisite for strong military capability; perhaps power-enhancing alliances and treaties with other states; perhaps intelligence and police work at home and abroad; perhaps measures to win respect abroad or to reshape potentially hostile regimes.

Domestic well-being. What about goals beyond security from physical attack? Should U.S. foreign policy also be concerned with the domestic well-being of American citizens, with how international affairs affect our jobs and incomes, the goods we can buy, the people who come to live in our neighborhoods, drugs or diseases spread from abroad, the air we breathe, or the weather we endure?

If so, is our well-being best served by international openness and free trade or by tariffs and protectionism? By free trade modified to safeguard American jobs and the world environment? What about immigration? Should immigration to the United States be encouraged as a source of skilled and unskilled labor, or should it be restricted in order to keep up the wages of native-born Americans and reduce cultural anxieties? How much foreign policy effort should go into stopping the importation of illegal drugs, slowing global warming, or ensuring supplies of oil and gasoline at reasonable prices?

In recent years, some observers have suggested that the concept of "national security" needs to be broadened—perhaps to "human security"—in order to include aims related to domestic well-being as well as security from attack.[5] Later in the book we will discuss Americans' rather strong views about what we will call "security of domestic well-being."

National interest or international justice? "National interest"—like "national security"—does not have a self-evident meaning. As political scientist Peter Trubowitz points out, "The very definition of the national interest is a product of politics. . . . There is no single national interest."[6] Different individuals and groups have quite different views of what is or is not in the U.S. national interest. Who gets to decide? (Perhaps the American people themselves, through democratic processes?)[7] Moreover, the term "interest" tends to focus attention on our individual or collective *self*-interest: our own security from attack, our economic welfare, our personal lifestyles. What about the welfare of people who live in other countries?

In a tradition sometimes associated with Woodrow Wilson, many Americans—often referred to as "idealists" or "liberals"—have argued that, whether or not it serves our own narrow self-interest, U.S. foreign policy should aim to help deprived or oppressed people in other countries.[8] In order to be consistent with our values, they say, we should help poor countries develop their economies, aid victims of famine or AIDS, protect people from human rights violations, and save them from tyranny. Economist Jeffrey Sachs, for example, has argued that it should be an urgent priority of the United States to meet the Millennium Development Goals set forth under UN auspices in 2000, in which the United States and other nations pledged to cut extreme world poverty in half and reduce child mortality by two-thirds within the following fifteen years by greatly increasing funds for development assistance. (U.S. official development assistance, at just 0.15 percent of our gross national income in 2003, was lower than that of any of the twenty other major donor nations.)[9] Others say we should save our resources to deal with problems at home.

What about defending human rights in other countries? For example, should the United States accept an international "responsibility to protect" people abroad who are suffering serious harm as a result of internal war, insurgency, repression, or state failure, when their own state is unwilling or unable to protect them? Michael Ignatieff and other members of an international commission have argued that we should accept a responsibility to prevent such suffering, to react (militarily, if necessary) when it occurs, and to help with rebuilding and reconciliation afterwards.[10] Others worry about infringements on other states' sovereignty or about the costs to Americans.

Sometimes goals of international justice may conflict with those of national self-interest, requiring choices and tradeoffs. At other times, they may go together. Neoconservatives like William Kristol and Lawrence Kaplan have argued that promoting "transformation" rather than coexistence with tyrannical regimes abroad (for example, bringing democracy to the Middle East) can help oppressed peoples in other countries while blunting threats to the United States, since liberal, democratic governments are less likely to promote violence or to attack us. (This idea is consistent with theories of "democratic peace.")[11] Some claim that combating world poverty will ultimately reduce security threats to the United States.

Global public goods? Altruistic and self-interested considerations may also come together in cases of "global public goods." Some objectives that the United States may seek through its foreign policy—such as peaceful regional balances of power, freedom of the seas, suppression of terrorism, open trade, control of infectious diseases, stability in financial markets, relief from global warming—are wholly or partly "public goods," in the sense that consumption is nonrival (it costs no more for many people to enjoy them than for a few to do so) and/or nonexclusionary (if the good is produced at all, it is not feasible to exclude anyone from consuming it).[12] These features make public goods quite desirable to have—for the United States and for other countries as well—but it is hard to ensure that they are produced.

Protection of the world environment is a quintessential example of a global public good. Practically everyone would benefit from curtailing global warming, for example, but no individual state may have sufficient incentive to help on its own. Instead, narrow self-interest may counsel each nation to act as a "free rider," cheerfully accepting others' efforts (if any) to limit carbon dioxide emissions, while themselves building cheap, dirty factories and power plants, polluting full steam ahead, and imposing much of the environmental cost on others. Only rules that somehow bind most—ideally, all—nations are likely to accomplish much.

Do we want U.S. foreign policy to pursue certain public goods? Should we, as potentially the biggest beneficiaries, actually take the lead in negotiating international treaties and seeking participation by all nations, even if the resulting agreements are "flawed" or imperfect? (The Bush administration has rejected several treaties signed by many other countries, including the Kyoto agreement on global warming, the International Criminal Court, the Comprehensive Nuclear Test Ban Treaty, and the convention banning land mines.) If not, what alternatives can we offer?

More broadly, what kinds of policies—military or diplomatic, multilateral or unilateral, legally binding or voluntary—should we use to achieve the goals mentioned above, including security from attack?

Military force, diplomacy, or "soft power"? Since the United States today has by far the most powerful military forces in the world, it may often be tempting to use U.S. military power to get what we want.

As we have noted, "realist" international relations theorists point to the key importance of military capability in international relations. This does not, however, mean they favor actually *using* force frequently or indiscriminately. Realists often prefer diplomacy and alliances to "balance" against aspiring hegemons, for example. Indeed, "structural" realists like Kenneth Waltz have argued that states should not aim for excessive military strength, which could alarm others into combining against them, but should instead try to maintain their positions in the international system through alliances and a peaceful balance of power.[13] Leading realists like Hans Morgenthau, John Mearsheimer, and Stephen Walt have opposed several U.S. military actions, including those in Vietnam and Iraq, as unnecessary, costly, distracting, and counterproductive.[14]

To an even greater extent, most "neoliberal" institutionalist theorists advocate using diplomatic and economic means when possible, rather than force, to get what the United States wants. This is particularly clear in the realm of economic relations, where political scientist Robert Keohane and others have praised webs of economic relationships, organized through institutions or legal and normative "regimes," as furthering the interests of the United States as well as those of other countries.[15] Neoliberals often argue that diplomatic and economic arrangements can help ensure security as well.

Taking this point a step further, political scientist and former Defense Department official Joseph Nye has emphasized the growing importance of "soft power" in achieving a broad range of American foreign policy goals. Soft power works by attraction and persuasion rather than coercion or material inducements. It involves gaining legitimacy, respect, and emulation through propagation of an appealing culture, faithful practice of widely shared political values, and a foreign policy that is respectful of others and promotes peace and democracy. Soft power, Nye says, can often get others to want the same outcomes we want, in contrast to arrogant, unilateral use of hard military power, which can alienate others, provoke resistance, and be self-defeating. Soft power can have an especially crucial role in promoting democracy, human rights, and open markets.[16]

Empire or republic? The United States now has military bases and troops deployed in all regions of the world. Our economic and cultural influence is felt everywhere. And we exert considerable influence over the governance of many countries. Does this mean we have become an "empire"?

President Bush has said no: "We're not an imperial power. We're a liberating power."[17] But other advocates of American power are less inhibited. Historian Niall Ferguson points out that President Bush's vision of bringing "freedom," "democracy," and "liberty" to other countries evokes just the kind of "universal civilizing mission" that has been a feature of all great empires. Moreover, the techniques of "indirect rule" employed by the United States in Iraq and elsewhere were also the preferred methods of the British empire. Ferguson has no quarrel with the idea of an American empire; he prefers it to the political disintegration into a Dark Age that he sees as the most likely alternative. He just wishes that Americans were more conscious of their position, more committed, and more able and willing to devote resources to the imperial enterprise.[18]

Others are appalled at the idea of an American empire. Even before the invasion of Iraq, political scientist John Ikenberry wrote of a "neo-imperial vision," which he called perilous and likely to fail. Political scientist Chalmers Johnson later wrote of the "sorrows of empire" and the "end of the republic," arguing that "militarism, the arrogance of power, and the euphemisms required to justify imperialism inevitably conflict with America's democratic structure of government and distort its culture and basic values." Secrecy surrounding covert actions undermines democratic control. If present trends continue, Johnson said, we will face a state of "perpetual war" and the loss of democracy and constitutional rights; "propaganda, disinformation, and glorification of war" will replace truthfulness; and economic "bankruptcy" will undermine the education, health, and safety of our fellow citizens.[19]

What kinds of force, when? Under the Charter of the United Nations, which the United States has signed as a legally binding treaty, UN members are obliged to refrain from the "threat or use of force" against any state, except in cases of individual or collective defense against "armed attack" or when authorized by the Security Council. Writing in the tradition of Christian "just war" theorists, Michael Walzer has argued that *preemptive* self-defense is justified in the face of serious threats of war, when failure to use force would place territorial integrity or political independence at serious risk, but he rejects merely *preventive* war in response to distant, prospective, or imaginary dangers.[20]

Has the possibility of devastating attacks by "rogue states" or by nonstate terrorists changed the situation? The 2002 National Security Strategy of the United States declared that "America will act against such emerging threats before they are fully formed." "We will disrupt and destroy terrorist organizations by . . . identifying and destroying the threat before it reaches our borders."[21] Was the invasion of Iraq justifiable for such reasons? Or did it amount to a speculative preventive attack, premised on intelligence that was overinterpreted, oversold, or false? Do we want to use military force under such circumstances?

What rules should apply to treatment of suspected terrorists? Is it justifiable to use torture to obtain critical information? Should we be allowed to lock up "enemy combatants" indefinitely without trial?

What about nuclear weapons? When and how might we use them? Several nations have declared a policy of "no first use," pledging not to employ nuclear weapons unless such weapons are first used against them, but the United States has never adopted such a policy. The March 2002 Nuclear Policy Review described plans to build a nuclear "robust earth penetrator" suitable for strikes on deeply buried bunkers, and the Pentagon has since expressed interest in "mini-nukes."[22] Should we plan to use nuclear weapons for tactical purposes?

Unilateral or multilateral action? Even before September 11, 2001, neoconservative columnist Charles Krauthammer had proclaimed a "new unilateralism," arguing that the United States can and should often act on its own, without enlisting help from others. The U.S. National Security Strategy put forth a year after the terrorist attacks declared, "We will not hesitate to act alone, if necessary, to exercise our right of self-defense by acting preemptively against such terrorists." Scholar and columnist Robert Kagan wrote that—on major strategic and international questions—"Americans are from Mars and Europeans are from Venus." Some American leaders have argued that our traditional European allies are too weak, too inward looking, and too obsessed with diplomatic and legal niceties to be of any use. Better to go it alone, avoiding the constraints and delays of multilateralism.[23]

On the other hand, even the vast power of the United States may not be sufficient to accomplish everything we want without assistance. Advocates of multilateralism point out the great benefits of burden sharing—getting others to help pay for mutually beneficial actions—and the advantages of increased legitimacy, which can weaken resistance and facilitate success. In the case of global public goods (including the regulation of economic, environmental, and political matters and even action against terrorism), multilateral action seems required by the very nature of the problems to be addressed. Joseph Nye has written of the "paradox of American power": the information revolution and globalization are transforming and shrinking our world, so that "we are not only bound to lead, but bound to cooperate."[24]

"Coalitions of the willing," treaties and alliances, or international organizations? To the extent that we work with other countries, should we do so on an ad hoc basis, bilaterally (one at a time) or with improvised "coalitions of the willing"? Or are there advantages to working through formal treaties, alliances, or universalistic international organizations?

"Coalitions of the willing" (such as the one assembled for the 2003 invasion of Iraq) have the advantage of minimizing constraints on U.S. freedom of action but will not necessarily be accorded legitimacy among the *unwilling*. And if bribery or coercion is necessary to secure official willingness, the result, even within the coalition, may be resentment or only grudging and ineffective cooperation. Formal alliances like NATO can act with more legitimacy, based on standing rules and procedures for when and how to act. By the same token, however, consensus may be hard to reach, and the United States may itself have to follow the rules that bind others. This is all the more true of international organizations like the United Nations, whose decisions enjoy the highest international legitimacy but are the most difficult for the United States to shape: all five permanent members of the Security Council have veto power over its decisions, and consensus requires a great deal of give and take. When, under what circumstances, should the United States pursue one or another of these forms of international cooperation?

International law and global governance? More broadly, should the United States be working toward a Kantian vision of the international rule of law, in which all nations are bound by the same obligations and procedures are established to enforce those obligations?[25] Or should we insist on preserving our own sovereignty and complete freedom of action? To what extent (if at all), and on what issues, should we be willing to accept constraints on ourselves in order to exert influence over the behavior of others? The Bush administration was generally reluctant to accept any such constraints.

LEARNING FROM HISTORY

American leaders, experts, and scholars—and, as we will see, the American public as well—have learned from history. Our opinions about foreign policy flow not just from the facts of the moment but also from knowledge and understanding acquired and passed along during more than two hundred years of history as a nation.

This does not mean that everyone learns the same thing from each world event, or that all disagreements get resolved by experience. Far from it. Debates like those discussed above have recurred again and again, often with very similar arguments made in very similar language. As the United States and the world have changed, however, *prevailing* views about U.S. foreign policy (the "winners" of the debates, if you will) have tended to change accordingly, sometimes for the long term. As a nation, we have learned from history. We have adapted to new circumstances. And we have learned specific lessons from experiences—occasionally bitter experiences—of particular world events.

Economic growth and the expansion of the United States. A very old dispute, going back to the very founding of the United States, concerns the extent to which the country should or should not play an active part in the world: what energy and resources, if any, should be devoted to actions beyond our borders. "Internationalists" have argued for an active diplomatic, economic, and sometimes military role abroad. "Isolationists," "neo-isolationists," and those focused on domestic priorities have favored concentrating our money and efforts at home. Defend our own shores and borders, they say, but refrain when possible from commitments abroad.

George Washington himself, in his farewell address to the nation, warned against "entangling alliances" that could draw us into petty quarrels among

European monarchies. During the first century of our existence U.S. foreign policy was in fact largely isolationist, at least in the sense that little action was taken outside North America (except for a few gunboat expeditions against pirates or into Central or South America). The United States did for the most part avoid entangling alliances and involvement in European squabbles; we were protected, to a large extent, by the Atlantic Ocean and the British fleet. International trade and investment from abroad were always important to us—and there were persistent sectional conflicts between southern, cotton-growing free traders and northern, industrial protectionists—but the United States eventually settled on a protectionist trade policy, imposing high tariffs on imported manufactured goods. Tariff duties constituted the chief source of federal government revenue and protected nascent U.S. industries against competition from cheap imports. The main business of America was economic development.[26]

In another sense, however, U.S. foreign policy was from the start quite activist or "internationalist," as the handful of newly united states along the Atlantic seaboard gained control of a large swath of North America and began to exert influence over the rest of the Americas. Hand in hand with economic development went vigorous diplomatic and military efforts to win land and territory. The land area of the country was doubled by the Louisiana Purchase of 1803; Florida was attacked and then bought from Spain; a "hands off the Americas" policy for Europe was articulated in the 1823 Monroe Doctrine; Native Americans were pushed westward or killed; immigrants swelled the workforce; and in a great rush of land acquisition between 1845 and 1848, Texas and "California" (everything between Texas and the Pacific Ocean) were taken from Mexico. Settlers flocked west, land was claimed, transcontinental railways were built, and soon the United States extended "from sea to shining sea"—and even north to Alaska. This expansion was said to fit the "Manifest Destiny" of Americans to spread civilization and progress across North America—and perhaps beyond.[27]

What lessons did Americans learn from our first hundred years of history? Despite conflicts over slavery, tariffs and trade, and just how far manifest destiny should carry us, certain conclusions became deeply rooted in the minds of most American leaders and (as best we can tell) citizens as well. The expanded United States came to be seen as our sacred homeland, to be defended against any attack or interference from abroad. Central and South America were considered as falling within a U.S. sphere of influence, not to be touched by Europeans or others. All tools of U.S. foreign policy, including military force, diplomatic negotiations, tariffs, and immigration policy, were aimed at territorial consolidation and economic development. Our political and economic systems (democracy and free enterprise) were judged to be good for us and good for people everywhere. All these views have largely persisted right up to our own times. A final lesson—that the United States should avoid entanglements with other nations—was partly reversed in the twentieth century, but it remains a cautionary ingredient of contemporary debates.

Emergence as a great power. By the end of the nineteenth century the United States had become a highly industrialized economic powerhouse and was ready to emerge as a major world power. The question of the day was whether it should seek control of lands beyond our shores, such as Cuba. Did Manifest Destiny imply empire? Most Americans decided it did not, at least not in the sense of direct colonial rule over others. True, the United States gained control over Cuba, the Philippines, and Hawaii after the 1898 war against Spain (exerting indirect rule over Cuba and the Philippines for decades and eventually incorporating Hawaii as a state) and later ran a number of "trusteeships" in the Pacific. But most Americans concluded that their nation, itself a former colony, should not become a colonial power. National independence for all peoples was embraced as a principle, one that echoes today in controversies about the future of Iraq.[28]

But the United States did indeed become a great world power, building a steam-powered "blue water" navy, dabbling in world diplomacy, and playing a major part in the World War I victory over Germany in 1918. Woodrow Wilson tried to lead the world toward open diplomacy, an end to colonialism, and peaceful international relations, overseen by a League of Nations, but was thwarted by other great powers, which kept their colonies and imposed a humiliating peace on Germany, and by his own Senate, which failed to ratify the League treaty. For some Americans, World War I looked in retrospect like a costly and disappointing overreaching of American power, and the chief lesson was that the United States should mostly stay at home. The interwar period was not purely isolationist (international trade blossomed, the U.S. participated in major disarmament conferences), but the United States pulled back from Wilsonian idealism. Isolationism became respectable.[29]

The triumph of internationalism. Some of the deepest and most enduring lessons that Americans have drawn from history involve the interwar period and World War II. The failure of the West to stop Hitler's early expansionism, followed by the enormously costly all-out war against Nazism and fascism, convinced overwhelming majorities of Americans that isolationism was untenable. A great power cannot stand aside from world events. After World War II, very few Americans favored complete demobilization of our armed forces or abandonment of bases abroad; few wanted to leave Europe to its own devices; few wanted to retreat to our homeland. The label "isolationist" became one of opprobrium, though of course disputes continued over the precise allocation of resources at home and abroad.

World War II itself was devastating, with scores of cities destroyed and many millions of people killed. Even though the United States was spared combat on its own territory (and emerged from the war stronger than ever, as one of only two superpowers in the world), American soldiers were killed, families disrupted, and the economy pinched. Preventing full-scale war in the future became the highest foreign policy priority for most Americans, especially after other countries acquired nuclear weapons.

The precise way in which World War II was won—by a host of "united nations" working together—was widely seen as offering lessons about how postwar peace could be maintained. Nearly all Americans rejected the communist ideology of the Soviet Union, but most had accepted the Soviets as crucial allies in the war—allies who in fact endured far more casualties than Americans did—and now saw them as necessary partners for peace, working through a new organization, the United Nations, established in 1946. After World War II the necessity for international activism backed by military strength, as well as the advantages of a cooperative, multilateral foreign policy, were widely accepted.[30]

Multilateralism and the Cold War. Most, though not all, Americans have maintained faith in cooperation, multilateralism, and international organizations throughout the period of Cold War with the Soviet Union and right up to the present. The United States fought the Cold War itself largely by cooperative, multilateral means: helping to rebuild Europe economically, forming the NATO military alliance, intervening in Korea under UN auspices, and building formal alliances around the world. We regularly engaged in dialogue and negotiation with the Soviets, signing several treaties on arms control and other matters.

Of course U.S. military power made containment of the Soviets possible. The mutual nuclear "balance of terror," together with NATO and other alliances, helped prevent any direct military confrontation between Russians and Americans for some fifty years. Stable boundaries between the two countries' spheres of influence were largely established by 1956, when the United States rejected a "roll-back" strategy and did not intervene in the Soviet suppression of the Hungarian revolt. Instead, the United States waited the Soviet Union out (and outspent it on arms) until it collapsed from within between 1989 and 1991. The only "hot" conflicts of the Cold War involved skirmishes on the edges of Asia and counterinsurgencies against "national liberation" movements in various developing countries.[31]

Certain Cold War events led to ambiguous "lessons" that are still contested today. The Korean War, for example, was seen by some Americans as a successful collective (UN-endorsed) effort to turn back communist North Korea's attack on the south in 1950. But it was seen by many other Americans as yielding only a costly stalemate in a country of little interest to the United States ("no more land wars in Asia," some proclaimed), or as improper interference in what was essentially a civil war fought across an artificially imposed boundary, the thirty-eighth parallel. Similarly, the lengthy and bloody U.S. combat in Vietnam was considered by some Americans to be a noble effort (perhaps sabotaged by unpatriotic media and a cowardly public) to protect the "dominoes" of Southeast Asia from communist conquest, while most Americans came to see it as a futile plunge into a quagmire, with some sixty thousand American lives wasted. Some thought the Vietnam War downright immoral, firebombing and poisoning the countryside and killing perhaps three million Vietnamese in order to prop up a corrupt regime against indigenous nationalists. Likewise, Americans differed about the propriety or effectiveness of various anticommunist alliances with right-wing (and often venal) dictators around the world, from Chiang Kai-Shek of Taiwan to Shah Pahlevi of Iran, Mobutu of the Congo, Franco of Spain, Trujillo of the Dominican Republic, and Marcos of the Philippines.[32]

Despite such controversies, however, most Americans accepted several lessons from the Cold War. First, the value of international engagement and military strength was confirmed; only active engagement in the world, backed by strong armed forces, can preserve U.S. interests. Second, the actual use of military force can and usually should be avoided. The Soviet Union, a nuclear-armed superpower brandishing a hated ideology, was contained and ultimately defeated without direct military conflict. Even Vietnam seemed to offer at least one moral that was accepted by nearly everyone (and later embodied in the "Powell Doctrine"): that the United States should use military force only for clear and achievable objectives that have broad support from society, and that we should then apply overwhelming force in order to prevail. Third, diplomacy and cooperative, multilateral policies should be preferred; formal alliances are crucial; and the United Nations can be very useful.[33]

These lessons apply to military and national security policy. But the value of cooperation, multilateralism, and international institutions also seemed apparent from the success of many economic and political measures. Tariffs were reduced and international trade promoted through the General Agreement on Tariffs and Trade and then the World Trade Organization. Financial stability and development assistance were organized by the International Monetary Fund and the World Bank. Epidemics were prevented by the World Health Organization. Cooperation seemed to work well on international postal service, aviation, agricultural assistance, refugees, and many other matters.

A new world order? Has all this historical learning become irrelevant because of fundamental changes in the world? We think not. More recent history has undoubtedly offered some new lessons and modified some old ones, but it has left most Americans with largely intact views of what the United States should seek in the world and how we should seek it.

Immediately after the end of the Cold War there was much talk about the emergence of the United States as the world's "sole superpower," and about the possibility of a "new American century" in which our will would prevail and our values could be spread everywhere. The Gulf War of 1991, in response to Iraq's invasion of Kuwait and threats to Saudi Arabia, seemed to show that no other nation would stand in our way: Russia and China went along with UN resolutions authorizing force; Arab countries as well as our European allies took part; and American tanks quickly chased Saddam Hussein's forces out of Kuwait, with hardly any U.S. casualties. But what were the lessons? That the United States could do whatever it wished? Or that only a broad international coalition, UN sponsorship, and limited objectives (liberation of Kuwait rather than regime change in Baghdad) could guarantee success? At the time, most Americans—though disappointed with Hussein's survival—thought the latter.

Then a series of nasty regional conflicts tested what the United States and other powers could or would do to protect human rights abroad. An intervention in Somalia went sour. Genocide in Rwanda was ignored, but ethnic cleansing in Bosnia and Kosovo was halted—under NATO rather than UN auspices. To many Americans, multilateral means (with the United States playing a limited role) seemed the best approach to humanitarian intervention.[34]

The 1990s were punctuated by a series of terrorist attacks on U.S. targets: the World Trade Center in 1993, embassies in Africa in 1998, the USS *Cole* in 2000. Some U.S. leaders (though not, as we will see, the American public) were slow to judge international terrorism to be a serious threat, but the September 2001 attacks united the country. That same fall the United States invaded Afghanistan and ousted the Taliban regime, which had been harboring al Qaeda terrorists. A year and a half later, claiming terrorist links and warning of nuclear dangers, the United States invaded Iraq.

It is still too early to expect Americans to reach a consensus on the lessons of Iraq. Already as we write, however—as a swift U.S.-led conquest of the country has been followed by more than two years of bloody insurgency—the evidence indicates that for most Americans the lessons may resemble those of the post–World War II period. Afghanistan, where the United States assembled broad international support in relatively successful pursuit of limited aims (to help local forces oust the Taliban and eliminate terrorist bases), seems to provide a painful contrast with Iraq, where the U.S. had very limited international support and pursued very broad aims, including rebuilding and democratizing a fractious society amid armed resistance. For most Americans, the "lessons of Iraq," like the "lessons of Vietnam," may well turn out to include wariness about the unilateral use of military force for complex or questionable ends.

Our main purpose in making this brief dash through American history has been to argue that most Americans, ordinary citizens as well as politicians and experts, have learned certain lessons from our national experiences that bear on the questions and debates discussed at the outset of this chapter. History has helped inform Americans' views of what sort of foreign policy the United States should pursue. In the next chapter we will cite this as one of several reasons why U.S. public opinion about foreign policy should be taken seriously: it is rooted in historical experience. In later chapters, however, we will also see that the lessons learned by our citizens and by our political leaders have not always been the same. We will argue that in many cases the public's views are actually superior, and that in any event they deserve more respect than they have been getting from decision makers.

Taking Public Opinion Seriously

In the following chapters we will show that large majorities of Americans favor a number of foreign policies designed to achieve security at home—security of domestic well-being—as well as security from attack and justice abroad, and that the public mostly favors cooperative, multilateral policies. We will also show that the actual foreign policies of the United States have often differed markedly from the policies that most Americans want. We will then argue that U.S. foreign policy would be more effective, and democracy in the United States healthier, if our government paid more attention to the views of its citizens.

But first we need to confront the objection that no one should *care* what sort of foreign policy the American public wants, because public opinion in general—and especially public opinion about foreign policy—is ephemeral and not worthy of serious attention. How can we assert the opposite?

Many American elites, including many foreign policy decision makers, scholars, and commentators, believe that the expressed opinions of the citizenry do not deserve much respect. Most ordinary people, their argument goes, do not devote serious time or attention to world affairs. Most do not have sufficient knowledge or skills to figure out how to protect U.S. national interests in a complex and rapidly changing world. Indeed—according to some skeptics—most people hold no real opinions at all about foreign policy: any responses they give to pollsters' questions are facile, thoughtless, top-of-the-head reactions, subject to drastic change the next time the same question is asked. Built on such shaky foundations, critics say, collective public opinion is unstable, unable to take the long view, and subject to emotional swings.

We disagree, for both theoretical and empirical reasons. Empirically, one of the main themes to unfold in this book is that the collective foreign policy preferences of the American public are in fact generally coherent, consistent, and stable and that—for the most part—they make a good deal of sense. The public's preferences regarding foreign policy tend to reflect widely shared historical experiences and shared goals and values, together with reasonable beliefs about other countries, reasonable perceptions of what threats and problems face the United States, and reasonable ideas about what kinds of policies work best.

Much of the book is devoted to analyzing what majorities of Americans want to do about a wide range of foreign policy issues, military, diplomatic, and economic. We put this portrait of current public opinion into the context of what the public has favored in the past, using three decades' worth of survey data. We also explore *why* Americans favor or oppose various policies, focusing on the goals they seek, the threats they perceive, their ideological and partisan commitments, and their feelings about specific countries. Within individuals' minds, these goals, perceptions, feelings, and basic attitudes tend to fit together into logically coherent patterns that we call "purposive belief systems."

As we describe the foreign policies favored by majorities of Americans, a second major empirical theme will begin to emerge: that the foreign policy the U.S. public wants is not always the foreign policy it gets. Again and again we will note cases in which the goals of ordinary Americans, and the specific means they favor for pursuing those goals (especially cooperative, multinational means), have differed markedly from actual U.S. foreign policy. In chapter 7 we will present systematic evidence of wide, persistent gaps—perhaps amounting to a "disconnect"—between the views of foreign policy decision makers and those of ordinary Americans. The authors believe that democratic theory and practical considerations both point toward the desirability of greater responsiveness by decision makers to the public.

Before we begin our empirical examination of U.S. public opinion on foreign policy and the connections or nonconnections between public opinion and policy makers, however, we need to explain, in general *theoretical* terms, why the critics are wrong and how it is possible that public opinion should be taken seriously. In this chapter we will also describe the data and methods used in the rest of the book.

DISDAIN FOR PUBLIC OPINION

Elected political leaders and the officials they appoint usually claim to serve the public. They mostly avoid saying unkind things about the voters who put them into office. Nonetheless, officials are often dismissive of "public opinion," especially as measured by opinion polls or surveys.

Skepticism about public opinion goes back at least to the founders of the United States, who feared the "passions" of ordinary citizens and tried to hedge them about with institutions designed to resist any hasty responsiveness to the public: an indirectly elected Senate, an indirectly elected president, and an appointed Supreme Court, each wielding separate powers, exerting checks and balances against each other and restraining the more popularly oriented House of Representatives. In Federalist Paper number 63, for example, James Madison argued that an institution such as the proposed Senate (whose members were originally to be selected by state legislatures rather than the voters) "may sometimes be necessary as a defense to the people against their own temporary errors and delusions." Similarly Alexander Hamilton, in defending an independent and energetic executive authority, declared that the republican principle "does not require an unqualified complaisance to every sudden breeze of passion, or to every transient impulse which the people may receive from the arts of men, who flatter their prejudices to betray their interests."[1] Had the founders lived to see two centuries of expansion in the meaning of "the people"—to include not only relatively affluent white, male property owners but also laborers, women, and even former slaves—they might have been still more disturbed by the idea of direct popular rule. (Then again, they might have modified their views, as they saw the results of widespread public education and property holding.)

One might expect democratic theorists to disagree with the founders, to call for elected officials to heed the wishes of their citizens and respond to ordinary people's policy preferences. Some democratic theorists like Robert Dahl—with whom we largely concur—do in fact advocate substantial government responsiveness to deliberative public opinion. But many others, including Edmund Burke, Joseph Schumpeter, and Giovanni Sartori, have argued that officials should act as trustees for, rather than delegates of, the citizens, and that democratic norms are satisfied if officials are chosen by and accountable to the citizenry, even if they act against the public's currently expressed wishes.[2]

Opposition to the idea of officials heeding public opinion has been particularly strong in the area of foreign policy. It has been expressed in stark terms by "realist" theorists of international relations (particularly classical realists), who advocate vigorous pursuit of "the national interest"—which they presume to be objectively ascertainable—no matter what the public may think. Hans Morgenthau, for example, argued that there is an "unavoidable gap" between the kind of thinking required for the successful conduct of foreign policy—an ability to take the long view and see the series of coordinated steps needed to achieve it, to accept small losses for great future advantage, to rationally evaluate constraints—and the "simple and moralistic" thinking of the general public, marred by erratically shifting "moods" and a hunger for quick results that sacrifices tomorrow's benefits.

Morgenthau urged officeholders to shield U.S. foreign policy from the distorting influence of public thinking even "at the risk of their own [political] futures." He declared that government "is the leader and not the slave of public opinion."[3]

Similarly, George Kennan spoke of the "erratic and subjective" nature of public reaction to foreign policy questions; he asserted that "public opinion . . . can be easily led astray into areas of emotionalism and subjectivity which make it a poor and inadequate guide for national action." Walter Lippmann, who had, before the advent of survey research, authored two books on the alleged deficiencies of public opinion, later (in a Cold War essay) warned that the "public opinion of the masses cannot be counted upon to apprehend regularly and promptly the reality of things"; the public lacks cognitive capacity, knowledge, experience, and seasoned judgment. He went so far as to assert that public opinion had "shown itself to be a dangerous master of decisions when the stakes are life and death" and was "deadly to the very survival of the state as a free society."[4]

Contemporary pundits and foreign policy decision makers are usually more cautious in their language, but they, too, often say that policy makers should ignore public opinion. Officials and commentators frequently insist that politicians should not "pander" to the opinions of the public, at least as manifested in polls. Even when debating such central domestic issues as Social Security or welfare reform, elected officials seldom discuss with any precision what the public wants; they rarely mention specific poll or survey results, and when they do cite public opinion they rather often get it wrong.[5]

Critics of public opinion have received some support from systematic surveys of the attitudes and behavior of individual Americans, particularly in the early years of survey research. In the 1940s, the Columbia school of sociologists found evidence that few citizens paid much attention to politics, even during a presidential election campaign; that many people were confused about candidates' stands on major issues; and that demographic characteristics and personal influences seemed to have more impact than policy issues upon voting decisions. In the 1950s, University of Michigan scholars confirmed that most citizens were poorly informed about politics and found that identification with a political party, rather than deliberation about policy issues, dominated political thinking and voting choices. Around the same time, Gabriel Almond cited fluctuating responses to "most important problem" survey questions as evidence for a "mood theory" of vacillating public opinion about foreign policy, and James Rosenau argued that only a small fraction of Americans (perhaps fewer than 10 percent) met the criteria of an "attentive public" with regard to foreign policy.[6]

A particularly telling blow against any idea of a real or stable public opinion seemed to be landed by Phillip Converse, who analyzed individuals' responses to policy preference questions that were repeated from one survey to the next in a University of Michigan panel study. Converse found that (on certain issues, at least) there was not much relation at all between what individuals said they favored in one survey and what the same people said two years or four years later. Their answers changed in ways that looked random, suggesting that they had no real opinions at all: only what he called "non-attitudes."[7]

Subsequent research has modified some of these findings. Christopher Achen and others have pointed out that some of the instability in individuals' recorded responses may result from errors in survey measurement, not the absence of opinions. William Caspary showed that the proportion of Americans saying they wanted to take an active part in world affairs remained quite stable over time, contrary to the mood theory. Citizens' confusion about candidates' stands on issues has varied from one election to another and seems to result partly from ambiguities in candidates' stands. And voting based on foreign policy and other issues began to look more prevalent once the sleepiness of the 1950s was replaced by the political tumult of the 1960s.[8]

Still, several of the conclusions of the early research have been confirmed. Many individual Americans *do* in fact give different answers at different times to the same survey question; whatever causes this, whether measurement error, respondents' uncertainty, or some mixture of the two, it casts doubt on the extent to which surveys produce reliable assessments of individuals' political opinions. Moreover, researchers have repeatedly found that the average American, who is often busy with work, family, and other concerns, does not know or care a great deal about politics. Michael Delli Carpini and Scott Keeter's exhaustive study—while questioning whether the average person actually needs to know political trivia, and while emphasizing the *possibility* of achieving an informed citizenry—also concluded that in many instances levels of political knowledge are "depressingly low." Fewer than half of Americans in their study correctly answered questions about certain apparently critical aspects of political institutions and processes: what percentage of Congress it takes to override a presidential veto (only 44 percent answered correctly), who sets interest rates (42 percent), what the electoral college is (35 percent), and how long terms of office are in the House (30 percent) and Senate (just 25 percent). Fewer than half of Americans correctly identified a number of prominent political figures, and only 35 percent were able to name both their U.S. senators. Fewer than half knew certain basic facts relevant to foreign or domestic policy, including the rough proportions of the federal budget that go to the military (21 percent correct), health care (17 percent), or Social Security (a minuscule 8 percent correct). In 1991, only 8 percent of Americans could name the United States' largest trading partner (it was Canada).[9]

When highly educated observers encounter such figures for the first time they tend to be appalled at the ignorance of the masses. Basic political facts—let alone the acronyms and buzzwords that are commonplace inside the Beltway and among readers of the New York Times—are beyond the ken of most ordinary people. But it turns out that a high level of political knowledge among individual citizens is not necessarily critical for the existence of a coherent, well-informed collective public opinion.

THE "RATIONAL PUBLIC" AND FOREIGN POLICY

In recent years an increasing body of evidence has indicated that aggregate or collective public opinion has characteristics quite different from the characteristics of most individual citizens' opinions. Collective opinion (as indicated, for example, by what percentage of the public favors a certain policy) tends to be rather stable over time. As a collectivity the public makes sharp distinctions among specific policies and does so in ways that are generally coherent and mutually consistent, apparently reflecting underlying beliefs and values. When collective public opinion changes, it usually does so in predictable and reasonable ways, in reaction to new information or to changes in the political world.

In The Rational Public, Benjamin Page and Robert Y. Shapiro examined more than one thousand survey questions about foreign and domestic policy that had been asked at least twice (with identical wording) between the 1930s and the 1980s. They found that collective opinion—in contrast to the vacillating opinions often expressed by individuals—seldom changed quickly by large amounts. More than half (58 percent) of the 1,128 repeated questions showed no significant change at all, and nearly half of the significant changes were smaller than ten percentage points. Public opinion more often changed abruptly on foreign than on domestic issues (generally in response to major international events), but it seldom fluctuated back and forth.[10] Moreover, they found that the public makes distinctions; levels of public support varied markedly depending on the specifics of policies: to which countries arms should be sold, under what circumstances abortions should be permitted, where U.S. troops should be used, what kind of gun control should be adopted, what types of military or economic aid should be given to particular countries, which desegregation measures should be enacted, and the like.[11] Conventional wisdom holds that public opinion is inconsistent (for example, the public is alleged to support both lower taxes and higher spending of virtually every kind); Page and Shapiro found little or no actual evidence of inconsistencies. They also found that nearly all significant changes in collective public opinion could be accounted for in terms of long-term population shifts or reasonable responses to world events and newly available information.

How can this "rationality" of collective public opinion (as Page and Shapiro loosely called it) be reconciled with the evidence that many individuals know little about politics and do not express firm views about it? The answer comes in two parts.

First, in *collective deliberation,* experts, commentators, and political figures tend to digest new political information and learn from history fairly efficiently, and the results are widely reported in the mass media. Intermittent attention to the media, together with personal experience and conversations among families, friends, and coworkers, can enable individuals to form sensible opinions about public policy based on the best available information and background knowledge, even when they know few specific facts themselves. People can follow simple cues or "heuristics," such as adopting the policy stands taken by prominent (and well-informed) figures whom they trust to share their values.[12] Thus the public as a whole tends to learn from historical experience, and broad conclusions are passed along from parents to children, from teachers to students, and from friends and neighbors to each other.

The role of direct personal experience in these processes should not be ignored. Members of the public learn from history not only through media reports of casualties in Korea, Vietnam, or Iraq, but also through their own wartime military service and the service, and deaths and maimings, of neighbors and family members.

Second, if collective deliberation leads most individuals to have at least a tendency to hold a sensible opinion about a particular policy—even while they remain only partly informed and uncertain, so that their expressed opinions may vacillate—the statistical *aggregation* of survey responses over a large population can cancel out random noise and reveal a meaningful, stable central tendency of opinion. If each individual has a tendency to favor a policy alternative consistent with his or her interests and values but gives survey responses that deviate from that preference (due to uncertainty, measurement error, or recently received bits of argument or information) in a fashion that is random and independent of other individuals' errors, then deviations in one direction by one individual will tend to be offset by deviations in the opposite direction by another. From one survey to the next, particular individuals may express shifting views in favor of or opposition to a policy, but the overall proportion of the public favoring that policy will stay about the same. And that proportion will rather faithfully reflect the proportion of individual Americans whose "real" or long-term preferences support the policy.[13]

These features of collective public opinion are particular examples of what James Surowiecki calls "the wisdom of crowds." In many cases, the collective opinions or collective decisions of groups—whether expressed through economic markets, jury deliberations, opinion polls, or votes by panels of experts—can be superior to those of any single individual in the group.[14]

The "rational public" perspective on collective public opinion, which is consistent with a substantial and growing body of empirical evidence, will both inform and be extended by our analysis of survey data concerning what kind of foreign policy Americans want. It helps give us confidence that when we report percentages of responses to survey questions, we are generally reporting sound indicators of real, meaningful collective public opinion.

Hazards in interpreting surveys. We do not, however, want to claim that aggregate responses to survey questions invariably convey an accurate picture of the public's true policy preferences. Nor do we wish to argue that those policy preferences are invariably wise or that they necessarily accord with what people would want if they had complete and accurate information about all relevant aspects of public policy. Various problems with survey technology and with the political information that is made available to the public can lead unwary interpreters of surveys to make incorrect inferences about collective public opinion.

The most serious problems have to do with two innocent-sounding statements we made above: that aggregate survey data can reveal true collective public opinion *if* individuals' survey responses deviate from their true preferences only in random ways that are "independent" of other peoples' deviations, and that, under similar conditions, survey-measured collective preferences will reflect the "best available" information. Individuals' errors are not always random or independent. Moreover, the best available information may not be very good: at times it may be a pack of lies. If biased or misleading information in the political system, or systematic errors in surveys, lead to nonrandom errors that affect many respondents in the same way, survey data can lead us astray about the authentic views of the citizenry. We will have more to say about this.

One supposed problem, however, is not in fact much of a problem at all. An aspect of opinion surveys that often worries nonexperts is the small number of respondents that is typically interviewed, compared with the enormous size of the U.S. population. How can the views of, say, seven hundred respondents possibly represent the thinking of a population of three hundred million people? Here survey research stands on fairly firm ground. So long as the sample is randomly chosen, statisticians have shown that it will usually be highly representative of the population: similar to the overall population in proportions of males to females, young to old, urban to rural residents, and so on. And it will be quite similar—within statistical "confidence intervals" that can be precisely calculated—in political attitudes. A properly drawn sample of modest size can serve as an amazingly accurate microcosm of the population.[15]

Of course the phrase "randomly chosen" glosses over certain difficulties. Most survey samples depart at least somewhat from true randomness. Cost considerations, for example, generally require that in-person respondents be geographically clustered, not scattered across the country, so that interviewers can easily get to them. (This is not true of telephone or Internet surveys, however.) People who are selected to be interviewed but who don't answer the phone or the doorbell may differ from those who do answer. And the number of nonrespondents to all kinds of surveys has been increasing, with more pressures on peoples' time, growing wariness of strangers, an onslaught of unsolicited communications, and the prevalence of caller ID (which makes it easy to skip unwanted calls). But researchers can generally deal with these problems through statistical adjustments, persistent callbacks, and careful "weighting" of the final pool of respondents. Most academic and commercial surveys in the United States do a respectable job of interviewing representative samples of Americans. Most of the time they produce collective response percentages that come within three or four percentage points of what they would find if every single adult American were interviewed—a remarkable achievement.

A more subtle representativeness problem is that, among respondents who are actually interviewed, those who have little interest or knowledge—and therefore frequently answer "don't know" or offer confused or mistaken responses—tend to be different from other Americans. They tend to be poorer, for example, and to have less formal education. Such people also tend to hold different underlying opinions and perhaps different "true interests" (e.g., they may have greater need for government services), which are then underrepresented in survey responses and in measures of collective public opinion. This problem is particularly marked with respect to issues of economic inequality and redistributive policies, where the opinions and needs of poor people may be especially relevant. On the other hand, scholars have found that the resulting distortions of collective public opinion are usually fairly small.[16]

A particularly important set of problems concerns exactly how survey questions are *worded*. A great deal of research has shown that differences in the precise wording of questions—even differences that seem, on their face, to be rather minor—can have a big effect on how people respond. It does not follow that a clever writer of survey questions can get absolutely any answer he wants from the public, or that people have no real opinions. (Indeed, even responses concerning extremely obscure matters or fictional policies made up by survey researchers can provide information about real public opinion.)[17] But it does mean that we need to pay close attention to the details of question wording in order to understand exactly what the responses mean. Moreover, some survey questions provide more useful information about collective policy preferences than others: some are misleading. Ask a stupid question and you may get a stupid answer.

In many cases, "question-wording effects" reflect nothing more than the unsurprising fact that people tend to give different responses when they are asked different questions. Altering a word or two, even saying "a" instead of "the," can make a significant difference in meaning. A dramatic example involves questions asked before and during World War II concerning "*the* League of Nations" (emphasis added)—which, in most Americans' minds, had been a disappointing failure—or "*a* League of Nations" (emphasis added)—perhaps a new and revitalized forum for world cooperation.[18] Obviously, a proposal to "forbid" handguns means something quite different from one to "register" handguns. To "use U.S. troops" does not mean the same thing as to "use force" or to "invade" a country. To "impose economic sanctions" on country X is not necessarily inconsistent with "engag[ing] in trade" with country X. "Military aid" is not the same as "selling military equipment." When interpreting any survey responses we need to pay attention to exactly what question was asked.

But other question-wording effects involve biased, one-sided, or tendentious wording that may push respondents to give a response different from their true opinions. Such questions are pernicious because they do not create random, independent errors that cancel each other out. Instead, they push most or all respondents in the same direction, biasing not only individuals' responses but also collective or aggregate responses. Invocation of popular authority figures, for example ("The President, the Secretary of Defense, and the Joint Chiefs of Staff favor a program to build fallout shelters for protection against nuclear attack. What do you think?"), tends to inflate apparent support for otherwise unpopular policies with which they are associated. Similarly, the addition to a question of a strong argument ("based on uncertain science," "trumped up charges may be brought"), or an implication about effects ("in order to combat terrorism") may bias responses, particularly if no counterargument is included.[19]

We are fortunate in this book to be able to report results based on survey questions that were mostly worded in a neutral or balanced, reasonably unbiased fashion likely to elicit responses that accurately reflect people's true long-term opinions. When exceptions occur we will discuss them.

Similar in effect to biased question wording are one-sided bursts of information or argument broadcast by the mass media, to which most or all respondents may be exposed just before a survey. This too does not produce independent random errors but systematically pushes many respondents in the same direction, away from expressing their long-term preferences. It is therefore important when interpreting survey results to bear in mind the context of recent news events that may temporarily have shifted peoples' opinions. We will attempt to do so.

More difficult to deal with are possible effects of media-reported information that may be biased not just temporarily but over the *long term*. Long-term biases could affect not only peoples' survey responses at a given moment but also what we have called their real or long-term policy preferences. Such biases could undermine the normative appeal of paying attention even to well-measured, long-term public opinion. If—over the long term—the best available information is biased, incorrect, or deliberately deceptive, we can no longer be confident that the policy preferences of the public will reflect peoples' true interests and values. The democratic ideal that government should respond to the public's policy preferences then loses much of its feasibility and its moral force.

It is well established that what is reported in the mass media has substantial effects on what people think about politically and what policy preferences they express.[20] There is also abundant evidence that—in the realm of foreign policy—the mass media tend to rely heavily on public officials as news sources and to voice opinions that are mostly in harmony with official foreign policy.[21] In some important cases—particularly involving wars or "crisis" situations, real or manufactured—U.S. presidents and other foreign policy leaders may have concealed or misrepresented crucial facts for a substantial period of time. The executive branch has a great deal of power to manipulate information. In such situations, opposition voices are often silent; foreign policy "bipartisanship" (or, less charitably, collusion between the two major parties) is maintained, and ordinary citizens have little choice but to rely on what the officials say.

If, for example, the president of the United States and members of his administration misleadingly declare that there have been "unprovoked attacks" on U.S. destroyers in the Gulf of Tonkin, many Americans may conclude there is reason for the U.S. to go to war in Vietnam. If the president and administration falsely or mistakenly imply that Saddam Hussein's Iraq has ties to anti-U.S. terrorists and has large quantities of potent—perhaps nuclear—weapons of mass destruction that pose an imminent threat to the

United States, many Americans are likely to be convinced. The public's willingness to invade Iraq is likely to increase. Yet it would be odd to celebrate a subsequent decision to invade Iraq as an instance of democratic responsiveness to public opinion.[22]

It is not easy for scholars or observers to identify such situations. There are often legitimate disputes over what is true or false, and motives are often murky—one cannot always detect untruths, let alone uncover intentional efforts at deception. Moreover, it is often difficult to pin down precisely how much or how little effect misleading rhetoric actually has had upon public opinion, so it is difficult to determine whether opinion has been manipulated. The best we can do (as we will do in the case of the Iraq war) is to point out possible cases of opinion manipulation and note that under such circumstances the idea of democratic responsiveness loses much of its meaning and public opinion is no longer a very useful guide to policy making.

Still, on the whole—most of the time, for most policy issues—we believe that the information available to the American public is sufficiently full, diverse, and accurate, and that the processes of collective deliberation and statistical aggregation work sufficiently well, that survey-measured collective public opinion is well worth paying attention to.[23] Public opinion has the potential to live up to the exalted role that populistic variants of democratic theory assign to it: as a chief input, perhaps *the* chief input, to policy making. The main reason this book describes in detail what sorts of foreign policies the American public wants is to make it easy for policy makers to respond to the preferences of their constituents, and easy to point the finger at those who fail to do so.

Purposive belief systems. In the course of describing the public's foreign policy preferences, we will also provide some new evidence that supports and elaborates upon the "rational public" perspective: namely, evidence that *individual* Americans tend to hold coherent, *purposive belief systems* concerning foreign policy, which (when individuals' opinions are aggregated) contribute to the existence of a coherent and consistent set of policy preferences at the collective level.[24] Some determined skeptics, still unpersuaded by the arguments about rational collective public opinion summarized above, have pointed out that statistical aggregation cannot accomplish anything unless there exists something to aggregate. One thousand times nothing is still nothing. Unless there is at least some tendency for individuals to have consistent and coherent opinions, collective consistency and coherence should not appear when individual opinions are added up. We propose to show that precisely such coherence and consistency does tend to exist within individual citizens' minds.

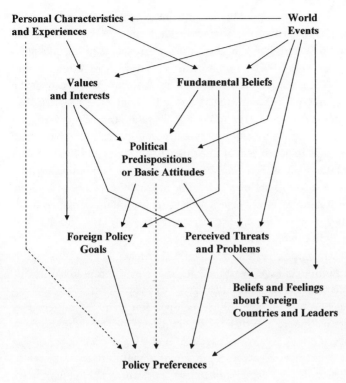

Fig. 1.1 Elements of purposive belief systems

We will not spell out any very elaborate theory in this book,[25] but the central idea of purposive belief systems is a simple one: that citizens tend to organize their foreign policy beliefs and attitudes in a *purposeful,* goal-oriented, instrumental fashion. Basic needs, values, and beliefs work together with a number of other political attitudes and predispositions—including political ideologies and party loyalties, perceptions of international threats and problems, specific foreign policy goals, and beliefs and feelings about specific foreign countries and leaders—to affect individuals' preferences concerning what sorts of foreign policies to pursue. These elements interact with each other in complex ways, but they tend to form *hierarchical, means-ends chains.* In these means-ends chains, specific policy preferences follow logically from foreign policy goals and perceptions about how best to achieve those goals. The goals and perceptions in turn flow from basic values and beliefs, which originate in personal characteristics and experiences. Figure 1.1 offers a sketch of how an individual's personal characteristics, values, beliefs, goals, policy preferences, and the like might affect each other.

The starting point is that—partly as a result of *personal characteristics* based on an individual's genetic makeup, early socialization, adult experiences, and position in the society and economy—individual Americans generally hold a set of *basic values* or objectives relevant to foreign policy. As we will see, these often include (with varying priorities) desires to protect the physical security of themselves and their country, concerns with economic and social security at home, and humanitarian or altruistic concerns about the welfare of people abroad. Individuals also tend to hold some *fundamental beliefs* about how the world works and how their values can be realized, such as whether the U.S. government can generally act effectively or not, whether foreign nations can be trusted, and the like. Basic values and fundamental beliefs feed into a set of *political predispositions*—or general political orientations, which we will sometimes call "basic attitudes"—such as an internationalist or isolationist worldview, a propensity toward unilateral or multilateral policy means, a liberal or conservative ideology, and identification with the Republican or Democratic Party.

These basic values, beliefs, and political orientations, together with outside stimuli—including world events and new information from the media—affect *perceptions of international threats and problems,* such as terrorism, nuclear proliferation, economic competition from abroad, environmental degradation, or poverty and AIDS in Africa. They also lead people to embrace specific *foreign policy goals,* such as combating terrorism, preserving Americans' jobs, protecting the global environment, or combating world hunger. Such goals and perceptions, in turn, may work together with *beliefs and feelings about particular foreign countries and leaders* (China, European countries, Saddam Hussein, African countries), with political predispositions, and perhaps with some residual effects of personal characteristics, to influence *specific foreign policy preferences* (for aid to Africa, invasion of Iraq, protection against job-threatening imports).

Most or all of the attitudinal and perceptual elements in figure 1.1 are affected over time by real-world events and circumstances, including the actions of other countries and feedback effects from U.S. foreign policies. They are also affected by media-reported cues from political elites. Historical learning takes place through many cognitive and affective pathways.

All of these values, beliefs, attitudes, goals, perceptions, and preferences can vary from one individual or social group to another. But in many cases there is a high level of consensus about them among Americans, so that collective public opinion itself exhibits something like a single, coherent collective belief system. That is, often large majorities of Americans share the same values, the same goals, and the same beliefs and perceptions, which lead to the same policy preferences. Steven Kull has pointed out that the various foreign policy positions taken by majorities of Americans tend to fit together logically and coherently, just as if they were all taken by a single, rather reasonable individual, "J. Q. Public." ("J. Q. Public," with help from

Kull, once gave an extensive interview on his/her foreign policy opinions to *Foreign Policy* magazine.[26]) We will often use language suggestive of a single collective belief system.

Previous research on both domestic and foreign policy has established some findings related to the idea of purposive belief systems. Stanley Feldman and others, for example, have shown that Americans' preferences concerning policies (mainly domestic) tend to be related to key underlying values. In the foreign policy realm, Eugene Wittkopf, William Chittick, Alvin Richman, and other scholars have shown that Americans' favored foreign policy goals and other attitudes tend to hang together in clusters or "dimensions" reflective of basic beliefs and values (hawkish or dovish internationalism, domestic concerns, humanitarianism, and the like). Jon Hurwitz and Mark Peffley have laid out a theory somewhat akin to our own, with substantial purposive elements, and have shown it to account rather well for the foreign policy attitudes of a local sample of Americans.[27]

In subsequent chapters we will use data from a 2002 national survey conducted for the Chicago Council on Foreign Relations (CCFR) in order to explore in some detail whether and how individual Americans' specific foreign policy preferences are affected by their personal characteristics, goals, attitudes, and perceptions. That is, we will see whether or not Americans actually tend to have purposive belief systems about foreign policy of the sort sketched in figure 1.1. The 2002 CCFR survey is particularly appropriate for this purpose. More than any other national survey we know of, it provides good measures of many (though unfortunately not all) of the key elements shown in figure 1.1. These include a large number of possible foreign policy *goals*, many possible *threats*, and *feelings* about many different foreign countries and leaders, along with the usual measures of respondents' personal characteristics and political predispositions. We will present evidence that individual Americans do indeed tend to have purposive belief systems that can account for policy preferences on many different issues, from military policy and the use of force abroad, to political and diplomatic relations with other countries, to international economic policies. This evidence adds to our understanding of individual political behavior as well as providing new support for the concept of rational collective public opinion.

But two caveats are in order. First, we certainly will not claim that every American holds a perfectly tight, logically organized purposive belief system. Only a significant *tendency* for attitudes and beliefs to hang together in that way is necessary to account for the coherence of collective public opinion. A tendency is what we find: a very substantial tendency in some cases, only a slight tendency in others. We will be interested in the extent of "constraint" in belief systems concerning particular policies, and in variations in constraint across policies.[28]

Second, we cannot always be sure what causes what. We want to discover exactly how much independent effect various factors have on policy preferences—that is, *why* individuals' take the policy stands they do. Relying on cross-sectional data, however (that is, relying on an opinion survey carried out at a particular moment in time, with all variables measured at that same time), we cannot always tell which factors were temporally or causally prior to others. We *can* usually be confident that personal characteristics like an individual's age, gender, religion, or education level affect his or her political attitudes, rather than vice versa, because such personal or demographic characteristics are relatively fixed and are generally unaffected by (are "exogenous to") political attitudes. But we cannot always be sure which attitudinal or perceptual elements affect which: whether, for example, people's foreign policy goals affect what threats they perceive, or perceived threats affect goals, or each affects the other. Nor can we rule out the possibility that specific policy preferences may sometimes affect broader goals, rather than the goals affecting policy preferences.[29]

Thus when we conduct multiple regression analyses and find large, statistically significant coefficients (or small, nonsignificant ones), we can judge whether or not the results are *consistent with* substantial independent effects of one factor on another and whether or not they are consistent with our theory of purposive belief systems. But we cannot conclusively test or "prove" the validity of the theory as sketched in figure 1.1, because we cannot always be sure that the directions of influence are the same as those indicated in the figure. When we use causal language about the "effects" of one factor on another, it should generally (except in the case of demographic variables) be interpreted in this way: we generally provide evidence that is necessary but not sufficient to establish causation. (On the other hand, findings about the extent of "constraint" in belief systems, or the extent to which factors "hang together," are not subject to this limitation.)

OUR SURVEY DATA

The data we use to describe and analyze Americans' opinions about foreign policy come chiefly from a series of nine national opinion studies that were conducted by the Gallup, Harris, and Knowledge Networks survey organizations for the Chicago Council on Foreign Relations every four years between 1974 and 2002, with an additional study in 2004.[30] Many questions were repeated, with exactly the same wording, from one survey to the next, so that trends in opinion over time can be assessed. Many questions—especially in 2002—concerned elements of purposive belief systems: foreign policy goals, perceived threats, feelings about foreign countries, and many specific foreign policy preferences.

Each of these CCFR studies included a "general public" survey of a large sample of respondents designed to be highly representative of all adult Americans, with about the same proportions of various subgroups—women and men, young and old, black and white, urban and rural, blue-collar and white-collar workers, Catholics and Protestants, and so forth—as in the population as a whole.[31] Because of this representativeness, we can be confident that the frequencies of responses to each survey question very closely approximate—usually within three or four percentage points—the proportions of responses that would be found if every single adult member of the U.S. population were asked the same question in the same way. That is, we can use these surveys with considerable confidence to assess what *all* adult Americans think, and what sorts of policies majorities of Americans have favored or opposed.

In addition, each CCFR study included a parallel survey (asking many of the same questions) of three hundred to four hundred "foreign policy leaders": people with special foreign policy responsibility or expertise who occupied prominent positions in government, interest groups, the media, think tanks, universities, and the like.[32] These "leader" surveys have allowed us to isolate the opinions of government officials concerned with foreign policy and to explore, in chapter 7, gaps between what officials favor and what ordinary citizens want.

This book focuses most closely on the CCFR general public survey conducted in the summer of 2002, which was cosponsored by the German Marshall Fund of the United States and carried out by Harris Interactive. This survey involved an unusually large sample of over thirty-two hundred respondents. It employed a sophisticated, rather complicated research design in which different sets of respondents were asked different sets of questions, so that a great many different questions could be asked of representative subsamples of roughly seven hundred or eleven hundred Americans.[33] (Certain key questions were asked of all 3,262 respondents.) This design made it possible to ask many more questions than can ordinarily be fit into a single survey: about twice as many questions as in a typical forty-five- or fifty-minute face-to-face survey, and about three times as many as in the standard twenty-five-minute telephone survey. As a result, the 2002 CCFR general public survey provides more complete and detailed cross-sectional data on Americans' foreign policy preferences than have ever before been collected. Thus we are able to present a more richly detailed picture of Americans' collective thinking about U.S. foreign policy than has ever before been presented. And we are able to put that picture into historical context, comparing Americans' opinions in 2002 both to their answers to identical survey questions over the preceding twenty-eight year period and to the answers given to a shorter survey two years later, in 2004. (Figures for years other than 2002 will mostly be reported in endnotes, with general trends described in the text.)

At the same time, the 2002 data have certain disadvantages. For one thing, comparisons with previous CCFR surveys must be made very carefully. The 2002 interviewing was done in the summer rather than (as in previous surveys) in the autumn of a congressional election year, when political attention tends to be somewhat higher. More importantly, cost considerations led the CCFR to shift in 2002 from purely in-person interviewing to a primarily telephone-interview design, with only a small in-person sample to establish comparability with the in-person surveys done previously. As we will note, there turned out to be some substantial "mode" differences between in-person and telephone responses in 2002. Both modes produced results that are valid and representative, and we generally use a combined data set that tends to mute differences between them. But precise inferences about opinion *changes* between earlier CCFR surveys and the 2002 survey must be made carefully, on the basis of precisely comparable in-person interviews.[34]

Similarly, the analysis of opinion changes *after* 2002 is complicated by yet another switch in survey mode in 2004, to a Web-based survey conducted by Knowledge Networks (KN). (Again cost considerations were a factor, as were concerns about the future of telephone surveys in an era of cell phones and caller ID.) The Web-based data, too, are highly representative of national samples of Americans; KN did not rely upon a biased (e.g., more affluent) sample of people who already had Internet access but instead selected a random sample of Americans and provided hardware and Internet access to those who lacked it.[35] Indeed there are some indications that Web-based respondents, working at their own pace in the privacy of their own homes, may give particularly deliberative and frank answers to survey questions. But again there were some mode effects, most notably a tendency for Web-based respondents to give cooler ratings than others did to foreign countries on a "feeling thermometer."[36]

Fortunately, the CCFR again made it possible to pin down the nature of mode effects fairly precisely. KN conducted a short Web-based pilot survey in 2002, permitting some comparisons with telephone and in-person responses to the same questions in the main CCFR survey that same year. The pilot survey also allows some direct, same-mode comparisons with 2004 Web-based results, permitting precise calculations of the extent (if any) of opinion change between 2002 and 2004. Moreover, in 2004 a small *telephone* survey was done by CCI, permitting same-mode comparisons with telephone-interview data from 2002 and additional calculations of opinion changes.[37] Using comparisons involving the 2002 KN pilot survey or the 2004 CCI telephone survey, as well as generalizations about mode effects based on comparisons of all three modes in 2002, we are able to discuss changes and nonchanges in opinion between 2002 and 2004 with considerable confidence. The results—there was not in fact much change between 2002 and 2004, except for certain opinions related to Iraq—will be described in the text, with details in the endnotes.

Readers who are interested in survey mode effects or in our techniques for drawing inferences about opinion changes from 1998 to 2002 (and from 2002 to 2004), will find a great deal of detail about these matters in the endnotes at the back of the book. The endnotes are mostly readable as a block, before or after the chapter they refer to, so that back-and-forth trips can be avoided. Readers who are less interested in such matters should feel free to ignore the notes altogether. You can be assured that all statements about opinion changes—or the absence of change—take survey mode effects into account.

A further difficulty in using the 2002 data is that the subsample design—in which different questions were asked of different (sometimes but not always overlapping) sets of respondents—greatly complicates the individual-level analysis of *relationships* among various beliefs and attitudes. In some cases there exist few respondents, or none at all, who were asked both of two particular questions. In such cases it is difficult or impossible to determine whether or not individuals who thought X also tended to believe Y. In many cases there exist few or no respondents who were asked *all* of a set of questions relevant to multivariate analysis of how a whole set of attitudes and beliefs did or did not relate to each other. To a large extent, multivariate analyses of the 2002 data must rely on a limited number of "core" questions that were all asked of all in-person respondents.[38]

Frustration about these difficulties will occasionally bubble up in the following pages. But of course we ourselves are largely responsible for them. From the start we accepted the negative consequences of mode changes and the subsample design, for the sake of being able to carry out cost-effective surveys with many respondents and very large numbers of questions. We have no regrets. Each reader can judge for her- or himself, but we are pleased at how well we have been able, despite the difficulties, to pin down opinion changes and to perform multivariate analyses.

In the chapters to come, we use the 2002 CCFR general public survey, supplemented by some polls and surveys conducted by other organizations around the same time, to look at percentage responses to many different policy preference questions. This produces a very comprehensive, detailed snapshot of exactly what kind of foreign policy the American public favored at one particular historical moment. It was an interesting moment. The Cold War was long past. The U.S. triumph in the 1991 Gulf War and the dazzling economic boom of the 1990s were both over. The terrorist attacks of September 11, 2001, had given foreign policy a new urgency and caused some Americans to look at foreign affairs in new ways; but enough time (roughly nine months) had passed since those attacks for any purely short-term effects to have had a chance to disappear.

Still, the summer of 2002 was just a single moment in history. It is important to put our snapshot into historical context. In order to do so, we use the previous CCFR surveys, going back to 1974, to see how Americans' opinions in 2002 compared with their opinions in the past. (For the sake of brevity and narrative flow, precise percentages from previous years are often given only in the endnotes, with the main points reported in the text.) Did the end of the Cold War transform U.S. public opinion? Did the September 11 attacks do so? Perhaps even more important, we use data from 2004 to see *how durable* or transient the scene depicted in our 2002 snapshot has been. (Again, precise percentages from 2004 are usually consigned to endnotes, where the complexities of mode effects can be dealt with.) Did impacts of the 2001 terrorist attacks fade away? Did the U.S. invasion of Iraq in early 2003, or its messy aftermath, transform public opinion afresh?

The answers may surprise some readers. Certain interesting changes have occurred, but the continuities in opinion are even more impressive. With the end of the Cold War the Soviet Union disappeared as the chief U.S. enemy, but other foes took its place; most of the major foreign policy goals that Americans sought, and most of the concrete policies they favored, remained very similar. The terrorist attacks of 2001 certainly galvanized the U.S. public and changed some opinions, but fewer than one might imagine. The Iraq war altered some attitudes related to Iraq itself, the Middle East, the promotion of democracy abroad, and some military matters—but usually not by a lot and often not at all. In short, the 2002 snapshot (with its 2004 update) has considerable relevance to the state of U.S. public opinion in the past and the present. We venture to guess that it will prove relevant in the future as well.

THE PLAN OF THE BOOK

As we proceed through different policy areas—military, diplomatic, and economic—we will also use the 2002 data to investigate *why* Americans believe what they do, using correlation and regression analyses to explore the strength or weakness of links among various beliefs, attitudes, and feelings in individual Americans' minds, and the effects of various factors on policy preferences. This will bear on the "purposive belief system" idea outlined in figure 1.1. Toward the end of the book we will make use of the surveys of "foreign policy leaders" from 2002 and previous years, in order to ascertain to what extent, and on what sorts of issues, there have been significant differences of opinion between U.S. foreign policy officials and ordinary citizens.

In chapter 2 we discuss some of the most important foreign policy attitudes and beliefs that Americans hold, especially the goals they embrace (particularly concerning security from attack, security of domestic well-being, and justice abroad) and how those goals have changed over time, the international threats that Americans perceive from terrorism and other sources, and the problems they consider most important.

Chapter 3 considers another key set of attitudes: feelings about particular foreign countries and world leaders. We explore which countries and leaders have been seen as friends and which as foes, and why.

Chapter 4 deals with the circumstances under which Americans favor or oppose using military force, with special attention to the roles of multilateral cooperation and of international organizations like the United Nations and NATO. It also considers policy preferences concerning military capabilities, including defense spending and bases abroad.

Chapter 5 turns to political relationships with other countries: diplomatic and other nonmilitary approaches to terrorism, diplomatic relations with other countries, international treaties and agreements, and cooperation through international organizations.

Chapter 6 deals with international economic policies, including trade, immigration, and foreign aid.

Chapter 7 analyzes the extent to which ordinary citizens and foreign policy decision makers have agreed or disagreed about foreign policy. We find substantial gaps between the two, which are discussed in relation to democratic theory and practical problems of governance.

Finally, chapter 8 summarizes and discusses our main conclusions.

CHAPTER TWO

The Goals of Security and Justice

According to democratic theory, *goals* shared by large majorities of citizens may be the aspect of public opinion to which policy makers ought to pay the closest attention. Even if ordinary citizens were unclear about the intricacies of specific policy choices, even if experts rather than the public might be better at devising detailed means for achieving foreign policy goals, surely—in a democracy—the goals themselves ought to be set by the citizenry. Nearly all strands of democratic theory, even the rather loose, Burkean or Schumpeterian variants that call upon leaders to act as trustees with only long-term accountability to the public (rather than immediate, delegate-style responsiveness to its wishes), generally accept the principle that citizens should set the goals.[1] Who, after all, can better judge peoples' values and interests than the people themselves? If a democratic government does not faithfully pursue its citizens' values and interests, what is democracy about? As it turns out, however, there are some marked differences between the foreign policy goals considered most important by ordinary Americans, and those given high priority by foreign policy decision makers.

In this chapter, analyzing three decades of opinion surveys for the Chicago Council on Foreign Relations,[2] we will see that several of the American public's top-ranked foreign policy goals involve physical *security against attack* by international terrorists or hostile foreign states. But nearly as important in the minds of ordinary Americans (though not in the minds of many international relations theorists and foreign policy leaders) are a cluster of goals related to *security of domestic well-being*: economic, social, and cultural security at home. Of distinctly lower priority—though still important—are a number of goals related to international *justice*: altruistic and humanitarian goals concerning the safety and well-being of people abroad. Later, in chapter 7, we will see that some of the biggest gaps between citizens and decision makers concern the importance of domestic well-being. (Other big gaps involve cooperative versus unilateral policies, and the use of armed force.)

As the world has changed, certain of the public's goals have changed accordingly. After the end of the Cold War, for example, goals involving security from attack shifted focus from preventing interstate wars to combating international terrorism. But more striking is the overall stability and continuity in foreign policy goals sought by the American public. The fundamental aims of security from attack, security of domestic well-being, and justice for people abroad have remained mostly the same for thirty years. The public's rankings of many specific goals have also shown remarkable continuity.

Peoples' perceptions of international *threats* and problems are closely related to their foreign policy goals. Here security from attack has been the chief concern, but problems related to domestic economic and social well-being have been highly salient as well. Perceptions of threats and problems have varied with changes in global realities, but again the continuity of basic concerns is striking.

For individual Americans, the foreign policy goals they think the United States should pursue are particularly central to their purposive belief systems. Goals constitute the ends or purposes toward which specific foreign policies are aimed as means. Both logically and in empirical fact, the goals that individuals seek and the threats they perceive are closely linked to their support for, or opposition to, concrete policy alternatives.

Why do some Americans emphasize particular goals and threats, while others place their priorities elsewhere? Not, for the most part, because of their personal or social characteristics. Women and men, the young and the old, and especially people of high and low levels of formal education do sometimes differ. More striking, however, is the fact of widespread agreement among people in all walks of life about foreign policy goals and threats. When we speak collectively of "the public" perceiving a threat or favoring a goal, this usually means the threat is perceived or the goal favored by majorities of Americans from all major social groupings—by young and old, rich and poor, women and men, urbanites and country dwellers, African Americans and whites, northerners and southerners, Catholics and Protestants.

Somewhat more important for understanding variations in individuals' foreign policy goals are differences among people with different political predispositions: between liberals and conservatives, Republicans and Democrats, and especially internationalists and isolationists. But we will see that there is often majority agreement about goals and threats—and even about concrete policies—among majorities of people who hold rather different beliefs and ideologies. Again, statements about attitudes of "the public" as a whole often apply to majorities of Americans from virtually all social and political groupings.

In this chapter we will use the CCFR data to describe what percentages of Americans have attributed how much importance to various possible goals and threats, how those percentages have changed over time, and how much effect various personal characteristics (especially level of formal education) and political predispositions have on the goals that individuals espouse.

AMERICANS' FOREIGN POLICY GOALS

The CCFR surveys provide uniquely comprehensive information about which foreign policy goals Americans do or do not want their government to pursue. In all nine surveys since 1974, interviewers have presented respondents with a diverse list of "possible foreign policy goals that the United States might have," and asked them whether they think each one should be "a very important foreign policy goal of the United States," "a somewhat important foreign policy goal," or "not an important goal at all." Many possible goals on the list have been repeated from one survey to the next, making it possible to track continuity or changes in opinion.

The percentage of the public saying that each goal should be "very important" can be used to form a ranking of how important or unimportant the American public as a whole considers various different goals, relative to each other.[3] Such a ranking for 2002 is given in table 2.1. (We will see that the rankings were quite similar—with a few interesting exceptions—in 2004.) Table 2.1 may well be the most important table in this book, because it tells a great deal about what kind of foreign policy Americans want. Each goal is assigned to one or more of the three general categories mentioned above (to be explained in more detail below): security from attack (labeled "S"), security of domestic well-being ("D"), and justice or humanitarian help for people abroad ("J"). These categories will be explained in more detail below.

In the June 2002 CCFR survey, conducted about nine months after the terrorist attacks of September 11, 2001, on the World Trade Center and the Pentagon, "combating international terrorism" was called "very important" by an overwhelming 91 percent of the U.S. public. Virtually the same proportion of Americans, 90 percent, said that "preventing the spread of nuclear weapons" should be a very important goal. These were the top two goals, reflecting the fact that, not surprisingly, Americans put a very high priority on attaining *security against attack* upon the United States. This does not, however, mean that people necessarily seek physical security through military might. Only a considerably lower 68 percent said that "maintaining superior military power worldwide" should be a very important goal of

Table 2.1. Goals for U.S. foreign policy

		Should be a "very important" goal (%)
S	Combating international terrorism	91
S	Preventing the spread of nuclear weapons	90
D	Protecting the jobs of American workers	85
D	Stopping the flow of illegal drugs into the United States	81
D	Securing adequate supplies of energy	75
D	Controlling and reducing illegal immigration	70
S	Maintaining superior military power worldwide	68
D, J	Improving the global environment	66
J	Combating world hunger	61
S, J	Strengthening the United Nations	57
S, J	Defending our allies' security	57
D, J	Safeguarding against global financial instability	54
D	Reducing our trade deficit with foreign countries	51
D	Protecting the interests of American business abroad	49
J	Promoting and defending human rights in other countries	47
J, S	Strengthening international law and institutions	43
J	Protecting weaker nations against foreign aggression	41
J, D	Promoting market economies abroad	36
J, S	Helping to bring a democratic form of government to other nations	34
J	Helping to improve the standard of living of less developed nations	30

Source: 2002 CCFR/GMF combined data set.

Note: **S** = Security from attack, **D** = Security of domestic well-being, **J** = Justice and help for people abroad.

U.S. foreign policy, while 57 percent felt that "strengthening the United Nations" should be a very important goal. In later chapters we will see evidence of strong public support for pursuing its goals—including combating terrorism and preventing nuclear proliferation—through cooperative, multilateral, and (when possible) diplomatic and political rather than military means.

More surprisingly (at least to those not familiar with past CCFR surveys), table 2.1 indicates that the American public in 2002 gave nearly as high a priority to several goals involving *security of domestic well-being*—that is, economic, social, and cultural security—as to security from armed attack. Fully

85 percent of Americans declared that "protecting the jobs of American workers" should be a very important foreign policy goal of the United States. A nearly equal 81 percent said that "stopping the flow of illegal drugs into the United States" should be very important. Seventy-five percent said the same about "securing adequate supplies of energy," while 70 percent attributed high importance to "controlling and reducing illegal immigration." "Improving the global environment," which has domestic as well as foreign implications, was called a very important goal by 66 percent of the public. These domestically oriented goals, concerned with security of well-being, clearly outweigh, in the minds of the U.S. public, such traditional national security concerns as "defending our allies' security," which just 57 percent said should be a very important goal. Majorities or near majorities of Americans also said that three other largely domestic goals should be very important: "safeguarding against global financial instability" (54 percent), "reducing our trade deficit with foreign countries" (51 percent), and "protecting the interests of American business abroad" (49 percent).

Certain goals related to domestic well-being, such as securing adequate supplies of energy, have been embraced by realist theorists of international relations as vital to the U.S. "national interest." But other such goals have not. Few international relations theorists focus on the importance to nation-states of protecting their citizens' jobs, stopping the inflow of drugs, or controlling illegal immigration. Nor do many U.S. foreign policy decision makers emphasize these concerns. But if they are serious about democracy, perhaps they should. Should not the American people themselves decide what is in the national interest?[4] Many of the "gaps" or "disconnects" between the policy preferences of decision makers and those of citizens, which will be analyzed in chapter 7, flow from these fundamental disagreements about what goals it is most important for U.S. foreign policy to pursue.

The American public gives decidedly lower priority to most altruistic or humanitarian goals concerned with helping people outside the United States, which we refer to under the (imperfect) rubric of promoting international *justice*. Certain mixed goals with altruistic elements (improving the global environment, strengthening the United Nations, defending allies' security) have consistently ranked rather high. Among purely altruistic goals, however, only "combating world hunger," which in 2002 61 percent of Americans said should be a very important goal of U.S. foreign policy, has come close in priority to the key objectives of attaining security against attack and security of domestic well-being. Other altruistic and humanitarian goals are mostly found at or near the bottom of the rankings. Only 47 percent of Americans, for example, said in 2002 that "promoting and defending human rights in other countries" should be a very important goal of U.S. foreign policy, putting it in fifteenth place out of the twenty possible goals that respondents were asked about. In sixteenth place was the rather abstract goal of "strengthening international law and institutions," called very important by just 43 percent. (In concrete cases, however, we will see that there is a very high level of public support for international organizations, especially the United Nations, and for international treaties and agreements.) "Protecting weaker nations against aggression," ranking seventeenth, was called a very important goal by 41 percent. Even lower, in nineteenth place, was "helping to bring a democratic form of government to other nations," which only 34 percent said should be a very important goal of U.S. foreign policy. Dead last came "helping to improve the standard of living of less developed nations," called very important by just 30 percent. ("Promoting market economies abroad"—which, depending on one's ideology, can be considered altruistic, in U.S. self-interest, or both—was also ranked near the bottom.)

There is no escaping the fact that most Americans put their own well-being and their own country's welfare ahead of the welfare of people who live abroad. At the same time, we should not conclude that the U.S. public does not care at all about human rights, democracy, or poverty in other countries. In each case, roughly one-third to one-half of Americans called these altruistic and humanitarian goals "very important," and many more said they should be at least "somewhat important." Indeed, if one adds together the "very" and "somewhat" important responses, fully 90 percent said that promoting and defending human rights in other countries should be an important goal of U.S. foreign policy. The comparable figure for strengthening international law and institutions was 86 percent; for protecting weaker nations against aggression, 91 percent; for helping to bring a democratic form of government to other nations, 83 percent; and for helping to improve the standard of living of less developed nations, 86 percent. In none of these cases did the proportion of Americans responding "not an important goal at all" rise above 15 percent.

We will see, in fact, that a strong humanitarian and altruistic thread runs through Americans' foreign policy preferences, producing strong support for humanitarian foreign aid, protection of threatened peoples, participating in peacekeeping forces, and the like. In short, most Americans want security for themselves first, but they also want justice for others. And, as later chapters will make clear, they generally want to pursue their own security through legal, cooperative, and multilateral means.

Clusters of goals. We have asserted that each foreign policy goal discussed above relates to certain basic objectives—security from attack, security of domestic well-being, or justice for people abroad—which presumably reflect the "basic values" postulated in figure 1.1. So far we have based this assertion on the evident meaning of the goal questions. It seems obvious, for example, that both nuclear proliferation and terrorism have something to do with security from armed attack.

A different approach involves asking empirically whether or not particular sets of goals actually tend to cluster together within individuals' minds. If, for example, an individual says that "combating world hunger" should be a very important goal of U.S. foreign policy, is he or she also likely to say that promoting and defending human rights in other countries or protecting weaker nations from foreign aggression should be very important?

The answer is yes. Foreign policy goals tend to cluster together in much the ways we have posited. A useful measure of this is the Pearson correlation coefficient, which tells, for a pair of goals, just how strongly or weakly responses about one goal—"very important," "somewhat important," or "not . . . important"—are associated with similar responses about another goal. Pearson's coefficient, r, takes a value of zero when there is no relationship at all and 1.00 when there is a perfect positive relationship (that is, if every individual who says goal A is "very important" says the same thing about goal B, and likewise for everyone who says A is "somewhat important" or "not important").

Particularly striking are the rather strong (though far from perfect) relationships among various justice-related, or humanitarian and altruistic, foreign policy goals. In 2002, those who thought it very important to "improv[e] the standard of living of less developed nations," for example, tended also to think that "combating world hunger," "promoting and defending human rights in other countries," "helping to bring a democratic form of government to other nations," "protecting weaker nations against foreign aggression," and "improving the global environment" should be very important goals of U.S. foreign policy. Pearson coefficients fell in the .35 to .45 range and were highly significant. Correlations among other pairs of justice-related goals were also generally high, but improving the standard of living of less developed nations, combating world hunger, and promoting and defending human rights appeared to stand at the center of this cluster.[5] (For precise figures, see table A1 in the appendix.)

Similarly—though less strongly—goals related to security from attack tended to go together: individuals who thought it very important to combat international terrorism also tended to think it very important to maintain superior military power worldwide and to prevent the spread of nuclear weapons. Those who wanted to maintain superior military power also tended to think that defending our allies' security should be a very important goal of U.S. foreign policy. (The military power goal also correlated positively with several domestic well-being goals.)

Likewise, those who embraced one goal related to security of domestic well-being also tended to embrace others. Those who said it was very important to control and reduce illegal immigration, for example, tended also to think that stopping the flow of illegal drugs into the United States, protecting the jobs of American workers, protecting the interest of American business abroad, securing adequate supplies of energy, and reducing our trade deficit should be very important goals of U.S. foreign policy, with correlations in the .20 to .33 range. Again, precise figures are given in table A1.

A more systematic way to identify clusters of variables is by performing "dimensional" analyses, or factor analyses, which examine relationships among all pairs of variables at once and infer common factors that may underlie them. The factors that researchers find vary in number and nature according to the particular methods used, and the names or labels given to them are necessarily somewhat arbitrary.[6] But several scholars who have factor-analyzed responses to the CCFR goals questions in various years have discovered patterns much like those we have described.

This line of work was pioneered by Eugene Wittkopf, who emphasized two factors (or "faces") of internationalism. Chittick, Billingsley, and Travis factor-analyzed the goals questions from the 1974, 1978, 1982, and 1986 CCFR surveys, using a principal-components model with orthogonal ("Varimax") rotation that requires factors to be uncorrelated with each other. In each year they found three main factors that closely resembled the clusters we have discussed. The first, which they labeled "identity" and associated with multilateralism, was essentially the same humanitarian, altruistic cluster of goals we refer to in terms of "justice." In nearly all years the highest-loading goals on that factor were combating world hunger, promoting human rights, and improving standards of living in developing countries. The second factor, which they labeled "security" and associated with militarism, closely resembled our own "security from attack" cluster. In those Cold War years, the goals of matching Soviet military power and containing communism were central to this factor. (Chittick and collaborators found that the goals of protecting weaker nations and bringing democracy to other countries sometimes loaded on the security factor but also loaded on the identity, or justice, factor.) The third factor, which they labeled "prosperity" and associated with internationalism/isolationism, was essentially the same as our "security of domestic well-being" cluster: protecting Americans' jobs, securing energy supplies, and keeping up the value of the dollar were most closely connected with it.[7]

Richman, Malone, and Nolle factor-analyzed the 1994 CCFR goals data using somewhat different methods: two types of exploratory factor analysis with oblique rather than orthogonal rotations (that is, the factors were allowed to be correlated with each other, which we find more plausible) and a confirmatory "LISREL" technique. But for post–Cold War 1994 they identified very nearly the same factors as Chittick, Billingsley, and Travis had found earlier. The chief difference, perhaps attributable to the different rotation method and looser criteria for accepting factors, was that what we call the "security of domestic well-being" cluster of goals broke into two separate factors: one involved improving the global environment, securing energy supplies, and reducing the trade deficit (and, oddly, preventing the spread of nuclear weapons and strengthening the UN); the other included protecting the jobs of American workers, reducing illegal immigration, and stopping the flow of drugs into the United States.[8]

Our own factor-analytic results for the 2002 and 2004 data bring matters up to date and confirm our categorization of foreign policy goals into the three major clusters. With the 2002 data, when we permitted factors to be correlated with each other by using an oblique rotation, as did Richman's group, but constrained the solution to three factors, the results fit our conceptual scheme almost perfectly.[9] The first factor, justice, had its highest loadings for improving standards of living, combating world hunger, improving the global environment, promoting and defending human rights, strengthening the UN, strengthening international law and institutions, protecting weaker nations against foreign aggression, and safeguarding against global financial instability. The second factor, security of domestic well-being, had its highest loadings for stopping the flow of illegal drugs, controlling and reducing illegal immigration, protecting the jobs of American workers, securing adequate supplies of energy, and protecting the interest of American business abroad. The third factor, security from attack, had high loadings for maintaining superior military power, defending our allies' security, combating international terrorism, and protecting weaker nations against foreign aggression. The three factors were all moderately related to each other. (For details, see table A2 in the appendix.) Our results for the shorter 2004 survey, displayed in table A3, were much the same: once again the same three distinct factors emerged, with essentially the same content.

Continuity in goals. The repetition of many identical goals questions in CCFR surveys over the years allows us to assess the extent of continuity or change in the foreign policy goals Americans have considered most important. There turns out to be a surprisingly high level of continuity.

As one would expect of a rational public, changes in the world have made a difference. Goals related to containing communism and the Soviet Union naturally faded at the end of the Cold War, and those concerned with nuclear proliferation and international terrorism soon rose to the top of the rankings. There have been some understandable ups and downs in goals related to energy and trade deficits as well as various altruistic aims. But the extent of continuity in basic objectives is striking. In every survey, including those of the Cold War years, goals involving security of domestic well-being have come at or near the top of the rankings, holding their own with goals related to security against attack. In every survey, purely altruistic and humanitarian justice-related goals have had substantial support but lower priority.

Tables 2.2 and 2.3 show the percentages of the public saying each goal should be "very important," for the Cold War and post–Cold War surveys respectively. The key transitional year of 1990 is included—with newly corrected data—in both tables.[10] Three Cold War–related goals—containing communism, matching Soviet military power, and worldwide arms control—that were last asked about in 1990 are included only in table 2.2.[11] Two post–Cold War goals that were *first* asked about in 1990—preventing the spread of nuclear weapons and improving the global environment— are included only in table 2.3, as are several goals that were added later. Once again, each goal is labeled according to its place in the security from attack, security of domestic well-being, and/or justice clusters of goals.

During the Cold War years the continuity is unmistakable. Several goals were called "very important" by nearly identical percentages of Americans in all five surveys (see table 2.2). The 1974 survey makes clear that security from attack was the top priority: the goals of "keeping peace in the world" (which would help other people as well as Americans) and the more purely U.S.-oriented "promoting and defending our own security" topped the ranking by substantial margins. Oddly, neither of these questions was repeated in later surveys, but there is every reason to expect that if they had been repeated they would have continued to enjoy very high levels of support. In each of the five Cold War–era surveys, about two-thirds of Americans said that "worldwide arms control"—a cooperative, nonmilitary approach to security from attack—should be a very important goal of U.S. foreign policy.

The related but distinct goal of "containing communism"—with its ideological baggage and its implication of shielding others rather than simply protecting the United States from attack—won significantly lower support from the public, though majorities of 54 to 60 percent considered it very important until the end of the Cold War, after which there was a sharp drop. "Defending our allies' security" (another goal involving benefits for others as well as the U.S.) was not very popular with the public in the Vietnam-traumatized year 1974, but it won bare majority support in 1978 through 1986, after which it too dropped. "Matching Soviet military power" followed the same path in the three surveys in which it appeared. It is notable that even in 1982, a time of high international tensions and President Reagan's intensive military buildup, the goals of containing communism and

Table 2.2. Cold War–era goals

		Should be a "very important" goal (%)				
		1974	1978	1982	1986	1990*
S, J	Keeping peace in the world	85	—	—	—	—
S	Promoting and defending our own security	83	—	—	—	—
D	Protecting the jobs of American workers	74	78	77	78	84
D	Securing adequate supplies of energy	75	78	70	69	76
D	Keeping up the value of the dollar	—	86	71	—	—
S, J	Worldwide arms control	64	64	64	69	68
J	Combating world hunger	61	59	58	63	—
D	Reducing our trade deficit with foreign countries	—	—	—	62	70
S, J	Containing communism	54	60	59	57	42
S, J	Defending our allies' security	33	50	50	56	43
S	Matching Soviet military power	—	—	49	53	40
S, J	Strengthening the United Nations	46	47	48	46	52
D	Protecting interests of American business abroad	39	45	44	43	46
J	Promoting and defending human rights in other countries	—	39	43	42	40
J	Helping to improve the standard of living in less developed countries	39	35	35	37	33
J	Protecting weaker nations against foreign aggression	28	34	34	32	32
J, S	Helping to bring democratic forms of government to other nations	28	26	29	30	28

Source: CCFR surveys.

Note: **S** = Security from attack, **D** = Security of domestic well-being, **J** = Justice and help for people abroad.

*1990 figures are newly revised, correcting a tabulation error.

matching Soviet military power (in contrast to worldwide arms control) enjoyed less than universal support from the American public.

During these same years, the public attributed great importance to foreign policy goals bearing on security of domestic well-being. "Protecting the jobs of American workers" was called a very important goal by three-quarters or more of the public throughout the period, and it stood at the very top of the rankings in 1982, 1986, and especially 1990, a recession year.

Close to three-quarters of respondents in all five surveys said that "securing adequate supplies of energy" should be a very important goal of U.S. foreign policy, especially at the time of the OPEC oil boycotts and high oil prices of the 1970s. "Keeping up the value of the dollar" topped the ranking in 1978, when stagflation and international competition were pressing concerns. "Reducing our trade deficit with foreign countries" was widely considered important when surveys began asking about it.

During the Cold War period—as in later years—the goal of "combating world hunger" was ranked highest among the purely altruistic or humanitarian justice goals; it was consistently called very important by about three-fifths of Americans. Other justice-related goals, such as promoting human rights, improving standards of living in less developed countries, protecting weaker nations against aggression, and bringing democratic forms of government to other nations, repeatedly came out at the bottom of the rankings, with little more than one-third of Americans saying they should be very important goals of U.S. foreign policy. (Again, however, many said they should be "somewhat important" goals.) Even "strengthening the United Nations," which mixes elements of altruism with security concerns, won less than majority support as very important during the 1970s and 1980s, when the General Assembly was widely perceived as anti-American; it rose, however, after the multinational Gulf War coalition came together under UN auspices in 1990.

One might imagine that "everything changed" in U.S. foreign policy with the end of the Cold War. The surveys from 1990 and later, however, show that Americans' basic foreign policy objectives remained surprisingly similar to what they had been before (see table 2.3). Table 2.3 should not be used to make precise cross-year comparisons of percentage figures involving 2002 or 2004, because the CCFR changed survey modes in those years, from purely in-person interviews in 1974 through 1998, to a combination of telephone and-in person interviews in 2002, to a Web-based survey in 2004. Comparisons of results from identical questions asked in all three modes in 2002 have established that there were substantial mode effects on responses regarding goals (telephone respondents tended to call more goals "very important," for example), so that one should—and we will—only compare percentages based on the same survey mode. But the *rankings* of goals appear to be comparable across modes. Table 2.3 makes clear that the American public ranked its foreign policy goals in much the same order after the end of the Cold War as before, and that there was a great deal of continuity in goal rankings every year between 1990 and 2004.

To be sure, after the Cold War there were real-world changes in the nature of international threats and changes in how the United States might achieve security from attack. The CCFR altered its survey questions, substituting

Table 2.3. Post–Cold War goals

		Should be a "very important" goal (%)				
		1990	1994	1998	2002*	2004*
S	Preventing the spread of nuclear weapons	84	82	82	90	73
S	Combating international terrorism	–	–	79	91	71
D	Protecting the jobs of American Workers	84	83	80	85	78
D	Stopping the flow of illegal drugs	–	85	81	81	63
D	Securing adequate supplies of energy	76	62	64	75	69
D	Controlling illegal immigration	–	72	55	70	59
D, J	Improving the global environment	73	58	53	66	47
J	Combating world hunger	–	56	62	61	43
D	Reducing our trade deficit	70	59	50	51	–
S	Maintaining superior military power	–	50	59	68	50
S, J	Strengthening the United Nations	52	51	45	57	38
D	Protecting interests of American business abroad	46	52	–	49	32
S, J	Defending our allies' security	43	41	44	57	–
J	Promoting human rights	40	34	39	47	–
D, J	Promoting market economies abroad	–	–	34	36	–
J, S	Protecting weaker nations	32	24	32	41	18
J	Improving standards of living	33	22	29	30	18
J, S	Bringing democratic government	28	25	29	34	14

Source: CCFR surveys.

Note: **S** = Security from attack, **D** = Security of domestic well-being, **J** = Justice and help for people abroad.

* Comparisons of percentages (though not rankings) involving 2002 and/or 2004 can be misleading because of survey mode differences. See the text and endnotes.

"preventing the spread of nuclear weapons" and "combating international terrorism" for the old Soviet-oriented security items. But the new threats, like the old, led to very high ranking of goals related to security from attack. Preventing nuclear proliferation has ranked at or near the top of all foreign policy goals throughout the period. Combating terrorism emerged as a highly ranked goal when it was first asked about in 1998 (just after the U.S. embassy bombings in Africa) and became the top goal in 2002, after the World Trade Center and Pentagon attacks of the previous year. Presumably for the same reason, the importance attributed to maintaining superior military power rose in 2002. The apparent increases in support for defending allies, protecting weaker nations, and several other relatively low-ranking goals, however, are artifacts of the 2002 change in survey modes; comparisons of in-person respondents in the two years show no significant opinion changes.[12] It is certainly not true that "everything changed," either after the end of the Cold War or after September 11, 2001.

By 2004, when there had been no new terrorist attacks on the United States and when the messy aftermath of the invasion of Iraq had caused growing disillusionment with U.S. foreign policy, the public put a somewhat lower priority on goals related to security from attack. According to same-mode survey data, the proportions of Americans attributing great importance to preventing the spread of nuclear weapons, combating international terrorism, and maintaining superior military power abroad dropped by 13, 12, and 17 percentage points, respectively—not quite as much as implied by the mixed-mode contrast in table 2.3 (and, as we will see, no more than most justice-related goals dropped), but quite a decline nonetheless.[13] Still, nonproliferation and combating terrorism stayed near the top of the goals rankings.

Domestic well-being has been a central concern of the American public in all post–Cold War surveys. Job protection ranked at or near the top every time (moving back into the number-one spot in 2004), with 80 to 85 percent of Americans generally saying it should be a very important goal of U.S. foreign policy. Securing adequate supplies of energy has also been considered very important, especially in surveys conducted in 1990 (during the run-up to the Gulf War), in 2002, and in 2004. New CCFR questions about stopping the flow of illegal drugs into the United States, controlling and reducing illegal immigration, and improving the global environment revealed very high support for those objectives as well, particularly for stopping drugs. Support for reducing immigration was highest in 1994, 2002, and 2004, when the U.S. economy was relatively shaky and job competition was seen as a threat; it was somewhat lower in boom-time 1998. Between 2002 and 2004, when same-mode survey comparisons show that every single goal received lower "very important" ratings, the domestic well-being goals dropped least.[14] As chapter 7 will make clear, these domestic well-being goals are given considerably lower priority by foreign policy decision makers than by ordinary citizens.

In the post–Cold War years, most of the purely altruistic justice-related goals continued to be rated as less important than the self-interested ones. The U.S. public was particularly ungenerous in 1994 (the year that produced the Gingrich-led conservative takeover of Congress, during a "jobless recovery" from economic recession), with significant drops for nearly all justice related goals: improving standards of living, promoting human rights, protecting weaker nations against aggression, and bringing democratic government to other nations.[15] These mostly rebounded in 1998 as the U.S. economy improved, but the impression from table 2.3 of an additional rise in 2002 is probably an artifact of the CCFR's switch in survey modes. By 2004 the proportions calling various justice-related goals "very important" had dropped markedly, by as much as 17 percentage points in the case of strengthening the UN and protecting weaker nations against foreign aggression.

INTERNATIONAL THREATS AND PROBLEMS

The foreign policy goals that people seek are closely connected, both in logic and in empirical fact, to the international threats and problems they perceive. Conceptually, a goal can be viewed as flowing from basic *values* (such as economic well-being, or physical security from attack), together with *beliefs* about opportunities for—or obstacles to—realizing those values. That is, in the hierarchical means-ends chains that constitute purposive belief systems, goals come a step or two lower than basic values. They focus on results that would realize one or more values, in conjunction with beliefs about particular ways in which those results could be achieved (e.g., a belief that security from attack can be achieved through "maintaining superior military power," or through "worldwide arms control").[16] Recall figure 1.1 in the previous chapter.

Similarly, perceptions of international *threats* or *problems* consist of beliefs about obstacles or challenges to the realization of particular values. Threats and problems differ from goals only in that they emphasize the negative: they focus on beliefs or perceptions concerning factors that might prevent the realization of particular values, such as the danger of attack from a heavily armed, hostile country, or economic competition from abroad that might lead to lower wages or job losses for American workers. Thus an exploration of the international threats and problems that Americans perceive is bound to cover much of the same ground as our discussion of Americans' foreign policy goals. Still, a brief look is worthwhile, both to confirm our account of the basic values or objectives that the public seeks from U.S. foreign policy, and to introduce additional elements of purposive belief systems that sometimes play important parts in organizing individuals' foreign policy attitudes and policy preferences.

In CCFR surveys over the years, members of the public have regularly been asked two open-ended questions: "What do you feel are the two or three biggest problems facing the country today?" and "What do you feel are the two or three biggest *foreign policy* problems facing the United States today?" (emphasis added).[17] Peoples' responses to these questions, when combined into general categories and counted, give measures of what sorts of international problems have most worried the American public at a given moment in time.

In the survey conducted in June 2002, for example, less than a year after the terrorist attacks on the World Trade Center and the Pentagon, about one third (33 percent) of all respondents spontaneously mentioned international terrorism as one of the two or three biggest foreign policy problems facing the United States. Smaller fractions of the public mentioned such related matters as arms control and nuclear weapons (5 percent), war (4 percent), or the situation in Afghanistan (3 percent), where the United States had just attacked and defeated al Qaeda terrorists and their Taliban hosts. The 33 percent figure for terrorism put it at the top of the public's foreign policy agenda in 2002, ahead of the general situation in the Middle East (cited by 12 percent of respondents) or Israel-Palestinian problems (9 percent), and well ahead of Americans' perennial concerns with foreign aid (8 percent), immigration (7 percent), or oil supplies (4 percent). (Only 3 percent of the public spontaneously mentioned Saddam Hussein's Iraq, which the Bush administration was just beginning to target publicly as a major concern.) More respondents cited terrorism as a big foreign policy problem than had mentioned any other single problem in any previous CCFR survey. Of course one could also note that this glass was nearly two-thirds empty: nine months after the 9/11 attacks, only a third of Americans spontaneously mentioned terrorism even as one of the *two or three* biggest foreign policy problems facing the United States.

In responses to the more general question, about problems facing the country (not limited to foreign policy), terrorism was cited as one of the two or three biggest problems by a relatively high 36 percent of the public: more than mentioned any other problem, domestic or foreign, and more than had ever cited a single foreign policy problem in any previous CCFR survey. When mentions of terrorism in 2002 are added to those of all other foreign policy problems in that year, they together constitute about two-fifths (41 percent) of all problem mentions, far more than in 1998 (16 percent) or in previous years. Thus in 2002 there were nearly as many mentions of terrorism and other foreign policy problems as there were mentions of the economy (then in the doldrums) and all other domestic concerns, including education, health care, drug abuse, crime, poverty, the environment, and racism. (The economy was cited in general terms by 22 percent of the public, unemployment by 9 percent.) Once again, however, the glass can be seen as partly empty: even so soon after the 9/11 attacks, more Americans were worried about domestic than foreign matters. This confirms our earlier finding that foreign policy goals related to security of domestic well-being have regularly held their own with goals related to security from attack. Still, we will see that the high level of public concern about international terrorism was accompanied by support from large majorities of Americans for a number of specific military and nonmilitary policies to combat terrorism.

Over the years, responses to the "biggest foreign policy problems" question have generally reflected world events and crises as reported in the headlines of the day. In the 1990 survey, for example, conducted shortly after the Iraqi invasion of Kuwait (which the first President Bush had vowed "will not stand"), many Americans mentioned the Middle East situation (21 percent) or Iraq (18 percent) as big problems. In 1986, many cited arms control (16 percent) or relations with the Soviet Union (22 percent); much the same thing was true in previous Cold War surveys. From the late 1970s to the beginning of the 1990s, trade deficits and the balance of payments were prominently mentioned as big problems, by 10 to 15 percent of respondents. In Vietnam-weary 1974, foreign affairs barely made the "country's biggest problems" radar screen; most of the 13 percent of Americans mentioning foreign policy said we should stop supporting other countries with foreign aid and instead take care of this country's needs.[18]

The open-ended "biggest problems" questions, which have generally been posed toward the beginning of the CCFR surveys (before a barrage of specific questions about foreign policy could influence respondents' thinking), have the advantage of eliciting spontaneous responses that reflect what ordinary Americans, rather than the designers of surveys, have been thinking. But they have the disadvantage—characteristic of open-ended questions—that they do not produce comparable information on how all interviewees feel about any one particular threat or problem. For that purpose it is useful to pose closed-ended questions that ask everyone to evaluate each of several potential *threats*.

Since 1990, CCFR surveys have regularly listed a number of "possible threats to the vital interest of the United States in the next 10 years" and asked whether respondents considered each a "critical threat," an "important but not critical threat," or "not an important threat at all." The same possible threats have often been repeated from one survey to the next in order to track opinion trends, but the lists have also been changed somewhat in order to keep up with world events. The percentage of Americans calling each possible threat "critical" can be used to form a ranking of how important or unimportant the public considers each possible threat to be.[19] Such a ranking for 2002 is given in table 2.4. Rankings for 2004 were quite similar, though most of the absolute percentages dropped markedly.[20]

By the "threat" measure, too, Americans in 2002 were highly concerned about terrorism. International terrorism was seen as a "critical" threat to the vital interest of the United States by an overwhelming 91 percent of all respondents. Chemical and biological weapons were seen as a critical threat by 86 percent, Iraq developing weapons of mass destruction by 86 percent,

Table 2.4. Perceived threats to the vital interest of the United States

	Threat is "critical" (%)
International terrorism	91
Chemical and biological weapons	86
Iraq developing weapons of mass destruction	86
Possibility of unfriendly countries becoming nuclear powers	85
AIDS, the Ebola virus, and other potential epidemics	68
Military conflict between Israel and its Arab neighbors	67
Islamic fundamentalism	61
Large numbers of immigrants and refugees coming into the U.S.	60
Development of China as a world power	56
Tensions between India and Pakistan	54
Global warming	46
World population growth	44
Economic competition from low-wage countries	31
Economic competition from Japan	29
Globalization	29
Political turmoil in Russia	27
Financial crises in other countries	25
Civil wars in Africa	24
Military power of Russia	23
Economic competition from Europe	13

Source: CCFR 2002 general public combined telephone and in-person data set.

and "the possibility of unfriendly countries becoming nuclear powers" by 85 percent of the public. "Islamic fundamentalism" was seen as a critical threat by 61 percent of Americans, up fully 23 percentage points since 1998.[21] Large majorities of Americans saw their homeland as seriously endangered. We will see that these perceptions of threats, like the associated goals, were related in individuals' minds to a number of specific policies aimed at combating terrorism.

By 2004, in the absence of further terrorist attacks and amid growing disillusionment about the invasion of Iraq and failure to find weapons of mass destruction there, nearly all perceptions of threats (except for certain economic, domestic well-being threats) dropped markedly. Perceptions of terrorism, chemical and biological weapons, unfriendly countries going nuclear, and Islamic fundamentalism as critical threats dropped by about 10, 17, 19, and 21 percentage points, respectively.

In 2002, three other geopolitical situations were also seen by majorities of Americans as posing a "critical threat" to vital U.S. interests. Military conflict between Israel and its Arab neighbors, long of great concern to the United States, was called a critical threat by 67 percent of the public. The development of China as a world power, which its rapid economic growth seemed to portend and which some Washington officials and pundits deplored, was seen as a critical threat by 56 percent. And tensions between India and Pakistan, two nuclear-armed countries reported to be close to war shortly before the survey was conducted, were called a critical threat by 54 percent. Again, we will see that individuals' perceptions of these threats were related to their concrete policy preferences. All these perceived threats dropped markedly by 2004, in part because of objective changes: tensions between India and Pakistan, in particular, were much lower.

The language of "critical threats" probably tends to direct respondents' attention to dangers of sudden violence or armed attack. Worries about domestic problems or justice abroad are less likely to come to mind in this context, so the CCFR "threat" questions probably give a less balanced picture of what Americans are concerned about than the "goals" questions. Still, table 2.4 indicates that large numbers of Americans are also concerned about perceived threats to their domestic well-being. Next to terrorism and weapons of mass destruction, the highest ranked threat in 2002 (called "critical" by 68 percent) was "AIDS, the Ebola virus, and other potential epidemics." AIDS is widely seen not only as afflicting many millions of people in Africa, Asia, and elsewhere, but also as endangering many Americans. Also widely seen as a critical threat, by 60 percent of the public, was "large numbers of immigrants and refugees coming into the U.S." As we will see, anxieties about immigration have economic, cultural, and security-related roots. Also called critical threats by substantial numbers of Americans in 2002 were global warming (46 percent) and world population growth (44 percent), both of which could impact domestic well-being in the United States as well as living conditions abroad. Those threat perceptions, like foreign policy goals, turn out to be strongly related in individuals' minds to specific policy preferences. It is noteworthy too that the only threats called critical by more Americans in 2004 than in 2002 were related to security of domestic well-being: economic competition from Europe and from low-wage countries.[22]

Individuals' perceptions of threats were related, in logically consistent ways, to the amount of importance they attributed to various foreign policy goals. For example, people in 2002 who perceived a critical threat from international terrorism, from chemical and biological weapons, from Iraq developing weapons of mass destruction, or from the possibility of unfriendly countries becoming nuclear powers, also tended to think that "combating international terrorism" should be a very important goal of U.S. foreign policy. Those who saw these threats as less important tended to consider the goal of combating terrorism as less important. (Pearson correlation coefficients were in the .24 to .36 range.[23]) The same threats were also related, though less strongly, to the goal of preventing the spread of nuclear weapons (correlations in the .13 to .27 range).[24]

Similarly, perceptions of a threat from "large numbers of immigrants and refugees coming into the United States" were very highly correlated with the goal of "controlling and reducing illegal immigration." The threat of global warming and the threat of population growth were closely related to the goal of "improving the global environment." Those most concerned about the threat of large number of immigrants and refugees coming into the country tended to call very important the goal of "protecting the jobs of American workers" (Pearson's *r* ranged from .25 to .56).[25]

These findings of empirical connections between the foreign policy goals that people seek and their perceptions of international threats are hardly earthshaking: the logical connections between the two are obvious. But they do not merely mean that individuals mechanically gave the same answers when similar questions were repeated moments later. The relationships involve survey questions that were rather widely separated in the questionnaire and formulated in substantially different terms. These relationships clearly contradict a "non-attitudes" perspective (which would expect such responses to be entirely random and unrelated) and, thus, constitute significant evidence for the existence of coherent, purposive foreign policy belief systems of the sort depicted in figure 1.1.

Over the years, the perceived importance of particular threats has risen and fallen with changes in real-world conditions. In the surveys of 1990 and 1994, for example, after a long boom in Japanese economic growth and exports, economic competition from Japan was seen by nearly two-thirds of Americans (60 percent and 62 percent, respectively) as a critical threat to the vital interest of the United States. As the U.S. economy improved and that of Japan declined, however, this dropped to 45 percent in 1998 and just 29 percent in 2002. Similarly, perceptions of economic competition from Europe as a critical threat gradually fell from 30 percent at the beginnings of the 1990s to 13 percent in 2002, and perceptions of economic competition from low-wage countries as a critical threat dipped a bit between 1998 and 2002,[26] though both rose slightly in 2004.

As noted previously, perceptions of Islamic fundamentalism as a critical threat jumped sharply between 1998 and 2002 after the World Trade Center attacks by Islamic terrorists. There were smaller rises in worry about unfriendly countries becoming nuclear powers (up 10 points), about chemical and biological weapons (up 10 points), and about international terrorism (up 7 points from an already very high level). Again, all these perceptions of threats dropped substantially by 2004, when no further terrorist attacks on the United States had occurred.

Even after the end of the Cold War, concern about the military power of Russia as a critical threat remained substantial (around 33 percent) until 2002, when Russia came to be seen as a reliable partner in fighting terrorism and the perception of threat declined. Anxiety about large numbers of immigrants and refugees coming into the U.S. stood at a high point in economically weak 1994, when 72 percent of Americans called it a critical threat, but it dropped sharply to 55 percent in prosperous 1998, rebounding somewhat in recessionary 2002.

We turn now from collective public opinion to issues concerning *individual* Americans' attitudes and behavior. The main points—especially the widespread consensus on foreign policy goals among different social groups, the normatively ambiguous effects of formal education, and the way political predispositions or "basic attitudes" (particularly the belief that the United States should take an active part in world affairs) fit into purposive belief systems—are relevant to our main argument that policy makers should pay attention to public opinion. But the details may be of more interest to students of individual behavior and political psychology than to readers chiefly interested in foreign policy.

WHO WANTS WHAT FROM FOREIGN POLICY

In seeking to understand *why* individuals place high or low priority on various foreign policy goals, it makes sense to look first at their personal and social characteristics. It turns out, though, that individuals' foreign policy goals—and foreign policy attitudes in general—are not very strongly anchored in their personal characteristics or social affiliations. There is a great deal of agreement across social groups. Often belief systems about foreign policy are relatively freestanding, based on values, beliefs, and ideologies—and presumably personal experience and historical learning as well—that are only faintly related to such demographic characteristics as gender, race, age, or income.

When we performed multiple regression analyses with the 2002 CCFR data, we found that the power of individuals' personal characteristics to predict how much importance they attributed to various foreign policy goals was very weak. We used a comprehensive set of fourteen demographic characteristics: gender, marital status, level of formal education, income, two measures of employment status, age, three racial/ethnic dichotomous variables (Hispanic, African-American, Asian), and four religious dichotomous variables (Evangelical, Catholic, Jewish, Muslim). For only four of the twenty goals—protecting jobs, stopping drugs, strengthening the UN, and improving the global environment—could more than 5 percent of the variance in importance ratings be accounted for by these demographic factors, and in no case did it reach 10 percent.[27] This certainly does not mean that peoples' foreign policy goals are rootless or ephemeral; we will see that they are often rather closely linked to a variety of other attitudes, including ideological positions and specific policy preferences. But neither goals nor threat perceptions—nor, indeed any but a handful of foreign policy attitudes and opinions we have studied—are deeply rooted in individuals' personal or social characteristics.[28]

By the same token, in these analyses of foreign policy goals, few personal or social characteristics had regression coefficients that would indicate substantial effects. Even though rather large numbers of respondents were analyzed, most estimated demographic coefficients were not significantly different from zero. Indeed, in thirteen of the twenty regression analyses, coefficients for only two or fewer of the fourteen demographic variables were significantly different from zero according to standard statistical criteria.[29] Still, these analyses produced some interesting results. Controlling for all the other demographic factors, for example, in 2002 the goal of protecting the jobs of American workers was considered significantly more important by people with less formal education, women, African Americans, lower-income people, and Catholics. Stopping illegal drugs was considered especially important (again controlling for other demographics) by evangelical Protestants, older people, Catholics, and women, but was downgraded by the highly educated. The goal of strengthening the UN was most enthusiastically embraced by women, lower-income people, and African Americans, but was rejected by evangelicals. Similarly, improving the global environment was most important to women, Hispanics, and lower-income people, and least important to evangelicals. The goal of bringing a democratic form of government to other nations was considered significantly more important by those of higher income, Catholics, African Americans, and Muslims, but less important by people with the most formal education.[30]

Because such demographic characteristics are relatively fixed and unlikely to be affected by individuals' foreign policy opinions, we can be particularly confident that these regression coefficients indicate independent *effects* of certain demographic characteristics upon individuals' espousal of certain foreign policy goals. We will briefly discuss some personal and social characteristics, noting any interesting effects, but also emphasizing that—contrary to some expectations—most personal characteristics have little or no effect. A possible exception involves individuals' levels of formal education.

The ambiguous effects of education and economic status. Formal education is sometimes thought to have crucial effects on foreign policy attitudes. Education is, of course, strongly related to cognitive skills and knowledge. *If* education has strong and pervasive effects on foreign policy opinions, and *if* those effects arise from greater knowledge or more powerful reasoning abilities, our argument that decision makers should pay attention to general public opinion must face a serious challenge. Why heed the general public? Why not just pay attention to the opinions of the highly educated elite?

Such a challenge has in fact been raised by a great deal of past research on public opinion and foreign policy. Particularly in the 1950s and 1960s, much research focused on alleged differences between an "attentive" and an inattentive public. Some scholars claimed that only a very small group of highly alert and well-informed citizens—perhaps constituting less than 10 percent of the American public—paid enough attention to what went on in the world, and had sufficient knowledge and cognitive skills, to form foreign policy preferences sufficiently coherent and reasonable that policy makers should take them into account.[31]

Our analyses do not provide much support for that idea. True, education level does have substantial *bivariate* (two variables at a time) relationships with goals and many other foreign policy attitudes. When other demographic factors (including income) are taken into account, however, the independent effects of education—though bigger than for any other demographic factor—turn out to be much more modest. Moreover, there is considerable ambiguity about exactly *why* these effects occur. Knowledge plays a part, but only a limited one. In some cases the root cause of education effects may have more to do with differences in social status and material self-interest that are associated with formal education. A further complicating factor is that highly educated people may be more aware of and more influenced by dominant social norms and mainstream communications networks than others are. This may lead them to accept whatever policies U.S. officials are promoting at the moment, whether or not those policies are based on correct information about world affairs. That is, the opinions of the highly educated may actually be the most easily manipulated by policy makers. To the extent that distinctive material self-interests or proneness to manipulation drive the opinions of the highly educated, it would be a mistake to accord them more respect than the opinions of other Americans.

When it comes to foreign policy goals, these ambiguities surrounding educational effects are on full display. If one looks at simple bivariate relationships between individuals' education levels and the importance they attribute to various goals—that is, if one just compares the opinions of highly educated people with those of the less educated—there appear to be many substantial differences. In 2002, on thirteen of the CCFR's twenty goals, there were differences of 9 percentage points or more (sometimes differences as high as 25 or 30 percentage points) between the proportions of highly educated and less-educated people that called a given goal "very important." When one controls for other demographic characteristics (including income and employment status) in multivariate regressions, however, these differences diminish and sometimes vanish. In our comprehensive demographic regressions, the coefficients for education were significantly different from zero for nine of the twenty goals—nearly half of them, more than for any other demographic variable—but in most cases they were quite modest in magnitude. This reduction in estimated impact, together with the substantive pattern of education effects, supports the inference that the social status and income correlates of formal education, rather than its cognitive and informational aspects, may underlie many of the differences in foreign policy goals.

The biggest education differences have to do with domestic well-being goals, which tend to affect lower-income and lower-status Americans more than those at the top of the heap. In 2002, for example, those who had not graduated from high school were much more likely than those who had done postgraduate work—by fully 34 percentage points (94 percent, compared to 60 percent)—to say that protecting the jobs of American workers should be a very important goal of U.S. foreign policy. This relationship held up in multiple regressions that controlled for thirteen other personal characteristics; in fact the standardized coefficient for education level in the job-protection regression, while not enormous ($-.21$), was among the largest for all the demographic variables in all our regressions for all twenty goals. But it is not clear that highly educated Americans assign a lower priority to job protection because of superior wisdom. This may instead reflect a difference in objective interests between people of different social classes. Americans with the least formal education consider themselves to be, and in fact have been, the most vulnerable to job and wage pressures from foreign economic competition.

Similarly, less-educated people—whose children are more exposed to drugs and drug-related crime and violence in their schools and neighborhoods—much more often than the highly educated, by 29 percentage points (92 percent, compared to 63 percent), said that stopping illegal drugs from entering the United States should be a very important foreign policy goal. This relationship, too, held up in multivariate analysis. Similarly, more formal education (controlling for other factors) led to less emphasis on the importance of controlling and reducing illegal immigration, which poses greater economic and cultural threats to lower-status

Americans, and to less emphasis on the domestic-prosperity goal of securing adequate supplies of energy.[32]

Beyond matters of economic class interest, having more formal education also made individuals less likely to endorse certain security-from-attack goals that are directly linked to the safety of Americans. In 2002, a higher level of education led people to attribute less importance to the goals of maintaining superior military power, combating international terrorism, and helping bring a democratic form of government to other countries. (As we will see, the latter is linked to security through the idea of "democratic peace," a widespread belief that democracies don't attack each other.) But education had no significant effects at all on the security-related goals of defending allies or protecting weaker nations from foreign aggression, both of which can entail high costs, in terms of U.S. casualties, that are largely borne by lower-status Americans.

It is also striking that more formal education had no significant tendency at all to lead people to attribute high importance to such justice-related, altruistic or humanitarian foreign policy goals as combating hunger, promoting human rights, improving the global environment, strengthening the United Nations, and strengthening international law. Whatever norms are promoted by higher education in the United States, they apparently do not include a sense of global citizenship or deep sympathy for people in other countries.

All in all, our analysis of education's effects on goals does not give a great deal of support to the idea that people with extensive formal education enjoy superior wisdom about what U.S. foreign policy should do, and that their opinions therefore deserve greater respect from policy makers. Instead, education-related differences in goals often tend to reflect differences in values that are related to peoples' social positions.

Additional evidence for this point comes from the fact that in some cases, when we controlled for education and all the other demographic factors, income itself had significant effects upon the goals that people considered important. Higher-income people were less concerned than lower-income people with protecting the jobs of American workers and were less likely to attribute great importance to the justice-related goals of strengthening the United Nations, strengthening international law and institutions, and improving the global environment. The class- and status-related aspects of education probably go beyond those captured by the (imperfectly measured) variable of family income.[33]

Limited effects of knowledge and exposure to the world. Individuals' positions in society, especially their incomes and levels of formal education, are related to their attentiveness to and information about world affairs. People with lots of money can more easily afford to go to college or send their children there, to make trips abroad, and to surround themselves with books, magazines, and computers that will help produce a well-informed view of the world. Thus there is a fairly strong empirical relationship between family income, on the one hand, and attentiveness and knowledge, on the other. But an important question is whether it is the money or the information that affects attitudes. In the case of foreign policy goals, exposure to the world and knowledge about it have very little independent effect, once level of formal education, income, employment status, and other personal characteristics are controlled for.

The telephone-based part of the 2002 CCFR survey included three knowledge measures relevant to foreign affairs: whether or not respondents could name the new European currency (about half knew it was the euro); how close they came to correctly estimating what proportion of the U.S. federal budget went to foreign aid (nearly everyone overestimated it, but some came much closer than others); and whether or not respondents reported that they had traveled outside the United States (about two-thirds said they had).

If knowledge about the world or exposure to it makes a difference in the foreign policy goals people seek, we would expect world travelers and those who are well informed to specify different goals as very important. In general, however, controlling for other personal characteristics, they did not. When we added these three information/exposure variables to our demographic regressions, the amount of variance explained (as indicated by adjusted R-squared) did not rise by even 1 percent except for three of the twenty goals—protecting jobs, maintaining superior military power, and protecting the interest of American business abroad. For thirteen of the goals, the proportion of variance explained—taking into account the random gains expected from adding any new independent variables—actually went *down*. Nor did the individual measures of information or international exposure have much independent impact upon the goals people sought. In a series of multiple regressions that included the knowledge/exposure variables plus the fourteen demographic factors and three ideological and partisan attitudes (to be discussed below), knowledge of the euro had a significant coefficient for seven of the twenty goals, most of them focused on humanitarian or domestic matters. But in every case the coefficient was *negative*: having more information or exposure made people consider the goals less important. The same was true of the four goals affected by more accurate perception of the size of the foreign aid budget. (Foreign travel independently affected ratings of only two goals, one positively and one negatively.)[34]

One might argue that highly informed people are more discriminating, more apt to select just a few goals to emphasize—or, conversely, that the less informed are rather facile in calling many goals "very important." But it is hard to discern any pattern of superior enlightenment in the goals that are differentially sought by the most highly informed. Rather than spurning the opinions of the whole American public as being based on little education and poor information, foreign policy decision makers might do well to consider the possibility that educational and informational differences largely reflect different values and interests, and that—in a democratic country—everyone's values and interests should have equal weight.

Women and men. Past research has uncovered a number of small but persistent gender differences in policy preferences, with women tending to be more opposed than men (in the bivariate sense) to the use of force and more supportive of certain social welfare policies.[35]

With respect to foreign policy goals, in the 2002 CCFR data we found no indication of women's being averse to the use of force, except perhaps their slight tendency to assign more importance to preventing nuclear proliferation; there were no significant gender differences with regard to international terrorism or military strength, perhaps because the September 11 attacks had moved women closer to the hawkishness of men. But women were significantly more likely than men—by about 9 to 13 percentage points—to call various altruistic or humanitarian goals "very important." In every case this tendency persisted in multivariate regressions that controlled for other demographic characteristics. In other words, gender had a real, independent (though not very large) effect on the prioritizing of a number of justice-related goals. Being female led to attributing greater importance to the goals of strengthening the United Nations, improving the global environment, strengthening international law and institutions, combating world hunger, and promoting human rights abroad (being unmarried had an additional impact on the human rights goal). In addition, being female led to somewhat more concern about three domestic well-being goals: protecting Americans jobs, protecting the interests of American business abroad, and stopping illegal drugs.[36]

Young and old. Various sorts of "generation gaps" between younger and older Americans have been observed in attitudes about domestic politics and policies, but age differences concerning foreign policy have generally been weak.[37] This was true in the 2002 CCFR survey data as well. In terms of simple bivariate relationships, age differences concerning foreign policy goals were numerous, though small. But they mostly vanished when other personal characteristics were controlled for. Consistent with the image of older Americans as being more supportive of the military and more conservative in social attitudes, however, the old in 2002 placed more importance than the young—controlling for other personal characteristics—on maintaining superior military power and especially on stopping illegal drugs and controlling and reducing illegal immigration.[38]

African Americans, Hispanics, and Asians. The racial and ethnic differences that frequently pervade disputes over U.S. domestic politics appear only faintly in the realm of foreign policy goals. The clearest trace we found was that a few more African Americans than whites, by 11 percentage points, said that protecting the jobs of American workers should be a very important goal. But African Americans also showed a small but significant tendency (which persisted in multivariate regressions) to embrace humanitarian values and sympathy with underdogs abroad. They attributed greater importance than whites, for example, to improving the standard of living in less developed countries, strengthening the United Nations, and bringing a democratic form of government to other nations.[39] As we will see, these values are reflected in African Americans' relatively high support for humanitarian foreign aid, especially to Africa.

Hispanics are even less distinctive in their foreign policy goals. Their clearest difference from other Americans in the 2002 survey was the lower importance they attributed to the goal of controlling and reducing illegal immigration, which of course has particular relevance to immigrants from Mexico and Central America. Controlling, as usual, for all other demographic characteristics, Hispanics also tended more than others to say that improving the global environment should be a very important goal of U.S. foreign policy.[40]

Rather few Asian Americans were interviewed in the 2002 CCFR survey. But their numbers were sufficient for multiple regressions to reveal one significant distinctive reaction to a foreign policy goal: Asian Americans tended to attribute less importance than did others to protecting weaker nations against foreign aggression.[41] It is not clear which "weaker nations" they had in mind but apparently not South Korea; as chapter 4 will indicate, Asian Americans tended, if anything, to be *more* supportive than others of using U.S. troops in the event of an invasion by North Korea.

Protestants, Catholics, Jews, and Muslims. In later chapters we will see that Americans of different religious faiths tend to have quite distinctive views of some foreign countries, foreign leaders, and U.S. policies, especially in the Middle East. Evangelical Protestants, Jews, and Muslims have differed markedly from other Americans in their opinions about Israel, Ariel Sharon, and certain (but not all) U.S. policies in the region. In terms of general foreign policy goals, however, religious-based differences—while sometimes significant—are weaker. In our multivariate regressions of foreign policy goals with demographic characteristics we included four dichotomous, yes/no variables, indicating whether or not respondents were, respectively, evangelical Protestants, Catholics, Jews, or Muslims. (The residual category included "moderate to liberal" Protestants, people of other religions, and people with no religion.)

With all other demographic factors controlled for, evangelicals tended to more strongly embrace the goals of stopping the flow of illegal drugs and combating international terrorism, and to be less supportive than others of the liberal or altruistic goals of improving the global environment and strengthening the United Nations.[42] We will see additional conservative effects of evangelicalism in later chapters.

Catholics in the United States, who constitute about one quarter of the population, no longer differ much in social and political attitudes from moderate to liberal Protestants. But—again controlling for all other demographic factors—they did tend to attribute a little more importance than others to the foreign policy goals of stopping illegal drugs, protecting the jobs of American workers, and helping bring a democratic form of government to other nations.[43]

The number of Jews in the 2002 survey was small but sufficient for multiple regressions to pick up one significantly distinctive reaction to foreign policy goals. More Jews than others, controlling for other demographic factors, tended to say that safeguarding against global financial instability should be a very important goal of U.S. foreign policy.[44] As we will see, being Jewish also had substantial effects on feelings about countries in the Middle East and on specific policy preferences related to the Middle East.

Very few Muslims were included in the 2002 CCFR survey, certainly not enough to characterize with any confidence the precise distribution of opinions among all American Muslims. But the fact that most of these people were selected by random-digit-dialing telephone techniques (meaning that they were geographically scattered rather than clustered in just one or two neighborhoods that personal interviewers visited), together with the great power of multivariate regressions to sort out the independent effects of multiple variables, made it possible to discern one distinctive effect upon goals of being Muslim. Controlling for other characteristics, American Muslims attributed significantly more importance than others did to the foreign policy goal of "promoting a democratic form of government in other nations."[45] Very likely they had in mind democratic reforms in the autocratic governments of the Middle East. In later chapters we will see that being Muslim had some very distinctive effects upon feelings about certain countries and upon certain specific policy preferences related to the Middle East.

Southerners, northerners, westerners, and easterners. During much of American history, people in different geographical regions of the country have taken quite distinctive—and often conflicting—positions on issues of U.S. foreign policy.[46] For many years it was generally safe to say that "the South is different": commodity-exporting southerners tended to be the leading internationalists, strongly favoring free trade. The South has also tended to have a strong military tradition, presumably solidified by the rise of the defense industry "Gunbelt" in that region.[47] Midwesterners were often seen as isolationists, and westerners (especially Rocky Mountain and Plains westerners) as cowboys, belligerent and quick at the trigger. Northeasterners were supposed to be liberal internationalists.

But now economic development and a common culture have spread throughout the country. Yankees have moved to the suburban South; cities and suburbs have grown in the West; the Midwest has connected closely with the global economy. Regional differences in foreign policy attitudes have become quite muted. Even in simple bivariate terms, of the twenty foreign policy goals the CCFR asked about in 2002 there were statistically significant differences among the four major regions—South, Northeast, Midwest, and West—on only seven.[48] And those differences were fairly small, usually amounting to only 10 or 12 percentage points.

Southerners, for example, tended to worry more than westerners about reducing our trade deficit (by 18 percentage points, the biggest regional difference) and about protecting American business abroad. Midwesterners were a little more concerned about maintaining superior military power than the stereotypically gun-happy westerners, and they were a bit quicker than westerners to call the domestic-impact goals of reducing illegal immigration and securing adequate energy supplies "very important." Northeasterners, who share with midwesterners the rigors of cold weather, shared also a somewhat greater than average concern about energy supplies. In a faint indication of northeasterners' supposed liberalism, they were also a little more likely than midwesterners to attribute great importance to defending human rights in other countries and strengthening the United Nations.

Again, however, most of these differences were small. This was true of all the personal and social characteristics we have discussed. As we will see in later chapters, demographic differences rarely account for much variation in specific policy preferences or other foreign policy opinions. Considerably more important are peoples' ways of thinking, including their basic values and political predispositions.

"BASIC ATTITUDES"

Certain ideological or partisan political predispositions of Americans—what we will call *basic attitudes*—apparently have much stronger effects on foreign policy goals and specific policy preferences than do peoples' personal characteristics. True, lacking experimental data, we cannot always be entirely sure which attitudes cause which.[49] Goals, perceived threats, and policy preferences may sometimes affect political predispositions rather than the other way around. But basic attitudes tend to be rather stable. They are often acquired at an early age and kept largely intact over long periods of time. Hence it is generally reasonable to assume, as we did in figure 1.1, that political predispositions are mainly *causes*, rather than effects, of individuals' foreign policy goals, perceived threats, and specific policy preferences.

The importance of political predispositions becomes evident when we compare our demographic regression analyses of goals with expanded regressions that add (to the fourteen variables measuring personal and social characteristics) three new independent variables: respondents' ideological ratings of themselves as "liberal" or "conservative," their identification with the Republican or Democratic party, and their general view that the United States should take an "active part" in, or "stay out" of, world affairs. In marked contrast to what happened when we added knowledge and exposure variables, when we added ideological and partisan predispositions to regressions the amount of variance explained rose for every one of the twenty goals. In several cases—especially the ideologically charged justice-related goals of improving the environment, promoting human rights, combating world hunger, strengthening the UN, and improving the standard of living of less developed nations—the proportion of variance accounted for increased by 6 to 9 percentage points. For three-quarters of the goals, the explanatory power of the regressions more than doubled.[50] In some cases this reflected a substantial effect on foreign policy goals of one or both of the two most pervasive correlates of domestic political opinions: liberal or conservative ideology and Republican or Democratic party identification. More often, however, it reflected a strong effect of responses to the deceptively simple but powerful question about whether or not the United States should take an active part in world affairs.

Ideology and party identification. In the contemporary United States, the most frequently used terms of ideological discourse are "liberal" or "conservative." These terms are used to refer to positions on a wide range of domestic policies and are fairly closely linked to whether people call themselves Democrats (as do most liberals) or Republicans (as do most conservatives).[51]

Most Americans can place themselves somewhere on a five-point liberal-conservative continuum—as "very" or "fairly" conservative, "middle of the road," or "fairly" or "very" liberal. Most also answer a series of questions in such a way as to put themselves somewhere on a seven-point party identification scale: from "strong" Republican, "not very strong" Republican, and independent "closer" to Republicans, through purely independent, to independent "closer" to Democrats, "not very strong" Democrat, and "strong" Democrat.

In the early years of survey research, liberalism and conservatism—as well as Democratic and Republican party identification—were chiefly associated with support for or opposition to an active federal government role in New Deal–style domestic social welfare policies, such as federal help with education, medical care, and Social Security. These economic-welfare issues remain significant in liberal and conservative ideology, but they have faded somewhat in relative importance since the 1960s, as new "social" or cultural issues concerning civil rights, the environment, women's rights and abortion, crime and gun control, gay rights, and the like have come to the fore. Now the terms "liberal" and "conservative" are often taken to refer most pointedly to social issues. But they continue to be closely linked to political party identification.

Liberalism and conservatism are less relevant to foreign policy than to domestic matters, but they do significantly affect a number of foreign policy attitudes, especially those with a clear justice-related, humanitarian or altruistic aspect, with strong connections to domestic social policies (e.g., foreign aid for birth control), or with implications for the use of military force (conservatives tend to support the use of force more than liberals do). These relationships are generally stronger than those involving any demographic factor other than level of formal education, and they generally persist when demographics and the other basic attitudes are controlled for. Party identification has substantial bivariate relationships with most of the same attitudes, but the relationships usually vanish when liberal/conservative ideology and other factors are controlled.

With respect to foreign policy goals, in 2002 self-declared liberals were (in bivariate terms) considerably more likely than conservatives to say that improving the global environment should be a very important goal: 85 percent of liberals said so, as against 52 percent of conservatives, a difference of 33 percentage points.[52] Nearly as big was the ideological divergence over promoting and defending human rights abroad; more liberals than conservatives considered this very important, by 23 percentage points. There were smaller but still substantial differences concerning improving standards of living in less developed countries, combating world hunger, and strengthening the United Nations. All these differences persisted in multiple regressions. That is, individuals' ideological liberalism or conservatism affected—independently of their demographic characteristics or the two other basic attitudes—the priorities that they put on several foreign policy goals.[53]

On security from attack concerns, conservatives were much more apt than liberals to endorse maintaining superior military power worldwide as a very important goal, by (in bivariate terms) 24 percentage points. Conservatives were also quicker to favor several domestic well-being goals that may involve a mixture of cultural anxiety and economic nationalism; more conservatives than liberals attributed great importance to controlling and reducing illegal immigration (by 17 points), stopping the flow of illegal drugs, securing adequate energy supplies, and protecting the interests of American business abroad. These relationships, too, persisted in multiple regressions.

Only for three of the twenty goals did party identification have a significant effect independent of liberal or conservative ideology and other factors. Everything else being equal, Democrats were more likely than Republicans to say that improving the global environment should be a very important goal of U.S. foreign policy. (Democrats had clashed repeatedly with President Bush and congressional Republicans over such matters as the Kyoto agreement on global warming.) Similarly, Democrats were substantially more apt than Republicans to call strengthening the United Nations a very important goal, another subject of dispute between the president and congressional Democrats. Party identification also affected the importance attributed to combating world hunger.[54]

In our later analyses of how individuals' specific policy preferences fit into purposive belief systems, we will see that liberal or conservative ideology sometimes plays a part independent of particular foreign policy goals. But ideology usually affects policy preferences by working *through* its relationships with particular goals and perceived threats, which are generally much better predictors of policy preferences.

Internationalism versus isolationism. As discussed earlier, most scholars no longer believe that internationalism is unidimensional. There are important differences, for example, between "hawkish" internationalists, who lean toward using military force abroad, and "dovish" internationalists, who favor diplomacy, foreign aid, and other peaceful methods.[55] Still, the active/nonactive distinction remains a crucial aspect of internationalist or isolationist attitudes and frequently affects foreign policy goals and preferences more strongly than does liberal or conservative ideology or party affiliation.

Since the 1940s, pollsters have repeatedly asked Americans, "Do you think it will be best for the future of the country if we take an active part in world affairs or if we stay out of world affairs?" Those who favor engagement (as 71 percent did in 2002) can be called "active part" internationalists, in contrast with the isolationists who say "stay out" (25 percent).

The proportion of the public saying "take an active part" is often used as a gauge of the level of internationalism among Americans. It has generally hovered around two-thirds, with some ups and downs in reaction to world events. It dropped after the unhappy experience of the Vietnam War, for example, and apparently reached a low point in the early years of the Reagan arms buildup, when many people feared confrontation with the Soviet Union. After the terrorist attacks of September 11, 2001, the proportion of internationalists appears to have risen to a high point comparable to that of the 1950s before settling, by 2004, around the usual two-thirds figure.[56]

By this measure, then, the American public is preponderantly internationalist. We will see that this general predisposition is translated into support by majorities of Americans for a wide range of activist and generally cooperative foreign policies, from basing U.S. troops abroad to using military force under various (mostly multilateral) circumstances, maintaining extensive diplomatic and trade relationships, giving humanitarian foreign aid, and participating in many international treaties and international organizations, especially the United Nations.

There are many large bivariate differences between the foreign policy opinions of internationalists and isolationists. Similar relationships generally hold up, though less strongly, in multivariate analysis. In terms of specific policy preferences, in 2002 "stay out" isolationists were much less eager than "active part" internationalists (in bivariate terms) to have long-term military bases abroad in any of the ten places that the CCFR asked about—by fully 35 percentage points (31 percent, compared to 66 percent) in the case of Turkey. They were much less favorable to foreign aid: economic aid in general (by 34 points), military aid (23 points), and economic aid to each of eight countries the survey asked about. Isolationists were also much less enthusiastic about using U.S. troops abroad in response to hypothetical invasion scenarios or (even more so) for peacekeeping: there was a 33-percentage-point difference with respect to peacekeeping in Afghanistan and a 32-point gap on Bosnia. Far fewer isolationists than internationalists wanted to expand NATO eastward to include any of the six countries that were asked about, with a 34-point difference concerning Russia. And fewer isolationists than internationalists (by 33 points) wanted to pay our UN dues in full. These are big differences.

Isolationists also tended to see fewer U.S. "vital interests" in countries around the world, to give lower "feeling thermometer" ratings to virtually all countries, and to see fewer critical threats from abroad.

Similar differences, mostly in the 15- to 20-percentage-point range, showed up with respect to foreign policy goals. These differences generally persisted when demographic and the other two basic attitudinal factors (liberalism or conservatism and party identification) were controlled for in multiple regressions. Indeed, in many cases—for eleven of the twenty goals—"active part" internationalism had the strongest independent effect of any of the seventeen independent variables we examined. This was true of many humanitarian or justice-related goals as well as some security goals; only with respect to domestic well-being goals was internationalism unconnected or (in one case) negatively related.

Holding constant individuals' demographic characteristics and their other basic attitudes, for example, more "active part" internationalists than isolationists attributed great importance to the justice-related goals of combating world hunger, protecting weaker nations against foreign aggression, promoting and defending human rights abroad, helping to bring a democratic form of government to other nations, and helping to improve the standard of living of less developed nations. There were also significant differences on strengthening international law and strengthening the United Nations. In the security realm, internationalists were more apt than isolationists to say that defending our allies' security and preventing the spread of nuclear weapons should be very important goals. Differences also occurred on maintaining superior military power and combating international terrorism.[57]

Not surprisingly, internationalism did not have a significantly positive effect on any domestic well-being goal, unless one counts safeguarding against global financial instability, which has an altruistic as well as a domestic-interest component. As one might expect, internationalism was *negatively* related to emphasizing the goal of reducing illegal immigration. All these relationships are consistent with the role of political predispositions—basic attitudes—in affecting foreign policy goals, as postulated in figure 1.1.

Lest we focus too heavily on individuals' variations in opinions, however, it bears repeating that the top-ranked foreign policy goals in table 2.1 were embraced by majorities of Americans from every walk of life and every major ideological persuasion, even self-professed "stay out" isolationists. Our description of what "the American public" wants from U.S. foreign policy reflects a high level of consensus across social and ideological divides.

CONCLUSION

Large majorities of Americans say—and have said for decades—that several specific foreign policy goals related to *security of domestic well-being* (protecting Americans' jobs, controlling immigration, stopping drugs, and the like) deserve very high priority in U.S. foreign policy. We will see that U.S. foreign policy decision makers have often differed markedly from the citizenry on these matters. Democratic theory would seem to call for more responsiveness. Large majorities of Americans also attribute high importance to *security from attack*, especially as a result of terrorism or nuclear proliferation (they have been less concerned with military strength and geopolitical struggles). Most also place substantial importance on various aspects of international *justice.*

Individuals' personal and social characteristics have relatively little effect on their foreign policy goals, except for the ambiguous impact of education: self-interest—based on economic and social status—and compliance with mainstream norms and official policy may have as much to do with education effects as enhanced knowledge does. This undermines the argument that decision makers should pay more attention to educated elites than to the general public.

More important in determining individuals' foreign policy goals are their political predispositions—liberal or conservative ideology, party identification, and especially "active part" internationalism or isolationism—which frequently work in the ways postulated in the "purposive belief system" diagram of figure 1.1.

*   *   *

A key point of this chapter has been the broad public consensus, cutting across social and ideological groupings, on what should be the most important goals of U.S. foreign policy. In later chapters we will describe the American public's collective opinions about many specific military, diplomatic, and international economic policies. We will also analyze how individuals' specific policy preferences are affected by their foreign policy goals, the threats they perceive to U.S. interests, their ideological predispositions, and other factors. Before doing that, however, we turn to another important set of foreign policy attitudes: Americans' feelings about foreign countries and world leaders.

CHAPTER THREE

Friends and Foes in the World

Feelings and emotions are sometimes dismissed as "irrational." Passions are said to interfere with sober, objective calculations about policy choices. But individuals' feelings about political actors or groups can actually play a constructive role in instrumentally oriented, purposive belief systems. This is so because people use feelings and emotions to sum up, rather efficiently, various judgments and beliefs that are logically relevant to their evaluations of specific policies.[1]

We will see in later chapters that Americans' feelings toward foreign countries and foreign leaders often serve as important elements in their foreign policy belief systems. Countries seen as hostile or threatening to the United States engender cold feelings and tend to be regarded as appropriate objects of wary preparedness, economic sanctions, or even military attack. Countries regarded as friendly elicit warm feelings and are viewed as suitable to be alliance partners, recipients of foreign aid (if needed), and providers of U.S. military bases. In individuals' minds, evaluations of foreign countries and their leaders often have substantial effects on specific policy preferences.

This chapter uses data from the 2002 and 2004 CCFR surveys to explore the positive or negative feelings that Americans express toward many different foreign countries and foreign leaders. We also look at earlier surveys to examine how such feelings have changed over a thirty-year period, finding that when major events occur, feelings about the particular countries involved tend to be adjusted accordingly, but that otherwise they generally have been rather stable. We go on to analyze how individuals' feelings about foreign countries and leaders are affected by their personal characteristics (especially their levels of formal education and their religious affiliations), their ideological and partisan attitudes (particularly their internationalism, or belief that the United States should take an "active part" in the world),

and their knowledge of world affairs. This will set the stage for analyzing, in later chapters, how individuals' feelings about foreign countries and
foreign leaders—along with the foreign policy goals they seek, the international threats they perceive, and their basic political attitudes and predispositions—tend to affect in reasonable ways their preferences concerning specific foreign policy alternatives.

Americans' perceptions of some foreign countries as friends, and others
as foes, form an important part of the picture of what sort of foreign policy
the American public wants.

AMERICANS' FEELING ABOUT FOREIGN COUNTRIES
AND LEADERS

The Chicago Council on Foreign Relations surveys have regularly asked respondents to quantify their feelings about foreign countries by giving each
country a score on a "feeling thermometer" that runs from 0 degrees ("very
cold, unfavorable") to 100 degrees ("very warm, favorable"), with the mid-
point, 50 degrees, representing feelings that are "not particularly warm
or cold." (Respondents were encouraged to pick any point on the whole
100-point scale.) In 2002, two separate sets of survey respondents were asked
to do this for fourteen countries each, and another subsample of respondents was asked to do it for various "people and organizations," including
the European Union, "the Muslim people," and "the Palestinians."[2] The 2004
Web-based survey asked the same question about a smaller set of eleven
countries or peoples.[3]

The average (mean) thermometer ratings given to each country conveniently sum up the overall warmth or coldness of the American public's feelings toward that country. Average ratings can be used to rank countries
from the most warmly to the most coolly regarded, as is done, for the 2002
survey, in table 3.1. Respondents' average ratings of foreign and U.S. leaders
on the same thermometer scale can be similarly displayed, as is done in
table 3.2.[4] Judging by comparable Web-based data in both 2002 and 2004,
the average ratings of countries in 2004 changed very little, so we are confident that our detailed portrait of perceived friends and foes, based on the
much more extensive 2002 data, remains generally up to date.[5] Exceptions
will be mentioned, with precise 2004 figures and discussions of mode
effects in the endnotes.

Of course we cannot be sure precisely what people have in mind when
they express "warm" or "cold" feelings toward foreign countries. When
Americans rate Italy very warmly, for example, some may be thinking about
Italian food, Roman ruins, or friendly Italian people rather than Italy's
politics or foreign policy. Cultural factors undoubtedly matter. Similarly,

Table 3.1. Americans' feelings about foreign countries and peoples

	Mean thermometer rating (degrees)	
Canada	77	Warm
Great Britain	76	
Italy	65	
Germany	61	
Japan, Mexico	60	
Russia, Israel, Brazil, France	55	
European Union	53	
Taiwan, Poland, South Africa	50	Neutral
The Muslim people	49	
China	48	
Argentina	47	
India, South Korea	46	
Turkey, Egypt	45	
Nigeria	42	
Colombia	36	
Cuba, the Palestinians	35	
North Korea	34	
Saudi Arabia	33	
Pakistan	31	
Afghanistan	29	
Iran	28	
Iraq	23	Cold

Source: 2002 CCFR/GMF U.S. public survey, combined telephone and in-person data.
Note: Entries are mean ratings on a 100-point "feeling thermometer," where 0 is very cold, 100 very warm, and 50 neutral.

evaluations of foreign leaders may partly reflect perceptions of their per-sonalities or styles rather than their policy stands. But the general patterns of thermometer rankings—and the relationships between individuals' ther-mometer ratings and their policy preferences—indicate that people often have in mind countries' political regimes (democratic or authoritarian, for example) and their foreign policies (e.g., friendly or hostile toward the United States), both of which are quite relevant to U.S. foreign policy. In some cases, attitudes toward countries' political leaders seem to be even more sharply focused upon politics and more closely related to policy pref-erences than are attitudes toward the countries themselves. As a general matter, feelings about foreign countries and leaders often appear to serve as "heuristics," or shortcuts, for a range of politically relevant beliefs and atti-

Table 3.2. Americans' feelings about U.S. and foreign world leaders

	Mean thermometer rating (degrees)	
Secretary of State Colin Powell	77	Warm
British prime minister Tony Blair	72	
President George W. Bush	72	
Secretary of Defense Donald Rumsfeld	67	
Pope John Paul II	61	
Russian president Vladimir Putin	56	
UN secretary general Kofi Annan	53	
German chancellor Gerhard Schroeder	52	
Israeli prime minister Ariel Sharon	51	
French president Jacques Chirac	51	
Japanese prime minister Junichiro Koizumi	50	Neutral
Former president Bill Clinton	49	
Chinese president Jiang Zemin	38	
Cuban president Fidel Castro	22	
Palestinian leader Yasir Arafat	22	
Iraqi president Saddam Hussein	8	Cold

Source: 2002 CCFR/GMF U.S. public survey, combined telephone and in-person data.
Note: Entries are mean ratings on a 100-point "feeling thermometer," where 0 is very cold, 100 very warm, and 50 neutral.

tudes that fit, in a largely instrumental fashion, into purposive belief systems about foreign policy.[6]

In the course of discussing feeling thermometer ratings we will also note whether or not large numbers of Americans have said that the United States has a "vital interest" in a particular country. Yes or no responses about vital interests are not usually very strongly linked to policy preferences. They do not allow for very refined distinctions, they tend to be facile (some respondents say the U.S. has vital interests practically everywhere), and they are somewhat ambiguous in meaning, particularly with respect to actual or potential foes (in what sense does one have an "interest" in an enemy?).

Still, individuals' assessments of vital interests are sometimes linked to support for or opposition to specific policies. And by comparing the different proportions of Americans that perceive vital interests in different countries, we can get a sense of which countries and regions are seen as more or less central to U.S. foreign policy. The short answer: more Americans tend to see vital interests in big countries that have substantial economic or military resources and are U.S. allies or competitors. (In 2002, these included Japan, Saudi Arabia, China, Russia, Israel, Great Britain, and Canada.) Many

Americans also perceive vital interests in countries regarded as potential regional threats, vulnerabilities, or trouble spots (Pakistan, Iraq, Iran, and Afghanistan). On the other hand, fewer Americans see vital U.S. interests in countries that are small, less developed, or located in the southern hemisphere (South Africa, Bosnia, Argentina, Brazil, Indonesia, Nigeria). Precise percentages are given in an endnote.[7]

Europe and North America. Reasonably enough, Americans tend to give very warm thermometer ratings to long-time U.S. friends and NATO allies in North America and Europe, together with Japan (see table 3.1). Large majorities of Americans—three-quarters or more—also said in 2002 that the United States has a vital interest in Japan, Great Britain, and Canada.

Canada—with a highly favorable average rating of 77 degrees—stood at the very top of the thermometer ratings in 2002, just as it had done in every CCFR survey since the feeling thermometer question was first asked in 1978. Canada's rating stayed at very nearly the same high level, in the 72-to-77-degree range, for each of seven quadrennial surveys.[8] Clearly Americans feel very close to their northern neighbor, with its strong cultural and economic ties to the United States.

Great Britain, which enjoys similarly close linguistic, cultural, economic, and military connections with the United States, in 2002 received an average rating of 76 degrees; as in every previous CCFR survey, Britain came in second only to Canada.[9] Its rating stayed essentially the same in 2004. After the September 11, 2001, attacks, Britain's strong support of the Bush administration's antiterrorism policies probably contributed to Americans' warm feelings. In 2002, British prime minister Tony Blair was rated more highly than any of the nine other foreign heads of government on the "American and foreign leaders" thermometer scale: at 72 degrees (up a substantial 13 degrees from four years earlier), he was tied with President George W. Bush (see table 3.2). Similarly, in the late 1980s, Margaret Thatcher, Ronald Reagan's great ally, had received very warm average ratings, in the high 60-degree range.[10]

A bit behind Canada and Great Britain in Americans' affections in 2002 came friends and allies Italy, Germany, Japan, and Mexico, with average thermometer ratings of 65, 61, 60, and 60 degrees, respectively. After the terrorist attacks of September 11, 2001, there appears to have been a "huddling effect," in which the American public drew closer to U.S. allies. The thermometer ratings of five of the six top-rated countries (all but Italy) rose significantly between the 1998 and 2002 surveys. And the ratings of those that were asked about in 2004 stayed as high or rose a bit more.[11] In harmony with this interpretation, in 2002 "the countries of the European Union" were judged to be "very reliable" or "somewhat reliable" partners in the war on terrorism by 77 percent of the U.S. public, more than so rated any of the six other countries asked about. Japan came not far behind at 69 percent. "Vital interest" ratings of Britain, Canada, and Mexico rose significantly between 1998 and 2002.[12]

In earlier Chicago Council surveys, NATO allies Italy and Germany regularly received high thermometer ratings, as did U.S. neighbor Mexico. Japan was a slightly more complicated case, perceived as a Cold War ally but sometimes also as an economic competitor. The average American expressed barely positive feelings toward Japan in the economically pressed years 1982, 1990, and 1994, but warmer feelings in more prosperous 1986 and 1998.[13] The political leaders of Germany and Japan, however, have generally been viewed more coolly than the countries themselves. In 2002, Japanese prime minister Junichiro Koizumi was little known by the U.S. public (an unusually high 40 percent said they were not familiar with him or had no opinion); those who rated him put Koizumi, on average, right at the 50-degree neutral point.[14]

A notch lower in thermometer scores in 2002, but well above the neutral point, came France, Brazil, Israel, and Russia, all with average ratings of 55 degrees. (Ratings of Israel rose a bit in 2004.[15]) Russia and Israel were widely seen as vital U.S. interests, but France and Brazil were not.[16]

In the early CCFR surveys Americans rated France a little higher than Italy or Germany, around 60 degrees. In the 1990s, however, France's average thermometer score dipped to 55 degrees, where it stayed for the summer 2002 survey. French Presidents Francois Mitterand and Jacques Chirac evoked neutral or slightly cool feelings.[17] Other polls conducted later in 2002 and in 2003 indicate that France's leadership in the UN Security Council of opposition to the U.S. invasion of Iraq—met by noisy anti-French outbursts on U.S. talk radio, boycotts of french fries, and the like—took a toll on average Americans' feelings toward France, which became significantly cooler. (At the same time, in most countries around the world attitudes toward the Bush administration and the United States became less favorable.) But Americans' feelings toward France appear subsequently to have moved back in a warmer direction.[18]

South America. Brazil, the largest country of South America—and a real or fantasy vacation destination for many Americans—has regularly won rather warm thermometer scores: ratings in the mid-50-degree range, only a bit below those of our North American neighbor Mexico. Argentina has been held in less high regard, with neutral to slightly cool average thermometer ratings. Colombia, associated in some Americans' minds with drug trafficking, violence, and corruption, in 2002 received a very cool average rating of 36 degrees. As we will see in chapter 4, many Americans, deeply concerned about drugs, favor using U.S. troops to fight Colombian "drug lords." It is presumably for this reason that Colombia was judged to be a "vital interest" of the United States by a substantial 62 percent of the U.S. public, considerably more than thought the same about other South American countries (just 36 percent for Brazil and 39 percent for Argentina).[19]

Perhaps the most important fact about the U.S. public's attitudes toward South America is that many people are not paying much attention. This is signaled not only by the low percentage of people who deem Brazil and Argentina to be vital U.S. interests, but also by the relatively high proportion of "don't know" responses (around 10 percent) to thermometer questions about those countries. Over the years, the CCFR has generally not thought it necessary to ask any questions at all about Chile, Venezuela, or other South American countries. To the U.S. public (and perhaps some U.S. policy makers as well) the continent of South America—much of it, much of the time—is nearly invisible.

Israel. Israel, viewed by many Americans as a Middle Eastern outpost of Western culture, free enterprise, and democracy, has generally won fairly warm thermometer scores: usually in the mid-50-degree range, considerably higher than those of the Palestinians or most Arab countries of the region. Most Americans' sympathies are clearly with the Israelis, and most consider Israel to be a vital U.S. interest. On the other hand, Israeli political leaders— particularly those seen as resistant to U.S. policies or as not fully dedicated to peaceful solutions, such as Menachem Begin (in 1982), Yitzhak Shamir, Benjamin Netanyahu, and Ariel Sharon (in 2002)—have been rated neutrally or slightly negatively.[20] We will also see that warm feelings toward Israel have not automatically translated into specific pro-Israel policy preferences. Most Americans want to be "even-handed" between Israel and the Palestinians.

Russia and the former Soviet bloc. Russia's average thermometer rating in 2002 was warm (55 degrees), up significantly from four years earlier. This presumably resulted from the antiterrorist alliance with the United States pursued by Russian president Vladimir Putin, who himself received a warm (56-degree) average rating. The U.S. public judged Russia to be second only to the countries of the European Union as a "reliable partner" in the war on terrorism, with 74 percent calling it very or somewhat reliable. And more than 80 percent of Americans called Russia a "vital interest" of the United States.

During the Cold War, not surprisingly, the Soviet Union regularly received cold thermometer ratings from the U.S. public: around 30 degrees, until its score jumped to 59 degrees as the Soviet Union broke up in 1990 under Mikhail Gorbachev (who that year enjoyed a very warm 64-degree rating, a shade above that of the first President Bush). Thermometer ratings of troubled postcommunist Russia then slowly eroded to a warmish and then neutral level before the 2002 rise. Interestingly, however, even during the Cold War period the Soviet Union was never despised as thoroughly by Americans as supposedly "rogue," pariah states like Iran or Iraq—or individual leaders like Idi Amin, Muammar Gadhafi, Fidel Castro, Ayatollah Khomeini, or Saddam Hussein—who were condemned by the U.S. government and received very hostile publicity.[21]

In terms of Americans' feelings, communist Cuba marched right in step with the Soviet Union during the Cold War, but its ratings continued to be cold (35 degrees in 2002) long after Russia had risen in Americans' esteem. Cuban premier Fidel Castro, the bête noire of American presidents from Dwight Eisenhower onward, was rated even more coldly, around 20 degrees.[22]

Like Cuba, isolated, communist-relic North Korea—with a recent history of U.S. objections to its nuclear weapons programs and accusations that it is a tyrannical, rogue state—has been given very cool (mid-30-degree) average thermometer ratings by the American public. President Bush's 2002 State of the Union mention of North Korea, Iraq, and Iran as constituting an "axis of evil," and even fresh alarms in 2004 about North Korea's possible possession of nuclear weapons, do not appear to have much affected Americans' already cold feelings toward the country.[23]

But the case of China shows that having a communist or socialist government does not in itself necessarily provoke particularly cold feelings from Americans. With little variation over the years (at least since the 1973 opening, the period covered by CCFR surveys), the People's Republic of China has generally received coolish to neutral—not cold—average thermometer ratings, mostly in the high 40-degree range, which rose a bit in 2004. Many Americans, despite reservations about human rights abuses and concerns about China's rise as a world power, have long admired Chinese culture and cuisine as well as the industriousness of Chinese immigrants to the United States. Some undoubtedly appreciate cheap consumer goods from China, and a few may be aware of China's key role in financing the twin U.S. deficits (in government budgets and trade flows). Feelings about Chinese Communist Party chairman Deng Xiaoping and president Jiang Zemin, however, were somewhat more negative. In terms of perceived "vital interests," China ranks near the top: in 2002, 83 percent of Americans, markedly more than in the 1990s, judged that the United States has a vital interest in China.[24]

Similarly Poland, with many successful immigrant sons and daughters in the United States, has regularly received neutral to warm (50-degree-plus) thermometer ratings—in the Cold War years and afterward—with a peak at 57 degrees in postcommunist 1990. And the Nicaragua of the 1980s, whose socialist Sandinista government was a target of insurgency by Reagan-backed *contra* rebels, got only moderately cool (mid-40-degree) ratings. But Nicaragua's president Daniel Ortega was rated substantially lower.[25]

Asia. Japan, as we have seen, is viewed by many Americans in much the same light as our closest European and North American allies. Despite periodic anxieties about economic competition, its pivotal position as the chief U.S. ally in Asia, together with its advanced economy, Westernized culture, and mostly democratic polity, have made Japan part of the inner circle of warmly regarded countries. In 2002, when respondents were asked to characterize relations between the United States and Japan as "friendly," "unfriendly," or neither, a solid majority (62 percent) said friendly; only 7 percent said unfriendly. As we will see in later chapters, substantial majorities of Americans favor having military bases in Japan and stationing large numbers of troops there, and there is now general equanimity about trade relations.

We have also seen that China is regarded more neutrally, perhaps ambivalently. China occupies a special position in the world, as a fast-growing economic power, a key trading partner for the United States, and a key investor in dollars. China is perceived as very important to the U.S. and is culturally admired, but at the same time it is viewed with wariness for its Communist Party dictatorship, poor human rights record, and low-wage economic competition. As we saw in chapter 2, a rather high proportion of Americans consider the rise in China as a great power to be a "critical threat" to the United States, and we will see in chapter 6 that perceptions of Chinese trade as "unfair" exceed those for any other country. Still, large majorities of Americans favor trade and diplomatic relations with China, and China's thermometer scores have not been cold.

India, a populous, democratic, and highly pluralistic country with potential for strong economic growth, has not so far elicited very warm feelings from the U.S. public. Both during the Cold War—when India led the "nonaligned" movement and was perceived by many Americans as too friendly to the Soviet Union—and for a while afterward, India's average thermometer scores held steady at a neutral-to-coolish 48 or 49 degrees, not very different from China's. They have dipped slightly from that level in recent years, perhaps because of concerns about India's nuclear arms and its standoff with Pakistan over Kashmir. With war between India and Pakistan appearing quite possible in 2002, perceptions of a vital U.S. interest in India jumped to 65 percent, after decades in the low to middle 30s.[26]

North Korea and its cold, "rogue state" thermometer ratings were discussed in connection with the former Soviet bloc. South Korea, a U.S. military and economic partner and the source of many thriving immigrants to the

United States, has nonetheless usually evoked only lukewarm to cool feelings from the American public, like those expressed toward India and China, though these feelings warmed somewhat in 2004. Likewise Taiwan has regularly had ratings that hovered right around the neutral, 50-degree point, despite being a U.S. trading partner, the recipient of extensive military arms sales, and now a democracy (and despite long being the embodiment to many U.S. conservatives of "free China"). The Philippines, with closer—albeit tangled—ties to the United States, has evoked warmer feelings. South Korea, Taiwan, the Philippines, and North Korea, however, were all seen in 2002 as vital interests by substantial majorities of Americans (69 percent, 65 percent, 62 percent, and 62 percent, respectively).[27]

Africa. Most countries in Africa, like most in South America, are barely visible to many Americans. Relatively few see vital U.S. interests in African countries. In 2002, just 53 percent did so in Egypt, 52 percent in Sudan, 49 percent in South Africa, and only 31 percent in Nigeria. "Not sure," "not familiar," or "no opinion" responses to thermometer questions tended to be relatively frequent (13 percent for Nigeria), as did exactly neutral, 50-degree responses (32 percent for both Nigeria and South Africa, 31 percent for Egypt), which may mix some highly uncertain responses with those that are genuinely neutral.[28]

South Africa during the apartheid period, in which whites tyrannized the black majority, received only moderately cool thermometer ratings from the U.S. public; subsequently, democratic South Africa has won only neutral to slightly warm feelings. This does not, however, mean that Americans were unaware of or unconcerned with the struggle. White president F. W. De Klerk—at the end of the apartheid era—received a cold rating of 39 degrees, whereas black liberation heroes Archbishop Desmond Tutu and especially Nelson Mandela were rated warmly: Mandela got a 60-degree average rating in 1998.[29] Again, the ratings of leaders seem more politically attuned, while country ratings may mix reactions to regimes with reactions to peoples.

Nigeria, a large, oil-producing West African country that has suffered from poverty, civil strife, and military dictatorship, has regularly received cool average thermometer ratings from Americans, in the mid-40-degree range. Egypt, a Middle Eastern as well as African country (and a key U.S. ally), has done somewhat better, sometimes rising into the mildly warm range—slightly above 50 degrees.[30]

We will see that individuals' feelings about these African countries affect their attitudes about foreign aid to Africa. But widespread awareness of AIDS and poverty in Africa, together with widespread embrace of the goal of combating world hunger, have been most central to producing broad support for increasing aid to African countries—the only countries for which such support exists.

The Arab and Muslim world. Most Americans have never felt particularly warm toward Arab or Muslim countries in the Middle East or elsewhere. This is true even of major strategic allies of the United States like Egypt, Saudi Arabia, Pakistan, and Turkey and has become all the more true since the terrorist attacks of September 11, 2001. Muslim countries and political leaders that are seen as hostile to the United States or Western values, or as having a connection with terrorism, are viewed quite negatively.

Americans' feelings toward Egypt—a keystone for peace between Arabs and Israel and the long-time number two recipient of U.S. foreign aid (after Israel)—have in the past sometimes risen into warm territory, but only by a little. Egypt's mean thermometer rating peaked at 53 degrees in 1978, the year President Anwar Sadat shared the Nobel Peace Prize with Israeli prime minister Menachem Begin, but fell below the neutral point by 2002. (Perceptions of Egypt as a vital U.S. interest also peaked in 1978, at 75 percent.) As we will see, Americans' support for giving Egypt foreign aid is very limited.

The story for Saudi Arabia is much the same. Despite the kingdom's status as a long-time U.S. ally and provider of key military bases during the Cold War, and its ownership of the largest oil reserves in the world, its average thermometer scores used to fluctuate around the neutral 50-degree point. They peaked at 53 degrees in 1990, when Saudi Arabia was threatened by Saddam Hussein's invasion of Kuwait and the Saudis welcomed U.S. troops for the counterattack on Iraq. As we will see, many Americans—large numbers of whom say that securing adequate supplies of energy should be a very important goal of U.S. foreign policy—have favored defending Saudi Arabia against Iraqi invasion. But most Americans have never felt very warm toward the authoritarian, fundamentalist Islamic state. Feelings drifted into cool territory during the 1990s before dropping precipitously (as discussed below) to coldness in 2002.[31]

Americans have also expressed neutral to cool feelings toward other Arab and Muslim countries whenever the Chicago Council has asked about them. In 1978, the average rating of Shah Pahlevi's Iran (a close U.S. ally) was just 50 degrees. In 1982, the rating of Jordan was 47 degrees; of Lebanon, 46 degrees; and of Syria (widely perceived to be an enemy of Israel) a very cool 42 degrees, which dropped to a cold 34 degrees in 1986. In 1998, feelings toward Pakistan (locked in nuclear-armed tension with India, but the object of U.S. strategic wooing) likewise averaged a very cool 42 degrees. In that same year even secular, somewhat democratic Turkey, a crucial NATO ally, got only a cool 45-degree average thermometer score.

So much for allies and neutrals in the Muslim world. When it comes to countries defined by U.S. officials as "rogue" states, threats to U.S. interests, or sponsors of terrorism, most Americans express quite cold feelings. Even colder feelings are directed at individual foreign leaders who have been demonized in the media.

After the Islamic revolution in Iran and the 1979–80 hostage crisis (in which U.S. embassy personnel were held by radical Iranian students who had state backing), Iran's average thermometer score plummeted from a neutral 50 degrees to a very cold 28 degrees. Ratings of "supreme leader" Ayatollah Khomeini were even colder. Iran's rating stayed at about the same cold level for the next two decades, despite the growth of a newly pro-Western young generation and the democratic election of reformist president Khattami (who was mostly stymied by powerful Islamic clerics). As in the case of North Korea, President Bush's designation of Iran as part of an "axis of evil" appears merely to have confirmed preexisting hostility from U.S. officials and the public.[32]

The 1990 invasion of Kuwait by Saddam Hussein's Iraq led to a quick reclassification of Iraq from a U.S. ally of convenience to a U.S. foe. The first President Bush compared the invasion of Kuwait to Hitler's aggression, and declared that it would "not stand." Beginning in autumn 1990, Iraq regularly received even colder thermometer ratings than Iran, in the middle to low 20-degree range. Hussein himself, vilified for his 1980s war against Iran (for which, however, the United States had given Iraq crucial support at the time), his gassing of Iranians and Kurdish Iraqis, his invasion of Kuwait and suppression of Shiite and Kurdish rebellions, and his allegedly continuing efforts to develop chemical, biological, and perhaps nuclear weapons, has evoked the coldest feelings that Americans have expressed toward any leader or country in the history of CCFR surveys: icy average thermometer ratings, between 1990 and 2002, of just 9, 11, 12, and 8 degrees.[33]

After the September 2001 terrorist attacks on the World Trade Center and the Pentagon, Americans' feelings toward several Arab and Muslim countries grew colder. Saudi Arabia provides the most dramatic example. The kingdom's already cool, 46-degree rating of 1998 dropped sharply to a cold 33 degrees in 2002 (with perhaps a small rebound by 2004).[34] After fifteen of the nineteen September 11 airplane hijackers were identified as being Saudi citizens, Saudi Arabia was widely accused by U.S. commentators of harboring feudal politics, fundamentalist Islamism, and tolerance (if not outright encouragement and funding) of terrorists. Only 31 percent of Americans said in 2002 that Saudi Arabia had been a "very" or "somewhat reliable" partner in the war on terrorism, the lowest figure for any of the seven countries asked about; 26 percent said "very unreliable." As we will see in chapter 4, majorities of Americans in that year opposed having U.S. bases in Saudi Arabia.

Similarly Pakistan, where President Pervez Musharraf had taken considerable personal risk to ally with the United States in the war against the Taliban in Afghanistan, was nonetheless seen in 2002 by many Americans as a hotbed of Islamic radicalism and a shelter for expelled Afghani Taliban, as well as a brandisher of nuclear weapons and encourager of terrorism in Kashmir. Pakistan was rated at a very cold 31 degrees, down a sharp eleven degrees since 1998. Only a minority of Americans, 43 percent, judged Pakistan to be a very or somewhat reliable partner in the war on terrorism (the only lower rating was Saudi Arabia's).

Even Afghanistan itself, which at the time of the 2002 CCFR survey had largely been purged of al Qaeda terrorists and liberated from the oppressive, fundamentalist Taliban regime, and which was presided over by U.S.-anointed president Hamid Karzai, received from the American public a quite cold, 29-degree average thermometer rating—about the same as that of Iran. (As we will see below, however, better-informed Americans tended to feel somewhat warmer than others toward both Afghanistan and Pakistan.) Likewise the beleaguered Palestinians, associated during their second intifada with terror attacks against Israeli civilians, got a cold 35-degree rating. Palestinian leader Yasir Arafat was rated at an even colder 22 degrees. Although Arafat had done somewhat better during the 1990s, a period of optimism surrounding the Oslo peace agreement, he always fell below the lukewarm or cool ratings accorded to most Israeli leaders.[35]

Still, cold feelings and associations with terrorism are by no means extended to all Muslims. On average in 2002, "the Muslim people" were rated at a neutral 49 degrees, neither warm nor cold (identical, as it happens, to the average rating of former president Bill Clinton). Few Americans in 2002, just 21 percent, told CCFR interviewers that "to a great degree" the World Trade Center attacks represented "the true teachings of Islam"; an additional 18 percent said "to some degree," but most said "not very much" (17 percent) or "not at all" (40 percent). Similarly, only 27 percent of Americans picked as closest to their own views a statement that Muslim traditions are "incompatible with Western ways" and that "violent conflict between the two civilizations is inevitable," while a solid 66 percent choose the statement "Because most Muslims are like people everywhere, we can find common ground and violent conflict between the civilizations is not inevitable." Neither a "clash of civilizations" nor a "war against Islam" was on most Americans' minds. (Ratings of Muslims apparently grew a bit cooler by 2004, however.[36])

The September 11 terrorist attacks and the Afghan war did, however, increase the importance that Americans attributed to several Arab and Muslim countries. The modest 45 percent who perceived a vital U.S. interest in Afghanistan in 1998 leaped to 73 percent in 2002, after U.S. troops attacked al Qaeda and the Taliban there. Over the same period the proportion of the U.S. public seeing a vital interest in Turkey jumped by 19 percentage points, and in Iran by 14 points. The Arab and Muslim worlds seem likely to stand near the center of the American public's (and U.S. decision makers') foreign policy concerns for some time to come.[37]

In the remainder of this chapter we again turn from the collective opinions of the American public to the question of how and why *individual* Americans vary in their views. We discuss the effects of education and knowledge, religious affiliations, and attitudes about how involved the United States should be in world affairs on individual's feelings about foreign countries. But we nonetheless find a broad consensus about different countries across nearly all social and ideological groups of Americans. As with the latter part of chapter 2, the details may be of more interest to students of individual behavior and political psychology than to readers chiefly interested in foreign policy.

WHO FEELS WARM TOWARD WHICH COUNTRIES

In this book we are chiefly interested in what sort of foreign policy the U.S. public as a whole—a majority of the public, or the average citizen—wants the United States to pursue. Indeed, one of our themes is that Americans of all sorts, from all walks of life, largely agree in identifying security and justice as the main goals of foreign policy and in favoring cooperative, multilateral means to attain them. Still, there are some interesting—though mostly rather small—differences in the ways individuals with different backgrounds and different points of view look at the world, including how they feel about world leaders and foreign countries.

In order to explore *why* people feel as they do, in terms of their personal and social characteristics, their basic political attitudes, and their knowledge of the world, we conducted three sets of ordinary-least-squares (OLS) regression analyses for thermometer ratings of each of the twenty-eight countries (plus the EU, Muslims, and Palestinians) and each of the sixteen world leaders that were included in the 2002 CCFR survey. As with the questions concerning goals, analyzed in the previous chapter, we began by examining the impact of fourteen more or less fixed demographic factors—age, education, income, employment status, gender, race, religion, ethnicity, and the like—then added variables concerning three basic, rather stable political attitudes: liberal or conservative ideology, party identification, and predisposition toward foreign policy activism or isolationism. Finally, along with the demographic and attitudinal variables we included three measures of exposure to or knowledge about world affairs.

In most of the book we focus on standardized coefficients, which help one assess the proportion of observed variation in dependent variables that is accounted for by observed variation in independent variables. This, however, is a particularly appropriate occasion to report *unstandardized* regression coefficients, which can reveal strong effects of membership even in very small groups that do not account for much variation in the population as a whole. Unstandardized coefficients estimate effects in terms of how many units of change in the dependent variable (in this case, how many degrees on the 100-degree thermometer scale) are associated with one unit of change in each independent variable (e.g., a one-year increase in age, or membership—versus nonmembership—in a religious group). For example, an estimated coefficient of 20.3 for the effect of being Catholic upon feelings toward Pope John Paul II would mean that, controlling for other factors, Catholics tended to give about 20-degree warmer thermometer ratings to the pope than did others. That the units of measurement here (degrees, years, membership status) are intuitively understandable, in contrast with many of the attitudinal variables we will consider in later chapters, also favors the use of unstandardized coefficients.[38]

On the whole, our results indicate that Americans' feelings toward most foreign countries—like their assessments of most foreign policy goals—are only modestly affected by their personal and social characteristics. Except in the cases of Great Britain and Poland, not even 10 percent of the variation in thermometer scores for any of the thirty-one countries or peoples could be accounted for by the fourteen demographic variables, and the average was only about 5 percent. The explanatory power of demographics was even lower for ratings of world leaders, except that feelings about U.S. officials like President Bush and former president Clinton were fairly strongly related to demographic factors connected to partisan and ideological affiliations.[39]

Adding the three basic attitudinal factors—liberal/conservative ideology, party identification, and "active part" internationalism—significantly increased the explanatory power of several regressions, but only the EU, Muslims, and Taiwan joined the short list of countries or peoples for which even 10 percent of the variance in thermometer scores was accounted for. (The inclusion of party and ideology did, however, have a big impact on the prediction of feelings toward several leaders: Clinton, Bush, Rumsfeld, Sharon, and Annan.) Adding measures of world-affairs information and exposure contributed little or nothing in most cases.[40]

Limited effects of personal and social characteristics. Although all the demographic factors taken together did not account for much of the variation in individuals' evaluations of countries or leaders, certain particular demographic characteristics did have interesting effects, including rather large and pervasive effects of education, smaller effects of age and gender, and substantial impacts of belonging to some religious groups.

Gender had mostly mild (though fairly widespread) impacts on thermometer ratings, including a tendency for men—controlling for other factors—to feel substantially warmer than women toward Vladimir Putin (the tough former head of the Soviet KGB) and a bit warmer toward Gerhard Schroeder, Taiwan, and perhaps Turkey, Japan, and Russia, while women tended to feel substantially less cold than men toward North Korea and a little warmer toward Italy and perhaps Nigeria and France. Most of these effects apparently worked through attitudinal or informational variables; they tended to shrink or disappear in expanded regressions when those variables were controlled for. The only clearly significant independent effect of marital status was that married people tended to feel 8 or 10 degrees cooler toward former president Bill Clinton, who had been revealed to be unfaithful to his wife in the Monica Lewinsky imbroglio.[41]

Economic status made little difference except for a tendency for employed people (as contrasted with homemakers, students, and retirees) to feel slightly more negative than others toward several countries, most notably Iran and North Korea. Conceivably members of the labor force felt more of a stake in accepting official definitions of U.S. enemies. The *unemployed,* however, did not express appreciably distinctive feelings, except for an odd tendency to dislike Poland and possibly Argentina and the pope. Income level, controlling for employment status and other demographic factors, had no appreciable impact at all.[42]

One consistent and moderately strong demographic effect was that older people—controlling for other factors—felt cooler than young people toward a number of countries: particularly countries in Africa, Latin America, Asia, and the Middle East but also France and Poland. (Older people felt *warmer* than the young toward Great Britain, however.) An increase of thirty years in age typically led to a 4- to 8-degree lower thermometer rating. These estimated effects nearly all persisted, and in some cases increased a bit, when attitudinal and informational as well as demographic factors were controlled for. Some aspect of the life cycle or generational experiences not captured by the CCFR attitudinal or informational variables apparently made older people feel less positive about many foreign countries, especially poor countries.[43]

Education and knowledge. Formal education had the most pervasive effects of any demographic factor on people's feelings toward foreign countries. Individuals with high levels of formal education tended to feel much warmer toward most countries than did people with little education. Controlling for income, employment, age, race, gender, religion, and all the other demographic factors, education levels had significant effects on individuals' ratings of twenty-six out of the thirty-one countries or peoples studied (though only on a few ratings of world leaders). Moving up just two levels on the six-point education scale—from high school graduate, say, through "some college" to college graduate—often led to rises in thermometer ratings of 6 to 8 degrees. Moving from the bottom (eighth grade or less) to the top (postgraduate study) of the education scale often meant an increase of 15 or 20 degrees in warmth. Some of the larger effects of a one-level increase in education, controlling for other demographic factors, are displayed in the left column of table 3.3.[44] Table 3.3 is rather dense and complicated: it displays the estimated effects of three different independent variables—education, knowledge, and internationalism—with, in the case of education, two different sets of control variables, upon feelings toward each of seventeen countries or peoples. Less quantitatively inclined readers will find the most important findings summarized in the text.

In chapter 2 we discussed some ambiguities in the observed relationships between education levels and foreign policy goals, which may often have reflected effects of individuals' socioeconomic status and material interests, or their socialization into mainstream norms, rather than their levels of cognitive skills or knowledge. Here, however, the story is rather different. Little if any of the impact of education on feelings about countries has to do with individuals' economic positions. Most is related to the greater tendency of highly educated people to know more about foreign affairs and to embrace the norm of "active part" internationalism.

The many substantial education effects shown in table 3.3 are largely independent of economic factors; they were all estimated with controls for employment status and income level. The key roles of both basic attitudinal and informational factors as intervening variables becomes evident when we look at the results of moving from demographics-only regressions (in the first column of table 3.3) to regressions that included attitudinal and informational variables (in the second column). With basic attitudes and information levels controlled for, the estimated direct, independent effects of education dropped markedly.[45] Roughly half of the drop in education coefficients occurred when the basic attitudinal variables (chiefly internationalism/isolationism) were added, and the other half with the addition of knowledge and exposure variables. But different countries differed in this respect: that is to say, education had its effects through different intervening variables for different sets of countries.

In the final, "full controls" regressions, when the estimated direct effects of education generally shrank or disappeared, significant effects of "active part" internationalism and of informational factors (chiefly as

Table 3.3. Effects of education, knowledge, and internationalism on feelings toward foreign countries and peoples

	Education (demographic controls only)	Education (full controls)	Knowledge (full controls)	Internationalism (full controls)
Muslims	5.8**	4.2**	6.3**	9.7**
Pakistan	4.5**	3.0**	6.3**	5.6*
Afghanistan	3.9**	n.s.	10.9**	7.8**
Mexico	3.5**	1.6+	3.8+	7.8**
India	3.5**	2.1*	n.s.	10.5**
Cuba	3.2**	2.4**	6.0**	n.s.
Palestinians	3.2**	1.9+	5.6*	5.9*
Nigeria	3.1**	2.3**	n.s.	4.1+
South Korea	2.8**	n.s.	6.3**	5.3*
Taiwan	2.7**	n.s.	7.3**	7.0**
Egypt	2.5**	2.0*	n.s.	4.0+
EU	2.9**	n.s.	n.s.	12.2**
Japan	2.9**	1.5+	n.s.	10.2**
Britain	2.8**	1.5+	4.9**	6.5**
Canada	2.5**	1.5+	n.s.	5.7**
Germany	2.3**	1.4+	n.s.	6.6**
Russia	2.3**	n.s.	n.s.	8.3**

Source: CCFR/GMF 2002 survey of the U.S. public, combined data.

Note: Entries are unstandardized coefficients from OLS regressions. Column headings specify the independent variable and control variables ("full controls" includes fourteen demographic characteristics, three basic attitudes, and three information/exposure measures). Dependent variables are ratings of various countries on a feeling thermometer that ranges from 0 degrees (very cold) to 100 degrees (very warm). Education level is measured on a six-point scale. Knowledge (knowledge of the euro) and internationalism (favoring an "active part" for the U.S. in world affairs) are 0-1 dummy variables.

$+p < .10$, $*p < .05$, $**p < .01$, by two-tailed test.

measured by knowledge of the euro) appeared and took their place (see the third and fourth columns of table 3.3). Controlling for everything else, *internationalism*—to be further discussed below—was rather strongly associated with warmer feelings toward most countries of the world, including the major nations in the bottom grouping of table 3.3: the EU, Japan, Russia, Germany, Britain, and Canada. But *knowledge* effects were mostly confined to the lower-visibility countries in the upper part of the table, especially countries that had—presumably without the awareness of the less informed—acted as key military and political partners to the United States.

As the third column of table 3.3 indicates, controlling for many other factors, better-informed respondents gave significantly warmer thermometer scores than the less-informed to Karzai's Afghanistan, military ally Taiwan, Musharraf's Pakistan, and South Korea; they also gave warmer ratings (not shown in the table) to NATO ally Turkey, trading partner China, and President Bush's antiterror partner Vladimir Putin. The better-informed felt somewhat warmer toward Cuba, with which U.S. agribusinesses were advocating fuller trade relations, and toward Muslims (crucial, in the minds of many experts, to success against terrorism), as well as toward Poland, Argentina, and Britain. In many of these cases, better-informed people made evaluations more in tune with the way that experts were assessing friends and foes of U.S. foreign policy interests. This constitutes at least some support for the early literature that emphasized the virtues of the highly informed "attentive public."[46] On the other hand, we have found little such evidence with respect to foreign policy goals or specific policy preferences. We do not consider these informational effects on feelings about foreign countries to be sufficient to warrant special deference by decision makers to the highly educated rather than the public as a whole when it comes to specific policies.

The impact of religion and ethnicity. In certain cases, controlling for other factors, individuals' ethnic and especially their religious affiliations significantly affect their feelings toward various countries and leaders. Some of these effects are consistent with simple "fellow feeling" predictions of group theory (that individuals tend to identify with, or feel close to, foreigners who share their own religious or ethnic affiliations) but not very strongly so. Other effects reflect distinctly instrumental, *political* calculations concerning which countries or leaders would help or hurt groups with which individuals empathize.[47]

Catholics, not surprisingly, tended—controlling for many other factors— to feel much warmer than others (by 21 degrees) toward the pope. They felt only slightly warmer toward predominantly Catholic Poland and Colombia (and possibly very slightly so toward Italy and Argentina) but not significantly warmer at all toward France, Mexico, Brazil, or Cuba.[48]

Being Hispanic led to substantially warmer feelings (by 14 degrees) toward Mexico—the country of origin and continued affiliation for many Hispanic immigrants—but not toward Argentina, Brazil, Colombia, or Cuba. Hispanics also showed a small tendency to *dislike* certain close U.S. allies (the European Union and Tony Blair) while feeling slightly warmer than others toward Yasir Arafat, Iran, and Saddam Hussein, hinting at an "outsider" perspective on U.S. foreign policy.[49]

Controlling for other factors, Asian Americans showed a tendency to feel a little less negative than others toward North Korea and a little more positive toward Japan and perhaps Prime Minister Koizumi, but their feelings were not significantly warmer toward Taiwan, South Korea, China, or Chinese president Zemin.[50]

Contrary to a simple "fellow feeling" hypothesis, African Americans (controlling for other characteristics) did not express particularly warm feelings toward African countries Egypt, Nigeria, or South Africa, nor toward UN secretary general Kofi Annan or Secretary of State Colin Powell. (As we will see in chapter 6, African Americans' liberalism—more than their racial or ethnic identity—has tended to make them more favorable than others to increasing foreign aid to African countries.) African Americans expressed significantly cooler (by 10 to 15 degrees) feelings toward U.S. allies Great Britain, Poland, Russia, Germany, Canada, and perhaps South Korea, suggesting a rather strong "outsider" foreign policy perspective and/or a primarily domestic orientation.[51]

By far the biggest religious or ethnic effects, however, were those of being Jewish or Muslim upon feelings about countries and leaders in the Middle East. These are summarized in table 3.4. As the table's first column indicates, controlling for their other characteristics Jewish Americans tended to feel considerably warmer toward Israel—the Jewish state, home to

Table 3.4. Effects of religion on feelings toward Middle Eastern countries and leaders

	Jewish	Muslim
Israel	30.2**	−3.4
Israeli Prime Minister Ariel Sharon	31.8**	−19.8
The Palestinians	−23.3**	48.9**
The Muslim people	−20.1**	51.6**
Yasir Arafat	−13.6*	3.2
Saudi Arabia	−18.1**	41.2**
Egypt	−12.6*	16.1
Iran	−10.2+	35.5**
Iraq	−5.8	33.5**
Iraqi President Saddam Hussein	−3.9	6.1
Afghanistan	−3.8	9.0
Pakistan	−5.2	37.5**
Turkey	−3.4	−5.6

Source: 2002 CCFR combined data.

Note: Entries are unstandardized OLS coefficients from regressions of 0–100 degree thermometer scales with 0-1 dummy variables for the indicated religious affiliation, with controls for the rest of fourteen demographic independent variables.

$+p < .10$, $*p < .05$, $**p < .01$

Jewish settlers and refugees from around the world—than did other Americans: by fully 30 degrees on the 100-degree thermometer scale. This would be enough to boost the average American's near-neutral 55-degree rating of Israel (recall table 3.1) to an extremely warm rating of 85 degrees, higher than the general-public rating for any country or leader in the world. Jews also tended to feel much warmer than others—by about 32 degrees—toward Israeli prime minister Ariel Sharon, whose hard-line military policies toward the Palestinians (in 2002) were highly controversial. Both these tendencies reached high levels of statistical significance despite the small number of Jews in the survey, and both stayed essentially intact with additional controls for respondents' basic political attitudes and knowledge of world affairs. (Indeed, Jews' tendency to feel warm toward Ariel Sharon *increased* when ideology was controlled for, since Jews tend to be liberal but liberals tended to dislike Sharon.)

By the same token, being Jewish led to much cooler than average feelings toward countries, peoples, and leaders viewed as enemies of Judaism, Zionism, or Israel. Being Jewish led to roughly 25-degree lower thermometer ratings of the Palestinians, who were then (in 2002) locked in violent conflict with the Israelis, and roughly 20-degree lower ratings of "the Muslim people" (perceived as mostly opposed to Israel) and Saudi Arabia (viewed as a major funder and supporter of the anti-Israel struggle). Jews also felt 14 or 15 degrees cooler than other Americans toward Egypt, then in a "cold peace" with Israel, and toward Palestinian president Yasir Arafat, whom the Sharon and Bush administrations had accused of complicity in terrorism and with whom they refused to deal. (The absence of significant effects on evaluations of Iraq or Saddam Hussein represents "floor effects": non-Jews were already highly negative.)

These distinctive feelings do not appear to reflect undiscriminating Jewish hostility toward Islam or Muslims, but rather political calculations related to Israel. Predominantly Muslim countries not opposed to Israel, such as Israel's strategic ally Turkey, or some distance from Israel, like Afghanistan and Pakistan, did not receive significantly more negative ratings from American Jews. (Being Jewish did, however, have negative effects on feelings toward Poland, Germany, France, and possibly the European Union—all viewed as sympathetic to the Palestinians and perhaps as harboring anti-Semitism. We also found positive effects on feelings toward pro-Israel U.S. presidents Bill Clinton and, once Jews' liberalism was controlled for, George Bush.[52])

The effects of being a Muslim American are, in some respects, mirror images of the effects of being Jewish (see the second column of table 3.4). Controlling for other characteristics, American Muslims tended to feel much warmer than others toward "the Muslim people" and the Palestinians: warmer by a remarkable 50 degrees or so, which could produce a leap from the neutral, 50-degree point (where the average American rated "the Muslim people") all the way to the top of the 100-degree thermometer scale. Muslims also tended to give much warmer ratings than did others—35 or 40 degrees warmer—to Saudi Arabia (a major center of Islam, with the holy city of Mecca), Pakistan (possibly the home country of some immigrant Muslim respondents), and Iran and Iraq (both centers of Shia Islam). These tendencies were highly significant statistically despite a very small sample of Muslims, and they stayed about the same with various sets of additional statistical controls.

But American Muslims, like Jews, made political distinctions. They expressed no particular enthusiasm for Arab leaders Saddam Hussein or Yasir Arafat. American Muslims tend to be strong democrats, friendly toward Muslim countries and peoples but not toward the authoritarian governments of the Middle East. Being Muslim did not lead to particularly negative feelings toward Israel, or even (at least not to a statistically significant extent) toward Sharon.

Americans who declared themselves to be "fundamentalist," "evangelical," "charismatic," or "Pentecostal" Protestants—whom we collectively label "evangelicals"—also expressed a few distinctive evaluations of leaders and foreign countries, though not nearly as distinctive as those of Jews and Muslims. Evangelicals tended (with controls for other demographic factors) to give 11-degree warmer ratings to Israel and 20-degree warmer ratings to Sharon, presumably because of a shared commitment to defend the Judeo-Christian holy land against perceived threats from Muslims. They gave slightly cooler than usual ratings to the European Union, a symbol of liberal, multinational values and a backer of the Palestinians. Evangelicals' active support of the Republican Party and hawkish foreign policy was manifested in their 20-degree warmer than usual thermometer ratings of President Bush and nearly as warm ratings of Secretary of Defense Rumsfeld. All these coefficients dropped when attitudinal and informational variables were added to the regressions, because part of the impact of evangelicalism worked through Republican party identification and conservative ideology.[53]

It bears repeating that the big effects of belonging to small religious minorities like American Jews or Muslims, while interesting and important (especially if their impact is magnified by organized interest groups), do not tell us a lot about the collective opinions of the American public as a whole. Within most large groups of Americans there is a high level of consensus about most friends and foes abroad.

Limited effects of party identification or liberalism/conservatism. As noted earlier, the predictive power of our regression analyses of feelings toward foreign countries and leaders rose markedly when we added three basic political attitudes or predispositions to our demographic regressions. Little of this change, however, was due to those staples of domestic U.S. politics, identification with the Republican or Democratic Party or self-identification as liberal or conservative. Most of it came from internationalism. In this respect, foreign policy opinions are quite different from opinions about domestic policy.

We found significant tendencies for Democrats (controlling for everything else) to express warmer feelings than Republicans toward perhaps half a dozen countries: France, Saudi Arabia, Argentina, and maybe South Africa, Cuba, and Turkey. The differences amount to as much as 10 degrees when one calculates the effect of being a "strong Democrat" as compared to being a "strong Republican." For all twenty-five other countries or peoples the coefficients for party identification were nonsignificant. Being a Democrat also led people to feel somewhat cooler toward Ariel Sharon and perhaps Vladimir Putin but did not significantly affect feelings toward any other foreign leader. (Not surprisingly, Democrats did feel much warmer than Republicans toward former Democratic president Bill Clinton—by a solid 37 degrees—and cooler toward Republican president George Bush and Secretary of Defense Donald Rumsfeld.)[54]

Similarly, there were only a few cases in which—controlling for everything else—self-identified liberals differed significantly from self-identified conservatives in their feelings toward foreign countries. The chief exceptions were Israel, toward which liberals had substantially cooler feelings than did conservatives, and Muslims, for whom the opposite was true. Liberals also expressed somewhat warmer feelings than conservatives toward the EU and European allies Italy and France and cooler feelings toward the conservatives' old friend Taiwan. But coefficients for the other twenty-five countries or peoples studied were not statistically significant.

Feelings toward world leaders, however, were more often related to ideology, not only for the obvious cases with strong links to domestic U.S. politics (Clinton, Bush, Rumsfeld), but also for several foreign leaders (Sharon, Castro, the pope, Arafat, and perhaps Annan). Liberals tended to feel substantially warmer than conservatives toward socialist Castro, Palestinian leader Arafat, and the UN's Annan; conservatives tended to feel warmer toward the culturally conservative pope and Israel's (then, in 2002) aggressively Zionist Sharon.[55] This fits with other evidence that Americans' feelings toward certain world leaders are as much or more politicized, and as relevant to policy preferences, as their feelings toward countries.

Pervasive effects of internationalism. By far the most pervasive and consistent relationships between basic political attitudes and feelings about foreign countries involve whether individuals are internationalists (saying that the United States should take an active part in world affairs) or isolationists (saying we should stay out of world affairs). Controlling for all other demographic, attitudinal, and informational factors—including education, which contributes substantially to internationalism—internationalists, much more than isolationists, express warm feelings toward a wide range of foreign countries and world leaders.

In many cases these differences are surprisingly large for such a simple, dichotomous variable in a multivariate setting (look back at the fourth column of table 3.3). In the 2002 data, for example, internationalism led to 12-degree warmer thermometer ratings of the EU; 10-degree warmer ratings of India, Japan, and the Muslim people; and 7- or 8-degree warmer ratings of Israel, Russia, Mexico, Afghanistan, Iraq, Saudi Arabia, Taiwan, Iran, and Germany. To a slightly lesser but still significant extent, internationalists expressed warmer feelings than isolationists toward Britain, China, Canada, and perhaps the Palestinians, Pakistan, South Korea, Brazil, Poland, and Argentina. Only for nine of the thirty-one countries or peoples did the coefficient for internationalism not reach the standard minimum level ($p < .05$) of statistical significance. Similarly, internationalists felt significantly warmer than isolationists (controlling for all other factors) toward thirteen of the sixteen world leaders: by 13 degrees in the case of UN secretary general Kofi Annan (a hero to humanitarian internationalists); by 7 to 9 degrees toward Clinton, Zemin, Powell, Koizumi, Rumsfeld, the pope, Arafat, and Chirac; by a bit less toward Bush and perhaps Schroeder and Blair. In full-control regressions, no other demographic, attitudinal, or informational factor rivaled an individual's internationalist or isolationist orientation as an independent predictor of warm feelings toward so many countries and leaders.[56]

We cannot be entirely sure about the causal processes involved here; it is possible that an accumulation of positive feelings and beliefs about various countries might lead to general support of international activism, rather than the reverse. But the most plausible interpretation is that a general orientation toward active international involvement leads to more positive feelings toward a wide range of foreign countries and world leaders, as well as to effects on the foreign policy goals discussed in the last chapter and on the specific policy preferences discussed in later chapters.

"Active part" internationalism largely stands on its own as an independent influence upon foreign policy opinions. It is entirely unrelated to liberal-conservative ideology and only weakly related to party identification. Internationalism is also relatively autonomous in personal and social terms. It is strongly affected by an individual's level of formal education—more education leads to more activism—with less than the usual ambiguity about why (both mainstream norms and knowledge of the world play a part). It is somewhat affected by age, income, and race; controlling for other demographic characteristics, older and wealthier people are more internationalist and African Americans less so. But the total impact of personal and social characteristics is limited.[57] To a large extent, an internationalist orientation appears to be acquired by learning—learning not only from formal education but also from family, friends, the media, personal experience, and history. And as we will see, "active part" internationalism, more than any other demographic characteristic or political predisposition, affects preferences concerning a number of specific foreign policies. Often it does so through its impact on the foreign policy goals that individuals seek, but sometimes it does so independently.[58]

CONCLUSION

Having devoted a fair amount of space to analyzing how differences in individual Americans' personal and social characteristics, basic political attitudes, and levels of knowledge lead to different feelings toward particular foreign countries and leaders, we should again emphasize that these individual differences are not our main point. The quite distinctive views of American Jews and Muslims involve the feelings of only small fractions of the population toward just a few Middle Eastern countries. Even differences in education levels and internationalist/isolationist orientations, the two factors with the broadest effects on thermometer ratings, generally produce only moderate differences in feelings. Much more important for our purposes is the extensive agreement, among Americans of practically all sorts, concerning which countries or leaders are regarded warmly, which coldly, and which more neutrally. It is the *collective* attitudes, feelings, goals, and beliefs of average Americans that we consider ultimately to be most important for providing a guide to policy makers.

Over the years, the clearly differentiated patterns in the American public's thermometer ratings of different countries and leaders—some quite warm, some very cold, others lining up at various points in between—indicate that many members of the public know enough to make clear distinctions among the world's major political actors. The high degree of stability over time in most ratings, whether high or low, suggests that many of these distinctions are firmly rooted in long-term beliefs and values. And sharp changes in average thermometer scores after such major events as the revolution in Iran, the breakup of the Soviet Union, or the 9/11 terrorist attacks indicate that the U.S. public tends to assimilate and take account of world events and new information (at least the information that is given them) in reasonable ways.[59]

Also bolstering the picture of a "rational public" is the fact that—as we will see in the following chapters—individuals' feelings about various countries and leaders tend to affect a number of specific policy preferences: which countries the United States should ally with, cooperate with in opposing terrorism, or engage in diplomatic relations or trade; where to have military bases or give economic aid; whom to defend; and even whom to consider attacking militarily. To the extent that thermometer-measured feelings are based on reasonable beliefs and attitudes about countries' political systems and about their needs, capacities, foreign policy intentions, and the like, such feelings can constitute useful elements within purposive belief systems. These aspects of individual behavior will help illuminate the coherent, rational foundations of collective public opinion.

We are now ready to consider what specific foreign policy measures are favored by the American public as a whole, beginning with the realm of military and defense policy.

CHAPTER FOUR

Military Strength and the Use of Force

The American public has been accused of isolationism, bloody-minded impulsiveness, and ill-informed "moods" that alternate between those two extremes. For many years officials and pundits proclaimed (with little evidence) that the public suffered from a "Vietnam syndrome": that the Vietnam War had made Americans so averse to U.S. casualties that they would not tolerate even a handful of combat deaths in peacekeeping operations in places like Somalia, Rwanda, or the Balkans.[1] After the terrorist attacks of September 2001, some observers expected that the American public would turn sharply inward and renounce engagement with the world; others expected popular demands for immediate, unilateral application of military force in every corner of the globe to eradicate real or imagined enemies.

Our data say otherwise. There is no evidence that majorities of Americans are pacifist or isolationist, or that they are belligerent unilateralists. Just as "realist" international relations theorists might hope (but not expect), most Americans are comfortable with the idea of the United States as the world's sole military superpower. Most support a high level of spending on the armed forces. Most favor commitments to military alliances like NATO, and most support the stationing of U.S. troops in long-term bases around the world. Most Americans also favor the use of armed force in certain circumstances, especially when directed against terrorism. And there is a very high level of support for U.S. participation in humanitarian and peacekeeping operations.

At the same time, there is little if any evidence of indiscriminate bloody-mindedness in the American public. Since the 2001 terrorist attacks there has been a substantial willingness to use force but only under particular conditions. Beyond relatively low-cost, direct operations against terrorists (e.g., using bombs or troops to destroy terrorist camps), most Americans prefer diplomatic methods, with major uses of force as a last resort. Before engaging in potentially high-cost wars against heavily armed states like Saddam Hussein's Iraq or Kim Jong Il's North Korea, large majorities of ordinary Americans—unlike some U.S. policy makers—want broad support from allies and the United Nations. Most favor *collective* security. Few are willing to go it alone. And enthusiasm for bases, defense spending, and military action has diminished somewhat since the invasion of Iraq.

Contrary to some arguments about public ignorance or "non-attitudes," the policies preferred by majorities of Americans form a generally coherent, consistent, and discriminating body of collective opinion about military capabilities and actions, opinion that is worth paying attention to. Moreover, analyses of variations in opinion among individuals indicate that preferences for specific military policies tend to follow, in logical ways, from the goals that people embrace and the threats that they worry about, as well as from broad values and beliefs concerning the expected costs and benefits of using force.

Such goals, values, and beliefs are in turn somewhat influenced by certain personal and group characteristics. Whites, men, evangelical Protestants, older people, and those with high levels of income and education, for example, tend to be more willing to use military force under various circumstances. So do conservatives, Republicans, "active part" internationalists, and people who embrace the goals of defending U.S. allies, maintaining superior military power worldwide, and protecting weaker nations against aggression. On the other hand, the use of U.S. armed forces for humanitarian and peacekeeping purposes is often favored more by women, African Americans, lower-income people, liberals, and others who want to combat world hunger, strengthen international law, and protect human rights.

Overall, however, there is broad agreement among Americans in virtually all social groups: they favor *prudent*—but only prudent—uses of military force, with help from allies and international organizations.[2] In our judgment, policy makers would do well to pay attention.

This chapter begins (and chapters 5 and 6 continue) a systematic description of the specific foreign policies that Americans want their government to pursue, thereby, we believe, providing useful guidance for government action. The chapters mainly draw upon data from the uniquely broad and detailed 2002 Chicago Council on Foreign Relations survey. The smaller 2004 CCFR survey and recent polls are used to note cases—mostly related to the Iraq war—in which collective opinion has changed since 2002, with precise figures and discussions of mode effects mostly relegated to endnotes. The text describes changes—and, more often, stability—in opinion over a thirty-year period, with precise data again generally given in the endnotes. About halfway through this chapter we turn to sustained analyses of purposive belief systems and the determinants of opinion variation among individual Americans, topics that will be treated only in a briefer and more integrated fashion in later chapters.

SUPERPOWER BUT NOT POLICEMAN OF THE WORLD

Most Americans accept the idea of the United States as the world's sole superpower. A very large majority, 83 percent, said in 2002 that it is either "very desirable" (41 percent) or "somewhat desirable" (42 percent) that the United States exert strong leadership in world affairs. A majority (52 percent) said that the United States should remain the only superpower, with just 33 percent saying that the European Union should also become a superpower. In 2004, a small majority said the United States should "make active efforts" to ensure that no other country becomes a superpower.[3]

To be sure, a solid majority of Americans (66 percent versus 27 percent) in 2002 viewed economic strength rather than military strength as more important in determining a country's overall power and influence. But this may just mean that economic strength is judged to be a *prerequisite* for military power. As we will see, large majorities of Americans want to maintain defense spending at the current level or increase it, want to maintain many long-term military bases abroad, and favor using military force under a variety of circumstances.

Still, substantial majorities reject a "world policeman" role for the United States. When asked in 2002, "Do you think that the United States has the responsibility to play the role of 'world policeman,' that is, to fight violations of international law and aggression wherever they occur?" only 34 percent said yes; 62 percent said no. A similarly solid majority (65 percent to 34 percent) said they agreed with the statement "The U.S. is playing the role of world policeman more than it should be." By 2004, after setbacks in Iraq, these sentiments appear to have grown even stronger.[4]

Nor do Americans generally favor a unilateral approach. In 2002, most rejected (56 percent to 39 percent) the notion of a division of labor in which the United States, with the strongest military, "should take the lead responsibility and supply most of the forces when it comes to military conflict," with Europe mainly assisting poor countries and trying to help reconstruct societies after a war. By a top-heavy majority of 71 percent to 17 percent, Americans also rejected the idea that "as the sole remaining superpower, the U.S. should continue to be the preeminent world leader in solving international problems," saying instead that "the U.S. should do its share in efforts to solve international problems together with other countries" (only 9 percent picked the third alternative, "the U.S. should withdraw from most efforts to solve international problems"). Just 31 percent of respondents said that, in responding to international crises, the United

States should "take action alone, if it does not have the support of its allies"; 61 percent said it should not act alone. In 2004, the public rejected the "preeminent world leader" idea by almost exactly the same margin as in 2002.[5] We will see that these are not just empty verbal responses. They reflect real opinions about the limits of U.S. power and the importance of multilateralism. These general sentiments carry through to specific preferences concerning concrete military policies.

USING ARMED FORCE

Fighting terrorism. Even before the terrorist attacks of September 11, 2001, majorities of Americans expressed willingness to used armed force against international terrorism. After 9/11 those majorities became very large. This follows logically from the fact that (as we saw in chapter 2) most Americans have called international terrorism a "critical threat" to the vital interest of the United States and have said that combating it should be a very important goal of U.S. foreign policy.

According to the 2002 CCFR survey, fully 92 percent of Americans approved of the use of U.S. troops "to destroy a terrorist camp" (see table 4.1).[6] To be sure, the wording of the question presumed success. And it seemed to

Table 4.1. Military action against terrorism

	Favor (%)	Oppose (%)
Approve of the use of U.S. troops to destroy a terrorist camp	92	6
Favor U.S. air strikes against terrorist training camps and other facilities to combat terrorism	87	10
Favor attacks by ground troops against terrorist camps and other facilities to combat terrorism	84	11
Favor the use of U.S. troops to assist the Philippine government to fight terrorism	78	19
Favor toppling unfriendly regimes that support terrorist groups threatening the U.S.	73	24
Favor assassination of individual terrorist leaders	66	26
Favor the use of U.S. troops if the government of Pakistan requested our help against a radical Islamic revolution	61	32

Source: 2002 CCFR/GMF U.S. public survey, combined telephone and in-person data set.
Note: Items are drawn from several different batteries of questions; exact wording is described in the text and endnotes.

imply a limited operation, conceivably with no casualties at all. Still, in response to a different question that inquired about a series of measures "to combat international terrorism," a hefty 84 percent of the public (up substantially since 1998) said they would favor "attacks by U.S. ground troops against terrorist training camps and other facilities."[7] The possibility of suffering some casualties, then, did not inhibit the public from risking U.S. troops in the context of a direct attack upon terrorists.

As table 4.1 indicates, in 2002 a very large majority (87 percent) also favored U.S. air strikes against terrorist training camps. And substantial majorities—around three-quarters of the public—favored using U.S. troops to help the Philippine government fight terrorism and favored "toppling" unfriendly regimes that support terrorist groups. About two-thirds even favored assassinating individual terrorist leaders. A majority of Americans (61 percent) also favored using troops if the government of Pakistan—which was armed with nuclear weapons and was considered a crucial though possibly vulnerable U.S. ally—"requested help against a radical Islamic revolution." In 2004, large majorities favored most of the same policies, despite a small drop-off after three years without terrorist attacks on the United States.[8] In these respects—though, as we will see, certainly not in all respects—the public seemed in harmony with the Bush administration's "war" on international terrorism.

Using troops for humanitarian and peacekeeping purposes. But terrorism was by no means the only focus of preferred military policies. Large majorities of Americans in 2002 also favored using U.S. armed forces for a variety of other purposes (see table 4.2). Large majorities, in the 76 percent to 81 percent range, for example, said they favored using U.S. troops to assist a population struck by famine, to stop a government from committing genocide and killing large numbers of its own people, to liberate hostages, or—remarkably— "to uphold international law." Much the same was true in 2004.[9] The high level of support for these humanitarian actions indicates that Americans are serious in saying that a number of justice-related objectives should be at least somewhat important goals of U.S. foreign policy. It is consistent with a "responsibility to protect" peoples abroad.

Similarly, three-quarters of Americans favored using U.S. troops as part of an international peacekeeping force in Afghanistan, and about two-thirds favored using troops to help enforce a peace agreement between Israel and the Palestinians, to help the UN pacify "a troubled part of the world," and to participate in the peacekeeping operation in Bosnia (where a few thousand U.S. troops were serving as part of a NATO operation). Understandably, there was less support for the vague and hazardous-sounding idea of using U.S. troops—perhaps alone—to bring peace to "a region where there is civil

Table 4.2. Troop use under various circumstances

	Favor (%)	Oppose (%)
Humanitarian operations		
To assist a population struck by famine	81	16
To liberate hostages	77	15
To stop a government from committing genocide and killing large numbers of its own people	77	19
To uphold international law	76	21
Peacekeeping		
To be part of an international peacekeeping force in Afghanistan	76	21
To be part of an international peacekeeping force to enforce a peace agreement between Israel and the Palestinians	65	30
To take part in a UN international peacekeeping force in a troubled part of the world rather than leaving this job to other countries	64	23
To participate in the peacekeeping operation in Bosnia ("strongly" and "somewhat" in favor combined)	64	33
To help bring peace to a region where there is civil war	48	43
Drugs and Oil		
To fight drug lords in Colombia	66	30
To ensure the supply of oil	65	30

Source: 2002 CCFR/GMF public survey, combined data.
Note: Items come from several different batteries of questions, which are described in the text and endnotes.

war," but even here approval outweighed disapproval (48 percent to 43 percent). By 2004, weariness with Iraq may have dented Americans' enthusiasm for peacekeeping somewhat, but majorities of Americans still favored using U.S. troops for international peacekeeping in Afghanistan and for the Israel-Palestinian and India-Pakistan conflicts. A very large majority, apparently unchanged from 2002, favored taking part in a "United Nations international peacekeeping force in a troubled part of the world."[10]

The American public's willingness to participate in many sorts of international peacekeeping operations contradicts claims of skittish aversion to such operations. No such generalized aversion was in fact supported by survey data even during the 1990s, when opponents of humanitarian intervention were saying the public would never stand for it.[11] As the "civil war" item suggests, however, a multilateral context is probably important to the public's willingness to engage in peacekeeping, and potential costs and benefits do matter.

Oil and drugs. Most Americans in 2002 also favored using U.S. troops to pursue two of their most highly ranked self-interested and domestically oriented foreign policy goals: securing adequate supplies of energy and stopping the flow of illegal drugs into the United States. About two-thirds of the U.S. public favored using U.S. troops to "fight drug lords in Colombia," where covert U.S. operations (perhaps related to oil as well as drugs) were in fact under way. Nearly two-thirds also favored using troops to "ensure the supply of oil," arguably a central issue in the confrontation at that time with Saddam Hussein's Iraq. In 2004, majorities of the public—probably somewhat smaller majorities—continued to favor both these uses of troops.[12] Certain foreign policy goals involving security of domestic well-being, then, are also considered important enough to justify using military force to pursue them.

It may be significant, however, that nearly all the military operations discussed above, from attacking terrorists to keeping the peace to fighting drug lords, might be conducted in limited ways with few U.S. casualties. What about more dangerous missions involving full-scale combat against opposing armies? In such cases the public is considerably more reluctant to commit U.S. troops and more insistent upon multilateral support.

Reacting to invasions multilaterally. Over the years, Chicago Council on Foreign Relations surveys have asked about the use of U.S. troops (without specifying multilateral action) in a variety of scenarios that would involve major combat. They have often found a high level of public opposition. In Vietnam-traumatized 1974, for example, when respondents were asked whether they would favor or oppose "U.S. military involvement, including the use of U.S. troops" in twelve different hypothetical circumstances, a majority favored involvement in only a single, quite unlikely, case: if Canada were invaded (77 percent favored U.S. involvement). Only 39 percent and 34 percent, respectively, favored using U.S. troops in case of an invasion of western Europe or the Russians taking over West Berlin. Still fewer supported troop use if Israel were being defeated by the Arabs (27 percent), if Communist China invaded Formosa (Taiwan) (17 percent), or if North Korea attacked South Korea (just 14 percent).[13]

By 1978, when some of the same hypothetical situations were asked about with slightly different wording,[14] responses were somewhat more favorable to using U.S. troops. A majority favored using troops to keep the Panama Canal open (58 percent) and to resist a Soviet invasion of western

Europe (54 percent). But with the rather fanciful Canadian case dropped from the survey, those were the only two of eleven scenarios with majority support for troop use. Just 48 percent favored defending West Berlin, and (reflecting a continued post-Vietnam distaste for land wars in Asia), only 21 percent and 20 percent wanted to defend South Korea and Taiwan, respectively.[15] In subsequent Cold War–era surveys support for using troops continued to rise somewhat, so that by 1986, 68 percent of the public favored defending western Europe, and 53 percent Japan, against a hypothetical Soviet invasion. But other troop uses remained unpopular.[16]

In 1990, with the Soviet Union falling apart, the improbable scenario of a Soviet invasion of western Europe found just 56 percent of Americans in favor of using U.S. troops.[17] But three months before the autumn CCFR survey Saddam Hussein's Iraq had invaded Kuwait, and the Chicago Council found that a solid 60 percent of Americans favored using U.S. troops if Iraq invaded oil-rich Saudi Arabia. A majority (57 percent) also said they would favor using troops if Iraq refused to withdraw from Kuwait. (Later surveys by other organizations leading up to the 1991 Gulf War generally indicated that small majorities of Americans favored war if Iraq did not withdraw from Kuwait, an action for which the United States had already lined up support from other countries and the United Nations. Support for the war then rose markedly after U.S. air attacks were successful and a quick ground invasion involved minimal U.S. casualties, though support declined somewhat when Hussein remained in power and brutally suppressed uprisings by the Iraqi Shiites and Kurds without U.S. intervention.[18]) In 1990 a long-term high of 45 percent of Americans favored using U.S. troops if Arab forces invaded Israel.[19] Nearly as large minorities (42 percent and 40 percent) favored using troops against a Soviet overthrow of a democratic government in eastern Europe or a Soviet invasion of Japan. Still, only 26 percent favored using U.S. troops if North Korea invaded South Korea.

In the next two CCFR surveys (1994 and 1998), support for defending Saudi Arabia against Iraq eroded a bit (to 52 percent and then 46 percent), as did willingness to defend Israel, while support for South Korea rose and then dropped back. With the Soviet Union gone, Saddam Hussein in a box, and no other plausible military threats to the United States in sight, there was no majority public support for U.S. troop use in any of the seven scenarios asked about in 1998: North Korea invading South Korea, Iraq invading Saudi Arabia, Arab forces invading Israel, Russia invading Poland, Cubans attempting to overthrow Castro, China invading Taiwan, or Serbian forces killing large numbers of Albanians in Kosovo.[20]

In 2002, respondents were asked to react to just four hypothetical invasion scenarios: Arab forces invading Israel, Iraq invading Saudi Arabia, North Korea invading South Korea, and China invading Taiwan.[21] In the

Table 4.3. Troop use in invasion scenarios

	Favor (%)	Oppose (%)
Without multilateral involvement specified:		
If Arab forces invaded Israel	48	45
If Iraq invaded Saudi Arabia	48	46
If North Korea invaded South Korea	36	56
If China invaded Taiwan	32	58
With multilateral involvement specified:		
If Iraq were to invade Saudi Arabia, would you favor or oppose the U.S. contributing military forces, together with other countries, to a UN-sponsored effort to reverse the aggression?	77	18
If North Korea were to attack South Korea, would you favor or oppose the U.S. contributing military forces, together with other countries, to a UN-sponsored effort to reverse the aggression?	57	35

Source: 2002 CCFR/GMF public survey, combined in-person and telephone data set.

post-9/11 environment, support for using troops may have risen a bit (probably not; the apparent increases were most likely artifacts of the change in survey modes), but even according to the combined telephone and in-person data, support for troop use did not reach a majority in any of these four cases (see table 4.3).[22] Only 48 percent of Americans favored using U.S. troops to defend Israel or Saudi Arabia, with 45 percent and 46 percent opposed, respectively. Only 36 percent said they favored using troops to defend South Korea, and 32 percent to defend Taiwan. Again in 2004, only minorities favored using U.S. troops to defend Israel, South Korea, or Taiwan.[23]

The history of responses to these questions indicates that the American public, at least in the post-Vietnam period for which we have data, has continued to oppose most uses of U.S. troops in major war situations likely to be costly in dollars and lives: the lives of ordinary citizens, of course, rather than of Washington decision makers. We will see in chapter 7 that there have been persistent, substantial gaps between citizens' and decision makers' views of these matters.

But the 2002 survey made clear another important fact, that an implication of *unilateral* action can play a crucial part in the public's opposition to using troops. When an independent subsample of respondents was asked about using U.S. troops in two of the same places but with an explicitly *multilateral* context—"contributing forces, together with other countries, to a UN-sponsored effort to reverse the aggression"—a large, 77 percent majority favored using U.S. troops to defend Saudi Arabia against an invasion by

Iraq, and a smaller majority of 57 percent even favored the apparently long-unpopular idea of defending South Korea (see table 4.3).[24] These increases in support for using troops—roughly 20 percentage points in the case of South Korea, nearly 30 in that of Saudi Arabia—indicate that, to the American public, multilateralism makes a big difference. The 2004 survey confirmed that an explicit reference to multilateralism increased support for defending South Korea by 21 percentage points.[25]

Attacking Saddam Hussein's Iraq. The same point applies to a crucial, very contentious issue of 2002: whether or not the United States should invade Iraq. At the time of the June CCFR survey, members of the Bush administration had already been charging that Iraq had ties with terrorism and either had in hand or was developing chemical, biological, and nuclear weapons that might be used against the United States. The administration had also begun secret contingency planning for an invasion of Iraq, though it had not yet launched its full-scale public relations offensive designed to build support for such action.[26]

In the 2002 survey, as we have seen, most Americans felt very cold toward Iraq and its leader. Saddam Hussein received a record-low average rating of just 8 degrees on the 100-degree feeling thermometer. Overwhelming majorities said that preventing the spread of nuclear weapons should be a very important goal of U.S. foreign policy (90 percent) and that Iraq's developing weapons of mass destruction was a critical threat to the vital interest of the United States (86 percent).Accordingly, when respondents were asked about various circumstances "that might justify using U.S. troops in other parts of the world," a large majority (75 percent) said they favored the use of U.S. troops "in order to overthrow Saddam Hussein's government in Iraq." To be sure, the wording of that question made the idea particularly appealing: "to overthrow" implied success, and there was no mention of the number of troops involved or the nature of the action. Respondents might have had in mind a small, quick, casualty-free Special Forces operation. But a flood of Iraq-related questions asked by other survey organizations from mid-2002 through early 2003 make clear that majorities—usually smaller majorities—favored a large-scale military operation against Iraq, so long as multilateral support was not excluded and the question did not emphasize the possibility of extensive costs in lives or money.

Again, however, multilateralism mattered. When a different CCFR question spelled out three alternative positions and inquired which "is closest to yours," a solid majority—65 percent—said, "The U.S. should only invade Iraq with UN approval and the support of its Allies." Only 20 percent said, "The U.S. should invade Iraq even if we have to go it alone" (13 percent said, "The U.S. should not invade Iraq"). In other words, when the issue of multilateral support was made explicit, it became clear that the U.S. public had little enthusiasm for invading Iraq unilaterally. A systematic statistical analysis of scores of prewar polls about Iraq has confirmed this finding.[27] In retrospect, the public seems to have had a good point: in the event, when the United States acted mostly on its own, it paid a high price.

Later in 2002—perhaps in part because surveys were making clear the American and European publics' preference for multilateralism,[28] as well as because of British insistence—the Bush administration turned to the UN Security Council. Ratcheting up its rhetoric ("we know" that Iraq has large stocks of chemical and biological weapons and is prepared to use them, and that an active nuclear weapons program is under way), the administration persuaded the world body to authorize stringent weapons inspections and to implicitly threaten the use of force ("serious consequences") if inspections were defied. After inspectors were readmitted to Iraq they found no major prohibited weapons but reported that Iraq had failed to cooperate fully. The Bush administration pushed hard for a second UN resolution explicitly authorizing the use of force, but it faced widespread opposition—including a veto threat from France—and pleas for giving inspectors more time. On March 19, 2003, President Bush went ahead and ordered the invasion of Iraq without such authorization. Just before the invasion, some survey evidence suggested that a bare majority of Americans had come to favor invading Iraq even without a new UN resolution.[29]

In order to understand the American public's acquiescence in the invasion of Iraq, however, it is important to bear in mind what the public had been told. The Bush administration implied that Iraq posed an imminent threat to the United States itself, alluding to the prospect of "mushroom clouds," an alleged program of drone airplanes that might deliver biological weapons to the east coast, and alleged ties with al Qaeda and other terrorist organizations that might be given "weapons of mass destruction." Moreover, the proposed invasion of Iraq was portrayed *not* as being unilateral but as involving a broad, multilateral "coalition of the willing," even though only Britain agreed to contribute substantial forces (most other "coalition" members, from Albania to Tuvalu, offered little but moral support). And the administration argued that it was *not* defying the United Nations but was in fact enforcing a long series of UN Iraq disarmament resolutions that other countries were too weak or too compromised to enforce. Much of this rhetoric was false or misleading.[30] Yet there is every reason to believe that the average American took it seriously. Many Americans, for example, were convinced that Saddam Hussein was "personally involved" in the attacks of 9/11.[31]

Should we take this as evidence of an "irrational" public? Surely not. Few U.S. politicians (Republican or Democratic), few pundits, and few media outlets presented substantial contrary evidence. Absent dissenting voices, Americans understandably tend to trust top government officials unless and until the officials clearly violate their trust. Given tightly controlled information, deceptive rhetoric, and two-party agreement or collusion, the rational public can be fooled.[32] This may happen with some frequency in foreign affairs. When it does, it would be wrong to blame the public, but expressed public opinion can no longer offer an independent guide to policy makers.

In any case, the prewar survey evidence does not contradict the American public's strong preference for multilateral and UN support in major military operations. Nor did polls during or after the Iraq war. Indeed, the failure of the invading U.S. forces to find any al Qaeda ties, stocks of chemical or biological weapons, or even active programs to develop chemical, biological or nuclear weapons, together with the turmoil and casualties of the occupation and the messiness of the "transition to democracy," undoubtedly reinforced the American public's already strong reluctance to use major military force unilaterally. In 2004, after the official rationale for invading Iraq had switched to democratization, a large majority opposed using U.S. troops "to install democratic governments in states where dictators rule."[33] In the Iraq case the public has learned from history, and the lesson has not favored the neoconservative agenda.

Security Council approval, allies, and unilateral uses of force. The 2004 CCFR survey asked a number of new questions about using military force that explored differences between unilateral and multilateral action. Large majorities of Americans said that the UN Security Council should "have the right to authorize the use of military force" for each of the following purposes: "to prevent severe human rights violations, such as genocide" (this had the highest level of support, 85 percent); "to stop a country from supporting terrorist groups"; "to defend a country that has been attacked"; "to prevent a country that does not have nuclear weapons from acquiring them"; and "to restore by force a democratic government that has been overthrown." (Despite the appealing proviso that the proposed action would *restore* democracy, this last case won only 60 percent support, 25 percentage points less than the one involving genocide.)[34]

But when respondents were asked whether "*a country* [presumably including the United States], without UN approval," should have the right to use military force for the same purposes, support in each case dropped by about 20 percentage points (only 15 points in the case of genocide). In the "restore . . . democratic government" scenario this was enough to transform clear majority support for the right to use force into clear majority opposition.[35]

The 2004 survey pursued similar themes with very similar results in regard to North Korea, which was thought surreptitiously to have developed nuclear weapons. Respondents were asked, "If the U.S. were to consider using military force to destroy North Korea's nuclear capability would it be necessary or not necessary to first get" particular sorts of approval: 74 percent said "approval of most U.S. allies" would be necessary; 68 percent, "approval of the UN Security Council"; and 58 percent, "approval from the South Korean government." A clever survey experiment pinned things down more precisely. Eight different subsets of respondents were asked, "Suppose North Korea continues to develop nuclear weapons. Please say whether you would support or oppose the United States using military force to destroy North Korea's nuclear weapons capability if . . . ," with each group of respondents given a different combination of approval or nonapproval by the UN Security Council and approval or opposition by "most U.S. allies" and by the South Korean government. Majorities of Americans favored using force in all cases except where both the UN and "most allies" were opposed. On average, postulated UN approval produced levels of support for using force about 19 percentage points higher than the absence of UN approval, and approval by allies led to about 11 points more support than allies' opposition. (Controlling for those factors, South Korea's views made little difference.)[36]

Using nuclear weapons. The willingness of the U.S. public to support a multilaterally authorized armed attack to prevent nuclear proliferation (despite the general legal right of countries to develop nuclear arms[37]) reflects Americans' deep fear and dislike of nuclear weapons. During the Cold War there was strong support for nuclear arms control. In every CCFR survey from 1974 through 1990, large majorities—about two-thirds of the public—said that "worldwide arms control" should be a very important goal of U.S. foreign policy. (By contrast, "matching Soviet military power" was called very important by at most a bare majority.)[38] During the 1980s, when the Reagan administration was rapidly building up U.S. nuclear arms and engaging in hostile rhetoric toward the Soviets, substantial and growing majorities of Americans (58 percent in 1982, 67 percent in 1986) favored the idea of a "mutual, verifiable freeze" on nuclear weapons "right now," if the Soviets would agree. Only a minority said "only after the U.S. builds up its nuclear weapons more" (21 percent in 1982, 14 percent in 1986) or "not at all" (12 percent in 1982, 11 percent in 1986).[39]

Since the end of the Cold War, every Chicago Council on Foreign Relations survey has found that the public puts "preventing the spread of nuclear weapons" at or near the top of the list of very important goals for U.S. foreign policy (recall table 2.3). Anxiety about the possibility of nuclear weapons falling into the hands of terrorists and being used against the United States has contributed to the high priority assigned to combating terrorism and to the public's willingness to contemplate going to war with Iraq or possibly North Korea.

The 2002 CCFR survey suggests that this abhorrence of nuclear weapons goes beyond concern for the security of the United States, however; it also touches upon issues of justice, including avoidance of using excessive force against people elsewhere. When respondents were presented with three alternative positions concerning "the possible use of nuclear weapons by the United States" and asked "which position comes closest to yours?" there was very little support for *first* use, as opposed to retaliatory use, of nuclear weapons. About one-fifth of the public (22 percent) said, "The U.S. should never use nuclear weapons under any circumstances." An additional 55 percent said, "The U.S. should only use nuclear weapons in response to a nuclear attack." Only about one-fifth of the public, 21 percent, said that "in certain circumstances, the U.S. should use nuclear weapons even if has not suffered a nuclear attack." Opinions were much the same in 2004.[40]

The public's opposition to the first use of nuclear weapons appears to go against the old Cold War–era doctrine of "massive [nuclear] retaliation" for any Soviet ground attack on NATO allies in Europe. More important, it signals likely public opposition to the implication of the Bush administration's 2002 National Security Strategy document, that the United States might use nuclear weapons for the penetration of deep bunkers and other tactical purposes in antiterrorist operations, even without nuclear provocation.[41]

MILITARY CAPABILITY

Consistent with their support for military action under various circumstances, most Americans favor maintaining the capability necessary for taking such action. The public favors substantial spending on the military and favors having extensive military bases around the world with large numbers of U.S. troops assigned to them. Most Americans like the general idea of a national missile defense but do not want to build such a system before it is proven to work. Following through on their preference for a cooperative and multilateral foreign policy, large majorities of the public favor maintaining or expanding *multilateral* military capabilities: maintaining a major U.S. commitment to NATO and expanding NATO to include a number of new member nations, encouraging strong leadership and defense spending by the European Union, and strengthening the United Nations' ability to react to crises by establishing joint training exercises and a rapid deployment force. But the public is not very supportive of the United States' giving military aid or even selling weapons abroad.

Spending on homeland security and defense. Perhaps the most important indicator of seriousness about military capability is willingness to pay for it. By that measure, the American public puts a very high priority on homeland security and gathering intelligence information about other countries, a priority nearly as high as it puts on domestic programs like health care and aid to education. It gives substantial—though notably less—support to defense spending but very little support to military aid to other nations.

Survey respondents in 2002 were read a list of "present government programs" and were asked whether each one should be expanded, cut back, or kept about the same. For "gathering intelligence information about other countries," a very high 66 percent said "expanded," up by 39 percentage points since 1998 and not far below the 77 percent who said they favored expanding health care or the 75 percent who wanted to expand aid to education (see table 4.4). Similarly, 65 percent of Americans said they wanted to expand "homeland security."[42] Some nine months after the terrorist attacks of September 11, 2001, the public's commitment to spending money for security against attack was unmistakable. By 2004—with fewer perceptions of imminent threats—these percentages had dropped a bit, but many more Americans still wanted to expand homeland security and intelligence gathering than wanted to cut back.[43]

Defense spending is a different story, with somewhat less popular support and a history of ups and downs. In the first CCFR survey, conducted in 1974, around the end of the unhappy U.S. involvement in Vietnam, only a small proportion of Americans (just 14 percent) favored expanding defense spending, with a much larger 42 percent wanting to cut back. Support for

Table 4.4. Expanding or cutting back government programs

	Expand	Keep about the same	Cut back
Health care	77	19	4
Aid to education	75	21	4
Programs to combat violence and crime	70	24	5
Gathering intelligence information about other countries	66	25	6
Homeland security	65	27	5
Social Security	64	30	3
Defense spending	44	38	15
Economic aid to other nations	14	35	48
Military aid to other nations	10	39	46

Source: 2002 CCFR/GMF general public survey, combined data set.

expansion rose markedly to 34 percent in 1978, during the "new Cold War" (other surveys show it peaked around 1980, after Iran's taking of U.S. hostages and the Soviet invasion of Afghanistan), but then fell steadily to a low point of 14 percent in 1990 (as the Cold War ended), before rising in 1994 and again in 1998. In five of the first seven CCFR surveys (all except 1978 and the virtual tie of 1998), the proportion of Americans wanting to cut back on defense spending exceeded the proportion wanting to expand it.[44] In post-9/11 2002, however, the proportion of the public saying that defense spending should be expanded jumped to 44 percent, the highest figure in all eight surveys (14 percentage points higher than in 1998) and the first time in twenty-four years that support for expansion clearly exceeded support for cutting back (which dropped to only 15 percent). Clearly, in 2002 many Americans favored increasing the military budget. Even though only a plurality picked the expansion response, it is reasonable to say that the "balance of opinion" "tilted" in that direction, and, indeed, that *most* Americans probably favored at least a small increase in spending.[45]

Still, the public's support for increased defense spending should not be exaggerated. For one thing, contemporaneous surveys by other organizations indicated that most Americans favored increased spending for defense against terrorism but thought the money could come from other parts of the military budget, without requiring an overall increase in spending.[46] For another thing, if the programs about which respondents were asked in the 2002 CCFR survey are ranked by the proportion of Americans wanting to expand them, defense spending comes in seventh out of nine, behind health, education, crime, intelligence, homeland security, and Social Security, and ahead only of economic aid and military aid (recall table 4.4). It seems reasonable to conclude that most Americans wanted to spend substantial sums on defense: probably somewhat more than the $305 billion that had been spent in 2001, perhaps more than the sharply increased figure of $349 billion in 2002, but quite possibly less than the extraordinary (and Iraq-inflated) figures of $405 billion in 2003 or $456 billion in 2004, when domestic programs were severely constrained.[47]

There are limits to the amount of money Americans want to spend on defense. By 2004, with military spending way up, with an easing of perceived threats, and with widespread disillusionment over the Iraq war, support for expansion of defense spending dropped significantly. Opinion barely tilted in the direction of expanding rather than cutting back; a large plurality preferred the status quo.[48]

National missile defense. The Bush administration came into office strongly committed to building a ground-based "national missile defense," ostensibly aimed at intercepting and destroying any nuclear missiles launched by "rogue states" like North Korea. (Some analysts here and abroad, however, considered the real target to be China.) Overriding objections from Russia and various U.S. allies, the administration abrogated the Anti-Ballistic Missile Treaty, which prohibited such systems, and moved to begin deployment as soon as possible, despite unsuccessful or rigged test results, expert doubts about feasibility, and the possibility of provoking a new arms race.[49]

The 2002 CCFR survey indicates that most Americans liked the general idea of a missile defense—understandably so, since it seemed to promise elimination of one of the most terrifying threats to Americans' physical security. But most had doubts about quick deployment. Given three alternatives, only a very small minority of the public (14 percent) said the United States should "not build a missile defense system at all," but only a minority (31 percent) said we should "build a missile defense system right away." A majority of Americans, 52 percent, said we should "do more research until such a system is proven to be effective."

This reaction closely mirrored the public's rather sensible response sixteen years earlier—in the 1986 CCFR survey—to President Reagan's proposal for a space-based missile defense system, known officially as the Strategic Defense Initiative but popularly known as "Star Wars." Star Wars had provoked similar doubts among experts. Asked a similar survey question at that time, an identically small 14 percent of the public said "the U.S. should abandon the project," a similar minority of 28 percent said "the U.S. should go ahead and build such a system," and a large plurality, 48 percent, said the United States should "go ahead with the research involved but make no decision at this time about building the system." As it turned out, Star Wars consumed many billions of dollars in research and development funds but never reached operational status.[50]

Military bases and troops abroad. Well after the disappearance of any threat from the Soviet Union, the United States continues to maintain what political scientist Chalmers Johnson has called an "empire of bases" around the world: an enormous network of military bases, devoted to electronic surveillance and to fighter and bomber aircraft as well as ground troops, spanning virtually all of the northern hemisphere and much of the southern. According to official sources assembled by Johnson, as of September 2001 the U.S. had 725 nonsecret bases in thirty-eight different countries. Each of seventeen large bases had a "plant replacement value" of more than $1.5 billion; altogether, the 725 bases had a replacement value of at least $118 billion. At that point, well before the Iraq war, the number of U.S. military personnel based abroad in 153 countries totaled 254,788; if civilians and dependents were included, the figure doubled to 531,227.[51]

Most Americans favor having a number of U.S. bases, though support has dropped recently. When respondents to the 2002 CCFR survey were asked in general terms about "long-term military bases overseas," the center of gravity of opinion favored the current (very large) number of bases or an increase: 57 percent said the United States should have "about as many as we have now" and 25 percent said "more bases overseas," while only 14 percent said fewer. More concretely, when asked about ten actual or potential locations for long-term U.S. military bases, a majority favored having bases in all but one of them, though the proportion in favor varied significantly from one location to another (see table 4.5).[52] Support was particularly high for bases on the soil of longtime allies or in well-established locations: 70 percent for Guantanamo Bay, Cuba (then in the news for holding terrorist suspects and detainees from the Afghan war); 69 percent for Germany, site of key NATO bases; 67 percent for South Korea, another Cold War stronghold; 66 percent for bases in the Philippines (former site of the navy's Subic Bay facilities); 65 percent for Saudi Arabia, longtime U.S. bastion in the Middle East; and 63 percent for Japan, where U.S. troops had stayed since World War II. Smaller majorities favored long-term U.S. military bases in Turkey (58 percent), Afghanistan (57 percent), and Pakistan (52 percent), all arguably critical to operations against terrorist groups. But only 41 percent of Americans favored bases in Uzbekistan, while an essentially equal 42 percent were opposed. Few Americans are likely to have known much about Uzbekistan, but it is possible that objections to the autocratic, human-rights-abusing Karimov government had filtered through to some members of the public, and that similar concerns limited support for bases in the other " 'stans."

Table 4.5. Long-term military bases abroad

	Should have bases (%)	Should not have bases (%)
Guantanamo Bay, Cuba	70	27
Germany	69	28
South Korea	67	27
Philippines	66	30
Saudi Arabia	65	32
Japan	63	33
Turkey	58	34
Afghanistan	57	40
Pakistan	52	41
Uzbekistan	41	42

Source: 2002 CCFR / GMF U.S. public survey, combined data set.

Support for maintaining numerous military bases around the world does not, however, mean that the public favors devoting unlimited resources to them. The balance of opinion in 2002 actually pointed toward stationing somewhat *lower*, rather than higher, numbers of troops abroad. When reminded that the United States then had about one hundred thousand troops in western Europe, 53 percent said that was "about right," but 33 percent said "too many"—considerably more than the 8 percent who said "too few." Even more strikingly, when reminded that the United States currently had about forty-four thousand troops in Japan (including Okinawa), 45 percent called that level "about right," while fully 43 percent said "too many," far overshadowing the 5 percent who said "too few." If even a small fraction of "about right" respondents thought that there were somewhat more U.S. troops in Japan than they wanted, a majority of Americans favored at least some decrease in troop levels.

By 2004, as part of a general pullback from military activism, the public—while continuing to support having substantial bases abroad—appears to have tilted toward favoring fewer bases as well as smaller numbers of troops. The 2004 Web-based survey indicated that majorities of Americans continued to favor having long-term military bases in South Korea, Guantanamo, Germany, and Japan, but opinion was more evenly divided about Saudi Arabia (where the U.S. was on the way out), Afghanistan, and Turkey. Majorities opposed long-term bases in Iraq, Pakistan, and especially Uzbekistan. Most Americans said that "if a majority of people in the Middle East want the U.S. to remove its military presence there," we should do so. Most said the thirty-seven thousand troops then in South Korea were "too many," and most thought that Washington's proposed reduction of one-third would have no significant effect on South Korea's security.[53]

The NATO alliance. In harmony with their preference for multilateral military action (which spreads costs, multiplies capabilities, and adds legitimacy) rather than unilateral action, most Americans favor formal alliances with other countries, especially the North Atlantic Treaty Organization (NATO). Throughout the Cold War period—even in Vietnam-weary 1974—at least 50 percent of respondents to Chicago Council surveys always said we should "keep our commitment [to NATO] what it is now," and an additional 5 or 10 percent wanted to increase it. Few wanted to decrease our commitment or withdraw entirely.[54]

Although the Soviet Union—NATO's original antagonist—no longer existed, 56 percent of Americans in the 2002 survey said NATO is "still essential to our country's security," with just 30 percent saying "it is no longer essential." Even more than in past CCFR surveys, a solid majority (65 percent) wanted to keep our commitment to NATO "what it is now"; 11 percent wanted to increase our commitment, 11 percent to decrease it, and 6 percent to withdraw entirely. Commitment to NATO stayed the same or dropped only a bit in 2004.[55]

Furthermore, majorities of Americans in 2002 wanted to expand NATO to include a number of countries then being considered for membership: Romania (56 percent in favor, 30 percent opposed); Slovakia—"formerly part of Czechoslovakia" (53 percent); the Baltic states—"that is, Lithuania, Estonia, and Latvia" (52 percent), Slovenia—"formerly part of Yugoslavia" (52 percent); and Bulgaria (50 percent, 34 percent opposed). (We will see that much of the support for NATO expansion rested on desires for *political* cooperation, rather than hopes of enlisting substantial military forces from these small countries.) Most remarkably, the highest proportion of Americans—fully 68 percent—favored including Russia in NATO. This was quite a testament to the end of the Cold War and the new perception of Russia as a reliable U.S. partner against terrorism. At the time of the 2002 survey, U.S. and NATO officials were taking only limited steps to develop friendly ties between Russia and NATO; formal admission to the alliance was not being discussed.

By the same token, most Americans want our European allies to play a substantial part in security issues. As we have seen, in 2002 most members of the public rejected the idea that the European Union "should become a superpower, like the United States," saying instead that "the U.S. should remain the only superpower" (52 percent to 33 percent). By a similar margin, however (56% to 39%), most Americans rejected the proposition that the U.S. should take the lead and supply most of the forces when it comes to military conflict, with European efforts instead focused on things like promoting development in poor countries and helping societies rebuild after wars. As we have also noted, most Americans (61 percent, compared to 34 percent) took the chief lesson of 9/11 to be that the United States needs to work more closely with other countries to fight terrorism, rather than acting on its own more. An even bigger majority (71 percent to 17 percent) said the U.S. should solve international problems together with other countries rather than continuing to be the preeminent world leader. And most (61 percent versus 31 percent) said that in international crises the United States should not act alone if it does not have the support of its allies.

Consistent with the idea of the Europeans' sharing military burdens with the United States, the American public in 2002 leaned somewhat toward favoring an increase in defense spending by European governments, with 38 percent saying that it should be expanded, 39 percent that it should be kept the same, and only 14 percent that it should be cut back.

UN military capability. In harmony with their support for a variety of UN peacekeeping operations, most Americans—unlike some U.S. government

officials—favor strengthening UN military capabilities to make such operations more speedy and effective. When asked in 2002 about "specific steps
that could be taken to strengthen the UN," a large majority (77 percent to
19 percent) favored "having joint training exercises of UN member countries
so that their militaries will be better prepared to work together in combat situations." More remarkably, a nearly identical majority (77 percent to 20 percent) favored "having UN members each commit 1,000 troops to a rapid deployment force that the UN Security Council can call up on short notice when
a crisis occurs." Similarly, in 2004 a large majority favored "having a standing
UN peacekeeping force selected, trained and commanded by the United
Nations." Solid majorities also favored "giving the UN the power to regulate
the international arms trade" and said the U.S. should be "more willing to
make decisions within the UN," even if this means that the United States "will
sometimes have to go along with a policy that is not its first choice." [56]

The idea of member-state contributions to a UN rapid deployment force—
provided for under the UN Charter (chapter 7, article 43)—had been resisted
for decades by the United States and other major powers. The CCFR findings
and other survey evidence suggest that the American public is considerably
more receptive to internationally controlled security arrangements than
most U.S. officials have been.[57]

Military aid and arms sales. Many or most Americans apparently *do not,* however, accept the idea of using military aid or arms sales to build up allies'
military capabilities. When the 2002 CCFR survey asked about expanding or
cutting nine different government programs, "military aid to other countries" got the least support: only 10 percent of the public said it should be
expanded, while 39 percent said kept the same and 46 percent said cut back
(recall table 4.4). In 2004, too, and in all previous CCFR surveys, large proportions of the public—up to 73 percent—have said that military aid to
other countries should be cut back.[58] Indeed, in response to a different question asked in the five surveys between 1974 and 1990, only small minorities
of respondents (generally less than 30 percent) said that "on the whole" they
favored our "giving military aid to other nations." (The question explained,
"By military aid I mean arms and equipment but not troops.")[59] When last
asked (in 1990) about military aid to specific countries like Israel, Egypt,
South Korea, and Turkey, very few Americans (on the order of just 2 to 8 percent) said it should be increased, while large pluralities or majorities said it
should be decreased or stopped altogether.[60] This appears to be another area
in which official U.S. policy has not been in agreement with the preferences
of the general public.

Since the demise of the Soviet Union and the U.S. success in the 1991 Persian Gulf War, the United States has become by far the world's biggest seller

of weapons to other countries. U.S. arms sales abroad totaled some $12 billion in 2001, more than double the total sales by runners-up Britain and Russia. Indeed, U.S. arms sales nearly equaled those of all other countries put together. U.S. weapons have been implicated in nearly all recent armed conflicts and civil wars.[61]

But the idea of "selling military equipment to other nations" has never evoked much enthusiasm from the American public. Presumably the danger of U.S. weapons falling into the wrong hands—encouraging bloodshed and perhaps facilitating attacks against Americans—is seen as outweighing the benefits of strengthening allies or making money through arms sales. Even in CCFR surveys during the Cold War, only about one-third of the public generally favored arms sales, while more than half opposed them. Support for arms sales dropped still lower in post-Cold War surveys. In 2002 just 18 percent favored arms sales, while 77 percent opposed them.[62]

Once more we now turn from collective public opinion to the determinants of *individual* variations in opinion, again finding that personal and social characteristics generally have only weak impacts on foreign policy opinions. We also discuss the ways in which purposive belief systems affect individuals' specific policy preferences on military matters, setting the stage for briefer reports of similar evidence concerning political and economic policies in chapters 5 and 6. Those who are not interested should feel free to skip ahead.

WHY INDIVIDUALS FAVOR OR OPPOSE USING MILITARY FORCE

As chapter 2 demonstrated, Americans' personal and social characteristics—with the ambiguous exception of education—generally have rather little effect on what foreign policy goals they consider most important. Even when fourteen demographic independent variables were included in multiple regression analyses, they did not account for a great deal of the variation in individuals' goals. Much the same is true for specific policy preferences.

To be sure, in bivariate terms—that is, when we consider just one characteristic at a time—there are some significant differences in opinion among population groups. For example, in 2002 men, whites, and people of higher income and higher education levels tended to favor the use of military force in various situations, from attacking terrorist camps to repelling invasions.[63] They also tended to favor higher defense spending and more military bases abroad. Women, on the other hand, were particularly supportive of participating in multilateral peacekeeping operations, using U.S. troops to "bring peace to a region where there is civil war," and contributing troops to a UN rapid deployment force. African Americans and young people also tended more than others to favor intervening to stop civil wars. Uses of U.S. troops to stop drugs or to ensure a supply of oil won the most backing from those with high school educations or less, midwesterners, and people of middle incomes.

But when we investigated the *independent effects* upon policy preferences of personal and social characteristics, by conducting a series of multiple regression analyses using all of our fourteen demographic variables at the same time, we did not find much. Certain personal characteristics—especially gender and religion—do have significant independent effects upon preferences about military policy. But most other demographic factors do not. This is even true, in large part, of individuals' levels of formal education. Moreover, none of our demographic regressions could account for very much of the variance in policy preferences—seldom even as much as 7 or 8 percent of it.[64] Citizens' preferences regarding foreign policy are generally not very strongly rooted in social or personal characteristics.

Much more directly linked to foreign policy preferences are various attitudes, beliefs, and perceptions that tend to fit together into what we have called *purposive belief systems.* When we added to our demographic regression analyses three political predispositions or "basic attitudes" (party identification, liberal/conservative ideology, and especially internationalism, expressed as a preference for the United States' taking an "active part" in world affairs), we could often account for much more of the variation in policy preferences, and any formerly substantial coefficients for demographic factors tended to become small or insignificant. This was even more true when (in a third step) we added to the regressions selected sets of relevant foreign policy goals people embraced, threats they perceived, and their feelings about particular foreign countries and leaders. Moreover, regression analyses which—in a fourth step—included *only* the three basic attitudes and a few selected goals, threats, feelings, and the like, while excluding demographic variables altogether, generally accounted for policy preferences just about as well as did the comprehensive regressions that included demographics.

In this and the next two chapters we will systematically use this methodology of four sequential types of regression analysis to investigate the nature and strength of purposive believe systems across a wide range of specific policy preferences. We will generally report *standardized* regression coefficients so that we can compare the magnitudes of effects by and upon differently scaled variables and ascertain which attitudes and beliefs most strongly affect policy preferences.

While our findings are not entirely without causal ambiguity, they do support our suggestion that logically relevant foreign policy goals, perceived threats, and other attitudes generally have the biggest and most direct impacts on foreign policy preferences (see fig. 1.1). To the limited extent that social and personal characteristics affect policy preferences, they mainly do so not directly but by working *through* attitudinal factors: through education's tendency to increase international activism, for example, or evangelical Protestantism's tendency to make people ideologically conservative, which in turn affect more specific foreign policy goals, threat perceptions, and the like.

Why people favor or oppose using U.S. troops if foreign countries are invaded. When it comes to high-risk, potentially high-cost military operations like using nuclear weapons or resisting hypothetical invasions of one nation by another, among demographic factors only gender and religion—especially evangelical Protestantism—regularly have independent effects on preferences. Preferences for troop use are more strongly and independently affected by espousal of "active part" internationalism, the embrace of certain foreign policy goals (especially defending U.S. allies and protecting weaker countries against foreign aggression), and favorable feelings about, or perceptions of vital U.S. interests in, the country being attacked.

Consider the question in the 2002 CCFR survey concerning respondents' opinions about using U.S. troops if North Korea invaded South Korea—a situation likely to involve full-scale combat and substantial casualties. Despite some rather strong bivariate relationships,[65] in a demographic multiple regression analysis only gender showed a strong independent effect on preferences for using troops, with men being substantially more likely to favor troop use; controlling for other characteristics, evangelical Protestants, Catholics, and perhaps Asians also tended to support the use of troops, but the effects were smaller (see the first column of table 4.6). All the demographic characteristics taken together accounted for a larger than usual portion of the variation in policy preferences, but still only about 8 percent of it (see the adjusted *R*-squared figure at the bottom of the column).

When the three "basic attitudes" were added to the regression it accounted for substantially more of the variance in preferences, 13 percent. "Active part" internationalism had a particularly strong estimated impact, with Republican party identification less important (see the second column of table 4.6). When more specific attitudinal elements were added—see the third column—the proportion of variance accounted for rose once again, to nearly 18 percent, and the coefficients for demographic factors other than gender no longer had anything but marginal statistical significance. Internationalism and the goals of protecting weaker nations and defending our allies were estimated to have particularly strong independent effects on favoring troop use. As usually turns out to be true, when specific goals were

Table 4.6. Sources of support for using U.S. troops if North Korea invaded South Korea

Independent variable	Variables included in regression			
	Demographics only	Demographics + basic attitudes	Demographics + attitudes + goals	Goals + attitudes only
Male	.22**	.20**	.19**	
Evangelical Protestant	11**	.06+	n.s.	
Catholic	.11**	.11**	.10+	
Asian	.06+	.07*	n.s.	
"Active part" internationalist		.22**	.15**	.17**
Conservative (self-rating)		n.s.	n.s.	n.s.
Republican party identification		.09*	n.s.	.11+
Thermometer rating, North Korea			n.s.	n.s.
Goal: protect weaker nations			.17**	.16**
Goal: defend allies			.18**	.20**
R	.305	.386	.473	.410
Adjusted R-squared	.079	.132	.175	.153
Degrees of freedom	896	892	340	340

Source: CCFR/GMF 2002 combined in-person and telephone general public data set.
Note: Entries are standardized OLS regression coefficients; logit and probit results were much the same. Demographic regressions included fourteen independent variables; except as noted, those with nonsignificant coefficients are not displayed. All included attitudinal variables are shown.
$+p < .10, *p < .05, **p < .01$

included in regressions the factors of liberal or conservative ideology and party identification had little estimated direct effect on policy preferences; instead they usually work through goals and other specific attitudes. Nor did feelings about the attacker, North Korea, make any significant difference. Presumably the hypothetical fact of an invasion of South Korea told people all that they needed to know about the aggressor. (Feelings about the country that is attacked generally make more difference, but the design of the CCFR survey unfortunately prevented us from including feelings about—or perceptions of vital U.S. interests in—South Korea in these regressions.[66])

The fourth column of table 4.6 presents evidence of a moderately strong purposive belief system shared by many Americans. It indicates that three logically relevant attitudes—"active part" internationalism, and the goals of protecting weaker nations from foreign aggression and defending our allies' security—each independently affected preferences concerning troop use. Together, the six attitudinal factors listed in the fourth column could account for nearly as much of the variance in preferences as could be accounted for when the fourteen demographic factors were also included.

As table 4.7 indicates, similar—indeed, somewhat stronger—patterns held for support for or opposition to using U.S. troops if Saddam Hussein's Iraq invaded Saudi Arabia. Again gender had a significant independent effect (being male led to more support for troop use), but as before other demographic factors faded away when attitudinal variables were included in multivariate analyses, indicating that the demographics mostly worked through the attitudes. Again the belief that the United States should take an "active part" in world affairs was potent, and again the logically relevant goals of defending U.S. allies and protecting weaker nations significantly affected policy preferences, as did the additional goal of "maintaining superior military power worldwide." Interestingly, the goal of "securing adequate supplies of energy" did *not* independently affect opinions about defending oil-rich Saudi Arabia. (The slogan "no blood for oil" may have some resonance among Americans.) But perceptions of U.S. vital interests in Saudi Arabia (not Israel) did matter.[67]

Again, the fourth column of table 4.7 presents substantial evidence of the existence of a purposive belief system. Five distinct attitudes, all logically pertinent, each substantially and independently affected individuals' support for or opposition to using U.S. troops to defend Saudi Arabia. This does not by any means imply that all—or even most—Americans held tightly constrained belief systems of this sort. But the ability of a handful of attitudinal factors by themselves to account for about 18 percent of the variance in dichotomous policy preferences suggests that these factors were related to each other in individuals' minds with sufficient strength to help produce the general coherence and consistency that we have observed in collective public opinion.[68] Coherent patterns in the beliefs and preferences of majorities of the public tend to reflect coherent patterns within the minds of individuals.

Americans' reactions to a hypothetical invasion of Israel by "Arab forces" also followed similar patterns. In multivariate analyses, the tendencies of men, evangelical Protestants, and perhaps Jews to favor using troops to defend Israel (and of African Americans to oppose troop use) disappeared when attitudinal factors were controlled for. "Active part" internationalism and Republican Party identification also ceased to be significantly related when more specific goals and feelings—including thermometer ratings of Israel, perceptions of a vital U.S. interest in Israel, and assessments of threat from military conflict between Israel and Arabs—were included in

Table 4.7. Sources of support for using U.S. troops if Saddam Hussein's Iraq invaded
Saudi Arabia

	Variables included in regression			
Independent variable	Demo-graphics only	Demo-graphics + basic attitudes	Demo-graphics + attitudes + goals	Goals + attitudes only
Male	.15**	.14**	.14**	
Evangelical Protestant	.08*	n.s.	n.s.	
African American	−.07*	n.s.	n.s.	
Muslim	−.06+	n.s.	n.s.	
Employed	.07+	.07+	n.s.	
"Active part" internationalist		.26**	.16**	.18**
Conservative (self-rating)		.08*	n.s.	n.s.
Republican party identification		n.s.	n.s.	n.s.
Goal: protect weaker nations			.11*	.11*
Goal: defend allies			.20**	.20**
Goal: superior military power			.11*	.11*
Goal: secure energy supplies			n.s.	n.s.
See vital interest in Saudi Arabia			.10*	.11*
See vital interest in Israel			n.s.	n.s.
R	.225	.340	.484	.447
Adjusted R-squared	.036	.099	.180	.179
Degrees of freedom	904	904	351	351

Source: CCFR/GMF 2002 combined in-person and telephone general public data set.
Note: Entries are standardized OLS regression coefficients; logit and probit results were very
similar. Demographic regressions included fourteen independent variables; except as noted,
those with nonsignificant coefficients are not displayed. All included attitudinal variables
are shown.
$+p < .10, *p < .05, **p < .01$

regressions. The crucial factors, just as one might expect of rational, instrumental belief systems, were feelings about Israel and the priority accorded
to the goals of defending U.S. allies and defending weaker nations against
foreign aggression.[69]

A hypothetical invasion of Taiwan by China elicited a similar pattern of
reactions. Bivariate evidence suggests that perceptions of a vital U.S. interest
in Taiwan (which could not be included in multivariate analyses) probably
played a substantial part in preferences for using U.S. troops. In multivariate
regressions, "active part" internationalism, conservatism, and the goals
of protecting weaker nations and defending U.S. allies all significantly

contributed to willingness to use troops. So did perceptions that tensions between India and Pakistan constituted a critical threat to the vital interest of the United States—presumably an indicator of general attention to and concern about security issues in Asia. But somewhat less variation in policy preferences could be accounted for than with the other invasion scenarios.[70]

Why people favor or oppose antiterrorist military operations. Similar patterns also appeared in responses to questions about using U.S. air power or troops against terrorist camps, assassinating individual terrorists, and the like, except that terrorism-related foreign policy goals understandably come to the fore. In our multiple regressions for opinions about "attacks by U.S. ground troops against terrorist training camps and other facilities" as a means of combating terrorism (reported in table 4.8), no demographic factor showed a clearly significant independent impact on preferences. (There were hints, though, that evangelicals tended to favor, and Jews to oppose, troop use.) The most important influences on opinions were logically relevant attitudes: the goals of maintaining superior military power worldwide, defending allies' security, and combating terrorism, together with the perceived threat of chemical and biological weapons and negative feelings about North Korea, which the Bush administration had declared capable of arming terrorist groups.[71]

Similarly, turning to a slightly different survey question, preferences for using U.S. troops "to destroy a terrorist camp" were strongly related to the goal of combating terrorism. The idea of combating terrorism by "toppling unfriendly regimes that support terrorist groups threatening the U.S." was most attractive (in bivariate terms) to whites, high-income people, men, conservatives, those who felt cold toward Iraq, and especially to those who saw "Iraq developing weapons of mass destruction" as a critical threat to the United States.[72]

Again, multivariate regressions on support for "U.S. air strikes against terrorist camps and other facilities" showed no clearly significant coefficient for any demographic characteristic except evangelical Protestantism, and that disappeared when attitudinal factors were controlled. The attitudes most closely and independently linked to preferences for air strikes were the goals of superior military power, preventing the spread of nuclear weapons, and defending allies, together with conservatism and the perceived threat of nuclear weapons falling into the hands of unfriendly countries.[73] Much the same was true of other kinds of antiterrorist actions, such as using U.S. troops to help Pakistan resist an Islamic revolution or to assist the Philippine government in fighting terrorism. Policy preferences in the Philippine case were particularly closely related to the importance attributed to the goal of combating international terrorism.

Table 4.8. Sources of support for attacks by U.S. ground troops against terrorist training camps

	Variables included in regression			
Independent variable	Demo-graphics only	Demo-graphics + basic attitudes	Demo-graphics + attitudes + goals	Goals + attitudes only
Evangelical	.06+	n.s.	n.s.	
Jewish	n.s.	n.s.	−.08+	
"Active part" internationalist		n.s.	n.s.	n.s.
Conservative (self-rating)		.11**	n.s.	n.s.
Republican party identification		n.s.	n.s.	n.s.
Goal: superior military power			.17**	.15**
Goal: defend allies			.16**	.16**
Goal: combat terrorism			.12*	.12*
Threat: chemical and biological weapons			.13*	.13**
Feelings toward North Korea			−.18**	−.17**
R	.124	.160	.432	.409
Adjusted R-squared	.000	.007	.133	.148
Degrees of freedom	936	936	356	356

Source: CCFR/GMF 2002 general public survey, combined in-person and telephone data set.

Note: Entries are standardized OLS regression coefficients. Logit and probit results were quite similar. Demographic regressions included fourteen independent variables; except as noted, those with nonsignificant coefficients are not displayed. All attitudinal factors that were included are shown.

$+p < .10, *p < .05, **p < .01$

Using force to stop drugs or ensure the oil supply. The policies of using U.S. military troops "to ensure the supply of oil" or "to fight drug lords in Colombia," which evoke more narrowly self-interested concerns focused on security of domestic well-being, attracted support from a somewhat different set of Americans. Judging by bivariate relationships (multiple regressions were not feasible because of non-overlap of respondents), those most supportive of fighting drug lords were less educated (high school only) and middle-income people, midwesterners (especially in contrast to westerners), people who had not traveled outside the United States, and (most notably) strong Republicans and conservatives. Similarly, the strongest supporters of using troops to ensure oil supplies tended to have less than high school education and to be midwesterners, strong Republicans, conservatives, and especially those who attributed high importance to the foreign policy goals of ensuring adequate supplies of energy, combating terrorism, maintaining superior military power, and defending allies.[74] The domestic, self-interested thrust of these policies is evident in the fact that "active part" internationalists did *not* particularly favor using troops to stop drugs or ensure energy supplies.

Why people favor or oppose peacekeeping and humanitarian uses of force. "Dovish" uses of military force for multilateral peacekeeping and other humanitarian purposes often evoke patterns of demographic support that are muted or reversed compared with those for "hawkish" uses. The most purely humanitarian uses of force, to deal with genocide or civil wars, win the most support from young people, women, and African Americans. As in other cases, demographic differences can mostly be accounted for by differing goals, values, and beliefs. Here the relevant goals and values center on justice-related altruistic or humanitarian concerns: for example, strengthening international law and institutions, strengthening the United Nations, protecting weaker nations against foreign aggression, and promoting human rights. Feelings about particular peoples or countries, such as Afghanistan, Muslims, or the Palestinians, also enter into preferences concerning peacekeeping operations in specific countries.

It is difficult or impossible to perform satisfactory multivariate analyses for some of these survey questions because of non-overlaps of respondents (when, for example, the goals questions were not asked of any respondents to a particular policy preference question). But analyses of responses to the general question of whether or not the United States should "take part" in "a United Nations international peacekeeping force in a troubled part of the world" tell much of the story. As table 4.9 shows, in a regression including fourteen demographic variables only two of them had clearly significant independent effects: having more formal education led people to support taking part in UN peacekeeping, and being evangelical Protestant led people to oppose it. (Muslims, curiously, may also have tended to oppose it.) When goals and other attitudinal factors were added as independent variables, even those demographic factors lost significance, indicating that—as usual—they worked mostly through attitudes, such as the internationalist inclinations of people with more formal education. "Active part" internationalism, which is generally associated with favoring dovish foreign policies, strongly affected support for peacekeeping. Also, controlling other factors, conservatives tended to oppose participation, liberals to favor it. Those who attributed great importance to the goal of protecting weaker nations against aggression (an altruistic as well as security-oriented goal) also tended to support peacekeeping. There were hints that the goal of promoting human

Table 4.9. Sources of support for participating in a UN peacekeeping force

Question: "In general, when the United States is asked to be part of a United Nations international peacekeeping force in a troubled part of the world, do you think we should take part, or should we leave this job to other countries?" Possible responses were "should take part," "should not take part," and (volunteered only) "depends on circumstances."

	Variables included in regression			
Independent variable	Demographics only	Demographics + basic attitudes	Demographics + attitudes + goals	Goals + attitudes only
Education level	.12**	n.s.	n.s.	
Evangelical Protestant	−.09**	−.07*	n.s.	
Muslim	−.06+	−.06+	n.s.	
"Active part" internationalist		.32**	.24**	.25**
Conservative (self-rating)		−.11**	n.s.	−.12**
Republican party identification		n.s.	n.s.	n.s.
Goal: protect weaker nations			.19**	.18**
Goal: promote human rights			.10+	.11+
R	.196	.383	.469	.444
Adjusted R-squared	.024	.131	.172	.181
Degrees of freedom	931	931	361	361

Source: CCFR/GMF 2002 general public survey, combined in-person and telephone data set.
Note: Entries are standardized OLS regression coefficients. Logit and probit results were quite similar. Demographic regressions included fourteen independent variables; except as noted, those with nonsignificant coefficients are not shown. All included attitudinal factors are displayed.
$+p < .10, *p < .05, **p < .01$

rights was relevant as well. Again attitudinal factors by themselves could account for a fairly substantial portion (18 percent) of the variance in policy preferences.

Multivariate analyses of the Afghan peacekeeping question (would you favor or oppose "the use of U.S. troops to be part of an international peacekeeping force in Afghanistan") had to rely on fewer respondents and include fewer independent variables, and they accounted for less variation in policy preferences. But an attitudes-only regression for the Afghan case revealed a pattern similar to that for the general item. "Active part" internationalism led strongly to favoring troop use. There were hints of effects also from favorable thermometer ratings of Afghanistan and embrace of the foreign policy goal of promoting and defending human rights in other countries.[75]

The quite different sources of support for dovish as opposed to hawkish sorts of military action are clearest when it comes to the most explicitly humanitarian occasions for using U.S. troops that the CCFR asked about: "to help bring peace to a region where there is civil war," "to uphold international law," "to assist a population struck by famine," and "to stop a government from committing genocide and killing large numbers of its own people." In each of those cases (focusing, of necessity, on bivariate relationships) women and minorities, the young, and those with less formal education tended to favor U.S. troop use. So did liberals and people who attributed great importance to the foreign policy goals of strengthening the United Nations, strengthening international law and institutions, and promoting human rights.

In the case of response to civil war, for example, troop use was supported by 66 percent of African Americans but only 45 percent of whites; 51 percent of women but 41 percent of men; 53 percent of liberals and moderates but 41 percent of conservatives; and fully 75 percent of those who considered the goal of "strengthening international law and institutions" very important, compared with only 47 percent of those who said it was somewhat important and just 28 percent of those who deemed it not important. In the famine case there were particularly strong relationships with the goals of combating world hunger and promoting human rights.[76]

WHY INDIVIDUALS FAVOR OR OPPOSE
BUILDING UP MILITARY STRENGTH

Since it is necessary for a country to have military capability before it can use military force, it is not surprising that the same sorts of people who tend to favor using force also generally favor building up capability for the same reasons. Once again individuals' personal and social characteristics have their (limited) effects mostly through logically relevant attitudes, including foreign policy goals. But these relationships are not always as strong as for issues of military action, since opinions about capability tend not to be as strongly held.

Most of the patterns are just what one would expect. The social and attitudinal sources of support for building up *multilateral* and UN-based forces for justice-related humanitarian and peacekeeping purposes, for example, tend to be quite different from the sources of support for solely U.S.-centered military capability, with its focus on security from attack and potential for unilateral use. There may be one surprise, however: Americans now appear to view the NATO alliance largely in terms of political rather than military objectives.

Who favors defense and intelligence programs, and why. In terms of simple bivariate relationships, defense spending, intelligence gathering, and homeland security programs—all at the heart of U.S. capability to provide security against attack—generally get the most support from the same sorts of people who tend to favor hawkish uses of force, such as whites and the college-educated. Even more closely related are people's goals, values, ideologies, perceptions of threats, and political orientations. In particular, Republicans, conservatives, and those who worry most about the threats of international terrorism,[77] Islamic fundamentalism, the rise of Chinese military power, or the Arab-Israeli conflict, as well as those who attribute the highest importance to the goals of maintaining superior U.S. military power or defending U.S. allies, are the most eager to expand such programs. (In 2002, 64 percent of strong Republicans but only 39 percent of strong Democrats favored expanding defense spending.) Attitudes toward the United Nations and "the Muslim people" also appear to make a difference.

Multivariate analyses reveal patterns much like those we have seen before. Take opinions about defense spending. As the first column of table 4.10 indicates, when fourteen different demographic factors were included in a regression, the only significant independent tendencies were for evangelicals and Catholics to favor increased defense spending, and for African Americans and perhaps Hispanics to oppose it. But these tendencies weakened or vanished when attitudinal variables were taken into account (the distinctive preferences of evangelicals, for example, partly reflect their tendency to be conservative and Republican). Defense spending was an unusually partisan issue (the Bush administration was pushing for a big buildup): party identification had a robust effect even when controlling for a number of attitudes and perceptions as well as demographic factors. The other important variables were logically relevant threats and goals, particularly the goal of maintaining superior military power, the perceived threats of China becoming a world power and of international terrorism, and the goal of defending allies' security. The marginally significant coefficient for the goal of restricting illegal immigration suggests that some people who focused on issues of domestic well-being tended to oppose increased military spending.[78]

Much the same thing was true of preferences regarding the homeland security program. In bivariate terms, support for expanding homeland security was especially strong among Catholics and people with higher incomes and more formal education. Multivariate analyses showed Catholicism to have an even bigger effect on favoring expansion than being evangelical. There were weaker tendencies for expansion of homeland security

Table 4.10. Sources of support for expanding defense spending

Independent variable	Demographics only	Demographics + basic attitudes	Demographics + attitudes + goals	Goals + attitudes only
			Variables included in regression	
Evangelical	.16**	.09*	n.s.	
Catholic	.09*	.08*	n.s.	
Hispanic	−.06+	n.s.	n.s.	
African American	−.12**	−.07*	n.s.	
"Active part" internationalist		.08*	n.s.	n.s.
Conservative (self-rating)		.10**	n.s.	n.s.
Republican party identification		.17**	.17**	.19**
Threat: China as a world power			.12*	.13**
Threat: international terrorism			.10*	.11*
Goal: superior military power			.15**	.15**
Goal: defend allies			.10*	.11*
Goal: restrict illegal immigration			−.10+	−.10+
R	.231	.324	.413	.393
Adjusted R-squared	.039	.088	.118	.135
Degrees of freedom	914	914	371	371

Source: CCFR/GMF 2002 general public survey, combined in-person and telephone data set.
Note: Entries are standardized OLS regression coefficients. Demographic regressions included fourteen independent variables; variables with nonsignificant coefficients are not displayed except as noted. All attitudinal variables included in regressions are displayed.
$+p < .10$, $*p < .05$, $**p < .01$

programs to be favored by women and Asians but to be *opposed* by the highly educated (controlling for other factors) and perhaps the unemployed. Party identification was irrelevant here, and the tendency of conservatives to favor expansion disappeared when specific threats and goals were accounted for. Ultimately, the crucial factors were quite pertinent ones: perceptions of the threat of international terrorism as "critical," and judgments that combating terrorism should be a very important goal of U.S. foreign policy.[79]

Multivariate analyses indicate that expansion of programs for "gathering intelligence information about other countries" also tended to be favored by evangelicals and perhaps Catholics (controlling for other factors), but these estimated effects, along with those of all three basic attitudes except conservatism, disappeared when threats and goals were taken into account.

Specific threats and goals, however, such as the threat of terrorism or of China as a world power, did not themselves have clear impacts.[80] The drops in size and significance of coefficients as we moved from defense spending to homeland security to intelligence gathering indicate that preferences concerning the more abstract sorts of capabilities may not be as strongly connected to demographic or attitudinal factors, or as closely embedded in purposive belief systems, as are preferences concerning the use of force.

Interestingly, preferences about *European* defense spending tended to follow bivariate patterns similar to those for U.S. military spending. Americans with higher incomes and more formal education, conservatives, "active part" internationalists, and especially strong Republicans (59 percent of them, compared with just 30 percent of strong Democrats), all tended to say that defense spending by European governments should be expanded. This suggests that many Americans may view European defense spending from a "burden-sharing" perspective, as complementary to American spending and likely to achieve the same goals, such as antiterrorism.[81]

Missile defense. In 2001 and 2002, missile defense was a particularly partisan issue. President Bush pushed hard for quick deployment of an antiballistic missile system and—against opposition from many Democrats—declared that the United States was no longer bound by the ABM treaty with Russia. In the summer 2002 CCFR survey, many more strong Republicans than strong Democrats (51 percent, compared to 20 percent), and somewhat more conservatives than liberals (38 percent versus 22 percent) thought a missile defense system should be built "right away," whereas more liberals, younger people, and higher-income people (as well as isolationists) thought that such a system should not be built at all.

Who wants military bases and troops abroad, and why. Support for having long-term military bases abroad and for basing substantial numbers of U.S. troops in western Europe and Japan tends to come (in bivariate terms) from the expected demographic groups (whites, men, people with higher incomes and more formal education), with the unusual wrinkle that young people are often considerably more supportive than older people. Support also tends to be associated with conservatism, identification with the Republican Party, and internationalism, as well as the goals of maintaining superior military power worldwide and (to a lesser extent) defending U.S allies. But all these relationships tend to be weak, suggesting that the issues of bases and troop deployments are not highly salient and not very strongly linked to Americans' main goals and values.

Patterns of support for military bases in 2002 differed somewhat depending on the specific countries where bases were located. The demographic and attitudinal differences tended to be sharpest for the cases of Afghanistan and especially Turkey, both arguably crucial for combating Islamic terrorism.[82] After the U.S. ouster of the Taliban regime in Afghanistan, the issue of U.S. bases there was apparently seen partly as a peacekeeping and humanitarian aid issue, since the priority attributed to goals of combating world hunger and strengthening international law and institutions related positively to support for U.S. bases in Afghanistan. With respect to bases in Uzbekistan, Saudi Arabia, and Pakistan (all countries with human rights problems), on the other hand, Americans' enthusiasm for strengthening international law and for combating hunger tended to be *negatively* related to support for U.S. military bases. In the cases of South Korea and Saudi Arabia, people who felt warm toward the host country tended to favor having U.S. bases there, while those who felt cooler tended to oppose bases—an understandable sentiment, though discordant with the Saudis' own growing opposition to U.S. bases (which were in fact removed shortly after the invasion of Iraq).

Americans apparently do not think of U.S. bases abroad primarily in terms of capacity to defend allies. Those who considered the goal of "defending our allies' security" to be very important were only a little more likely to favor bases than were those who did not. (Strikingly, in the case of South Korea, potentially vulnerable to well-armed North Korea, there was no significant relationship at all.[83]) Nor was the goal of "protecting weaker nations against foreign aggression" much related to attitudes about most bases.

Why individuals favor or oppose NATO. The North Atlantic Treaty Organization (NATO) is apparently no longer seen mainly as a military alliance devoted to collective self defense against potential aggressor states, but more as a multilateral political organization. In bivariate terms, some of the same sorts of people who tended to favor increased defense spending and a strong U.S. military—the college-educated, conservatives—actually tended to want to *decrease* the level of U.S. commitment to NATO. And the goal of maintaining superior U.S. military power worldwide was related to NATO commitment in a slightly *negative* fashion, while the more altruistic and humanitarian, Justice-related goals of strengthening international law and institutions and combating world hunger, were positively related. There was a particularly strong bivariate relationship between wanting to increase the U.S. commitment to NATO and giving warm "feeling thermometer" ratings to the United Nations.

The tendency of Americans to view NATO in political rather than military terms is confirmed by multivariate analyses of the "commitment to NATO" question. "Active part" internationalism and especially the goal of strengthening the United Nations had the strongest coefficients.[84]

By the same token, Americans' support for expanding NATO to include new members from central and eastern Europe seems to have had less to do with supplementing U.S. military strength than with integrating ex-Communist countries into the West politically. True (in bivariate terms), higher-income people, internationalists, and the college-educated tended to favor admitting to NATO most of the six countries or groups of countries they were asked about. But the security from attack goal of maintaining superior U.S. military power worldwide was *negatively* related to support for expanding NATO to include the Baltic countries, Romania, Slovakia, Bulgaria, or Russia. Instead, the justice-related goals of strengthening international law, combating world hunger, and promoting and defending human rights all tended to be positively associated with support for admitting new members to NATO.

Who favors UN military capability. Support for strengthening United Nations military capabilities, too, tends to come from people who generally embrace humanitarian and altruistic goals and multilateral means, rather than from hawkish advocates of unilateral U.S. power. In the 2002 CCFR survey, joint training exercises by UN members won somewhat more backing (in bivariate terms) from "active part" internationalists than from isolationists, and from Democratic leaners as opposed to strong Republicans. (But whites were more supportive than blacks.) The commitment of a thousand U.S. troops to a UN rapid deployment force was favored substantially more by strong Democrats than by strong Republicans (by 86 percent, compared with 66 percent) and somewhat more by liberals than by conservatives and by women than by men.[85]

CONCLUSION

We have seen some significant differences among demographic groups in favoring or opposing the use of military force. And controlling for many personal and social characteristics at once, certain demographic characteristics have had significant independent *effects* on policy preferences. In particular, being male or an evangelical Protestant (and in some cases being a Catholic) tends to lead one to favor "hawkish," unilateral uses of force, while being female, a "liberal to moderate" Protestant, or (in some cases) a member of a minority group inclines one toward certain "dovish" uses of force like participation in UN peacekeeping.

But the estimated effects of personal and social characteristics are mostly small. They generally decrease or disappear altogether when attitudinal factors are taken into account. This indicates that demographic factors generally exert their influence on policy preferences *indirectly*, working through basic attitudes such as "active part" internationalism, party loyalties, or liberal or conservative ideology (for example, evangelicals' conservatism and Republicanism), and especially through specific perceived threats and foreign policy goals. Moreover, it is the attitudinal factors—connected with each other in purposive belief systems—that most strongly and directly affect individuals' policy preferences.

Individuals' preferences concerning military policies generally flow from logically relevant perceptions of threats, espousal of foreign policy goals, and feelings about specific countries. Preferences for hawkish security-related policies (attacking terrorists, resisting invasions of foreign countries, and the like), for example, have resulted from perceptions of terrorist threats as critical and from the goals of combating terrorism, maintaining superior military power, and defending allies. Preferences concerning dovish, justice-related policies, on the other hand (such as UN peacekeeping operations and humanitarian intervention to prevent civil war, famine, or genocide), have followed from the goals of protecting weaker nations, protecting human rights, and strengthening international law. One striking finding is that commitments to NATO and even to maintaining certain U.S. military bases abroad tend to be based more on political than on military considerations, and to garner more support from doves than from hawks.

Similar patterns generally apply to preferences about military *capabilities*. The same sorts of people who favor military actions tend also to favor increased defense spending and other policies that can make such actions possible, and for the same reasons. The relative weakness of these statistical relationships suggest that preferences concerning capability policies may tend to be less strongly held and less closely linked in purposive belief systems than are preferences concerning the use of force. But even here, purposive belief systems shared by many individuals appear to be strong enough to account for logical coherence in collective public opinion. The American public as a whole generally favors having the capabilities needed to pursue the military actions it wants.

Our discussion of what sorts of individuals tend to support or oppose various military policies, and why, has naturally highlighted the sharpest instances of disagreement, the biggest differences between social or ideological groups. But what should not be lost in this discussion is the high degree of public *consensus* about most of these matters. With some exceptions we have noted—such as the unusually big disagreement between Republicans and Democrats over defense spending—there has actually been agreement among majorities of Americans from virtually all social or ideological groupings (Republicans as well as Democrats, liberals as well as conservatives) on most essential matters of military policy. Large majorities of Americans agree that the use of force is appropriate under a number of circumstances, especially to combat terrorism, and that substantial military capabilities are called for. Large majorities also agree that multilateral and UN-authorized action is preferable to the unilateral use of force, and that the U.S. military should be used for humanitarian, or justice-related, purposes, as well as to ensure security from attack. Again, we believe that policy makers would do well to pay attention to these views.

The multilateralism that pervades Americans' attitudes about military matters—evident in the reluctance to use U.S. forces unilaterally and in the strong support for UN peacekeeping and an expanded NATO—emerges just as clearly when it comes to international political relationships, the subject of the next chapter. Most Americans want the chief ends of U.S. foreign policy to be the pursuit of security and justice. Most want the primary means to be diplomatic, cooperative, and multilateral.

CHAPTER FIVE

Political Cooperation

In recent years the United States has been widely accused of pursuing a unilateral, "go it alone" foreign policy. The two administrations of President George W. Bush, in particular, sometimes seemed to spurn and deride international institutions, to reject diplomacy in favor of military force, and to oppose international treaties and agreements concerning arms control, the environment, and human rights.[1]

Most Americans, however, reject unilateralism in favor of international cooperation and multilateralism. In effect (though not in self-description) most are neoliberal institutionalists. Indeed, most Americans appear to believe in elements of what can be called "global governance": webs of international laws and institutions that serve broad U.S. interests while also furthering the interests of people worldwide and sometimes constraining the United States. Most Americans prefer cooperative, multilateral, and diplomatic methods as the chief means to pursue their foreign policy goals.[2]

In the last chapter we saw that the U.S. public puts a high value on multilateralism in cases of military action and the use of force. Support from allies and the United Nations is considered very important before entering into major military engagements. In this chapter we will see that the public also seeks international cooperation when it comes to *political* relationships. Large majorities of Americans favor having diplomatic relations with countries that are potential foes. They favor a variety of diplomatic and multilateral measures to combat terrorism; express a high level of support for the United Nations; favor various concrete measures to increase the UN's capability and effectiveness; and back international treaties—several of which have been rejected by U.S. government officials—concerning the control of nuclear weapons, the prohibition of land mines, measures against global warming, and the International Criminal Court. Most Americans also favor using diplomatic means to promote human rights and democracy abroad.

The evidence from three decades of Chicago Council on Foreign Relations surveys indicates that such strong support for international cooperation has been an enduring feature of U.S. public opinion. Even during tense periods of the Cold War, most Americans wanted to negotiate with and reach agreements with the Soviet Union and other potential adversaries, to work closely with allies, and to pursue diplomatic solutions to foreign policy problems. The terrorist attacks of September 11, 2001, changed Americans' views of the world in certain respects, but for the most part their cooperative inclinations have held steady.

Individuals' policy preferences concerning international cooperation—like other aspects of foreign policy—tend to fit into coherent, "purposive belief systems" of the sort we discussed in chapter 1. Policy preferences generally reflect the goals that people want U.S. foreign policy to pursue, the threats and problems they perceive around the world, their feelings about particular countries, their inclinations toward international activism or isolationism, and—in some cases—their party loyalties and liberal or conservative ideologies. For example, those who attach particular importance to justice- and cooperation-related goals, such as strengthening the United Nations, strengthening international law and institutions, improving the global environment, promoting and defending human rights abroad, and combating world hunger, tend also to favor a variety of specific cooperative policies. The same is true of people with warm feelings toward the United Nations, the European Union, and various foreign countries; those who favor the United States' taking an active part in world affairs; and liberals and Democrats.

On most of these issues, however, the similarities among Americans are more important than the differences. Majorities even of conservatives and Republicans favor a wide range of cooperative international policies. Such cooperative and multilateral policies have, of course, been pursued by a number of Republican as well as Democratic administrations, including those of Dwight D. Eisenhower, Richard M. Nixon, and George H. W. Bush ("Bush I"). We believe that current policy makers would do well to heed the public's voice.

DIPLOMACY AND MULTILATERAL DECISION MAKING

As we noted earlier, most Americans in 2002—by a 71 percent to 17 percent margin—rejected the idea that, as the sole remaining superpower, the United States should "continue to be the preeminent world leader in solving international problems," saying instead that it should "do its share in efforts to solve international problems together with other countries." Similarly, most Americans, by a 61 percent to 31 percent margin, rejected the proposition that in responding to international crises the United States should "take action alone, if it does not have the support of its allies"; most said that it should not act alone. In 2004 the "do its share" response remained predominant.[3]

Support for cooperation with European and other allies. In 2001 and 2002, well before disagreements surfaced over the Iraq war, a number of tensions built up between the Bush administration and European governments, over such matters as U.S. rejection of treaties on global warming, antiballistic missiles, and the International Criminal Court; European agricultural protectionism and restrictions on genetically modified organisms; and U.S. barriers to trade in steel and agricultural products. Despite these government-level disagreements, however, the American public's inclination to cooperate internationally applies particularly strongly to the countries of the European Union, which enjoy warm feeling thermometer ratings and are seen as the most reliable partners against terrorism. A large majority in the summer of 2002, for example, considered it "very desirable" (31 percent) or at least "somewhat desirable" (48 percent) that the European Union "exert strong leadership in world affairs"; only 17 percent considered this undesirable.

After the 2002–2003 disputes in the UN Security Council over policies toward Iraq (continued UN weapons inspections versus war), Americans' feelings about certain European countries—especially France, which led the opposition to war—cooled somewhat, at least temporarily. A post-invasion Pew survey found more negative than positive feelings about France. But by 2004 Americans' feelings about Germany, another strong opponent of the Iraq war, were as warm or warmer than they had been in the summer of 2002.[4] In any case, there are no indications of a decline in Americans' general desire to cooperate with Europe.

To most Americans, cooperation with Europe apparently means not just perfunctory consultation but genuinely joint decision making, including willingness to compromise. In 2002, a solid majority of the public (70 percent) agreed with the statement that "when dealing with common problems, the U.S. and the European Union should be more willing to make decisions jointly, even if this means that the U.S., as well as Europe, will sometimes have to go along with a policy that is not its first choice." Only 27 percent disagreed.

At the same time, there are limits. Rather few Americans (just 33 percent) in 2002 said the European Union should "become a superpower, like the United States," while 52 percent said the United States should remain the only superpower. (Of course the fact that only a bare majority of Americans favored the U.S. remaining the sole superpower may signal greater openness to power sharing than some enthusiasts of U.S. supremacy might expect.) As we will see in table 5.4, the European Union itself received only a slightly warm average thermometer rating of 53 degrees, substantially cooler than the separate ratings of Britain, Italy, and Germany. And only a modest plurality of 45 percent said the European Union "needs to be strengthened," which put it next to the bottom of the eight international institutions asked about, above only the International Monetary Fund. The 2004 CCFR survey produced similar results.[5] These mixed findings suggest that most Americans may want to work with Europe on the basis of something close to the current balance of power, with more extensive consultations and joint decision making but not a major upsurge in European influence.

Desires for cooperation with allies extend well beyond Europe. Japan, for example, has long been seen as a key friend of the United States. In 2002 Japan enjoyed a very warm, 60-degree average thermometer rating, and 62 percent of the public called relations between the United States and Japan "friendly" while only 7 percent said "unfriendly." As we saw in chapter 3, after the end of the Cold War Russia also emerged in the public mind as a friend, an economic partner, and a reliable ally against terrorism. Closer to home, Mexico and especially Canada enjoy high regard from the U.S. public.

Within the U.S. public, support for joint decision making and a strong role for Europe is significantly stronger among liberals, and especially Democrats, than among conservatives and Republicans. For example, in 2002 about 80 percent of Democrats, compared with only a little over 60 percent of Republicans, favored making joint decisions with the European Union. But even among those who called themselves "strong" Republicans, a majority (53 percent) favored joint decision making. When we performed our usual set of four multiple regression analyses, the initial results confirmed the impact of party affiliation. Controlling for fourteen demographic factors and two other basic attitudes, being a Democrat led to more support for joint decision making with Europe (see the second column of table 5.1). The results suggest that being an "active part" internationalist or a Catholic may also have contributed to support for joint decision making, while being an evangelical Protestant or an African American may have contributed to opposition. But the chief message of table 5.1 is a familiar one: that demographic characteristics and basic political orientations like party identification seldom have much independent effect on policy preferences, and when they do they mostly work through specific foreign policy goals. For example, Democrats apparently favored joint decision making with Europe somewhat more than Republicans did because they tended more often to embrace cooperative foreign policy goals. When individuals' foreign policy goals were included in regressions, much more of the variation in policy preferences

Table 5.1. Sources of support for joint decision making with the European Union

dependent variable	Variables included in regression			
	Demographics only	Demographics + basic attitudes	Demographics + attitudes + goals	Goals + attitudes only
Evangelical Protestant	−.08+	n.s.	n.s.	
African American	n.s.	−.09+	n.s.	
Catholic	n.s.	.07+	n.s.	
"Active part"				
internationalist		.09*	n.s.	n.s.
Liberal self-rating		n.s.	n.s.	n.s.
Democratic party identification		.13**	n.s.	n.s.
Goal: protect weaker nations			.16+	.18*
Goal: strengthen the UN			.17*	.15*
Goal: superior military power			−.18*	−.17*
Goal: control illegal immigration			−.17*	−.17*
Goal: improve standard of living of less developed nations			n.s.	.13 ($p = .107$)
Goal: promote human rights			n.s.	n.s.
Goal: combat terrorism			n.s.	n.s.
	.157	.243	.464	.432
Adjusted R-squared	.003	.033	.096	.139
degrees of freedom	639	639	181	181

Source: CCFR/GMF 2002 general public survey, combined in-person and telephone data set.

Note: Entries are standardized OLS regression coefficients. Controls as indicated. Demographic regressions included fourteen independent variables, but only those with significant coefficients are displayed. All attitudinal variables included are shown.

$p < .10$, *$p < .05$, **$p < .01$

was accounted for, and the coefficients for demographic and basic attitudinal factors lost their statistical significance (contrast the third and fourth columns of table 5.1 with the first and second columns, noting the changes in coefficients and in adjusted R-squared values).[6] This is consistent with our argument about purposive belief systems.

Regression analyses that include foreign policy goals also help illuminate just what people expect to gain or lose from joint decision making with Europe. Controlling for other factors, respondents who rated the goal of protecting weaker nations from foreign aggression or the goal of strengthening the United Nations as very important tended to support making joint decisions with the EU, whereas those who emphasized the goals of maintaining superior U.S. military power worldwide or restricting illegal immigration (the latter signaling a focus on domestic interests or suspicion of foreigners) were more likely to oppose joint decision making. Taking these factors into account, there was only the barest hint that the desire for joint decision making was linked to an interest in improving standards of living in less developed nations, and the goals of combating terrorism or promoting human rights had no appreciable effects at all (see the third and fourth columns of table 5.1). The key factors seem to be general support for international organizations and a preference for multilateral rather than unilateral approaches to conventional security issues.

Analyses of support for the related idea that the EU should be "strengthened" produced results that again fit with our notion of purposive belief systems but suggest slightly different motivations, mainly involving economics rather than security. Support resulted from favoring the goals of strengthening the United Nations (that is, general international cooperation), safeguarding against global financial instability, or combating world hunger.[7]

As we noted in the previous chapter, the North Atlantic Treaty Organization (NATO) is now apparently seen not only as a military alliance but also as an arena for collaborative political decision making about such matters as democratization abroad, economic relations, world health, and the environment. The strongest motivations for wanting NATO to be "strengthened" came from attributing high importance to the foreign policy goals of strengthening the UN, safeguarding against global financial instability, and possibly bringing democratic government to other nations, as well as that of maintaining superior military power worldwide.[8] Similarly, desires to "increase our commitment" to NATO appear to result from giving high thermometer ratings to the United Nations, embracing the goals of strengthening the UN or bringing democracy to other countries, and worrying about the threats of global warming, AIDS, or civil wars in Africa, as much as or more than worrying about the threat of chemical and biological weapons.[9]

The similar sources of popular support for the United Nations, NATO, and the EU suggest that many Americans see them all in similar ways—perhaps as part of a single, general system of global governance, a system that is beneficial for a variety of U.S. interests and deserves protection against unilateralist impulses.[10]

Diplomatic relations, even with enemies. Even when dealing with nations perceived as enemies, such as the countries that President George W. Bush dubbed the "axis of evil"—Saddam Hussein's Iraq, Iran, and North Korea—most Americans want to maintain diplomatic relations and to hold open the possibility of negotiations rather than conflict. In 2002 substantial majorities favored having diplomatic relations with North Korea (65 percent to 32 percent) and with Iran (58 percent to 38 percent). Even Iraq, which at that time was more feared and despised by Americans than any other country in the world and was subject to escalating threats of U.S. invasion, won a bare plurality (49 percent to 47 percent) of support for having diplomatic relations.[11]

Similarly, a solid majority of Americans (65 percent) favored having diplomatic relations with Cuba, a longtime U.S. nemesis; only 31 percent were opposed, despite most people's negative feelings toward that country and its leader, Fidel Castro. This pro-diplomatic-relations sentiment was in harmony with the long-standing desires of U.S. agribusiness and other firms to trade with Cuba, and with the arguments of human rights activists that engagement rather than isolation of Cuba would be more likely to improve conditions there. But it ran up against opposition from well-organized conservative Cuban exiles and from all recent U.S. administrations, including those of presidents Clinton and Bush.

Public support for diplomatic relations with countries not seen as official enemies runs even higher. Despite concerns about human rights in China and neutral to cool feelings about that country, for example, a very large majority of Americans (80 percent) favored having diplomatic relations with China, while only 18 percent were opposed.

Diplomatic relations with adversary or potentially adversary countries tend to be supported especially strongly by people with high levels of formal education and people with more information about the world, which apparently leads to greater appreciation of the advantages of diplomacy. (This is an unusual case in which information does affect policy preferences.) A particularly extreme example is that in 2002 fully 80 percent of those who had done postgraduate work, but only 46 percent of those with less than a high school education, favored having diplomatic relations with Cuba. There was generally more support for diplomatic relations with adversary countries among individuals who had traveled abroad or who displayed substantial knowledge of foreign affairs. Such ideological predispositions as "active part" internationalism and self-identification as liberal play only a small part in preferences about diplomatic relations. Much more important is cooperative internationalism, as manifested (for example) in warm thermometer ratings of the United Nations and the European Union, as opposed to hawkish reliance upon force. Sometimes people's feelings about the particular regimes and/or countries that are the potential participants in diplomatic relations are also important, as are their feelings about related peoples, leaders, and geographic regions.

In the case of Cuba, for example, multiple regressions that included demographic factors and basic attitudes showed independent positive effects of education level, being male, and "active part" internationalism, with negative effects of being Catholic or evangelical Protestant. In a purely attitudinal regression, thermometer ratings of Castro, perceptions of a vital interest in Brazil (presumably an indicator of perceived importance of Latin America generally), and travel abroad all had significant positive effects on favoring diplomatic relations, while support for assassinating terrorist leaders had a negative estimated effect.[12]

Similarly, support for having diplomatic relations with Iran, according to multiple regressions that included demographics and basic attitudes, was positively affected by being highly educated, male, an "active part" internationalist, and (perhaps) a liberal, while being Catholic, evangelical, or (perhaps) Asian tended to lead to opposition. Only subsets of specific attitudinal variables could be included together in regressions, but even so they accounted for more variation in preferences. Several such variables— especially evaluations of Jiang Zemin (perhaps an indicator of feelings toward important countries with nondemocratic regimes) and Ariel Sharon (who viewed Iran as a key enemy of Israel), as well as advocacy of assassinating terrorist leaders and knowledge of the euro—appeared to have substantial independent effects on preferences about diplomatic relations with Iran.[13] Again the independent role of information, though a bit smaller than in the Cuban case, was unusually substantial.

Diplomatic approaches to terrorism. As we saw in the previous chapter, most Americans favor using military force to destroy terrorist camps, to topple regimes that support terrorists, and the like. But support for diplomatic measures to combat terrorism is equally high or higher. There is reason to believe that most Americans prefer using diplomatic rather than military means whenever possible.[14]

When questioned about measures to combat terrorism in the 2002 survey, for example, fully 89 percent of the public favored "diplomatic efforts to apprehend suspects and dismantle terrorist training camps" (only 9 percent were opposed), compared with the 87 percent who favored U.S. air strikes and the 84 percent who favored attacks by U.S. ground troops against "terrorist training camps and other facilities."[15] A substantial majority of 80 percent favored "diplomatic efforts to improve U.S. relations with potential adversary countries" (15 percent opposed). Apparently believing that world poverty helps provide a breeding ground for terrorism, 78 percent said they favored "helping poor countries develop their economies" in order to combat terrorism (with only 19 percent opposed).[16] Despite widespread negative feelings about Yasir Arafat and the Palestinians, a solid 66 percent of Americans favored "making a major effort to be evenhanded in the Israeli-Palestinian conflict," with 29 percent opposed. Fewer Americans, but still a

Table 5.2. Diplomatic and nonmilitary measures for combating terrorism

Question: "In order to combat international terrorism, please say whether you favor or oppose each of the following measures" (options were split into two distinct batteries).

	Favor (%)	Oppose (%)
Diplomatic efforts to apprehend suspects and dismantle terrorist training camps	89	9
Setting up an international system to cut off funding for terrorism	89	10
Working through the UN to strengthen international laws against terrorism and to make sure UN members enforce them	88	10
Trial of suspected terrorists in an International Criminal Court	83	14
Diplomatic efforts to improve U.S. relations with potential adversary countries	80	15
Helping poor countries develop their economies	78	19
Restricting immigration into the U.S.	77	21
Making a major effort to be evenhanded in the Israeli-Palestinian conflict	66	29
Sharing intelligence information with other countries	58	39
Using racial profiling at airport security checks	54	43

Source: 2002 CCFR survey combined data set.

majority (58 percent, with 39 percent opposed), favored "sharing intelligence information with other countries." (Opponents presumably feared leaks or misuse of U.S. intelligence in others' hands.) See table 5.2.

Large majorities also favored several multilateral, nonmilitary approaches to terrorism: 89 percent favored "setting up an international system to cut off funding for terrorism," and 88 percent favored "working through the UN to strengthen international laws against terrorism and to make sure UN members enforce them," with only 10 percent opposed in each case. In apparent contrast to Bush administration policies (which have involved incommunicado detentions on the Guantanamo naval base and elsewhere, and the use of U.S. military tribunals), 83 percent of the public favored the "trial of suspected terrorists in an International Criminal Court"; just 14 percent opposed that idea. (Major, systematic terrorist acts occurring after July 2002 would presumably fall under the jurisdiction of the newly established ICC, as "crimes against humanity."[17])

There was also majority support for two nonmilitary measures against terrorism that could be undertaken unilaterally at home: 77 percent of

Americans favored "restricting immigration into the U.S." in order to combat terrorism. (We will see in the next chapter that opposition to immigration now springs from fears of admitting potential terrorists, as well as from job concerns and cultural anxieties.) A small majority (54 percent to 43 percent) in 2002 even favored "using racial profiling in airport security checks" as a measure to combat terrorism, though this appears to have reversed by 2004.

The 2004 CCFR survey similarly revealed very high support for diplomatic measures against terrorism: especially for working through the UN to strengthen international laws against terrorism and for trying suspected terrorists in the International Criminal Court. Again support for diplomacy was as high or higher than for military measures. Indeed, the size of majorities favoring several military actions against terrorism dropped significantly—perhaps reflecting growing disillusionment with the Iraq war— while support for most diplomatic measures appears to have held steady. Moreover, there was new evidence that a very large majority of Americans opposes torture of terrorism suspects.[18]

Most Americans apparently do not see diplomatic measures as mutually exclusive with the use of force but rather as supplements or complements to it, or—as we have suggested—as methods of first resort, preferable to force when possible. In 2002 there were few negative relationships between support for forceful approaches and support for diplomatic approaches to terrorism. The individuals most enthusiastic about diplomatic approaches to terrorism tended to be those who most strongly supported diplomatic and cooperative measures in general: those who attributed great importance to the foreign policy goals of strengthening international laws and institutions, strengthening the UN, combating world hunger, improving standards of living, protecting the global environment, promoting markets and democracy abroad, and safeguarding against global financial instability.[19]

"Improv[ing] U.S. relations with adversary countries" as a means of combating terrorism not surprisingly won the most backing (in bivariate terms) from those who favored diplomatic relations with Iran, Iraq, or Cuba, and from those who favored a Palestinian state, participation in the International Criminal Court, or participation in UN peacekeeping, as well as (to a moderate extent) supporters of various altruistic foreign policy goals. Regression analyses confirm the independent impacts of a number of these factors, as well as the goals of promoting markets abroad and especially securing adequate supplies of energy. Though tending to reject "blood for oil" (recall chapter 4), some Americans appear to have made a strategic calculation that improving relations with adversaries in the Middle East could help ensure U.S. access to oil.[20]

Support for trying suspected terrorists in an International Criminal Court and for diplomatic efforts to apprehend terrorists and dismantle training camps were greatest among people who embraced international institutions and the altruistic foreign policy goals listed above. There were high bivariate correlations with the goal of strengthening international law—over 80 percent of respondents who attributed at least some importance to that goal favored trying terrorists in an ICC, while only 55 percent of those who deemed it "not important at all" did so—and with thermometer ratings of Kofi Annan, the goal of improving the environment, and the goal of combating world hunger. Multiple regressions indicate that several of these factors (and, oddly, the goal of protecting jobs of American workers) independently affected attitudes about the ICC.[21]

Specific antiterrorism measures of different types draw support or opposition from different sets of people. Most cooperative measures, including working through the UN to strengthen international laws against terrorism, tend to win the most backing (in the bivariate sense) from "active part" internationalists, people with high levels of formal education, and (less strongly) from liberals to middle-of-the-roaders and from Democrats. But the unilateral and politically controversial measures of racial profiling at airports and restricting immigration were supported most in 2002 by whites (57 percent of whom favored racial profiling, as compared to only 31 percent of African Americans) and by conservatives and Republicans. Sharing intelligence information with other countries, too, won more backing from whites (61 percent) than from African-Americans (39 percent), who may be particularly sensitive to spying because of FBI harassment of Martin Luther King Jr. and others. This issue also provoked unusually sharp differences by education level: 85 percent of those with postgraduate education but only 24 percent of those with less than high school favored intelligence sharing. So did 68 percent of world travelers versus just 35 percent of non-travelers, suggesting that information and sophistication about world affairs may tend to reassure people that shared U.S. secrets will not generally go astray.

Again, however, the main point is that most Americans, from nearly all walks of life and with all sorts of political attitudes, favor a wide range of diplomatic and multilateral approaches to combating terrorism, though they are willing to turn to military force if necessary.

Dealing evenhandedly with Israel and the Palestinians. As we saw in chapter 2, when survey respondents in 2002 were asked to evaluate various potential threats to the vital interest of the United States, "military conflict between Israel and its Arab neighbors" was rated as a "critical" threat by 67 percent, putting it below the threats of international terrorism and weapons of mass destruction but above all other traditional security threats, including the development of China as a world power and tensions between nuclear-armed

India and Pakistan. Many Americans care a great deal about what happens in the Middle East.

As the feeling thermometer ratings discussed in chapter 3 indicate, many more Americans sympathize with the Israelis than with the Palestinians, and Palestinian leader Yasir Arafat was very unpopular. At the same time, however, there is no sign that most Americans favor a military solution to the problem, such as a long-term Israeli military occupation or the expulsion of Palestinians from the West Bank and Gaza. Instead, most favor the United States' taking an evenhanded position, encouraging negotiations and compromise that will lead to a homeland for the Palestinians.

In the 2002 CCFR survey, a plurality of Americans (40 percent to 35 percent) said they favored "the establishment of an independent Palestinian state on the West Bank and the Gaza Strip." The margin of support had dropped a bit between 1998 and 2002, perhaps in response to the second intifada or heightened sensitivity to terrorism after September 11.[22] The public was evenly divided, 46 percent to 45 percent, on whether or not the United States should "actively work to help establish a Palestinian state," but a solid majority (58 percent to 30 percent) said that "President Bush's endorsement of an independent Palestinian state" was "a good idea" rather than "not a good idea."[23] Of course, invoking the name of a popular president as favoring a policy tends to increase the level of expressed support for that policy, especially among his fellow partisans. Moreover, some respondents may have merely approved Bush's *verbal* endorsement of a Palestinian state without actually favoring its realization. Still, these questions taken together indicate that a substantial portion of the U.S. public has supported a Palestinian state since well before the Bush administration's official commitment (in 2003, after the invasion of Iraq) to a two-state solution.

When asked in 2002 whether, in the Middle East conflict, the United States should "take Israel's side, take the Palestinians' side, or not take either side," a solid majority of 71 percent said "not take either side," while only 25 percent favored taking Israel's side and a bare 1 percent the Palestinians' side. Most Americans, however (58 percent), thought that in fact the United States "generally takes Israel's side," while only 4 percent said that it generally sides with the Palestinians and 30 percent said it takes neither side. The implication is that actual U.S. policy at that time was somewhat more pro-Israel than the average American wanted. A slight plurality of Americans even favored what would then have been seen in Washington as a rather drastic step: "When the U.S. disapproves of Israeli military operations against the Palestinians," 46 percent said they favored "telling Israel not to use U.S.-provided battlefield weapons," while 44 percent opposed that policy.

A large majority of Americans (83 percent to 11 percent), said that in the Middle East conflict they would "like to see the European Union be more involved in the negotiations while also bearing more of the political and economic costs." Such involvement had long been opposed by Israel and, for the most part, by the United States. Not long after the 2002 CCFR survey was conducted, however, the United States began to work with the European Union, Russia, and the United Nations on a plan for a peaceful solution of the conflict. After the invasion of Iraq, the "road map" was made public and the Bush administration made some efforts to persuade the new Palestinian prime minister and Ariel Sharon's government in Israel to follow it.

The American public favors certain additional U.S. policies aimed at furthering peace in the Middle East. In 2002, in the context of a series of questions about using U.S. troops under various circumstances, a large majority (65 percent to 30 percent) favored their use as "part of an international peacekeeping force to enforce a peace agreement between Israel and the Palestinians." In harmony with the CCFR question, mentioned above, regarding Israeli use of "U.S.-provided battlefield weapons," a mid-2003 survey by the Program on International Policy Attitudes (PIPA) found that substantial majorities of Americans favored withholding military and economic aid from the Israelis or the Palestinians if either failed to take the steps called for in the road map.[24]

Responses to the much more limited Middle East questions in the 2004 CCFR study were consistent with most of the above-mentioned patterns but also revealed certain changes in opinion after the invasion of Iraq. There was a sharp drop of 24 percentage points—to just 43 percent—in the proportion of Americans calling military conflict between Israel and its Arab neighbors a "critical threat" to the vital interest of the United States, and fewer favored using U.S. troops to enforce a peace agreement between Israel and the Palestinians. Thermometer ratings of Israel rose a bit, but so did the proportion of Americans saying that the United States should "not take either side" in the conflict.[25] Frustrations about Iraq appear to have lowered Americans' enthusiasm for engagement in the region as a whole.

Among Americans, support for Israel is not seen as requiring anti-Palestinian policies. In 2002, seeing a U.S. "vital interest" in Israel or rating Israel warmly on the feeling thermometer was not at all associated with opposing an independent Palestinian state. Indeed, warm ratings of Israel were *positively* associated with favoring the United States' "actively working" for a Palestinian state. And Jewish respondents, though overwhelmingly pro-Israel, rather strongly tended to favor a Palestinian state: 72 percent did so, as contrasted with only 44 percent of Catholics and 38 percent of Protestants. They may have judged that the establishment of a Palestinian state would dampen conflict and enhance Israel's security.[26]

At the same time, Americans' attitudes about these issues were quite strongly affected by their feelings toward the Palestinians and toward "the

Muslim people."[27] Understandably, those who felt warm toward the Palestinians tended to favor creating a state for them, whereas those who felt cold did not. Multiple regressions that included thermometer ratings of the Palestinians indicated that those feelings had much more effect on policy preferences than any other factor, though there were also indications of an independent impact of "active part" internationalism and perhaps Democratic party identification and the goal of securing adequate supplies of energy.[28]

Feelings about the Palestinians probably sum up a variety of perceptions and attitudes relevant to the Middle East. By doing regression analyses that excluded those feelings but included specific goals we were able to get a more clear idea of just what Americans seek to accomplish through U.S. policies toward the Middle East. As table 5.3 indicates, support for actively working for a Palestinian state tended to result from embrace of the humanitarian goals of "promoting and defending human rights in other countries" and "improving the standard of living of less developed nations," goals of clear relevance to Palestinians living in poverty and under military occupation. To an unusual extent, "active part" internationalism—which is associated with support for a variety of cooperative and altruistic foreign policies (especially humanitarian foreign aid)—also independently affected this policy preference, as did Democratic party identification and perhaps (controlling for everything else) *conservative* ideology.

Also striking in the third and fourth columns of table 5.3 are the results concerning two self-interested goals that a strategically calculating American might seek in the Middle East: combating terrorism and securing oil supplies. The terrorism goal was totally *unrelated* to support for or opposition to actively working toward a Palestinian state, indicating no net tendency for Americans to seek such a state in order to defuse Palestinian terrorist attacks or to oppose such a state so as not to "reward" terrorism. On the other hand, embracing the goal of securing adequate energy supplies *did* tend to contribute to favoring active efforts for a Palestinian state. There may well be a real-world connection between the two, given anti-U.S. spillovers of Arab and Muslim resentment at the Israeli occupation of the West Bank and Gaza. Again, in the pursuit of oil, diplomacy seems to be more attractive to Americans than military force.

While table 5.3 clearly indicates that being Jewish has no distinctive independent effect on attitudes about working for Palestinian statehood, it does reveal some unusually strong impacts of other personal and social characteristics. Controlling for all fourteen demographic factors (column 1) and also for basic political attitudes (column 2), being older, having a higher income, being Muslim, and perhaps being male each independently

Table 5.3. Sources of support for U.S. actively working for a Palestinian State

Independent variable	Variables included in regression			
	Demographics only	Demographics + basic attitudes	Demographics + attitudes + goals	Goals + attitudes only
Age	.17**	.13**	.14*	
Income	.13**	.13**	.13+	
Muslim	.09*	.09*	n.s.	
Jewish	n.s.	n.s.	n.s.	
Evangelical	−.09*	−.08+	n.s.	
Asian	−.09*	−.09*	n.s.	
Male	.07+	.08+	n.s.	
"Active part" internationalist		.19**	.13*	.18**
Conservative ideology (self rating)		.09*	.12+	.12+
Democratic Party identification		.21**	.19**	.17*
Goal: secure energy supplies			.12*	.11+
Goal: promote human rights			.16*	.14*
Goal: improve standard of living of less developed nations			.12+	.13*
Goal: combat terrorism			n.s.	n.s.
R	.278	.376	.459	.374
Adjusted R-squared	.055	.115	.144	.117
Degrees of freedom	580	580	272	272

Source: CCFR/GMF 2002 general public survey, combined in-person and telephone data set.
Note: Entries are standardized OLS regression coefficients. Controls as indicated. Demographic regressions included fourteen independent variables; except as indicated, only those with significant coefficients are displayed. All attitudinal variables included are shown.
$+p < .10$, $*p < .05$, $**p < .01$

contributed to favoring Palestinian statehood, while being an evangelical Protestant or an Asian American contributed to opposition. Yet even here, as in so many other cases, the estimated direct impact of demographic factors tended to fade in importance when attitudinal factors were included (column 3). The goals people embraced and (to an unusual extent) their basic political attitudes more closely and directly affected their policy preferences, just as the idea of purposive belief systems suggests they would.

SUPPORT FOR THE UNITED NATIONS
AND INTERNATIONAL INSTITUTIONS

During the 1990s, U.S. relations with the United Nations came under considerable strain when prominent conservative Republicans expressed contempt for that organization. North Carolina's Jesse Helms, chairman of the Senate Foreign Relations Committee, blocked payment of U.S. dues to the UN until various U.S.-imposed "reforms" were enacted. During the George W. Bush administration tensions reemerged, particularly over the refusal of several nations in the UN Security Council (including France, Russia, and China, each of which has veto power) to authorize the U.S./British invasion of Iraq. President Bush declared that the Security Council was in danger of becoming "irrelevant," and administration officials resisted giving the UN a major role in the postwar reconstruction of Iraq or the development of a new Iraqi government.

The U.S. public takes a different view. Ever since the closing years of World War II, when the United States helped create the United Nations, most ordinary Americans have had high hopes and aspirations for the organization. Again and again over the years, large majorities of Americans—often in contrast to their government officials—have expressed a high level of regard for the UN, have supported U.S. membership in and "full cooperation" with it, and have favored various measures to strengthen the organization, including contributing troops to a UN emergency force. Americans' support for the UN dipped somewhat in the mid-1960s and for a decade or so after that, as newly admitted nations in Africa and Asia, formerly Western colonies, declared their "nonalignment" in the Cold War and pushed for resolutions and actions contrary to some official U.S. policies. Even at the low point around 1976, however, Gallup found that a majority of Americans (53 percent) wanted to "cooperate fully" with the UN, and NORC found that 80 percent or more wanted to continue U.S. membership in the organization. The movement to "get the UN out of the U.S. and the U.S. out of the UN" (at one time led by conservative icon Barry Goldwater) never made much headway with the American public. Pro-UN sentiment then increased further as Mikhail Gorbachev's USSR embraced international cooperation and the Cold War wound down.[29]

As we saw in chapter 2, each of the eight CCFR surveys beginning in 1974 found about half of the U.S. public saying that "strengthening the United Nations" should be a "very important" goal of U.S. foreign policy; 57 percent said so in 2002.[30] Only 13 percent said it should not be an important goal at all. In terms of average feeling thermometer scores, the United Nations in 2002 scored a very warm 64 degrees, which put it at the top of twelve organizations, groups, or peoples that were asked about—most of which are

Table 5.4. Feelings toward international organizations and groups

Organization	Mean thermometer rating
United Nations	64
International human rights groups	63
International environmental groups	57
World Trade Organization (WTO)	55
European Union	53
World Bank	51
Multinational corporations	49
World Court	49
International Monetary Fund (IMF)	48
Protestors against globalization	45

Source: 2002 CCFR/GMF public survey, combined data set; telephone-only subsample ($N = 703$).
Note: Entries are mean ratings on a 100-point "feeling thermometer," where 0 is very cold, 100 very warm, and 50 neutral.

shown in table 5.4.[31] In fact the average thermometer rating of the UN was also higher than those of every one of the twenty-eight countries discussed in chapter 3, except for top-ranked Canada, Great Britain, and Italy. This is a remarkable manifestation of the high regard in which most Americans hold the United Nations.

A large majority of Americans (77 percent) also said they favored strengthening the United Nations, even in the context of a question that cast some doubt upon the proposition: "Some say that because of the increasing interaction between countries, we need to strengthen international institutions to deal with shared problems. Others say that this would only create bigger, unwieldy bureaucracies. Here are some international institutions. For each one, please tell me if it needs to be strengthened or not."[32] The United Nations—along with one of its specialized agencies, the World Health Organization—came out at the top of the list of eight organizations, well ahead, for example, of the WTO, the World Bank, and the IMF (see table 5.5). These economics-oriented organizations will be discussed in the following chapter, but it is notable that pluralities of Americans favored strengthening every one of the eight international organizations they were asked about, including NATO, the World Court, and the European Union. Thermometer scores and other evidence indicate that such sentiments signal basic support for the organizations and their missions, along with a desire for them to have increased capabilities.

Most Americans are willing to put U.S. tax dollars into the UN. In the 2002 survey a solid majority (58 percent to 32 percent) said it favored the

Table 5.5. Strengthening international institutions

	"Needs to be strengthened" (%)	"Does not need to be strengthened" (%)
World Health Organization (WHO)	80	15
United Nations	77	21
World Trade Organization (WTO)	63	30
NATO	61	29
World Court	56	29
World Bank	49	39
European Union	45	40
International Monetary Fund (IMF)	42	38

Source: 2002 CCFR/GMF general public survey combined data set; telephone-only subsample (*N* = 752).

United States' "paying its UN (United Nations) dues in full," a matter that had become highly contentious in the 1990s when Helms and others resisted paying accumulated unpaid dues until various UN policies and organizational arrangements were changed, including a reduction in continuing U.S. financial obligations. At the very end of that decade, under the threat of losing its UN voting rights, the United States finally agreed to pay some (though far from all) of the $1.7 billion the UN said it owed.[33] But the controversy has continued ever since.

Large majorities of Americans have also favored concrete measures to strengthen the United Nations militarily (as we saw in chapter 4), through joint training exercises by members and through member contributions of a thousand troops each to a rapid deployment force. Remarkably, in the allegedly tax-averse United States, in 2002 a small majority of Americans (51 percent to 42 percent) even supported "giving the UN the power to fund its activities by imposing a small tax on such things as the international sale of arms or oil." Popular support for the idea of providing the UN with a direct power to tax, reminiscent of a key feature of the U.S. Constitution that distinguished it from the ineffectual Articles of Confederation, should hearten struggling World Federalists.[34] This idea does not appear to have been seriously considered among decision makers in Washington. It represents one of many apparent divergences concerning the United Nations between the American public and the makers of U.S. foreign policy.

Acrimony over Iraq in the UN Security Council before the winter 2003 invasion, and President Bush's charge that the Security Council was becoming "irrelevant" because it was not enforcing its own resolutions concerning Iraqi disarmament (while many other nations argued that UN weapons inspections were working well and that there was no hurry to go to war), undoubtedly diminished some Americans' regard for the UN, at least temporarily. A twenty-nation survey conducted for Pew shortly after the invasion, for example, found that Americans' positive ratings of the UN had dropped and that fewer people saw it as a positive influence in the world. (A similar decline in regard for the UN occurred in other countries as well, presumably not because of efforts in the Security Council to avoid war but because those efforts failed. Negative opinions of the Bush administration, U.S. unilateralism, and the United States itself rose sharply between summer 2002 and spring 2003 in nearly all the countries surveyed.)[35]

Indications are, however, that any anti-UN backlash among Americans was quite limited. A PIPA/KN poll in late April 2003 found that 88 percent of Americans still thought that seeking UN authorization for military action against Iraq had been "the right thing to do," rather than a mistake. Substantial majorities said that the United States should *not* feel more free in the future to use force without UN authorization (61 percent) and favored the UN rather than the U.S. taking the lead in dealing with Syria (61 percent), Iran (57 percent), and North Korea (67 percent). Regarding Iraq itself, clear majorities of Americans—contrary to U.S. official policy—favored the United Nations' directing humanitarian relief and economic reconstruction (57 percent) and continuing the oil-for-food program (70 percent). Only 29 percent said the U.S. military should be responsible for relief and reconstruction efforts. Even for maintaining civil order in Iraq, 54 percent preferred "a UN police force of police officers from various countries" rather than the U.S. military. In a separate PIPA/KN poll two months later, the proportions of Americans wanting the UN to take the lead on building a new government in Iraq and on economic reconstruction had risen to 64 percent and 69 percent, respectively.[36] Thus various post–Iraq war proclamations that the "grand experiment" of the UN Security Council had "failed" appear rather distant from the views of the American public.[37]

By the time of the 2004 CCFR Web-based survey, judgments that strengthening the UN should be a very important goal of U.S. foreign policy had dropped markedly—by 17 percentage points—since 2002, but similar drops were characteristic of nearly all foreign policy goals except those most narrowly focused on domestic well-being. Disenchantment with the Iraq war appears to have led to a rather general pullback from foreign policy activism. An apparent drop in UN thermometer scores, though, was probably an artifact of the change to the Web-based survey mode. Public support for concrete policy measures to strengthen the UN remained high: a large majority favored having "a standing UN peacekeeping force selected, trained and commanded by the United Nations"; a solid majority favored giving the UN "the power to regulate the international arms trade"; and a plurality continued to favor giving the UN the power to fund its activities by imposing a small tax.

A large majority of Americans in 2004 said the United Nations, rather than the U.S., should have the "stronger role" in helping Iraqis to write a new constitution and build a democratic government. An even larger majority favored giving the World Health Organization "the authority to intervene in a country to respond to a crisis that threatens world health, even if that country disagrees." A solid majority agreed that, when dealing with international problems, "the U.S. should be more willing to make decisions within the United Nations even if this means that the United States will sometimes have to go along with a policy that is not its first choice." A majority of the American public favored making a "general commitment to accept the decisions of the World Court" rather than deciding whether or not to accept jurisdiction on a case-by-case basis. And a majority favored the strong step of abolishing the absolute veto power of the United States and other permanent members of the UN Security Council.[38] Without question, then, most Americans continue to give strong support to the United Nations and its agencies. Most are willing to accept constraints on U.S. power in the context of collective international decision making.

Turning to the question of *why* individual Americans tend to favor or oppose the United Nations, the answers are familiar. The warmest thermometer ratings for the UN, and the highest proportions of people wanting to strengthen that organization and to pay UN dues in full, are found (in the bivariate sense) among the same groups that most strongly support other kinds of international cooperation: the highly educated, women, "active part" internationalists, liberals, and Democrats. In 2002, for example, 90 percent of strong Democrats and 89 percent of liberals, but just 54 percent of strong Republicans and 67 percent of self-described conservatives, said the UN should be strengthened. Yet majorities even among conservatives and strong Republicans felt positively about the UN, favored strengthening it, and favored paying UN dues in full. This suggests that the anti-UN policies pursued by some Republican office holders may reflect the views of party activists (who tend to hold extreme opinions) rather than those of rank-and-file party members.

On UN-related issues, as on other aspects of foreign policy, there is strong evidence of coherent, purposive belief systems among members of the public. Pro- or anti-UN attitudes tend to hang together consistently within individuals' minds. For example, UN thermometer ratings in 2002 correlated quite highly and positively with opinions about the importance of the foreign policy goal of strengthening the United Nations, which were even more strongly related to the sentiment that the UN "needs to be strengthened." As obvious as this may seem, it contradicts a great deal of conventional wisdom about "random" foreign policy attitudes.[39] Policy preferences about the UN also tended to reflect various justice-related humanitarian and altruistic foreign policy goals, including the goals of improving the global environment, combating world hunger, and promoting and defending human rights in other countries.

A comprehensive regression analysis of why people thought the UN "needs to be strengthened," for example, indicates that individuals' embrace of the foreign policy goal of strengthening the United Nations had by far the biggest effect (not surprisingly), but the goal of improving the global environment also contributed substantially to support, and the nationalist goal of restricting immigration led to opposition. Even controlling for many attitudinal and demographic factors, being female led to support for strengthening the UN, and Democratic party affiliation also had a small direct effect. Other regressions suggest that information levels may have had an impact as well.[40]

For the more concrete issue of paying UN dues in full, table 5.6 indicates that Americans want several different things from the UN and are willing

Table 5.6. Sources of support for paying UN dues in full

dependent variable	Demographics only	Demographics + basic attitudes	Demographics + attitudes + goals	Goals + attitudes only
female	.12**	.11**	n.s.	
Education level	.16**	.13**	.11*	
"Active part" internationalist		.16**	.10*	.12**
Liberal ideology (self-rating)		.14**	n.s.	n.s.
Democratic party identification		.10*	n.s.	n.s.
Goal: strengthen the UN			.23**	.23**
Goal: improve global environment			.11*	.11*
Goal: superior military power			−.11*	−.11*
Goal: combat world hunger			n.s.	n.s.
Favor U.S. peacekeeping in Bosnia			.12*	.13**
Oppose tightening Muslim immigration			.09+	.12*
	.242	.346	.478	.454
Adjusted R-squared	.035	.093	.185	.190
Degrees of freedom	579	579	419	419

Source: CCFR/GMF 2002 general public survey, combined in-person and telephone data set.
Note: Entries are standardized OLS regression coefficients. Controls as indicated. Demographic regressions included fourteen independent variables, but only those with significant coefficients are shown. All included attitudinal variables are displayed.
$^+p < .10$, $^*p < .05$, $^{**}p < .01$

to pay for them. Not only the general goal of "strengthening the United Nations" but also the goal of improving the global environment, support for peacekeeping, and a general predisposition toward "active part" internationalism each independently contributed to support for paying UN dues. So did *opposition* to the nationalistic desire to restrict Muslim immigration in order to combat terrorism and downplaying the unilaterally oriented goal of maintaining superior U.S. military power.[41] Table 5.6 tells our usual story about purposive belief systems: only a couple of personal characteristics (being female or highly educated) had independent effects. Demographic factors and basic political orientations mostly affected policy preferences through their impact on foreign policy goals and specific, logically relevant attitudes. Goals and other attitudes went the furthest toward explaining the variance in preferences, accounting for more than five times as much of it as did demographic characteristics (19 percent versus 3.5 percent).

STRONG BACKING FOR INTERNATIONAL TREATIES AND AGREEMENTS

International treaties are often designed to provide global "public goods": desirable ends for which international cooperation is necessary, like the control of nuclear arms races, reduction of global warming, or nonproliferation of weapons of mass destruction. No single country acting alone can accomplish such goals. Even if most nations would like to pursue them, the actions of just a few noncooperating "free-rider" countries (seeking gains from unilateral military buildups, arms sales, or cheap polluting industries) could undercut collective objectives. Only near-universal adherence to international agreements is sure to produce success.[42] Most Americans appear to accept this logic. For as long as opinion surveys have inquired into the matter, majorities of the American public have favored a wide range of international treaties and agreements.

Arms control treaties during the Cold War and now. Arms control treaties have always won particularly strong popular support and continue to do so. During and shortly after World War II, for example, most Americans favored putting all countries' nuclear weapons under international control, an idea that U.S. officials succeeded in defusing only by means of the Baruch Plan.[43]

During the Cold War, majorities of Americans regularly said they favored various proposed or actual treaties concerning the control of weapons, especially nuclear weapons. In the 1974 CCFR survey, for example, 77 percent favored "substantially limiting the number of nuclear missiles each country [the U.S. and the Soviet Union] has." In 1978, 71 percent favored "signing another arms agreement to limit some nuclear weapons on both sides," and

62 percent even favored "signing an agreement to *ban all* nuclear weapons on both sides" (emphasis in the original). In 1982, when the Reagan administration was pursuing a rapid arms buildup and tensions with the Soviet Union ran high, a large majority (77 percent) favored "negotiating arms agreements between the U.S. and the Soviet Union." (Majorities also favored resuming cultural and educational exchanges, and opposed prohibiting the exchange of scientists or restricting U.S.-Soviet trade.)[44]

In that same year, 1982, the idea of a mutual "nuclear freeze" gained considerable support from the American public. When CCFR respondents were given three options concerning the idea of a "mutual, verifiable freeze on nuclear weapons, that is, a freeze agreed to by both sides, with inspections," only 26 percent of the public said that "the U.S. should continue to build nuclear weapons regardless of what the Soviets do." About half (49 percent) said "the U.S. should stop building nuclear weapons only if the Soviet Union agrees to do so," while an additional 19 percent said "the U.S. should stop building nuclear weapons even if the Soviet Union does not." In response to a different question, a solid majority (58 percent) favored a mutual freeze "right now, if the Soviets would agree," rather than only after the U.S. built up its nuclear weapons more, or not at all. By 1986, support for arms control rose still further, with 80 percent favoring "negotiating arms control agreements" (only 13 percent opposed), and 67 percent favoring a nuclear freeze "right now."[45]

Strong public support for arms control agreements continued after the end of the Cold War right up to the present. Americans have increasingly worried about the possible proliferation of weapons—especially nuclear weapons—into the hands of "rogue" states or terrorists. As we saw in chapter 2, Americans' most urgent foreign policy goals and their strongest perceptions of threats to the United States involve terrorism and weapons of mass destruction. Thus in 2002 a very large majority (81 percent to 14 percent) said that the U.S. should participate in "the treaty that would prohibit nuclear weapon test explosions worldwide," that is, the Comprehensive Nuclear Test Ban Treaty (CNTBT), designed to make it difficult for countries to design or improve nuclear weapons or check their reliability.[46] The CNTBT, accepted by most other countries, had been signed by the United States under President Clinton but not ratified by the U.S. Senate; it was opposed by President George W. Bush and many Republican officials.[47] Table 5.7 summarizes public support in 2002 for that and other treaties.

Similarly, a substantial majority of the public (75 percent to 19 percent) favored U.S. participation in "the treaty that bans the use of all land mines." Millions of cheap land mines planted during conflicts in Cambodia, Angola, Afghanistan, and elsewhere have killed or maimed tens or hundreds of thousands of innocent civilians, sparking an anti–land mine campaign, led

Table 5.7. International treaties and agreements

	U.S. should participate (%)	U.S. should not participate (%)
The treaty that would prohibit nuclear weapon test explosions worldwide	81	14
The treaty that bans all use of land mines	75	19
The agreement to establish an International Criminal Court that would try individuals for war crimes, genocide, or crimes against humanity if their own country won't try them	71	22
[Longer ICC question*]	65	28
The Kyoto agreement to reduce global warming	64	21
[Longer global warming question*]	70	25

Source: 2002 CCFR/GMF general public survey, combined data set.
* The longer questions, which included pro and con arguments, are described in the text.

by the International Campaign to Ban Landmines, Nobel Prize winner Jody Williams, and the Vietnam Veterans of America Foundation, which mobilized government support and prodded many governments (143 of them by mid-2004) to ratify the treaty.[48] This agreement too was signed under President Clinton but rejected by other U.S. policy makers, chiefly because of the Pentagon's desire to keep using land mines on the border between South and North Korea, while arguing that sophisticated U.S. land mines can be deactivated after they are no longer needed.

The U.S. public apparently also approved of the Anti-Ballistic Missile (ABM) Treaty with the Soviet Union; it did not give high marks to President George W. Bush's decision to abrogate the treaty and proceed with a national missile defense. In 2002, only 41 percent said the Bush administration's handling of the ABM treaty was "excellent" or "good," while 43 percent said "fair" or "poor."

In 2004, the strong majority support for both the Comprehensive Nuclear Test Ban Treaty and the land mines treaty held steady or rose a bit.[49]

The reasons for support for or opposition to these treaties generally follow familiar patterns. As the multiple regression results displayed in table 5.8 indicate, for example, individuals' support in 2002 for the Comprehensive Nuclear Test Ban Treaty was independently affected by being

Table 5.8. Sources of support for Comprehensive Nuclear Test Ban Treaty

	Variables included in regression			
Independent variable	Demographics only	Demographics + basic attitudes	Demographics + attitudes + goals	Goals + attitudes only
Catholic	.09*	.10**	.10+	
Education level	.07+	n.s.	n.s.	
"Active part" internationalism		.11**	n.s.	.08+
Liberal ideology (self-rating)		.08*	n.s.	n.s.
Democratic party identification		.07+	n.s.	n.s.
Goal: prevent spread of nuclear weapons			.27**	.26**
Threat: global warming			.16**	.15**
Goal: improve global environment			.10+	.10+
R	.148	.220	.408	.381
Adjusted R-squared	.007	.031	.119	.131
Degrees of freedom	928	928	371	371

Source: CCFR/GMF 2002 general public survey, combined in-person and telephone data set.
Note: Entries are standardized OLS regression coefficients. Controls as indicated. Demographic regressions included fourteen independent variables; only those with significant coefficients are shown. All attitudinal variables included in regressions are displayed.
$+p < .10, *p < .05, **p < .01$

Catholic (the church has consistently favored nuclear arms control). But by far the strongest factor leading to support for the CNTBT was the judgment that preventing the spread of nuclear weapons should be a very important goal of U.S. foreign policy: a clear, if unsurprising, example of how Americans tend to form their policy preferences in a purposive, goal-oriented way. The perceived threat of global warming (a sign of general environmental concerns) and possibly the goal of improving the global environment also had independent effects, indicating that Americans worry about the environmental as well as the security aspects of nuclear testing. Controlling for these goals and threats, "active part" internationalism, liberalism, and Democratic party identification, which initially appeared important, made little or no difference (contrast the second and third columns of table 5.8). Here, as in so many other cases, specific goals more directly affected policy preferences than did general ideological predispositions.

Similarly, the treaty banning land mines won distinctively high support from better-educated people, women, Democrats, and liberals, as well as from older people—who may have remembered gruesome U.S. casualties

from land mines in Korea and Vietnam. Again, however, substantial majorities of all social and political groups favored both the Comprehensive
Nuclear Test Ban Treaty and the land mines treaty. Even among those who
wanted to stay out of world affairs, for example, 74 percent favored the former, as did 75 percent of strong Republicans. Regression analyses indicate
that support for the land mines treaty reflected not only concerns about human death and destruction (as indicated by the goal of preventing the spread
of nuclear weapons and by the threat of unfriendly countries becoming nuclear powers) but also environmental concerns, as expressed in the goal of
improving the global environment. Controlling for those factors, neither
"active part" internationalism nor liberalism nor Democratic affiliation any
longer made a significant difference.[50]

Multilateral approaches to energy and the environment. Issues involving energy
supplies and the world environment are very important to many Americans. At least since the 1970s the public has favored a variety of treaties and
cooperative efforts to deal with them. In 1974, for example, when the OPEC
oil boycott had driven oil prices sharply upward, 83 percent of the U.S. public told CCFR interviewers that they favored "undertaking joint efforts [with
the Soviet Union] to solve the world energy shortage" (with only 10 percent
opposed), and 80 percent said oil-consuming nations should "get together"
to develop strategies that would make us less dependent on the decisions
of foreign oil-producing countries. (An identical 80 percent favored this
course even if it meant cutting back on gasoline consumption by 10 percent,
but support dropped to 54 percent if it meant "spending U.S. tax dollars" to
support it.)[51]

In 2002, 66 percent of Americans said that "improving the global environment" should be a very important goal of U.S. foreign policy, and
79 percent said that global warming was a "critical" or an "important but
not critical" threat to the vital interest of the United States. "International
environmental groups" received a warm average thermometer rating of
57 degrees. In harmony with these feelings, a solid 64 percent said that the
U.S. should participate in "the Kyoto agreement to reduce global warming"
(recall table 5.6).

This is particularly striking because the Kyoto Protocol, though negoti-
ated with extensive U.S. input and ratified or assented to by some ninety-
four countries at the time of the 2002 survey, had been renounced and
strongly criticized by President Bush, who instead encouraged a voluntary
carbon-emissions reduction by U.S. industry, which critics predicted would
have little effect.[52] In the CCFR survey, the Bush administration's handling
of global warming was called "excellent" or "good" by only 25 percent of the
public, with 65 percent saying "fair" or "poor"; this put it at the very bottom

of fourteen areas of administration performance that were asked about.[53] This appears to signal another substantial gap between what American citizens favor and what the U.S. government has been doing.

In order to be certain that respondents knew what the Kyoto agreement entailed and were aware of major arguments for and against it, and to avoid invoking any positive or negative associations of the word "Kyoto" itself by omitting that word, a separate subsample of interviewees in 2002 was asked a longer question:[54]

> An international treaty calls on the U.S. (United States) and other industrialized nations to cut back on their emissions from power plants and cars in order to reduce global warming, also known as the greenhouse effect. Some people say this would hurt the U.S. economy and is based on uncertain science. Others say this is needed to protect the environment and could create new business opportunities. What's your view—do you think the United States should or should not join this treaty requiring less emissions from U.S. power plants and cars?

Despite the inclusion in this question of strong-sounding arguments against the Kyoto Protocol ("hurt the U.S. economy," "uncertain science"), public support was actually somewhat higher: 70 percent said the U.S. should join the treaty, while only 25 percent said it should not join.

When the short Kyoto question was repeated in the 2004 survey, public support for the treaty was steady or up a bit from 2002.[55]

In 2002, the usual groups of international cooperators—with a few variations—were most supportive of the Kyoto agreement. Young Americans are particularly attuned to the environment: in simple bivariate terms, 77 percent of eighteen- to twenty-nine-year-olds, but only 48 percent of those sixty-five or older, said (in response to the long question) that the US should "join this treaty requiring less emissions from U.S. power plants and cars." Women and the highly educated were somewhat more supportive than men or those with less formal education, and evangelical Protestants tended to oppose the Kyoto agreement. Partisan and ideological differences were unusually strong on this issue, presumably because of the highly visible debates in Washington: 84 percent of strong Democrats but only 52 percent of strong Republicans supported the treaty, as did 85 percent of liberals but only 53 percent of conservatives. Still, majorities or pluralities of virtually every social or attitudinal group—including conservatives, strong Republicans, and the elderly—said they favored joining the treaty.

As in most other cases, our regression analyses (using the short Kyoto question so that goals could be included) indicated that only a few of these social characteristics or basic political orientations independently affected policy preferences. The few that did, did so indirectly, working through

Table 5.9. Sources of support for Kyoto agreement on global warming

Independent variable	Demo-graphics only	Demo-graphics + basic attitudes	Demo-graphics + attitudes + goals	Goals + attitudes only
		Variables included in regression		
Female	.06+	n.s.	n.s.	
Evangelical Protestant		−.21**	−.13**	n.s.
Married	−.08*	n.s.	n.s.	
"Active part" internationalist		.06+	n.s.	n.s.
Liberal ideology (self-rating)		.14**	n.s.	.11*
Democratic party identification		.24**	.12+	.11*
Threat: global warming			.44**	.45**
Goal: improve global environment			.14**	.13**
Goal: strengthen international law			.08+	.09+
R	.271	.409	.614	.602
Adjusted R-squared	.057	.150	.331	.349
Degrees of freedom	829	829	291	291

Source: CCFR/GMF 2002 general public survey, combined in-person and telephone data set. Short Kyoto question.

Note: Entries are standardized OLS regression coefficients. Logit estimates were quite similar. Controls as indicated. Demographic regressions included fourteen independent variables, but only those with significant coefficients are shown. All attitudinal variables included in regressions are displayed.

$+p < .10, *p < .05, **p < .01$

more specific attitudes about foreign policy goals, threat perceptions, and the like. Evangelicals' opposition to the treaty, for example, apparently reflected their conservatism and Republicanism, which in turn led to downplaying environmental goals and threats. As the third and fourth columns of table 5.9 indicate, the strongest independent source of support for the Kyoto agreement—quite understandably—was from those who considered global warming to be a "critical threat" to the vital interest of the United States.[56] The foreign policy goal of improving the global environment also mattered, and the goal of strengthening international law and institutions may have added something as well. With these goals and threats taken into account, liberalism and Democratic party identification added only a bit to support. Once again, policy preferences tended to flow in a purposive fashion from goals and other attitudes—which accounted for an unusually high 35 percent of the variance.

Human rights and international criminal justice. Although human rights are not at the top of the American people's agenda (in 2002 only 47 percent said that promoting and defending human rights in other countries should be a "very important" goal of U.S. foreign policy), there is nonetheless substantial support for action that would promote such rights. "International human rights groups" received a quite warm average rating of 63 degrees on the feeling thermometer, one of the highest ratings in the survey, nearly matching that of the United Nations. As we have seen, large majorities of Americans favored various sorts of peacekeeping and humanitarian uses of U.S. armed forces, including the 77 percent who favored their use "to stop a government from committing genocide and killing large numbers of its own people."

There is also a high level of public support for using international legal tribunals to protect human rights and to try accused abusers. As we have seen, in the context of combating terrorism 83 percent of the public in 2002 favored "trial of suspected terrorists in an International Criminal Court." Similarly, in answer to the questions about U.S. participation in four international treaties and agreements, a solid 71 percent (with only 22 percent opposed) said that the U.S. should participate in "the agreement to establish an International Criminal Court that would try individuals for war crimes, genocide, or crimes against humanity if their own country won't try them" (recall table 5.6).

This represents another clear contrast between the views of average Americans and those of the Bush administration. In multiyear negotiations over the ICC treaty the U.S. had won substantial concessions; the treaty made clear that national courts had primary jurisdiction and that only a circumscribed list of extreme violations of human rights (war crimes, genocide, and crimes against humanity) could be prosecuted at the ICC. Near the end of his presidential term President Clinton signed on. But the Bush administration strongly denounced the ICC, "unsigned" the agreement, and urged other countries not to join it. When the agreement nonetheless went into effect in April 2002, with more than sixty nations having ratified it,[57] the United States pushed a temporary exemption for American peacekeepers through the UN Security Council (threatening to scuttle several UN peacekeeping operations otherwise). The saga continued after the summer 2002 CCFR survey, as the U.S. government mounted a high-pressure, worldwide campaign for long-term bilateral agreements not to subject any American nationals located in the countries with which the pacts were made to ICC jurisdiction. Many small countries like Azerbaijan, Bhutan, Gabon, Maldives, and Tuvalu—and, more importantly, Afghanistan and Bosnia, where American troops were actually operating—signed such agreements, often under the threat that otherwise military aid would be cut off under the so-called American Servicemen's Protection Act. (The U.S. ambassador to the Bahamas, for example, warned that Bahamanians could lose U.S. aid earmarked for paving and lighting the airport runway in Inagua if they did not sign.) A total of about eighty countries had signed bilateral U.S.-immunity agreements (some in secret) by mid-2004, even as the total number of countries ratifying the ICC itself continued to grow, reaching ninety-four (plus forty-five signatories that had not yet ratified). In that same year, after prisoner abuse scandals in Iraq and elsewhere had cast a darker shadow on the U.S. administration's motives, the United States failed to win an extension from the Security Council of the U.S.-peacekeeper exemption.[58]

Given the political controversies surrounding the ICC, a separate subsample of CCFR 2002 survey respondents was asked a longer question that explicitly took note of the Bush administration's key argument against the treaty:[59]

> A permanent International Criminal Court has been established by the UN (United Nations) to try individuals suspected of war crimes, genocide, and crimes against humanity. Some say the U.S. (United States) should not support the Court because trumped up charges may be brought against Americans, for example, U.S. soldiers who use force in the course of a peacekeeping operation. Others say that the U.S. should support the court because the world needs a better way to prosecute war criminals, many of whom go unpunished today. Do you think the U.S. should or should not support the permanent international criminal court?

Support for the ICC was a bit lower in response to this question than for the shorter version, presumably because of the strong (some would say misleading) reference to trials of Americans on "trumped up charges" and the omission of any mention of the priority given to home-country courts.[60] Still, even in response to this question, a solid 65 percent of the public said that the United States "should support" the permanent ICC, while only 28 percent said it should not do so.

In 2004, when the short ICC question was repeated, public support for participating in the treaty remained at essentially the same high level.[61]

Many of the political and social groups of Americans that generally favor international cooperation tended to support the ICC in 2002: liberals, Democrats, "active part" internationalists, the highly educated, and Catholics favored it, while evangelicals tended to oppose it. But those tendencies were small and mostly disappeared in multiple regressions. By far the biggest independent contributors to support for the ICC were the foreign policy goals of strengthening international law and institutions and strengthening the United Nations.[62]

PROMOTION OF DEMOCRACY ABROAD

Rather few Americans in 2002—just 34 percent—said that "helping to bring a democratic form of government to other nations" should be a very important goal of U.S. foreign policy. But a large majority said that this should be at least a "somewhat important" goal; only 15 percent said "not an important goal at all." Not many survey questions are available to see whether or how people translated this goal into concrete foreign policies. But when respondents were asked in 2002 about a list of "some types of foreign aid" (most which were related to health, population growth, or economic development), a solid majority of 64 percent favored, while only 27 percent opposed, "assistance to promote democracy abroad."

Not surprisingly—and again in harmony with the idea that Americans tend to hold coherent, purposive belief systems about foreign policies— individuals' support for "assistance to promote democracy abroad" was strongly affected by endorsement of the foreign policy goal of bringing democratic government to other nations. Our analyses also suggest that many Americans may accept the theory of "democratic peace" (namely, that democratic countries do not attack each other militarily), so that the promotion of democracy may help prevent aggression or conflict—between Arabs and Israelis, for example. In comprehensive multiple regressions, both the perceived threat of military conflict between Israel and its Arab neighbors and the goal of protecting weaker nations against foreign aggression, as well as (more strongly) the goal of bringing democratic governments to other nations, led independently to support for aid to promote democracy. No other factors were clearly significant.[63]

One dramatic but controversial way to promote democracy abroad is through "nation building" in the wake of military conquest. But this is not always easy, as became clear in Afghanistan after the autumn 2001 war and in Iraq after the U.S.-British invasion of winter 2003. One study of sixteen past U.S. efforts to build democracy after military interventions refers to the record as "daunting," with only four clear successes: in Japan and German (after total victory in an all-out world war, and with the investment of many billions of dollars and years of effort by many thousands of U.S. occupiers), and in tiny Grenada and Panama. More often, such obstacles as ethnic fragmentation, lack of state capacity, inexperience with constitutionalism, and conflicts of national interests with those of the United States have led within a few years to a breakdown of democracy and frequently to misrule, widespread poverty, and brutal dictatorships.[64]

Greater legitimacy for nation building efforts generally results from multinational involvement, especially through the United Nations. It is presumably for that reason that, even shortly after the victorious U.S. invasion of Iraq, a survey found clear majorities of the American public in favor of having the UN direct humanitarian relief, economic reconstruction, and civil order in Iraq. A large majority (73 percent) said it was necessary to get the participation of a substantial number of other countries in the process of reconstruction, with 66 percent saying it was necessary to get Arab countries involved.[65] U.S. officials, however, insisted upon keeping broad authority over Iraq in their own hands until Iraqis could take over. This arrangement was endorsed—as a fait accompli—by UN Security Council Resolution 1483, passed with near unanimity (with Syria absent) on May 22, 2003, and followed a year later by a partial turnover of sovereignty to Iraqis.[66]

By the time of the summer 2004 CCFR survey—when fighting and disorder continued in Iraq, the road to democracy there looked bumpy indeed, and much of the U.S. public had grown disillusioned—Americans' enthusiasm for the unilateral promotion of democracy abroad had waned markedly. The already small proportion of the public attributing high importance to the foreign policy goal of promoting democracy shrank still further. Support for "assistance to promote democracy abroad" fell by 16 percentage points, much more than for any of the five other types of aid the CCFR asked about. Only a minority of 40 percent said that "a country, without UN approval"—presumably including the United States—should have the right to use military force to "restore" a democratic government that has been overthrown (a purpose for which a solid 60 percent majority said the UN Security Council should have the right to authorize the use of military force). As we have noted, a large majority had long favored the United Nations rather than the United States having the stronger role in democratizing Iraq. Even the rather mild idea that the U.S. should "put greater pressure" on countries in the Middle East like Saudi Arabia and Egypt "to become more democratic" was supported by only about one-third of the public, with a majority opposed.[67]

The U.S. public gives very little support to the neoconservative program of spreading democracy at the point of a gun, or indeed in any other unilateral fashion. In the political realm, as in virtually all other aspects of foreign policy, most Americans prefer multilateralism and international cooperation to unilateral action. This tendency appears to have been accentuated by the Iraq experience.

THE PUZZLE OF DISAGREEMENTS
BETWEEN CITIZENS AND OFFICIALS

In this chapter—even more than in the previous one—we have noted a number of clear contrasts between the foreign policies actually pursued by U.S. officials and the policies favored by most Americans. How is this possible? How, in a democracy like ours, can officials be elected and reelected if their policies defy the wishes of the citizenry? We will address this question more fully in chapter 7, after we present systematic data on just how frequently citizens and officials have disagreed over the years about various foreign policy issues. Here, however, we can briefly mention some reasons why such disagreements occur and persist.

The most fundamental point is that—whatever we may wish—the United States is *not* in fact a majoritarian democracy. There is no guarantee that policies favored by majorities of citizens (even quite large majorities) will be enacted into law or carried out. This is true of domestic as well as foreign policy. The founders of the United States did not intend to establish a majoritarian democracy. They wrote into the Constitution many barriers to majority rule, some of which (e.g., the pro-rural, small-state bias of the Senate that results from giving each state two senators) still persist.[68] Over the last two hundred years voting rights have been extended to most previously disenfranchised groups, and the citizenry has won a more direct role in elections for the presidency and the Senate. But there remains a great deal of political inequality. It is by no means the case that each American citizen has equal influence ("one person, one vote") over the making of public policy.[69] The reasons for this (some of them contested among political scientists) probably include the following:

1. Highly unequal economic and other resources among individuals are translated into unequal political influence, through campaign contributions, lobbying, publicity campaigns, voting turnout, and other means.

2. *The costs of political information* make it hard for citizens to be certain of what effects alternative policies would have, what the government is doing, or what stands politicians take. This opens the way for misleading advertising and public relations campaigns by interest groups, corporate media, parties, and officials, which can manipulate preferences, distort perceptions of what officials and politicians stand for, or divert voters away from public policy onto spurious issues of "character" and the like. It also discourages citizens from participating in politics and permits a surreptitious antipopular influence on policy by interest groups, party activists, and others outside the public's view.[70]

3. *The two-party system,* deeply embedded in constitutional and legal provisions, permits explicit or implicit bipartisan agreements to defy the popular will (e.g., on certain economic issues, discussed in the next chapter). It gives power to party activists and money givers who influence which candidates the voters are allowed to choose between. The two-party system has also contributed to the absence in the United States of a working-people's party that could (as in much of the advanced industrial world) mobilize ordinary citizens.

4. *Noncompetitive elections,* especially for the House of Representatives, blunt the power of citizens. District boundaries are gerrymandered so that each party has many "safe seats" in the House; very few districts can swing either way. This empowers extremist party activists and money givers, who can influence party nominations and thereby pick candidates who will win but who stand for some policies that most voters oppose. As a result, House majorities have often backed policies quite distant from the will of the citizenry, such as the unilateral rather than multilateral foreign policies discussed in this chapter. This partisan extremism spills over into other branches of government, by affecting presidential nominations and career paths to the Senate.

5. *Burdensome personal registration of voters* and other legal provisions (such as the lack of a national holiday for voting) discourage participation in elections, especially among lower-income citizens, thus biasing the composition of the electorate and distorting the voice of the public.

6. *An unbalanced set of organized interest groups* favors certain ethnic organizations (not always representative of their members) and—especially—large business corporations. Multinational corporations with vast resources, facing global economic competition, sometimes push for and obtain economic policies opposed by ordinary citizens. This is accentuated by the weakness of organized labor and is facilitated by business-funded foundations and think tanks.

Most of the above factors apply to domestic as well as foreign policy. Foreign policy, more than domestic, may be subject to two additional impediments to majority rule:

7. *Particularly scarce information on many foreign policy issues.* In many international situations, including armed interventions, there can be inherent uncertainty about future events and about the likely consequences of alternative U.S. actions. This makes it hard for citizens to translate their values and interests confidently into policy preferences, so they may have to defer to officials at first and rely on later, retrospective judgments for any hope of democratic control. Similarly, the low visibility and high costs of getting information about, say, Uzbekistan or the ICC may make it difficult to find out what the government is doing and therefore hard to hold officials accountable.

8. *Information control by the executive branch.* In foreign affairs the president and executive branch often control the flow of information, sometimes having—or claiming to have—unique access to secret information. This can permit them to manipulate opinion and engineer consent, at least temporarily, to policies that would be unpopular if the public were fully informed. Such may have been the case with allegations of al Qaeda ties and nuclear dangers from Saddam Hussein's Iraq. In less visible cases (perhaps

including the Kyoto agreement and the ICC) the executive can sometimes distort relevant facts or simply conceal its own unpopular actions.

On some issues of relatively low salience and minor consequences, officials may get away with pursuing unpopular policies for a long time. On more important matters, much probably depends on the *results* of policy actions. If disliked policies eventually produce unmistakably negative results—extensive war casualties with little gain, or catastrophic climate changes, for example—incumbent officials may be punished at the polls, as they were for the Vietnam War. But the electoral punishment that tends to follow policy disasters is a blunt and inefficient instrument. It is insufficient for timely enforcement of democratic policy making unless decision makers correctly anticipate that punishment is coming—which, of course, they do not always do. When they do not, unsuccessful and unpopular policies can drag on for a long time, at great cost, before the officials are replaced.

In any event, we consider large, persistent gaps between the wishes of citizens and the actions of their leaders to be normatively troubling. And in practical terms, such gaps often involve policies pursued by narrow clusters of elites that may not be sustainable in the long run, because of lack of popular support. We will have more to say about these matters in chapters 7 and 8.

*   *   *

The chief lesson of this chapter is that most Americans, from virtually all walks of life, favor a wide variety of cooperative international policies. Security and justice are the chief foreign policy objectives of the public. Cooperative diplomatic and multilateral measures are the favored means for attaining those objectives.

A second lesson is that in this policy realm, like the others we have studied, individual Americans tend to hold coherent, purposive belief systems about foreign policy that help produce coherent patterns in collective public opinion. The coherence of public opinion makes it particularly worth paying attention to.

When it comes to cooperative, multilateral political relationships—perhaps more than any other aspect of foreign policy—it is our judgment that current U.S. policy would be markedly improved if decision makers listened more closely to the voice of the public.

CHAPTER SIX

Economic Well-Being
and Economic Justice

Americans' opinions about economic relations with other countries reflect some of their most deeply held foreign policy goals and values: their desires to protect the physical security of the United States, to promote justice abroad, and especially to ensure Americans' own security of domestic well-being. Citizens' top-ranked goals of combating international terrorism and protecting the jobs of American workers, for example, infuse their attitudes about international trade and immigration. Support for free trade is conditioned on helping Americans' whose jobs are threatened, as well as protecting the environment and insisting on acceptable labor standards abroad. Long-held skepticism about immigration due to job fears and cultural anxieties has been fortified in recent years by concern about terrorists entering the country.

Contrary to much conventional wisdom, the U.S. public does not reject the idea of foreign aid. Instead, opposition to existing aid programs focuses on strategic and military uses of aid and also reflects extreme overestimates of the amount of aid that is actually given. In harmony with widely shared justice-related goals, many types of humanitarian aid are favored by large majorities of Americans. These include food and medical assistance, development aid, and help to reduce population growth and to prevent and treat AIDs, especially in Africa.

Some of the international economic policies favored by large majorities of the American public, however, particularly those concerning protection of Americans' jobs, restrictions on immigration, and provision of humanitarian aid abroad, do not appear to have been fully embraced by U.S. policy makers or enacted into policy. In some cases official U.S. foreign policy has conflicted with policy preferences held by large majorities of Americans.

APPROVAL OF GLOBALIZATION

Increased economic globalization—that is, increased international trade, capital flows, and immigration—is one of the major features of recent world history. Tariffs and legal barriers against cross-border trade and investment have fallen. Formerly closed communist countries like China and Russia have opened their doors to capitalist enterprises. New information technology and lowered transportation costs have made international transactions much quicker and cheaper.

There have been sharp disagreements over the benefits and costs of globalization. Many observers, including most U.S. economists, celebrate what they see as gains to consumers and businesses in rich countries as well as rapid economic growth and modernization in the developing world. But others fear rising inequality and losses of jobs and income by workers in wealthy countries. Still others deplore "economic totalism"—the consumerist homogenization of "McWorld," which they see as eroding civil society and democracy—or lament environmental damage and loss of cultural diversity.[1]

On balance, most Americans now take a positive view of globalization. Fears of economic competition from Japan, Europe, and low-wage countries, which reached high levels during the early and middle 1990s (with a startling 62 percent of the public calling economic competition from Japan a "critical threat" to the vital interest of the United States in 1994), dropped markedly during the U.S. economic boom of the late 1990s and have stayed fairly low at the beginning of the twenty-first century. In 2002, only 29 percent perceived economic competition from Japan as a critical threat; 31 percent saw economic competition from "low wage countries" as a critical threat, and just 13 percent saw such a threat from Europe. The figures for Europe and perhaps low-wage countries may have risen a bit, but only a bit, in 2004.[2]

Similarly, perceptions that Japan or the European Union practice "unfair trade" with the United States dropped markedly between 1990 and 2002: from 71 percent to 41 percent for Japan, and from 40 percent to 20 percent for the European Union. In 2002 respondents were asked the same question about China, Mexico, and Canada as well; a majority saw unfair trade only in the case of China. The same was true in 2004, when South Korea was added to the survey: a bare majority of Americans saw China, but no other country, as an unfair trader.[3]

Nor does the danger of international financial crises, arguably heightened by the new global economic interdependence, seem to worry many Americans. In 2002, although 54 percent said that "safeguarding against global financial instability" should be a very important goal of U.S. foreign policy, only 25 percent said that "financial crises in other countries" were a critical threat to the United States. Most of the damage from the 1997–98 Asian financial crises had long since been repaired, and actual or potential crises in Argentina, Brazil, Venezuela, and elsewhere were not highly visible at the time of the survey.

By the late 1990s, many more Americans considered economic globalization to be "mostly good" for the United States than considered it "mostly bad." This continued to be true in 2002, by a solid 56 percent to 27 percent margin, and also in 2004.[4] "Protestors against globalization" received a mean thermometer rating in 2002 of a cool 45 degrees, lower than ten other international organizations and groups. At the same time, however, very few Americans—only 14 percent—said it should be a goal of the United States to "actively promote" globalization; another 35 percent wanted simply to "allow it to continue," while a substantial 39 percent wanted to slow it down (24 percent) or try to reverse it (15 percent).

When asked whether globalization was "good" or "bad" for various specific groups or objects, large majorities in 2002 said it was good for people in other countries: for "providing jobs and strengthening the economy in poor countries" and for "democracy and human rights abroad" (see table 6.1). Smaller majorities said globalization was good in various ways for themselves or for other Americans: for "consumers like you," for "American companies," for "the U.S. economy," and for "your own standard of living"—no more than 30 percent of the public said that globalization is bad in any of these respects. A majority even thought globalization good for "maintaining

Table 6.1. Perceived impacts of globalization

Percentages of respondents saying they think that, overall, globalization is good or bad for the following:	Good	Bad
Providing jobs and strengthening the economy in poor countries	64	21
Democracy and human rights abroad	61	20
Consumers like you	55	27
American companies	55	30
Maintaining cultural diversity in the world	53	28
The U.S. economy	52	30
Your own standard of living	51	28
Creating jobs in the U.S.	43	41
The environment	42	37
Job security for American workers	32	51

Source: 2002 CCFR/GMF survey, combined in-person and telephone data set.
Note: In addition to "not sure" responses, small proportions of respondents volunteered "equally good or bad" or "neither good nor bad."

cultural diversity in the world" (presumably because of increased cross-national sharing of cultural variety, rather than preservation of sharp differences), and a plurality thought it good for "the environment." But sentiment about whether globalization is good or bad for "creating jobs in the U.S." was evenly balanced (43 percent to 41 percent), and a majority (51 percent to 32 percent) said that globalization was bad for "job security for American workers."[5]

When individual Americans judge whether or not globalization is, on the whole, "mostly good or mostly bad for the United States," they pay most attention to their own economic interests and those of the United States generally. Our multiple regressions indicate that in 2002 people were especially influenced by whether they saw globalization as good for "consumers like you," for "the U.S. economy," and for "your own standard of living." Altruistic factors involving the economies of poor countries, democracy and human rights, cultural diversity, or the environment had little or no impact.[6] On the more policy-relevant, less U.S.-centric question of whether the United States should "actively promote" globalization, however, some altruistic or justice-related considerations (democracy and human rights, cultural diversity, the economies of poor countries) did enter in, though U.S.-focused economic thinking remained dominant.[7]

Jobs are important to people. As we saw in chapter 2, 85 percent of the U.S. public in 2002 said that "protecting the jobs of American workers" should be a very important goal of U.S. foreign policy, putting it third in priority among twenty goals, behind only combating terrorism and preventing the spread of nuclear weapons. And job protection became the top-ranked goal in 2004. Many Americans worry about how globalization will affect their own and their neighbors' job security. Such concerns play an important part in the public's policy preferences regarding international trade and immigration.

SUPPORT FOR INTERNATIONAL TRADE
WITH SAFEGUARDS

If U.S. economists agree about anything, they agree that free trade is good. Surely, the reasoning goes, every participant must gain from any voluntary trade in which he or she engages, or else he or she would not take part in it. Granted, some nonparticipants in a given trade might be harmed by "externalities" (closings of factories and losses of jobs, for example), but the overall gains from trade are—at least in principle—supposed to be sufficient to compensate any such losers.

Still, at least since the pioneering 1941 article by Wolfgang Stolper and Paul Samuelson, economists have recognized that cheap imports from low-wage countries may drive down the wages, or eliminate the jobs, of workers who make similar goods in richer countries. And of course there is no guarantee of compensation for such losses: even if gains from trade provide resources that could be used for compensation, businesses generally lack any incentive to offer it to workers. The theory of "factor price equalization" suggests that—given free trade and cheap transportation of goods—the wages of workers throughout the world should move toward a single, equilibrium level, perhaps a much lower level than that once enjoyed by manufacturing workers in rich countries.[8]

Debates continue over whether free trade alone invariably leads to factor price equalization. Even if it does not, however, a single world market with free mobility of capital and labor, as well as free trade in goods, surely would. Edward Leamer has likened high U.S. wages to a tall column of water in a confined tank: when the free trade spigot at the bottom is opened, water (wage payments) naturally flows out into the much lower—and much larger—pool of the international labor market, with its hundreds of millions of skilled and energetic but low-paid workers in China, India, Indonesia, and elsewhere.[9]

Ordinary Americans have long felt ambivalent or conflicted about international trade. They like the general idea of free trade and cheap imports but worry about threats to Americans' jobs, the global environment, and working conditions abroad. This was evident in the 2004 CCFR survey: substantial majorities said that, overall, international trade was good for "consumers like you," "your own standard of living," "American companies," and "the U.S. economy," but the public was evenly divided about "the environment," and substantial majorities said trade was bad for "creating jobs in the U.S." and for "job security for American workers." A large majority also said that "outsourcing" U.S. jobs to low-wage countries is "mostly a bad thing."[10]

These concerns affect concrete preferences about trade policies. One frequently asked survey question mentions arguments for and against tariffs and restrictions on imported goods: "it has been argued that if all countries would eliminate their tariffs and restrictions on imported goods, the costs of goods would go down for everyone"; but, it notes, "others have said that such tariffs and restrictions are necessary to protect certain manufacturing jobs in certain industries from the competition of less expensive imports." Respondents are then asked whether they generally "sympathize more with those who want to eliminate tariffs or those who think such tariffs are necessary." By this measure, most Americans oppose completely free trade. A substantial plurality in the CCFR surveys in which the question was asked (beginning in 1978) has always picked the "tariffs are necessary" side. In 2002, 50 percent said "tariffs are necessary," while 38 percent said "eliminate tariffs."[11]

Clearly, however, job worries stand at the heart of opposition to free trade. When they are assuaged, opinion looks very different. For example, when a different set of respondents in 2002 was not forced into this dichotomous choice but was allowed to choose among three alternatives—"I favor free trade and I believe that it is necessary for the government to have programs to help workers who lose their jobs," "I favor free trade and I believe that it is *not* necessary for the government to have programs to help workers who lose their jobs" (emphasis added), and "I do not favor free trade"—the first option (free trade plus job help) won by a landslide: 73 percent of the public favored it, with only 16 percent for pure free trade without jobs programs, and a bare 9 percent opposed to free trade altogether.[12] Given three slightly different (and probably better-phrased) alternatives in 2004, a moderate plurality favored agreements to lower trade barriers "provided the government has programs to help workers who lose their jobs," while only a similarly small minority favored lowering barriers without such programs.[13]

An overwhelming 93 percent of the public in 2002 (and 94 percent in 2004) said that "countries that are part of international trade agreements should . . . be required to maintain minimum standards for working conditions." This may reflect concerns about U.S. jobs and wages (higher working standards abroad imply higher labor costs and product prices there, hence less competitive pressure on the United States); it may also be motivated partly by justice-related concerns about the fate of workers abroad. Individuals who favored working-conditions standards tended, slightly, to see economic competition from Japan or Europe as critical threats and also to see global warming as a critical threat.[14]

It seems doubtful that U.S. trade negotiators and policy makers have responded fully to Americans' job concerns. There does exist a program, which grew substantially in the 1990s, designed to help with the adjustment and retraining of workers who are displaced by import competition. At the same time, under Democratic and Republican administrations alike, the pursuit of free trade has sometimes seemed to enjoy a higher priority than the protection of domestic employment or working conditions abroad. The first Clinton administration, for example, started out with a major push for the North American Free Trade Agreement (NAFTA)—which lacked provisions for strong regulation of working standards in Mexico—while sharply cutting its promised "job stimulus" program. (Most Americans in 2004 said that NAFTA had been good for the Mexican economy and for creating jobs in Mexico [though Mexicans surveyed at the same time disagreed]; good for U.S. consumers, U.S. companies, and respondents' standard of living; but bad for the environment, for creating jobs in the United States, and especially for job security for American workers.)[15] And the George W. Bush administration pushed for and received "fast track" authority to negotiate a broader free trade agreement with Central America.

Most Americans—an overwhelming 94 percent in 2002 and 91 percent in 2004—also said that "countries that are part of international trade agreements should . . . be required to maintain minimum standards for protection of the environment." As we have noted, "protecting the global environment," while not as high a priority as job protection, was seen as a very important U.S. foreign policy goal by a substantial 66 percent of the public. (Another 29 percent said "somewhat important.") Individuals who favored environmental standards tended to see global warming as a critical threat and, slightly, to call themselves liberals.[16] It is difficult to argue that U.S. trade negotiators, presidents, or Congresses have pursued such environmental provisions with great vigor. The Clinton administration's revisions of NAFTA, for example, nodded in the direction of the environment but included no strong enforcement provisions.

Perhaps in sympathy with other countries' health and environmental concerns, most Americans—66 percent, with only 26 percent opposed—said in 2002 that the European Union and Japan should be able to require labeling of genetically modified food, "even if this might keep consumers from purchasing food imported from the U.S." Americans were themselves divided about the use of biotechnology in agriculture and food production, with nearly equal proportions supportive of it and opposed (48 percent and 45 percent, respectively).

There are further indications that feelings about international fairness and justice enter into attitudes related to trade. In recent years developing countries have complained of hypocrisy as the United States has sought open markets for its own exports but has continued to hinder foreign competitors, especially through large subsidies to domestic producers of agricultural commodities like cotton. In 2004, only a bare majority of Americans judged that the United States "practices fair trade" with poor countries, and about two-thirds of the public disagreed with the statement that "rich countries are playing fair in trade negotiations with poor countries." A substantial majority favored farm subsidies but only to small farmers and only in "bad years": the public overwhelmingly opposed the long-standing policy of providing government subsidies to large farming businesses on a regular annual basis.[17]

Consistent with their conditional support for free trade and globalization, Americans in 2002 gave a fairly warm, 55-degree average thermometer rating to the World Trade Organization.[18] A substantial majority (63 percent) said the WTO should be "strengthened," putting it below only the WHO and the UN among eight organizations listed. Feelings about the WTO, like most other foreign policy attitudes we have studied, are not very deeply rooted in individual's group memberships or social characteristics but are embedded in purposive belief systems. Our standard, fourteen-variable demographic regression analysis could not account for any appreciable part of the variance in feelings; only women and possibly Asian Americans showed significant (but small) tendencies to feel warmer toward the WTO than others did (see the first column of table 6.2). But feelings about the WTO follow from general support for multilateralism and international organizations, especially as signaled by feelings about the European Union and the goal of strengthening the United Nations. These attitudes about the EU and the UN, the belief that globalization creates jobs in the United States, and possibly concerns about energy supplies had substantial independent effects on feelings about the WTO according to full regressions controlling for demographics and basic

Table 6.2. Sources of feelings about the World Trade Organization

Dependent variable: Rating of the WTO on a 0- to 100-degree feeling thermometer

	Variables included in regression			
Independent variable	Demo-graphics only	Demo-graphics + basic attitudes	Demo-graphics + attitudes + goals	Goals + attitudes only
Woman	.10*	.10*	n.s.	
Asian	n.s.	.07+	n.s.	
"Active part" internationalism		.21**	n.s.	n.s.
Liberal/conservative self-rating		n.s.	n.s.	n.s.
Party identification		n.s.	n.s.	n.s.
Thermometer rating of European Union			.42**	.40**
Goal: strengthen the UN			.28**	.29**
Goal: secure energy supplies			n.s.	.12+
Globalization good for creating jobs in the U.S.			.14+	.15*
R	.149	.259	.632	.621
Adjusted R-squared	−.003	.038	.287	.351
Degrees of freedom	566	566	133	133

Source: CCFR/GMF 2002 general public survey, combined in-person and telephone data set.
Note: Entries are standardized OLS regression coefficients. Controls as indicated. Demographic regressions included fourteen independent variables; except as indicated, only those with significant coefficients are displayed. All attitudinal variables included in regressions are shown.
$+p < .10$, $*p < .05$, $**p < .01$

political orientations. By themselves, attitudinal factors accounted for an unusually high proportion—over one-third—of the variation in ratings of the WTO (see the third and fourth columns).

Most Americans are willing to take collective obligations to the WTO seriously, accepting rulings that constrain the United States as well as other countries. Asked in 2002 about a situation in which "another country files a complaint with the World Trade Organization and it rules against the U.S.," 64 percent said that as a general rule, yes, the U.S. should comply with that decision (24 percent said no). As many or more Americans said the same thing in 2004, when a large majority also said that in "international economic organizations like the World Bank, the International Monetary Fund and the World Trade Organization," decisions should "always be made by a majority" of members: the United States should not have a veto.[19]

Again, individuals' opinions about compliance with WTO rulings are not much affected by their social characteristics, except that having more formal education leads to favoring compliance, while being an evangelical Protestant (and perhaps being older) tends to lead to opposition. But this issue, with its provocative implication of constraints on U.S. sovereignty, evokes responses that line up unusually strongly along the basic ideological fault lines of American politics. Controlling for our fourteen demographic factors, being a liberal, a Democrat, or an "active part" internationalist each independently contributed to favoring compliance with WTO rulings, while being a conservative, a Republican, or a "stay out" isolationist contributed to opposition. In addition, a reciprocity norm with our European trade partners may come into play: controlling for all the other factors, believing that countries of the European Union "practice fair trade" contributed to favoring compliance with WTO rulings, while perceptions of unfair trade by Europeans contributed to opposition.[20]

Economic sanctions and trade with specific countries. Most Americans favor economic sanctions against specific countries that are seen as enemies of the United States or as flagrant violators of human rights. In 2002, for example, 66 percent favored economic sanctions against Saddam Hussein's Iraq, 63 percent against Iran, 58 percent against North Korea, 51 percent against Cuba, and—despite official policy running in the opposite direction—51 percent against China.[21] There were, however, signs of a thaw with respect to Cuba, with which a number of U.S. businesses were eager to trade: opposition to sanctions had grown by 11 percentage points since 1998, reaching 41 percent.[22]

Just as one would expect, the individual Americans who feel most negatively about a country or its leader are the most likely to favor economic sanctions against that country. Those in 2002 who most disliked Fidel Castro, for example, rather strongly tended to favor sanctions against Cuba. Similar patterns held for ratings of Iran, North Korea, China, Chinese president Jiang Zemin, Iraq, and then-president Saddam Hussein with respect to sanctions against the relevant countries. In the case of Iraq (and, to a lesser extent, Iran and North Korea) bivariate correlations indicate that perceptions of critical threats from nuclear proliferation, international terrorism, and Iraqi weapons of mass destruction were also moderately related to support for sanctions, but some of those relationships weakened or vanished when other factors were controlled for in multiple regressions.

Our regression analyses reveal some subtle and interesting patterns in individuals' support for or opposition to sanctions. In the case of Cuba, for example, hopes for U.S. economic gains from trade apparently counterbalance dislike of the Castro regime, producing the fairly even division of opinion for and against sanctions.[23] In the case of Iraq, calculations' about Israel's security seem to enter the picture: thermometer ratings of Israeli prime minister Ariel Sharon contributed to support for sanctions independently of peoples' feelings about Iraq itself.[24]

When it comes to Iran, concerns about terrorism, negative feelings about Iran, and geopolitical considerations involving Israel all contribute to support for economic sanctions. Individuals' social characteristics make little or no difference. But "active part" internationalism (with an unusually hawkish effect in this case) contributes to favoring sanctions, while self-identified liberalism contributes to opposition. Even more strongly—controlling for all other demographic and attitudinal factors—feeling warmer toward Iran tends to lead to opposing sanctions, while intense opposition to terrorism or warm feelings toward Israel (whose governments have seen Iran as a major threat) lead to favoring sanctions against Iran.[25]

The American public's readiness to use economic sanctions, despite indications that they tend to be ineffective against regimes but harmful to innocent civilians unless they are universally enforced and carefully targeted, has been apparent throughout the history of CCFR surveys. In one case of effective sanctions, a majority (57 percent) of the U.S. public in 1986 favored either banning "all trade with or investment in South Africa" (29 percent) or imposing "limited economic sanctions" (28 percent) if the South African government did not dismantle its apartheid system. Only 23 percent said "we should take no position," and a bare 8 percent said we should support the South African government.[26]

Of course "economic sanctions" need not entail the prohibition of all trade or, indeed, limiting trade at all: sanctions might, for example, be narrowly targeted against specific kinds of foreign investments or against travel abroad by elites, and the public may have something of this sort in mind. Despite the public sentiment in favor of sanctions, a separate series of questions in 2002 asking whether people favored or opposed "engaging in trade with the following countries" elicited a strong majority (71 percent to 26 percent) in favor of trading with China and a narrow majority (52 percent to 46 percent) for trading with Cuba, with which the United States had banned trade for decades. On the other hand, a large majority (72 percent to 26 percent) opposed trade with Saddam Hussein's Iraq, and smaller majorities opposed trade with the other two members of President Bush's "axis of evil," Iran and North Korea. Results in 2004 were similar.[27]

Even more than in the case of economic sanctions, individual Americans' attitudes about trade with particular countries are strongly related to their feelings about those countries and their political leaders. In bivariate terms, respondents in 2002 who felt relatively positive (or less negative) about Fidel Castro, Iraq, China, Iran, and North Korea were substantially more likely to favor trade with the relevant countries. Those favoring trade with a particular country also tended to favor having diplomatic relations with that country.[28]

Again, however, multiple regressions reveal more subtle patterns. In the case of Cuba, support for trade has unusually substantial roots in individuals' social characteristics. Independently of other characteristics, being male or having more formal education contributes to favoring trade with Cuba, while being evangelical or Catholic contributes to opposition. (Controlling for religion, being Hispanic makes no significant difference.) Among basic political attitudes, only self-rated liberalism significantly affects favoring trade. Liberalism and the demographic characteristics appear to work chiefly through two factors that account for a substantial fraction of the variance in policy preferences: feelings toward Fidel Castro, and support for or opposition to the idea of combating terrorism by "improving U.S. relations with adversary countries."[29]

Trade with China tends to win support (independently of other factors) from the well-educated, liberals, and "active part" internationalists, with indications of opposition from evangelicals and (oddly) Hispanics. As usual, demographic factors work mostly through attitudes, in this case particularly the perception of a vital U.S. interest in China, with hints of opposition from those who see a critical threat to the United States from China's development as a world power or a threat from economic competition from low-wage countries.[30]

In the cases of both Iran and Iraq, support for trade is a mirror image of support for economic sanctions. It reflects an independent impact of geopolitical concerns involving Israel as well as feelings about Iran and Iraq themselves.[31]

WORRIES ABOUT IMMIGRATION

Although nearly all Americans are descended from immigrants, through-out our history *new* immigrants (at least non-Anglo-Saxon immigrants) have generally encountered substantial opposition. Even Irish Americans, whose descendants are now seen as thoroughly Americanized and highly success-ful, were in the early nineteenth century often reviled as criminals or drunk-ards and stigmatized as "black" or "the race." Later in the nineteenth century Asian immigrants (many of them brought to the American West to build rail-roads) suffered severe discrimination and eventually legal exclusion. At the beginning of the twentieth century, waves of Catholic or Jewish, non-English-speaking immigrants from southern and eastern Europe aroused fears about "foreignness," political corruption, and (particularly after World War I) sus-ceptibility to socialism or anarchy. More recently immigrants from Mexico and Latin America, especially those without documents, have faced resent-ment and hostility.[32]

In CCFR surveys that have asked about the issue (starting in 1994) ma-jorities of the U.S. public have always said that "controlling and reducing illegal immigration" should be a very important goal of U.S. foreign policy. In 2002, 70 percent said so. *Legal* immigration faces substantial opposition as well. In each survey since 1994, majorities—60 percent in 2002—have called "large numbers of immigrants and refugees coming into the U.S." a "critical threat" to the country's vital interest. Asked whether legal immi-gration into the United States should be kept at its present level, increased, or decreased, 55 percent in 2002 said "decreased," while only 15 percent said "increased." By all three of these measures anti-immigration senti-ments dipped somewhat between 2002 and 2004, but they continued to be expressed by majorities of Americans.[33]

One reason for opposition to immigration is concern about competition for jobs. Immigrant workers, it is feared, may depress wages and cause un-employment. Such worries tend to rise when economic times are hard. Both the priority assigned to the goal of controlling illegal immigration and per-ceptions that large numbers of immigrants are a critical threat declined between economically sluggish 1994 and boom-year 1998, but figures rose again in recession-plagued 2002,[34] only to ease off again by 2004. Individuals who said that protecting the jobs of American workers should be a very im-portant goal had a modest but significant tendency (in the bivariate sense) to want to decrease the number of legal immigrants. The same was true of lower-income individuals and those with lower levels of formal education.[35]

The actual effects of immigration upon wages and employment have been disputed among economists, some of whom see immigration as a source of lower prices for goods and services, higher business profits, and economic growth. But standard economic theory indicates that an increase in the supply of labor due to immigration should lower the price of labor—namely wages—for native-born workers who compete with immigrants. The best econometric evidence indicates that this is in fact the case. George Borjas has calculated that the upsurge of immigration between 1980 and 2000 reduced the average annual earnings of native-born American men by about $1,700, or roughly 4 percent. Those hardest hit were workers with low skill levels who competed directly with low-skill immigrants from Mexico. Native-born workers without a high school diploma lost, on average, 7.4 percent of their weekly wages. The impact was also high on African Americans (who lost 4.5 percent of wages) and native-born Hispanics (who lost 5.0 percent).[36] Immigration's pinch is especially important for low-end service workers, who (because their work cannot be manufactured abroad and imported) are relatively immune to wage squeezes from the two other engines of economic globalization, international trade and capital mobility. Thus it is not unreasonable for members of the U.S. public to worry about the economic consequences of immigration, or to believe that U.S. immigration policy has been oriented more toward serving the desires of U.S. businesses (including agribusiness) for cheap labor, than toward alleviating the worries of American workers.

Another source of concern about immigration is cultural anxiety: unease about sharing workplaces, neighborhoods, and schools with people who look and act "different" and perhaps speak a foreign language. The same lower-income and less-educated people who worry about job competition tend also to harbor cultural anxieties—in part, no doubt, because they (in contrast to higher-income enthusiasts for immigration) are more likely to have contact with recent immigrants in their schools and neighborhoods. The present authors generally favor immigration, believing that it brings us cultural diversity and economic energy, but we recognize that cultural anxieties, like job concerns, are real. Americans who gave Mexico cooler ratings on the feeling thermometer in 2002 had a small but significant tendency (again in the bivariate sense) to want to reduce the number of legal immigrants into the United States. The same thing was even more true of those who rated "the Muslim people" coldly.[37]

Since September 11, 2001, when nineteen young Arab men visiting the United States crashed airliners into the World Trade Center and the Pentagon, concern about Muslim immigrants has reflected not only cultural anxieties but also worries about international terrorism. In the summer 2002 CCFR survey, a large majority of the public (76 percent to 22 percent) said that "based on the events of September 11 . . . U.S. immigration laws should be tightened to restrict the number of immigrants from Arab or Muslim countries into the United States." When asked about various measures to combat international terrorism, 77 percent said they favored "restricting immigration into the U.S." Despite traditional U.S. sensitivity to the preservation of civil rights and civil liberties, a small majority of 54 percent to 43 percent even favored "using racial profiling in airport security checks." Support for tightening laws to restrict the number of Arab or Muslim immigrants was especially high (again in a bivariate sense) among individuals who gave cool thermometer ratings to the Muslim people, thought that the 9/11 attacks represented the "true teachings of Islam," or considered Muslim ways incompatible with Western ways and violent conflict inevitable, though it was also high among those who considered protecting the jobs of American workers to be a very important goal and individuals with lower levels of formal education.[38] The post-9/11 U.S. government policies of racial profiling at airports, registration of Arab immigrants and visitors, intrusive surveillance, and detention of illegal or suspect immigrants, then, appear— for better or worse—to have had substantial public support.

For some Americans, the association between Muslim immigrants and terrorism goes beyond the undeniable fact that the 9/11 attackers were Muslim extremists and implicates Islam itself. In the 2002 CCFR survey, a substantial minority of the public—39 percent—said that the attacks on the World Trade Center and the Pentagon represented "the true teachings of Islam," either "to a great degree" (21 percent) or "to some degree" (18 percent). (Of course "to some degree" represents a rather mild indictment; Muslims in medieval times might well have said something similar about Christianity and the destructive Crusades into the Middle East.) But a majority of Americans—57 percent—rejected this view, saying that the attacks reflected Islam "not very much" (17 percent) or "not at all" (40 percent).

As we noted in chapter 4, in 2002 a solid majority of Americans (by 66 percent to 27 percent) also rejected the "clash of civilizations" notion that "because Muslim religious, social and political traditions are incompatible with Western ways, violent conflict between the two civilizations is inevitable." Most said, instead, that "because most Muslims are like people everywhere, we can find common ground and violent conflict between the civilizations is not inevitable." Moreover, the 49-degree average thermometer rating of "the Muslim people" indicated lukewarm average feelings, but not widespread hostility; 36 percent of the public gave Muslims ratings above the 50-degree neutral point, 32 percent ratings below. (Average ratings of Muslims may have dropped a bit, but only a bit, by 2004.)[39] There is no evidence that the U.S. public wants to end or drastically cut immigration by Muslims.

In order to sort out the relative importance of economic worries, cultural anxieties, and concerns about terrorism in shaping Americans' attitudes about immigration, we included measures of all three in multiple regression analyses of individuals' attitudes about "controlling and reducing illegal immigration."[40] In a demographics-only regression, a few of our fourteen demographic factors proved to have moderately important effects (though less so than for trade with Cuba). Being older led people to attribute greater importance to the goal of controlling and reducing illegal immigration, while being Hispanic or having more formal education led to less enthusiasm for restrictions (see the first column of table 6.3). Still, even in this case personal and social characteristics did not account for much variance in policy preferences. And they apparently worked chiefly through specific, logically relevant political beliefs and attitudes; except for age, the demographic coefficients lost statistical significance when individuals' foreign policy goals and other attitudinal factors were included in regressions. As usual, goals, threats, and feelings with logical connections to policy preferences accounted for a substantial portion of the variation in those preferences, a considerably larger portion than personal or social characteristics did (about six times as much).

Table 6.3 neatly exemplifies many of the findings about purposive belief systems that we have emphasized throughout the book. As the third and fourth columns make clear, all three types of concerns—economic, cultural, and terrorism-related—are independently and substantially related to opinions about immigration policy. Economic and terrorism-related concerns appear to have roughly equal impact, with cultural anxieties perhaps somewhat less important. The goal of protecting Americans' jobs leads to opposition to immigration, as does the goal of reducing the trade deficit (which apparently taps general domestic economic concerns). But worries about terrorism are equally important. Perceptions of terrorism as a critical threat, and willingness to assassinate individual terrorist leaders (an indicator of particularly strong concern about terrorism) both have substantial, highly significant effects.

Feelings about Mexico also significantly affect attitudes toward immigration: cool feelings lead to opposition. This indicates that cultural anxieties play a part as well, since our regression controls for economic concerns. (Feelings about Muslims unfortunately could not be included in the analysis.[41]) It is striking, however, that thermometer ratings of China, which would presumably reflect any cultural anxiety about Asian immigrants, are not in fact related at all to attitudes about immigration when other factors are controlled for. The public apparently reacts quite differently to Asian immigrants than to Hispanics. An unusual finding is that liberal ideology independently contributes to favoring immigration even after job worries, concerns about terrorism, and cultural anxieties are taken into account.

Table 6.3. Sources of attitudes about immigration

Dependent variable: importance of the foreign policy goal of "controlling and reducing illegal immigration"

Independent variable	*Demographics only*	*Demographics + basic attitudes*	*Demographics + attitudes + goals*	*Goals + attitudes only*
		Variables included in regression		
Age	.12**	.13**	.14*	
Education level	−.12**	−.10**	n.s.	
Hispanic	−.10**	−.10**	n.s.	
Employed	n.s.	.07+	n.s.	
"Active part" internationalism		−.07*	n.s.	n.s.
Liberal self-rating		−.16**	−.12*	−.18**
Party identification		n.s.	n.s.	n.s.
Economic concerns:				
Goal: protect American jobs			.21**	.20**
Goal: reduce trade deficit			.15**	.17**
Terrorism concerns:				
Threat of terrorism			.17**	.17**
Support for assassination of terrorist leaders			.21**	.20**
Cultural anxieties:				
Thermometer rating of Mexico			−.14**	−.15**
Thermometer rating of China			n.s.	n.s.
R	.223	.285	.516	.489
Adjusted R-squared	.035	.064	.214	.219
Degrees of freedom	936	936	343	343

Source: CCFR/GMF 2002 general public survey, combined in-person and telephone data set.
Note: Entries are standardized OLS regression coefficients. Controls as indicated. Demographic regressions included fourteen independent variables, but (except as indicated) only those with significant coefficients are displayed. All attitudinal variables included in regressions are shown.
$+p < .10, *p < .05, **p < .01$

SUPPORT FOR HUMANITARIAN BUT NOT STRATEGIC FOREIGN AID

There is an enormous gap in living standards between the world's richest countries and the poorest countries, especially those in Africa. At the beginning of the twenty-first century, while the United States had a gross domestic product of about $36,000 per person per year (and Norway's and Ireland's were a bit higher), the per capita GDP of Zambia was only $840 a year, that of Malawi was $580, and Sierra Leone's was just $520. Whereas an American baby at birth could be expected to live about seventy-seven years (and babies in twenty-six other affluent countries could expect to live even longer), babies born in Mozambique had life expectancies of only thirty-nine years, in Sierra Leone thirty-four years, and in Zambia just thirty-three years. Illiteracy, barely detectable among adults in wealthy countries, afflicted about 60 percent of adults in Ethiopia, Senegal, Gambia, and several other African countries, and reached 83 percent in Niger. In Mali, Nigeria, the Central African Republic, Zambia, and Niger, more than 60 percent of the population lived on the purchasing-power equivalent of less than one dollar per day.[42]

Since the early years of the Cold War, when the United States began competing with the Soviet Union for "hearts and minds" in developing countries, the U.S. has boasted of efforts to help poor people around the globe. Yet much U.S. aid has been military, and the biggest recipients of economic aid have been countries of perceived strategic military or political importance to the United States—first in Europe and Japan; then South Korea, Taiwan, and South Vietnam; more recently Israel, Egypt, and other geopolitically important countries—rather than the neediest countries.

Moreover, the total economic aid effort of the United States, as a proportion of its economy, has consistently lagged behind that of other advanced countries. In 2002, for example, the United States ranked dead last among twenty-one rich countries in the aid component of the Commitment to Development Index. Our skimpy 13 cents per American per day in governmental aid was dwarfed by the 57 cents per day in government aid from each Netherlander, the 61 cents from each Swede, the 84 cents from each Dane, and the remarkable $1.02 from each Norwegian. True, our much-touted private giving was higher than in many countries, but at 5 cents per person per day it was not enough to raise the United States' dismal ranking. And it was outclassed by the average Norwegian's private giving of 24 cents per day.[43]

Conventional wisdom holds that the paucity of U.S. foreign aid has reflected ordinary Americans' aversion to aid—that the American public adamantly opposes foreign aid of virtually any sort. At first glance some survey data do seem to support this view. In general terms, the balance of Americans' opinions has always tilted toward reducing rather than increasing overall aid programs, and more people want to decrease than to increase aid to most specific countries or regions. A closer look, however, reveals that the opposition is partly based on extreme overestimates of how much money the United States is actually spending on aid. And opposition is mostly directed toward "waste" or toward military and strategic uses of aid. Survey questions that focus on justice-related humanitarian and altruistic forms of foreign aid, such as help with food supplies, medical care, and economic development, show a high level of public support.[44]

Opposition to strategic or "wasteful" aid. When Americans are asked simply whether they favor or oppose "our giving economic aid to other nations," opinion has been fairly closely divided, with a plurality or small majority generally favoring it: 54 percent favored aid, with 38 percent opposed, in 2002.[45] But when respondents are given a list of federal government programs and asked whether they feel each one should be expanded, cut back, or kept about the same, many people say that "economic aid to other nations" should be cut back. In all nine CCFR surveys between 1974 and 2004 at least 48 percent have said "cut back," with 50 percent or more saying so in five of the surveys (see table 6.4). In every case, "cut back" responses have greatly outweighed support for expansion, suggesting that the balance of opinion has always favored at least some reduction in aid. In 2002, 48 percent of respondents wanted to cut back aid, 35 percent to keep it about the same, and only 14 percent to expand it; results were about the same in 2004.[46]

A similar picture emerges when people are asked specifically whether economic aid "to the following people or nations" should be increased, decreased, kept about the same, or stopped altogether. With respect to nearly every country or people, in nearly every year since 1990 (when these

Table 6.4. Cutting back or expanding economic aid to other nations

Year	Should be cut back (%)	Should be kept about the same (%)	Should be expanded (%)	Not sure (%)
1974	55	28	10	7
1978	50	31	11	8
1982	54	31	8	7
1986	48	35	11	6
1990	61	27	7	5
1994	58	28	9	5
1998	48	36	13	3
2002	48	35	14	3
2004	49	38	10	3

Source: CCFR surveys. 2004 data from the CCI telephone survey.

questions were first asked by the CCFR), many more members of the public have said economic aid should be decreased or stopped altogether than have said increased.[47] In 2002, the proportion saying aid should be decreased or stopped was 54 percent for the Palestinians, 51 percent for Pakistan, 45 percent for Afghanistan, 41 percent for Israel, 38 percent for Egypt, 39 percent for India, 32 percent for Russia. In each of these cases at least twice as many people favored decreasing or stopping aid as favored increasing it, which suggests that the median respondent probably favored at least some reduction in aid.[48] Only when asked about "African countries" did more Americans say economic aid should be increased (35 percent) than said it should be decreased or stopped (22 percent). As we will see below, the African exception reflects humanitarian, justice-related motives.

The picture changes when we ask exactly *why* people oppose aid or want to reduce the amount. For one thing, Steven Kull and his associates at the Program on International Policy Attitudes (PIPA) have shown that most Americans greatly overestimate the fraction of the federal government budget that is currently spent on aid, and most say they favor a budget allocation that turns out to be considerably larger than the present one.[49] The 2002 CCFR survey confirmed this. When respondents were asked, "Just based on what you know, please tell me your hunch about what percentage of the federal budget goes to foreign aid," the median response was 20 percent. This is far more—astoundingly more—than the less than one-half of 1 percent of the budget that actually goes for foreign economic aid.[50] (One might ask where such gross misperceptions come from. A possible answer is noisy rhetoric from aid opponents, which makes aid programs seem bigger and more important than they are. The same point probably applies to overestimates of amounts spent on "welfare.")

When a subset of respondents was asked "What do you think would be an appropriate percentage of the federal budget to go to foreign aid, if any?" the median response was 10 percent: considerably less than people thought was currently being spent, but more than twenty times the actual level of spending.[51] Since many people have difficulty working with percentages and since no tradeoffs with other budget priorities were posed, we should probably not take the 10 percent figure too seriously as the precise level of foreign economic aid that the average American favors. Still, the contrast between 10 percent and the actual budget level of less than half of 1 percent suggests that if everyone had accurate knowledge of current spending levels, more Americans would probably favor increases in economic aid. Almost certainly they would be willing to give more than 13 cents per person per day. PIPA has found that survey and focus group respondents who are given correct budget numbers often drop their stand that too much is being spent or that aid should be cut. Similarly, Americans tend to overestimate the generosity of U.S. aid compared with that of other industrialized countries.[52] If more knew that the United States has ranked at the very bottom among wealthy countries in terms of foreign aid as a proportion of GDP, it seems likely that more people would support increases in aid.

Another element in Americans' opposition to foreign aid is concern that much aid is wasted, going to corrupt or dictatorial regimes and not getting to people who need it. An early CCFR survey that explored this issue found, for example, that 67 percent believed economic aid generally "benefits the rich more than the poor in other countries"; at the same time, fully 79 percent said they favored giving economic aid if they were "sure that it ended up helping the people of those countries." In a 2001 PIPA study, 77 percent of Americans said that too much U.S. foreign aid goes to governments "that are not very democratic and have poor human rights records." Respondents' median estimates were that only 10 percent of U.S. aid money to poor countries "ends up helping the people who really need it," whereas 50 percent "ends up in the hands of corrupt government officials."[53] No doubt the public's estimate of the extent of waste and corruption is grossly exaggerated; surely more than 10 percent of aid to poor countries actually reaches the needy. But there is plenty of reason to believe that misuse and outright theft of aid has in fact been a problem, especially when it goes, for geopolitical reasons, to corrupt or repressive regimes. If it were clear to the public that aid was effectively designed and targeted, public support would undoubtedly be greater.[54]

In the 1970s and 1980s, large majorities—around 75 percent—of the American public also told CCFR interviewers that economic aid to other countries generally gets us "too involved in other countries' affairs." In 1982, when the Reagan administration was pushing to help Nicaragua's "Contra" rebels, 57 percent of the public thought that U.S. economic aid to Central America was "likely to lead to U.S. military involvement in that area." In those economically pressed times, majorities of Americans also said that economic aid did not contribute to national security, did not help our economy, and generally was "not worth the economic cost." These self-interested factors were particularly strongly related to individuals' opposition to aid.[55]

More broadly, most Americans are simply uncomfortable with strategic uses of foreign aid, whether economic or military. Even during the tense years of the "new Cold War" in the late 1970s and early 1980s, only about a third of respondents said they believed that either economic or military aid helped prevent the spread of communism or improved our national security.[56] Most Americans worry that current U.S. aid programs (which have been overwhelmingly military and strategic) promote waste, corruption, and dependency and support undemocratic regimes that abuse human rights.

Support for humanitarian aid. When it comes to humanitarian forms of foreign aid, however, the picture is quite different. As we saw in chapter 2, a substantial majority of Americans—61 percent in 2002, though significantly fewer in 2004—have said that "combating world hunger" should be a very important goal of U.S. foreign policy. A lesser number (30 percent in 2002, and still fewer in 2004) have said the same about "helping to improve the standard of living of less developed nations," though very large majorities—86 percent in 2002—have said this goal should be at least somewhat important.[57] The data on Americans' support for specific types of humanitarian aid indicate that there is substantial concern about economic justice for the poor of the world.

Particularly popular is the idea of "food and medical assistance to people in needy countries." In 2002 fully 84 percent favored such assistance, with only 12 percent opposed (see table 6.5).[58] "Assistance with the prevention and treatment of AIDS in poor countries" was favored by 79 percent and opposed by only 18 percent. "Aid that helps needy countries develop their economies" won nearly as much backing, 74 percent, with support rising to 78 percent when a similar question was asked in the context of combating terrorism. Favorable responses were nearly as frequent in 2004.[59] It appears that the public would favor expansion of the very skimpy U.S. programs of these types, particularly (as we saw above) in African countries, where the AIDS crisis has been devastating.

Table 6.5. Support for humanitarian foreign aid

Type of aid	Favor (%)	Oppose (%)
Food and medical assistance to people in needy countries	84	12
Aid for women's education in poor countries to help reduce population growth	80	17
Assistance with the prevention and treatment of AIDS in poor countries	79	18
Aid that helps needy countries develop their economies	74	21
Aid for birth control in poor countries to help reduce population growth	71	25
Assistance to promote democracy abroad	64	27

Source: 2002 CCFR/GMF survey, combined data set.

President Bush's announcement in March 2002 of a substantial increase in anti-AIDS and developmental aid through a Millennium Challenge Account (emphasizing recipients' own capacities and responsibilities) would seem to be in harmony with the wishes of the public. The program started slowly, however. Only by early 2005 had fifteen of the seventeen eligible countries finally overcome various hurdles and submitted proposals laying out their development plans; most were still waiting for payments at the beginning of 2006. Moreover, much less money was appropriated than had been promised. Although total developmental and humanitarian aid increased significantly during Bush's first term, it continued to focus on geopolitical targets rather than the world's poorest countries. And aid outlays remained at a very low level: just $13.8 billion in fiscal year 2004, only about 0.6 percent of the federal budget or 0.12 percent of GDP—about one-sixth of the UN-recommended fraction.[60]

Also winning high levels of public support are aid programs designed to reduce population growth. As table 6.5 indicates, "aid for women's education in poor countries to help reduce population growth" was favored by 80 percent of the public in 2002. Strikingly, even when the controversial issue of birth control was explicitly introduced, a large majority still favored such aid: 71 percent favored "aid for birth control in poor countries to help reduce population growth," while just 25 percent opposed it. The 2004 figures on both issues were essentially the same.[61] In this respect the wishes of the public appear to conflict with policies of the Bush administration, which made major efforts to withhold U.S. aid from any international organizations involved in abortion or birth control.

As we have noted, African countries were the only specific aid recipients for which pluralities of Americans in 2002 clearly wanted the amount of economic aid to be increased rather than decreased or stopped. Multiple regression analyses indicate that the motivations for favoring such an increase include the goals of combating world hunger and improving the standard of living of less developed nations (see the third and fourth columns of table 6.6). Independent of that, being an "active part" internationalist or a self-described liberal tends to lead to favoring increased aid to Africa. Feelings about African countries, as measured on our thermometer scale, make a difference as well. Interestingly, the specific African countries that the public has in mind apparently span the continent geographically, politically, and religiously: feelings about Egypt, Nigeria, and South Africa each have an independent effect on opinions about aid.[62]

Table 6.6, the final piece of evidence we will present concerning purposive belief systems, deserves a close look. In certain respects the findings are unusual. Policy preferences concerning aid to Africa, like those related to trade with Cuba, are substantially rooted in individuals' personal and social

Table 6.6. Sources of support for increasing economic aid to African countries

Independent variable	Demographics only	Demographics + basic attitudes	Demographics + attitudes + goals	Goals + attitudes only
			Variables included in regression	
Education level	.20**	.15**	.11*	
African American	.10**	.09**	n.s.	
Married	−.10**	−.09**	−.07*	
Age	−.10**	−.13**	n.s.	
Income	.09*	.08*	.08+	
Employed	−.09*	−.11**	−.08+	
Female	.06*	.05+	n.s.	
Jewish	.06+	n.s.	n.s.	
Muslim	.06+	.07*	n.s.	
Hispanic	.05+	n.s.	n.s.	
Evangelical	n.s.	.10**	.09*	
Catholic	n.s.	.08*	n.s.	
"Active part" internationalist		.25**	.16**	.18**
Liberal self-rating		.14**	.10*	.09*
Democratic party identification		.10**	n.s.	n.s.
Goal: combat world hunger			.16**	.17**
Goal: improve standard of living of less developed countries			.11*	.11*
Thermometer rating of South Africa			.17**	.17**
Thermometer rating of Nigeria			.14**	.18**
Thermometer rating of Egypt			.10*	.10*
R	.316	.441	.616	.582
Adjusted R-squared	.086	.179	.349	.327
Degrees of freedom	911	911	467	467

Source: CCFR/GMF 2002 general public survey, combined in-person and telephone data set.

Note: Entries are standardized OLS regression coefficients. Controls as indicated. Demographic regressions included fourteen independent variables; except as indicated, only those with significant coefficients are displayed. All attitudinal variables included in regressions are shown.

$+p < .10$, $*p < .05$, $**p < .01$

characteristics. This has not been true of most other foreign policy issues we have investigated. Our demographics-only regression, reported in the first column of the table, indicates that (controlling for other characteristics) being highly educated, having a higher income, or being African American or female inclines people to favor increasing aid to African countries, while being older, married, or employed (all indicators of established positions in society) inclines people to prefer that aid be kept the same, reduced, or ended. There are also intriguing hints that their own minority or "outsider" status may lead individuals to favor increasing aid to African countries, where some of the poorest of the world's poor people live. Not only being African American or a woman, but perhaps also being Jewish, Muslim, or Hispanic independently inclines people to favor increasing aid to Africa. Once individuals' basic political orientations (e.g., evangelicals' conservatism) are controlled for, the humanitarian beliefs associated with being evangelical or Catholic also have a positive impact.

It is also unusual that some of these demographic factors (especially educational level, being married, and being an evangelical Protestant) still have independent effects on opinions when a number of political attitudes and beliefs are controlled for. And to an unusual extent, basic political orientations ("active part" internationalism and liberalism) continue to have significant independent effects on policy preferences when specific foreign policy goals and feelings about African countries are taken into account. Attitudes about aid to Africa appear to be solidly connected with domestic social and political cleavages.

But despite these unusual features, table 6.6 again supports the main points we have repeatedly made about purposive belief systems. When political attitudes are included in regressions, the demographic coefficients tend to drop in magnitude or lose significance altogether, indicating that demographic factors mostly work *through* political attitudes. That is, personal and social characteristics tend to shape political attitudes, which in turn affect specific policy preferences, just as we suggested in chapter 1. Here, as in our other comprehensive regression analyses, political attitudes generally have bigger coefficients than demographic factors. They always account for more of the variance in policy preferences: even in this case, nearly four times as much (contrast the adjusted R-squared figure in the first column of table 6.6 with that in the fourth column). When all fourteen demographic variables were dropped from the regression and only attitudes remained, virtually the same amount of variance was accounted for (compare the third and fourth columns). Most of the explanatory power, then, comes from specific, logically relevant goals and feelings.

In the case of aid to African countries, key factors include the highly relevant goals of alleviating world hunger and improving the standard of living of poor countries, as well as thermometer-measured feelings about Nigeria, South Africa, and Egypt. These feeling thermometer ratings undoubtedly reflect the extent of individuals' sympathy and fellow feeling for African people (clearly relevant to aid giving), but they are not necessarily just "emotional"; they may also capture such cognitive factors as awareness of Africans' material needs (awareness that is probably also reflected in the pro-aid impact of education) and perhaps belief in African countries' ability to make good use of aid. The pattern of relationships suggests that policy preferences are indeed embedded in *purposive* belief systems in a logically coherent fashion.

We do not want to overstate our argument, however. Even in the case of economic aid to Africa, where relevant goals and feelings and basic political orientations can account for an unusually high proportion of the variance in individuals' policy preferences (about one-third of it), the bulk of variation in expressed preferences remains unaccounted for, perhaps a product of measurement error or idiosyncrasy or randomness. We do not claim that most Americans hold tightly constrained, neatly and logically connected belief systems about foreign policy. Instead, we argue that (1) the extent of constraint is much greater than many scholars have thought; (2) the connections are often logical and purposive; and (3) relevant beliefs and attitudes often have sufficiently strong effects on individuals' policy preferences to account for the coherent *collective* belief systems that characterize a "rational public."[63]

Returning to the substance of Americans' opinions about foreign aid, an important issue concerns whether aid should be delivered bilaterally or multilaterally. When bilateral aid comes from a single powerful country, there is a danger that strategic political aims will overwhelm developmental effectiveness. But a plethora of separate bilateral aid arrangements involving various countries and nongovernmental organizations can result in excessive paperwork for recipient states, poor coordination among donors, and ineffectiveness. A possible solution is to have aid programs centrally administered by multilateral institutions like the World Bank's International Development Association, the African Development Fund, or the Asian Development Fund. The United States has made some nods in that direction.[64]

CCFR surveys have provided several indications of U.S. public support for multilateral approaches to foreign aid. In addition to the generally high esteem for the United Nations and cooperative internationalism described in chapter 5, the public in 2002 gave a neutral to warmish 51-degree average thermometer rating to the World Bank, the chief multilateral dispenser of economic development aid. A plurality—not quite a majority—of 49 percent to 39 percent also said that the World Bank "needs to be strengthened."

On the other hand, the International Monetary Fund (IMF) in 2002 received a slightly cooler, 48-degree average thermometer rating. Only 42 percent of respondents said the IMF needs to be strengthened, with 38 percent saying it does not. This put the IMF at the bottom of eight international organizations on the "needs to be strengthened" question (see chapter 5, table 5.5), and below eight other international organizations on the thermometer scale, a low position it retained in 2004.[65] It suggests that criticisms of the IMF's stringent loan conditions (insisting on "structural adjustment," including privatization of state-run enterprises, cutting budgets for social services, and the like) may have filtered through to the U.S. public.[66]

All in all, the data indicate that the American public is considerably more favorable toward humanitarian-oriented foreign aid than one might infer from the rhetoric of U.S. politicians and pundits, or from the tiny portion of the federal budget actually devoted to aid.

CONCLUSION

The main point of this chapter is that the American public favors certain policies—including increasing humanitarian foreign aid and restricting immigration and international trade—that have not been fully accepted by U.S. foreign policy decision makers. Particularly in the cases of trade and immigration, there is some evidence that the discrepancy results from the power of business corporations to influence policy in opposition to the public's wishes.[67]

These aspects of public opinion often upset elites, who argue that ordinary Americans are unaware of their true interests in free trade and immigration, both of which are said to contribute to lower prices and faster economic growth. The present authors are not unsympathetic to such arguments. But it is important not to let one's own economic position sway judgments of what is in the best interest of the country as a whole. The objective evidence indicates that many Americans do in fact have legitimate reasons to worry about the effects of trade and immigration on their domestic well-being. And the survey data show that citizens' policy preferences on these matters are in fact founded on clearly relevant goals and concerns.

On balance we believe that U.S. trade and immigration policy would better serve the interests of most Americans if decision makers paid more heed to the public's expressed wishes, at least to the extent of keeping the magnitude of immigration under control and ensuring that gains from trade are used to compensate those hurt by trade.

With less ambivalence we can say the same thing about aid policy. Closer adherence to the public's desires for less strategic and military aid—which has helped prop up some very distasteful regimes around the world—and for more humanitarian aid to Africa would surely have net benefits. It is hard to defend the fact that the richest country in the world is also the stingiest in terms of aiding the world's poor.

This chapter concludes our description of the collective foreign policy preferences of Americans in the military, political, and economic realms and our analysis of the ways in which individuals' preferences are embedded in purposive belief systems. In the next chapter we consider more systematically the extent to which the preferences of U.S. foreign policy decision makers differ from those of the general public, and the implications of those divergences for American democracy.

CHAPTER SEVEN

A Disconnect between Policy Makers and the Public?

With Lawrence R. Jacobs

Should foreign policy decision makers heed the views of the general public? Many observers have said no, asserting that the public lacks the ability to make sensible decisions on matters of national life and death; decision makers, they say, should pursue the national interest according to their own best judgment, even if that contradicts the wishes of the public. Others, including the present authors—bolstered by the evidence in previous chapters—are much more optimistic about the public's capacity to form reasonable opinions. We believe that democracy requires substantial responsiveness to what citizens want and that the results of pursuing a democratic foreign policy are likely to be good.

But even those who are skeptical about the wisdom of the public generally acknowledge that large discrepancies between what decision makers do and what the public wants are undesirable and potentially dangerous. Lack of public support for official foreign policy can send bad signals to international adversaries, constrain policy choices, upset policy continuity, and destabilize political leadership. Thus most skeptics about public opinion argue that it is important to "educate" the public, to bring their views into harmony with official policy.

Nearly all observers, then, agree on a key point: that foreign policy decision makers and the general public should not disagree—at least not often, deeply, and persistently. In the long run, at least, policy makers and the public should come into substantial agreement, either because policy makers respond to what citizens want or because they persuade citizens to agree with their judgments.

In this chapter, however, we will show with systematic data what various examples in earlier chapters have already suggested: that over the last thirty years there have been many substantial disagreements or gaps between foreign policy decision makers and the U.S. public. Indeed there has been something like a "disconnect" between the two. Moreover, there has been no discernible tendency for the gaps to narrow or disappear over time. We see this as presenting serious problems for democratic values and as constituting a challenge for formulating an effective foreign policy.

SHOULD POLICY MAKERS RESPOND TO PUBLIC OPINION?

Many observers and commentators insist that officials, in making foreign policy, need not generally respond to what ordinary citizens want. Classical realists, in particular, have argued that policy makers should exercise discretion independent of the public's preferences, because of the dire stakes involved, the need for secrecy and dispatch, and the necessity for specialized skills, knowledge, and experience. As we noted in chapter 1, for example, Hans Morgenthau spoke of an "unavoidable gap" between the kind of thinking required for the successful conduct of foreign policy and the kind used by the mass public, which (he said) embraced "simple moralistic and legalistic terms of absolute good and absolute evil" and erratically changed its views due to shifting "moods" and a hunger for "quick results" that "sacrifice tomorrow's real benefit."[1]

Similarly, Walter Lippmann warned that the "public opinion of the masses cannot be counted upon to apprehend regularly and promptly the reality of things." The public, he asserted, simply did not have the "kind of knowledge—not to speak of an experience and seasoned judgment—which cannot be had by glancing [at media reports]." Lippmann concluded that public opinion had "shown itself to be a dangerous master of decisions when the stakes are life and death" and was "deadly to the very survival of the state as a free society."[2] George Kennan agreed that "public opinion . . . can be easily led astray into areas of emotionalism and subjectivity which make it a poor and inadequate guide for national action." He concluded that "a good deal of our trouble seems to have stemmed from the extent to which the executive has felt itself beholden to . . . the erratic and subjective nature of public reaction to foreign policy questions."[3]

Our view is quite different. For one thing, Americans' opinions about foreign policy simply do not now (if they ever did) fit these pessimistic characterizations. The "mood theory" of an erratic public opinion has been thoroughly discredited.[4] Increasingly, scholars have concluded that the problem of meager knowledge among most average citizens need not prevent *collective* public opinion from being generally stable and consistent and reflecting the best available information. This is so because citizens are able to use heuristics and cues from well-informed people to form sound opinions, and also because random variations in individuals' opinions (so long as they are independent of each other) tend to cancel out in the aggregate.[5]

We believe that the evidence presented so far in this book supports and extends a "rational public" view of Americans' opinions concerning foreign policy. Three decades of Chicago Council on Foreign Relations surveys do not reveal a moody, erratic public opinion. Far from it; they display very substantial continuity. The goals respondents have deemed most important, and policy options they have favored, have remained much the same for a long time. The public has consistently emphasized key issues related to security and justice, among others nuclear arms control and nonproliferation, protection of Americans' jobs, and combating world hunger. Moreover, when collective opinions have changed, they have done so in reasonable ways, in response to changed world circumstances, such as the end of the Cold War or the rise of international terrorism. We see no sign of Morgenthau's erratic "mood" changes.

Nor do we see evidence of Kennan's "emotionalism and subjectivity." The American public tends to draw sharp distinctions among policy alternatives (favoring humanitarian foreign aid, for example, while opposing military and strategic aid, and distinguishing clearly among different countries or regions). Collective opinions are mostly consistent with each other, forming a reasonably coherent whole that reflects shared beliefs and values. Moreover, we have seen that *individuals'* opinions tend to reflect, in a purposive or instrumental fashion, the values they hold, the goals they seek, and the threats they perceive.

In our judgment, the findings of stable, consistent, and coherent collective public opinion point toward a relatively populistic brand of democratic theory that calls upon elected government officials (and those they appoint) to respond to the policy preferences of the citizenry. To allow officials simply to ignore what the public wants would risk ignoring values that their constituents hold dear. To assume that officials always know best—despite copious examples of error and miscalculation, from Vietnam to Iraq—would be more dangerous than listening to the public. And it would be undemocratic.

To be sure, an alternative line of democratic theory, represented by Edmund Burke, Joseph Schumpeter, and Giovanni Sartori, argues that officials should exercise their own judgment, restrained only by knowing that they will be held accountable to the citizenry in periodic, competitive elections; this may bring about responsiveness to "latent" or "anticipated" (rather than current) public opinion. We are more persuaded by Robert Dahl and others who advocate a high degree of responsiveness to citizens' deliberative policy preferences. But in any case, even looser sorts of democratic theory prescribe eventual harmony between leaders and public.[6]

A number of international relations scholars have pointed out that, as a practical matter, officials must pay *some* attention to public opinion. One

possible explanation for "democratic peace" (the phenomenon that democratic countries rarely fight each other), for example, may be that elected officials calculate that going to war requires broad public support if they are
to avoid electoral punishment.[7] Some students of American foreign policy
appreciate that public support and society-wide legitimacy provide the
foundation for stable and effective foreign policy.[8] And a large body of literature has indicated that officials do in fact respond to public opinion, at least
to some extent.[9]

Even the realists generally recognize the importance of public support
in bolstering the country's willingness to bear financial and other costs
of diplomatic and military action. For this reason they advocate efforts by
leaders to change or "educate" public opinion. Morgenthau, for example,
argued that government officials must "marshal public opinion" to secure
public approval for the policies that best serve the country's interests. It is
the "historic mission of the government" to provide "informed and responsible leadership." "[The] government must realize," he emphasized, "that it
is the leader and not the slave of public opinion." In his view, public opinion
is not a "static thing" but a "dynamic, ever changing entity" that leaders
"continuously creat[e] and recreat[e]." [10]

Persuasive efforts of the sort that Morgenthau advocated, if effective,
should eventually produce a high degree of harmony between foreign policy leaders and the general public. Thus practically everyone, including populistic democrats, "trustee"-style democrats, and classical realists, agrees
that it is desirable that foreign policy leaders and ordinary citizens should
end up in substantial agreement on the kinds of foreign policies that the
nation should pursue. This brings us to the question we will attempt to answer in this chapter: To what extent do foreign policy decision makers and
the U.S. public actually agree or disagree?

STUDYING "GAPS" BETWEEN DECISION MAKERS
AND THE PUBLIC

In previous chapters we have mentioned a number of apparent disagreements between actual U.S. foreign policy and the policies that majorities of
Americans say they want, such as participation in international agreements
concerning global warming, a comprehensive nuclear test ban, the prohibition of land mines, and the International Criminal Court. But are such
discrepancies unusual? How often do they occur?

An effective way to assess the size and frequency of gaps between policy
makers and the public is to compare their responses to identically worded
survey questions concerning their preferences on a broad set of foreign policy alternatives. Fortunately, each of the eight CCFR studies between 1974

and 2002 involved a survey of elite "foreign policy leaders" (including decision makers in the executive branch, the House of Representatives, and the U.S. Senate) as well as the general public surveys we have analyzed in previous chapters. Many of the same questions were asked of both leaders and the public, so we are able to select actual decision makers from the "leader" sample and compare their responses—on hundreds of international economic, defense, and diplomatic issues—with those of the general public.[11]

These data have both strengths and limitations. The decision makers surveyed were not randomly selected; respondents were chosen from institutional positions with foreign policy responsibilities, more often middle-level bureaucrats and members of Congress than the very top decision makers in the White House and the Department of Defense. The number of government officials interviewed in a given year was not very large (averaging about seventy-eight).[12] The samples of policy makers do add up across surveys, however, to more than six hundred respondents. And they have the advantage of being drawn in a consistent manner across years, because of continuity in survey organizations and research teams as well as conscious efforts to produce comparable data.

The most crucial advantage of using these survey data is that they permit us to make precise, direct comparisons of policy preferences between policy makers and citizens, using their responses to identical questions asked at the same time. Previous researchers have found it very difficult to devise measures of foreign policy and public opinion that are directly comparable with each other. They have often struggled to match polls of the mass public with some kind of indicator of (or sometimes just a subjective judgment about) government policy. To be sure, our data on policy makers' expressed preferences are not inevitably indicative of actual policy. But close scrutiny of the data indicates that policy makers' responses have usually reflected the positions and actions of the institutions in which they hold office and that rectification of any discrepancies would tend to strengthen rather than weaken our findings of extensive gaps between policy makers and public.[13] We believe that the problem of possible slippage between these survey responses and actual foreign policy is outweighed by the enormous advantage of being able to obtain precise, quantitative measures of differences of opinion between citizens and policy makers.

The scope and duration of the parallel surveys enable us to make a number of different kinds of comparisons. In addition to judging overall levels of agreement or disagreement between policy makers and the public, we can compare levels of agreement in different time periods, for distinct types of policy issues, for sets of policy makers from different institutions, and for different institutional contexts (e.g., unified versus divided party control of the executive and legislative branches of government).

Each quadrennial pair of parallel surveys included, on average, 145 common survey items—that is, 145 policy-relevant questions that were asked, with identical wording, both of policy makers and of the general public—for a total of 1,153 common questions over the years.[14]

In addition to tracking the extent of policy-opinion agreement or disagreement for all issues in a given survey (and for the whole twenty-eight-year period), we separately investigated the level of agreement for each of three critical policy domains, which roughly correspond to the three previous chapters of this book: diplomatic policy, defense policy, and economic policy. The diplomatic area includes questions concerning relations with other countries and with international organizations as well as general evaluations of America's vital interests and foreign policy goals; defense questions deal with topics including the recruitment and deployment of troops, military aid, and the development, procurement, and transfer to other countries of military hardware); and the economic category encompasses issues related to trade, tariffs, and the protection and promotion of American jobs and businesses.[15] We also separately calculated opinion differences between the general public and three distinct groups of policy makers: officials in the House of Representatives, in the Senate, and in the administration.

We used two different types of measures to compare the preferences of policy makers with those of the public. First, we calculated the frequency of *disagreements* between the two groups as a proportion of the total number of common items. For each survey question, the percentage of policy makers taking a particular stand was subtracted from the percentage of the public taking that same stand ("don't know" or "no opinion" responses were excluded), and any difference of 10 percentage points or more was taken as constituting a "disagreement." [16] We then counted the number of such disagreements and reported them as a percentage of the total number of common items. For instance, in 2002, we found 100 survey questions on which the public and policy makers disagreed by 10 percentage points or more, out of a total of 149 common items, producing a proportion of disagreement of 67 percent. We also calculated proportions of disagreements for subsets of policy makers and for the three separate policy areas. For instance, the proportion for diplomatic policy in 1974 was 75 percent—45 disagreements out of a total of 60 common items for this policy domain.

Our second summary measure is the proportion of survey items on which a disagreement of 10 points or more existed and *majorities* of policy makers took positions opposite to those of majorities of the public. For instance, in 2002 a majority of policy makers disagreed with a majority of the public on 39 of 149 common items, or 26 percent of them. From the perspective of democratic theory, the frequency of these *opposing majorities* may be of particular interest. We believe, however, that the frequency of disagreements between the preferences of policy makers and citizens is also important, especially because (as we will see shortly) they are often quite large.

NUMEROUS AND PERSISTENT DISAGREEMENTS

The data indicate that, over a thirty-year period, foreign policy decision makers in the administration, the U.S. Senate, and the House of Representatives have frequently and persistently disagreed with the views of the U.S. public. In short, there appear to be many gaps: a substantial "democratic deficit," if not a disconnect between leaders and public.

Table 7.1 shows that during the whole 1974–2002 period, policy makers disagreed with the public by 10 percentage points or more on fully 73 percent—nearly three-quarters—of the 1,153 survey questions that both leaders and citizens were asked. Data from each of the eight pairs of surveys indicate that the frequency of leader-opinion divergence has been fairly consistent over time, ranging only from 67 percent, in 2002, to 78 percent, in 1990.

Not only have there been a large number of foreign policy issues on which decision makers and the public have differed, but the magnitude of those differences (as measured by percentage point differences in support levels between the two groups) have been sizeable. As table 7.2 indicates, in 80 percent of the disagreements over the three-decade period, the level of support among decision makers has differed from that among the public by 15 percentage points or more. In more than half of the disagreements (58 percent) the levels differed by 20 points or more. Moreover, the magnitudes of disagreement have been fairly consistent across all eight surveys. In every single pair of surveys, more than half the disagreements between decision makers and public involved 20 percentage points or more. The magnitude and consistency of these differences is remarkable. Changing counting rules or cutoff points, or making other methodological adjustments, does not meaningfully affect the results. It is hard to avoid the conclusion that there has been a rather wide gulf, on many issues, between the foreign policy preferences of government officials and those of the American citizenry.

Of course some might argue that gaps of 20 or even 30 or 40 percentage points might not matter, so long as both the public and the leaders ended up on the same side of each issue. If 90 percent of policy makers but "only" 60 percent of the general public favored some particular policy, why should anyone worry about the difference? We do not agree with this perspective, because we believe that a high or low percentage of support for some policy on a survey question with limited choices (often only two choices) usually reveals something about what specific policy the *average* person would

Table 7.1. Frequency of disagreements between policy makers and the public

	1974	1978	1982	1986	1990	1994	1998	2002	All years
Percentage of opinion items on which officials and public disagreed	75	74	73	68	78	72	70	67	73
	(184/246)	(117/158)	(105/143)	(63/93)	(106/136)	(83/116)	(78/112)	(100/149)	(836/1,153)

Note: A disagreement is defined as an instance in which the response frequencies of policy makers differed by 10 percentage points or more from those of the general public when asked identically worded questions. Numbers of disagreements and of common opinion items are given in parentheses.

Table 7.2. Magnitude of disagreements between policy makers and the public (%)

Size of disagreement	1974	1978	1982	1986	1990	1994	1998	2002	All years
10–14 points	21	15	16	21	26	17	28	20	20
15–19 points	24	21	28	16	18	19	19	23	22
20–24 points	21	20	14	17	15	20	13	11	17
25–29 points	15	12	10	16	15	17	10	15	14
30–34 points	5	14	5	13	8	5	13	9	8
35–39 points	5	9	13	6	5	5	10	6	7
40–44 points	3	4	3	3	2	10	3	7	4
45–49 points	3	2	3	2	8	4	3	3	3
50 points or more	2	4	8	6	2	4	1	6	4
Total	100	100	100	100	100	100	100	100	100
Number of common items	(184)	(117)	(105)	(63)	(106)	(83)	(78)	(100)	(836)
5 points or more	79	85	84	79	74	83	72	80	80
20 points or more	54	64	56	63	56	64	53	57	58

Note: Entries are percentages of all disagreements between policy makers and the public that had a given size in terms of percentage point differences in response frequencies by the two groups.

favor. We believe, for example, that if 90 percent of policy makers but only 60 percent of citizens favor "increasing" foreign aid to a particular country, the average policy maker is likely to favor a significantly larger increase than the average citizen does. Even if majorities seem to agree, therefore, we consider percentage point gaps to represent meaningful differences about precisely what sorts of foreign policies the United States should pursue.[17]

Still, the idea of a majority occupies a special place in democratic theory. It seems important to check how often *majorities* of foreign policy decision makers disagree with majorities of citizens on these survey questions. When we do so, we see that the answer is, *rather often*. Table 7.3 shows that over the 1974–2002 period as a whole, majorities of policy makers took stands opposed by majorities of the general public on 26 percent—about one-quarter—of the 1,153 common items. This has been true year in and year out; there has not been a great deal of variation, in the different Chicago Council surveys, between the lowest proportion of opposing majorities (20 percent, in 1986) and the highest (31 percent, in 1998).

To be sure, one could emphasize that the glass is three-quarters full rather than pointing out that it is one-quarter empty. But we consider the fact that most public officials say they want to go in the *opposite direction* from what most members of the public want, on so many important foreign policy

Table 7.3. Frequency of opposing majorities between policy makers and public

	1974	1978	1982	1986	1990	1994	1998	2002	All years
Percentage of common items with opposing majorities	28	22	27	20	27	28	31	26	26
	(68/246)	(34/158)	(38/143)	(19/93)	(37/136)	(33/116)	(35/112)	(39/149)	(303/1,153)

Note: An "opposing majority" is an instance in which the response frequencies of policy makers and the public differed by 10 percentage points or more on identically worded questions and majorities of the two groups took opposite sides of the issue. Entries are numbers of opposing majorities expressed as percentages of all opinion items asked of both groups. Numbers of opposing majorities and of common items are given in parentheses.

issues—including major issues of war and peace and economic relations—to be rather sobering. Neither democratic responsiveness nor education of the public by leaders seems to be functioning with anything close to perfection.

VARIATIONS IN CITIZEN-LEADER DISAGREEMENTS

Over the whole three-decade period, then, and in each of the eight separate CCFR studies, there have been substantial disagreements between policy makers and the general public. But has the extent of disagreement varied based on such factors as the partisan control of Congress and the White House, the type of policy maker, or the particular policy area? A series of more refined comparisons simply bolsters the case that a substantial and pervasive democratic deficit exists across the board.

Party control and divided government. Politicians are recruited and their careers are advanced by political parties; they often hold distinctive public philosophies that reflect the core ideas of their party. Which political party controls the legislative chambers and the White House, therefore, and whether there is unified or divided party government, might be expected to affect officials' responsiveness to the policy preferences of the mass public. To test this idea, we regrouped the proportions of citizen/official disagreements and opposed majorities in the CCFR studies according to whether, and to what extent, the legislative and executive branches were unified (with the president's political party controlling both chambers of Congress) or were divided at the time.

Contrary to expectation, neither measure of policy makers' disagreements with public opinion appears to be related to political control of the lawmaking branches. Partisan control of government was divided (that is, different parties controlled the presidency and at least one chamber of Congress) during both a low point (1986) *and* the high point (1990) of leader-opinion disagreements. The average proportion of disagreements between policy makers and public did not differ appreciably between the six instances of divided government (71 percent) and the two instances of unified government (73 percent). Likewise, the average proportion of opposing majorities has been very nearly the same in the six instances of divided government (27 percent) as in the two instances of unified government (25 percent).

Nor does the overall extent of leader-citizen disagreement appear to be related to *which* party controls the House and Senate, or by how big a margin. The two parties may tend to disagree with the public on different issues; we do not have enough cases to tell. But a substantial overall disparity between policy makers' preferences and those of citizens has been evident under different forms of political control and during both Democratic and

Republican presidencies. Unified Democratic governments appear to be no more or less responsive to citizens' wishes than divided governments with Republican presidents.

Variations by type of policy. Aggregate comparisons of the preferences of policy makers and the mass public might mask important variations by policy area. Policy makers might, for example, be more responsive to public opinion on issues that have direct pocketbook impacts on ordinary Americans, such as economic policies affecting jobs or trade. On the other hand, some international relations scholars have emphasized that economic considerations may motivate powerful interest groups (especially business groups) to influence policy making, perhaps outweighing the public. Or corporate interest groups may have such distinctive preferences on economic matters that even a moderate influence on policy would produce unusually big gaps with the public.[18] We explored such possibilities by breaking down our comparisons into three policy domains—economic, defense, and diplomatic.

Economic policies. There have indeed been some variations across issues. Table 7.4 indicates that policy makers' sharpest disconnect from public opinion does, as expected by some interest group analysts, occur in the economic realm, presumably because business corporations care most about economic policies, differ sharply from the public on many of them, and have substantial influence over what government does. The public-policy maker disagreement on economic issues averaged 81 percent across the eight surveys, reaching a remarkable peak of 95 percent disagreement in 1994. Likewise, table 7.5 indicates that majorities of policy makers and of the general public took opposite sides on fully one-third of all economic policy questions (33 percent), with a peak of 50 percent in 1994—a year in which the Democrats controlled both Congress and the presidency. Foreign policy gaps between officials and citizens are thoroughly bipartisan.[19]

Policy makers' divergence from the public on economic policy can be illustrated with a few specifics from that peak year. In 1994 officials departed

Table 7.4. Frequency of policy maker/public disagreements by policy type

Policy type	1974	1978	1982	1986	1990	1994	1998	2002	All years
Economic policy	89	73	86	79	75	95	68	77	81
Defense policy	65	80	83	66	90	74	52	49	70
Diplomatic policy	75	71	66	60	75	60	74	75	70

Note: Entries are percentages of common items within a given policy domain on which policy makers and the public differed by 10 percentage points or more.

Table 7.5. Frequency of opposing majorities by policy type

Policy type	1974	1978	1982	1986	1990	1994	1998	2002	All years
Economic policy	36	21	43	21	29	50	32	31	33
Defense policy	29	40	36	21	29	22	33	13	28
Diplomatic policy	23	13	19	20	21	21	29	32	22

Note: Entries are percentages of common items within a given policy domain on which majorities of policy makers took the opposite sides from majorities of the public.

from the majority of citizens who thought that the protection of American jobs should be a very important foreign policy goal (just 42 percent of officials versus 84 percent of the public). Large majorities of government officials bucked public opinion by favoring the elimination of tariffs (91 percent versus only 40 percent of the public) and judging that Europe genuinely practiced free trade (71 percent versus 48 percent). Officials were also much more certain that NAFTA was "mostly good" (91 percent versus 62 percent). Ordinary Americans ranked the threats of economic competition from Japan and Europe higher than did policy makers and were more disposed to cut back economic aid, both overall and to several specific countries (with the exception of those in Africa).

Although the economic policy gaps between decision makers and the public were especially sharp in 1994, similar patterns pervade all the surveys. Again and again, officials have disagreed with some of the public's key opinions that we described in chapter 6. Most importantly, officials have been much less concerned with the goal of protecting Americans' jobs, consistently one of the top-ranked goals in the public surveys. Officials have been much less receptive to tariffs, restrictions on immigration, and other measures that ordinary Americans see as related to job protection. In 2002, for example, many more members of the public than policy makers preferred to decrease even legal immigration (57 percent, compared to 8 percent), and more were alarmed about threats posed by population growth (45 percent to 18 percent) and globalization (33 percent to 17 percent). Year after year, foreign policy decision makers have also been much more ready than the public to spend tax money on foreign policy programs (especially foreign aid) and less eager to spend it on domestic programs like Social Security, medical care, and aid to education.

Defense policies. On average over the years, policy makers have not differed quite as often from the public on defense or diplomatic foreign policies as on economic ones, though average proportions of disagreement stand at 70 percent in both areas. Opposing majorities have also been less common, and only a little more frequent on defense issues (28 percent) than on diplomatic issues (22 percent). (See tables 7.4 and 7.5.)

But table 7.4 shows that policy makers were out of harmony with the public on defense issues to an unusually great extent in 1990, disagreeing on fully 90 percent of the common items. A large part of that divergence stemmed from policy makers' having concluded more quickly than the public that the Cold War was over and the Soviet Union no longer a threat, but that continued support for long-standing defense alliances remained important. For example, officials were substantially less inclined to evaluate the Soviet Union as a threat and more favorable toward cutting back defense spending, but were more supportive than the public of providing military aid and equipment to other countries and more willing to use troops to defend traditional allies. In addition, policy makers in 1990 were more supportive of using U.S. troops to counter both the actual Iraqi invasion of Kuwait (21 percent of the public rated that action as "excellent," compared with 49 percent of officials—among whom most opposition came from Congress, especially the House) and a hypothetical Iraqi invasion of Saudi Arabia (by a 92 percent to 67 percent margin).

The level of leader-citizen disagreement on defense issues dropped sharply, to only about one-half of all common items (52 percent and 49 percent) in 1998 and 2002, largely because both policy makers and the public favored strong defense in reaction to terrorist attacks. The frequency of opposed majorities on defense matters dropped to an all-time low of just 13 percent in 2002 (see table 7.5). Even then, however, significant gaps remained. For example, the public and policy makers disagreed about certain hawkish methods of combating terrorism (as we will see, they disagreed about several dovish or diplomatic methods as well): more citizens than officials favored assassination of suspected terrorist leaders (72 percent, compared to 59 percent) and racial profiling at airports (56 percent to 42 percent).

Over the years, the public has often been considerably more resistant than decision makers to the idea of using U.S. troops abroad (for example, in reaction to various hypothetical invasions; recall the data in chapter 4). That remained true in 2002. Some of this reluctance undoubtedly reflects public concern about risking the lives of U.S. troops, who are more often the sons, daughters, or friends of ordinary Americans than of public officials. In addition, however, the public appears more sensitive than officials to other costs of armed conflict, including harm to non-Americans. The public has also regularly been more opposed to military aid, and even to *selling* weapons abroad, than officials have.

Diplomatic policies. Disagreements between decision makers and the public have generally been least frequent (at least in terms of opposed majorities) in the diplomatic realm (see tables 7.4 and 7.5). Even there, however, substantial gaps have often occurred, especially reflecting greater support among the public than among officials for the United Nations, for negotiating with adversaries, and for treaties and agreements on arms control and other matters.

In 2002, when citizen/official disagreements were less frequent than usual on defense policy, tables 7.4 and 7.5 indicate that policy makers and the public disagreed unusually often on diplomatic matters. The public's strong multilateralism and support for international organizations and agreements, as we pointed out in chapter 5, contrasted rather sharply with the Bush administration's tendencies toward unilateralism. For example, government officials were much more supportive than the public of the general idea that the United States should "go it alone" (favored by 58 percent of officials versus 33 percent of the public) and considerably less supportive than the public of strengthening the United Nations (16 percent, compared to 58 percent) or participating in the Kyoto agreement on global warming (49 percent to 75 percent), the International Criminal Court (45 percent to 76 percent), or the Landmines Convention (56 percent to 80 percent). In the context of combating terrorism, more members of the public favored trying suspected terrorists in an International Criminal Court (86 percent did so, compared to 63 percent of policy makers), while government officials were more in favor of sharing intelligence information (95 percent of officials versus 60 percent of the public), improving relations with adversaries (99 percent to 85 percent), helping poor countries develop their economies (97 percent to 80 percent), and being evenhanded in the Palestinian-Israeli conflict (95 percent to 70 percent). (Note, however, that large majorities of both the public and the surveyed officials favored most of these dovish measures against terrorism.)

Although the degree to which policy makers disagree with citizens has varied somewhat across policy domains and over time, our most important finding remains the high overall extent and persistence of disagreement. It is striking to see in table 7.4 that, looking at the three clusters of diplomatic, economic, and defense issues across all eight surveys between 1974 and 2002, the proportion of disagreements between policy makers and the public dropped below two-thirds (66 percent) only five out of a possible twenty-four times. Not once did the proportion of disagreements fall below 49 percent (that is, about half) of the questions that citizens and policy makers were asked in common.

Different institutions: House, Senate, and administration. Realist and rational-choice theories of international relations tend to treat governments as "unitary actors," on the assumption that all relevant policy makers, evaluating the same set of international conditions, generally adopt similar policy positions. Our samples for separate groups of policy makers are rather small, but we are able to use the data at least in a suggestive fashion to examine the policy preferences of three different sets of policy makers—officials from the House of Representatives, the Senate, and the administration—for evidence bearing on the unitary actor assumption. As is often the case with elite interviewing, the prominence of the respondents is critical; the officials studied are not necessarily statistically representative, but their responses do indicate the preferences of authoritative policy makers in their respective branches of government.[20]

Our data suggest that there have been some significant differences among different sets of policy makers on certain critical foreign policy issues. Data from 2002 illustrate these differences. Members of the House of Representatives were a bit more supportive than senators and administration officials of "go[ing] it alone" with respect to Iraq (by 7 and 14 percentage points, respectively) but also substantially more supportive of the Kyoto agreement (by 23 and 28 points). Administration officials were more supportive than House and Senate members of using nuclear weapons (by 17 and 7 points, respectively).

Meanwhile, senators, with their crucial treaty-ratification responsibilities, were *less* supportive than members of the House or administration officials of the treaty banning land mines (by 28 and 31 points, respectively) and of participating in the International Criminal Court (by 16 and 14 points), but *more* supportive of requiring standards for working and environmental conditions as part of international trade agreements.

These results are suggestive of important differences among policy makers. On many issues, certain clusters of policy makers adopt positions that are close to those of the public, while others do not. For instance, Senate officials almost exactly matched the public's views on requiring working standards in international trade agreements, while the administration was some distance away. The connection or nonconnection of public views to those of policy makers is undoubtedly complicated by differences among sets of government officials, each of which typically exerts a conditional veto power over policy. (Sometimes an absolute veto, as in the case of senators and treaties.) For the same reason, foreign policy decision making may often be more complicated than "unitary actor" theories envision.

CONVERGENCE OVER TIME BETWEEN POLICY MAKERS AND THE PUBLIC?

Democratic theorists and analysts of foreign relations often emphasize the temporal dimension of policy makers' relationships with public opinion. Classical realists expect policy makers to "educate" the public when it disagrees with them, changing citizens' stands over time so that they come to support the government's position. Some democratic theorists suggest that policy makers should respond to "latent" or *anticipated* public opinion: that is, they ought sometimes to adopt positions that are currently unpopular, anticipating that future public opinion—based on further experience and information—will move toward their view.[21] Other democratic theorists expect officials to respond to the public only in the long run, gradually moving toward the public's views.

All these lines of thought share the expectation that, over time, disagreements between policy makers and the public should diminish. But we have already seen reasons to doubt this prediction. As tables 7.1 and 7.3 indicated, there has been no discernible tendency for the frequency of disagreements between policy makers and the public, or the frequency of opposing majorities, to decrease over the three decades of Chicago Council on Foreign Relations surveys. The frequency and size of gaps between leaders and citizens have remained much the same.

Still, that finding is not inconsistent with the possibility that gaps on particular policy issues generally narrow over time, and that those issues are then replaced by new ones, again entailing big initial gaps, which then diminish in their turn. In order to test the convergence hypothesis more directly, we need to look at what happens over time with respect to individual issues. We therefore examined a set of specific issues on which we have extensive data over time, important, highly salient issues on which the preferences of government officials differed from those of the public (at some point in time) by especially large amounts—by 30 to 50 percentage points. Presumably on issues like these, involving potentially severe disjunctions between citizens' wishes and public policy and thus risks of electoral retribution, policy makers would pay special attention to correctly anticipating future opinion, or would be prodded into responsiveness, or would devote special efforts to persuading the public.

Table 7.6 shows the differences (in percentage points), for each CCFR survey, between the proportions of ordinary Americans and the proportions of government officials taking a given position on half a dozen headline issues, including job protection, the use of U.S. troops in hypothetical battles abroad, and strengthening the United Nations. Table 7.6 offers little or no evidence of convergence between policy makers and the public over time. In fact, looking just at the starting and ending points of each time series (1974 and 2002), in each of the six cases there was a net *increase* in the magnitude of opinion difference between policy makers and the public. On the three troop-use questions this increase was quite substantial, going from no significant gap at all to a gap of 28 to 51 percentage points. On two of the questions (job protection and economic aid) the increase is too small to take very seriously, but there is certainly no indication of convergence.

Table 7.6. Magnitude of differences over time between the public and policy makers on selected issues

	1974	1978	1982	1986	1990	1994	1998	2002
Protecting U.S. jobs very important foreign policy goal	47	44	38	30	49	42	33	52
Favor economic aid	−38	−33	−41	−32	−39	−35	−41	−41
Favor U.S. troop use if North Korea invaded South Korea	no gap	−37	−53	−53	−46	−40	−50	−51
Favor U.S. troop use if Arab forces invaded Israel	no gap	no gap	−22	−40	−29	−27	−27	−28
Favor U.S. troop use if China invaded Taiwan	no gap	no gap	no gap	not asked	not asked	not asked	−34	−28
Strengthening UN very important foreign policy goal	30	36	27	38	45	44	21	42

Note: Entries represent the percentage of the public taking a particular position on an issue minus the percentage of policy makers taking the same position. Positive figures indicate greater support among the public than among policy makers for the stated position; negative figures mean a higher proportion of policy makers favored it.

Bear in mind that these issues were chosen for the existence of large gaps *at some point* (any point) in a time series. If anticipatory responsiveness *or* delayed responsiveness *or* education of the public were working well, presumably the largest gaps would tend to occur toward the beginnings of the time series (before those processes had time to work), not toward the ends. To be sure, one can pick through table 7.6 and find some instances of citizen-leader differences declining from one survey to the next, but in every case these instances were counterbalanced by subsequent increases. On these important issues, then, there is no sign that the views of policy makers and the public have converged, even over a nearly thirty-year period. Leader-citizen differences seem to be quite persistent.

These findings, though based on just a few cases, look somewhat damaging to the theories of classical realists like Morgenthau, who have urged the makers of foreign policy to "mobilize" public support. If officials have tried to do so in these cases, they have not had much success. Our findings also cast doubt upon whether U.S. foreign policy decision makers always abide by even the looser forms of democratic theory. They do not seem to have narrowed these wide gaps between themselves and the public, either by gradual responsiveness to public opinion or by correctly anticipating that public opinion would come into harmony with their own views.

CAUSES AND CONSEQUENCES OF CITIZEN-LEADER GAPS

Our evidence of frequent and persistent disagreements between influential makers of foreign policy and the U.S. public challenges the optimism of classical realists regarding the efficacy of leaders at educating or persuading the public. It also casts doubt on others' claims that public opinion strongly constrains foreign policy making. In fact, government officials' preferences (and, we believe, the foreign policies they pursue) are often out of step with public opinion. Often they remain out of step for years or decades. Why have there been so many large, persistent gaps?

As we see it, the explanations fall into two groups. First, the gaps are not avoided or closed by policy makers more fully *responding* to the preferences of the public for the reasons sketched at the end of chapter 5: highly unequal distributions of economic and other resources among citizens, which translate into unequal political influence; the costs of political information (especially high concerning foreign policy), which muffle the public's voice and permit distortions and misrepresentations by officials and other elites; a two-party system that does not mobilize lower-income citizens, permits bipartisan collusion, narrows voting choices, and gives power to party activists and money givers with extreme views; noncompetitive elections that blunt the power of citizens; electoral rules that discourage and bias public participation; and influence by organized interest groups, especially large business corporations that often push for economic policies opposed by the public. Second, gaps are not closed by officials "educating" or *persuading* the public because education campaigns are very difficult and usually not very effective. Indeed they are sometimes not even attempted, perhaps because they are not expected to succeed.

Here we will discuss the reasons for lack of democratic responsiveness under two general rubrics: (1) the ability of decision makers to get away with nonresponsiveness without much fear of electoral retribution, and (2) the fact that competing influences often push them away from doing what the public wants. We will then turn to the limits of educating or persuading the public.

The ease of ignoring the public. Vote-seeking politicians undoubtedly do have *some* motivation to respond to public opinion on foreign policy. The public perceives differences between candidates on foreign policies, and these perceptions tend to affect their evaluations of the candidates.[22] Moreover, some international developments regularly impinge on the daily lives of Americans, as is evident in the public's strong support for protecting jobs and its alarm about immigration.

But electoral incentives for policy responsiveness can be muffled or evaded. As Richard Fenno and others remind us, politicians use "explanations" to "develo[p] the leeway for activity undertaken in Washington" and to dodge retribution by voters as they pursue their own policy goals. Lawmakers may also take advantage of arcane legislative procedures and the sheer number and diversity of issues to obscure their responsibility for costly decisions.[23] The executive branch can use its information control to conceal or misrepresent what it is doing abroad. This diminishes the ability of voters to hold officials accountable.

Foreign policy presents a special set of conditions that may particularly blunt electoral incentives for officeholders to engage in policy responsiveness. Although many citizens hold meaningful attitudes about foreign policies and know the positions of candidates, the relative certainty and intensity of public attitudes, and the clarity of their perceptions on foreign policy, may generally be weaker than those pertaining to such domestic policies as health care and job creation. Thus citizens may be less prone to insist on responsiveness and more apt to defer to the executive. Moreover, prevailing interpretations of the U.S. Constitution, combined with the executive's control over information and the nature of U.S. institutional arrangements, may encourage congressional and judicial deference as well to unilateral presidential actions on foreign affairs, and especially on national security issues.[24]

Being shielded from voter retribution, then, may enable even electorally mindful politicians to slight the preferences of the mass public and instead respond to the intense preferences of well-organized interest groups, activists, and money givers. The diffuse and uncertain threat posed by foreign policy–oriented voters may often be less intimidating (and may in fact have less impact on officials' electoral success) than concentrated pressure and tangible threats of retribution from party activists, interest groups, financial contributors, and businesses threatening disinvestment from the United States. A resulting "bias in representation," in which business groups often prevail, is suggested by a substantial body of research in international relations and is consistent with our evidence of large and persistent leader-public gaps.[25]

Politicians' deviations from the public's wishes are apparently facilitated by a tendency for politicians to misperceive (or perhaps rationalize) what those wishes are. Steven Kull and I. M. Destler have shown that members of Congress often insist that ordinary Americans hold opinions that they do not in fact hold: a pervasive isolationism, for example; opposition to multilateral peacekeeping operations; opposition to all foreign aid. Such misperceptions can conveniently allow politicians to portray themselves—even to think of themselves—as responding to the public when they are not actually doing so. The misperceptions tend to persist even when officials are confronted with strong evidence to the contrary, including surveys of opinion in their own districts.[26] The 2004 CCFR study confirmed and extended these findings. When "foreign policy leaders" were asked where they thought the U.S. public stood on eleven different issues, they correctly perceived what a majority of the public favored in only two of the eleven cases. Most leaders grossly underestimated public support for collective decision making within the UN, giving the UN the power to tax, participating in UN peacekeeping operations and in international agreements such the ICC and the Kyoto Protocol, and complying with adverse WTO decisions.[27]

Competing influences on policy makers. The leeway that decision makers have to ignore the public is important because they often have incentives to do so: incentives to respond instead to a variety of other influences. These include the organized interest groups, party activists, and campaign contributors we have mentioned. They also include the views of pundits and foreign policy "experts," and policy makers' own values and ideologies.

As we have noted, several past studies of relationships between public opinion and the making of foreign policy have indicated that the public has substantial influence on policy. But few of these studies took explicit account of alternative hypotheses or possible competing factors, so the findings may be spurious. That is, the apparent impact of public opinion may simply reflect the fact that the public sometimes agrees with the wishes of other actors who carry the real weight with policy makers. Indeed, when Jacobs and Page included the preferences of competing actors in a regression analysis they found that business executives and foreign policy experts (themselves probably influenced by organized interests) had a big effect on foreign policy decision makers, but the influence of the public was barely discernible.[28]

Failure to "educate" or persuade the public. Our second type of explanation for the persistence of large gaps between the views of policy makers and the public involves the failure of decision makers to bring ordinary Americans' foreign policy preferences into line with their own preferences through education or persuasion. Classical realists appear to be wrong about the ease of "educating" the public. Or, if they are right, leaders do not make sufficient efforts at education to close the many large gaps we have observed.

There are reasons to believe that such persuasive efforts face serious obstacles. The public's collective policy preferences, including its foreign policy views, have been found to be generally stable, rarely changing or fluctuating by large margins except in response to world events.[29] The institutional context of democratic states may be especially inhospitable and resistant to government-initiated political education because of the difficulty of sending clear and coherent messages for the public to heed. Divisions among policy makers may often produce multiple, competing messages aimed at the public. Professional norms, legal protections, and commercial pressures within the media encourage the press to collect and circulate information that challenges the messages even of presidents on contentious policies.[30]

True, one can find examples in which unified, persistent, and energetic efforts by officials appear to have shifted public opinion. This was probably the case in the run-up to the U.S. invasion of Iraq, when the Bush administration overcame opposition to the war by arguing that Saddam Hussein's Iraq posed an imminent threat to the United States (particularly because of an allegedly reconstituted nuclear weapons program and alleged ties to al Qaeda terrorists), that past UN resolutions justified U.S. action, and that a multilateral "coalition of the willing" had been assembled. But such persuasive successes can prove temporary, if based on shaky evidence and not confirmed by clearly positive results. In any case, campaigns of that kind require large amounts of time and effort. Neither attempts nor successes of that sort are common. Morgenthau and other classical realists may have significantly underestimated the obstacles facing presidents and other government officials who would like to mobilize public support behind policies that they have formulated independently of, or contrary to, the public's wishes.

By the same token, we believe that the *manipulation* of public opinion— in the sense of using false or misleading arguments or information to turn the public against its true interests (the preferences it would hold if information were accurate and complete)—is also very difficult. This is a key reason why we consider collective public opinion generally to offer a useful guide to decision making: it amounts to something more than just an echo chamber for elite wishes.[31] Indeed the very existence and persistence of gaps between public and official opinion argues for the largely autonomous, "authentic" nature of public opinion. There seem to be two main types of exceptions. In certain real or manufactured international "crisis" situations in which the executive has strong information control and bipartisan backing (as in the Iraq case), it may be able to manipulate the public into consent— short-run consent, at least—to its policies. In certain other, longer-run situations, unified elites—working through compliant media, foundations, think tanks, and academia—may be able eventually to shift the public's views. But the shortfall of decades' worth of efforts to convince the citizenry of the virtues of completely free international trade suggests that even here, there are limits.

Turning to the consequences of gaps, we see them as mostly negative.

Should wise leaders override an uninformed citizenry? Even if the realists are wrong about the ease of "mobilizing" or "educating" the public, they might still be correct in seeing gaps as just a practical problem, not a normative one—not, that is, a reason to object to policies that contravene the public's wishes. Perhaps public opinion on foreign policy issues is often so ill-informed that it is not worth paying attention to. Perhaps decision makers more accurately perceive what is in the national interest, knowing better (for example) how to advance the country's position in the international system by maximizing its military strength relative to its competitors'. Perhaps the public's lack of knowledge and experience, and its inability to set aside emotions and rationally size up the country's interests, make it essential to insulate some government decisions from influence by the citizenry.

We cannot entirely dismiss this view of gaps. The American public is not always right. As we have noted, for example, some of the public's disagreements with policy makers over defense policies at the beginning of the 1990s probably resulted from officials more quickly and accurately understanding the implications of the end of the Cold War. We have also seen that the public has held some gross misperceptions about the nature and extent of U.S. foreign aid. In these and certain other cases, policy makers may have been right and the expressed preferences of the public wrong. Some gaps may be explicable on these grounds and may therefore be less normatively troubling.

But these, we believe, are exceptions. A theme of this book has been that Americans' collective policy preferences concerning foreign affairs have generally been sensible, coherent, and logically related to a reasonable set of foreign policy goals. Often public opinion reflects the best available information. There is no guarantee that officials can do better than the public itself at discerning or defining the national interest. Instead, officials may go off on mistaken or self-interested ventures. We believe that gaps between the preferences of citizens and those of decision makers often reflect differences in the *values* and the *objective interests* of the two groups (differing reactions to job losses or to military casualties, for example), rather than differences in information, knowledge, or expertise.

This interpretation is bolstered by our findings about the very limited impact of levels of information or of formal education upon citizens' foreign policy preferences. If officials' superior wisdom were the main source of gaps between their policy preferences and those of the general public, one would expect that the most highly educated and best informed citizens would hold different policy preferences—preferences more like those of officials—than their fellow citizens do. But we have found that education and information (controlling for other factors) have had only sporadic effects, mainly related to the evaluations of obscure policies and low-salience foreign countries. When we controlled for income, ethnicity, religion, gender, and other demographic characteristics, again and again we found that formal education had no more than moderate effects on policy preferences. The effects it did have generally diminished greatly or vanished when we took account of ideology (especially "active part" internationalism) and specific foreign policy goals. That is, the effects of education on foreign policy preferences seemed often to work through individuals' *goals, values,* and *ideologies*—presumably because levels of formal education reflect people's social positions and their material self-interests—not through information or expertise.

Why, in a democracy, should the goals and values of officials or high-status individuals count for more than those of other citizens? When interests differ, political equality would seem to be an essential characteristic of democracy. Who can be better trusted to define the "public interest" than the public itself?

Dangers of gaps between officials and citizens. Returning to practical rather than normative issues, two serious risks are created by any persistent tendency of policy makers to ignore public opinion or to exaggerate the ease of molding it. First, policy that extensively and consistently flouts public opinion goes out on a shaky limb. The greatest concern of classical realists is not that citizen-leader disconnects signal a failure of democracy but that they may cause the public to oppose and impede the government's conduct of foreign policy. Numerous large citizen-leader disagreements may increase the risk that government officials will find, at some point, that they have committed the United States to a long-term military or diplomatic position that lacks public support and becomes the target of divisive domestic opposition.[32]

The case of the Johnson administration's handling of Vietnam is instructive. The U.S. public is sometimes accused of having become disillusioned with the war and having "deserted" the administration. Archival evidence indicates, however, that the Johnson administration closely monitored public opinion and, in important respects, quite deliberately turned its back on the preferences of most Americans from the very outset of military escalation. The public's turn against the Vietnam war should thus be seen not as a case of the public's deserting government officials but as the opposite: an example of policy makers' knowingly disregarding the public's preferences in the false expectation that they would eventually be able to "educate" the public to support their position.[33]

When officials adopt policies opposed by the public, they place American foreign policy on a weak foundation. Although it may take unusually strong electoral upheavals or social movements to actually overturn established policies, a sharp opinion-policy divergence means that policies that draw intense media coverage and become salient may elicit significant opposition, eroding long-term trust in government officials and institutions and perhaps leading to excessive gun-shyness with respect to future policies.

A second danger of opinion-policy disparities is that government officials may excessively inflate expectations in efforts to "mobilize" the public. Decisive leadership of the sort that Morgenthau and others recommend seems to call for the enunciation of clear, sweeping goals and optimistic visions. But if appealing rhetoric turns out to contrast with ambiguous and costly realities in the actual implementation of policy, the public may be deeply disappointed. President Johnson was caught in just this kind of painful dilemma. On the one hand, he was repeatedly urged by his aides to emphasize progress in Vietnam in order to discredit the "widespread impression . . . that the war may go on for years."[34] On the other hand, officials warned that the administration's optimistic promotion of its initiatives produced a "psychological escalation" that would inevitably be met by a "let down in the public's thinking" when the initiatives failed to clearly produce the promised objectives—peace or military victory.[35] Johnson and the country paid a steep price for this disillusionment.

Disillusionment of a similar—though, so far, milder—sort has resulted from the bloody and chaotic aftermath of the 2003 invasion of Iraq, in which many highly publicized prewar expectations have proved to be hollow: that American forces would be welcomed with flowers rather than resistance; that low and rapidly diminishing numbers of U.S. troops would be sufficient to keep order; that Iraqi oil money would pay for reconstruction; and so on. The political, economic, and social costs to the Bush administration and to the United States are likely to prove significant.

Given our findings, one might counsel public officials to take seriously the practical dangers of foreign policies endemically distant from the preferences of citizens.

A more democratic foreign policy. The chief point we want to make about gaps between public opinion and official policy is, however, a different one. The persistence over time of large gaps between policy makers and citizens makes clear that officials can, in fact, sometimes get away with ignoring the public's wishes for a long period. But we believe they should not generally do so.

To the extent that the public's collective preferences are based upon sound information but values or interests different from those of political leaders or influential interest groups (and we believe this is often the case), policy makers ought to pay more attention to the wishes of ordinary citizens. The resulting policies would be more democratic, more satisfying to more Americans, and (in many or most cases, we believe) more effective for the country as a whole.

To the extent that the American public is mistaken about certain matters, the proper course in a democracy is for officials not simply to defy the public's will and evade any negative consequences, but to ensure that better information is provided. This is not always easy to achieve but it is worth considerable effort. It is worth noting that some of the misinformation that has distorted certain of the public's policy preferences (concerning foreign aid, for example, or Iraq) has come from politicians and public officials themselves. To clear up popular misconceptions about foreign policy it would be helpful to raise the level of public rhetoric by politicians and others. In any event, we consider large and persistent gaps between the preferences or actions of policy makers and the wishes of ordinary citizens to be normatively very troubling.

CHAPTER EIGHT

Conclusion: Foreign Policy and Democracy

Our findings that the American public has stable, consistent, and sensible preferences concerning a wide range of foreign policies, and that those preferences are based on coherent, logical, purposive belief systems, contradict a good deal of conventional wisdom. But they support the main argument of this book: that the officials who make U.S. foreign policy should pay more attention to what the public wants.

As we have seen, the evidence from thirty years of opinion surveys makes clear that most Americans want U.S. foreign policy to pursue goals involving security of domestic well-being and international justice, not just security from attack. They want to do so chiefly through *cooperative,* multilateral means—including participation in international treaties and agreements and collective decision making within international organizations.

The evidence indicates that—contrary to the assertions of many scholars, pundits, and political elites—collective public opinion about foreign policy is not inconsistent, capricious, fluctuating, or unreasonable. Instead, Americans' collective responses to hundreds of different survey questions over the years have, for the most part, been coherent and mutually consistent, durable over time, and (given the information available to the citizenry) sensible. Despite limited attention and low levels of knowledge about the details of foreign affairs, the average U.S. citizen is able to form coherent, reasonable views on many matters of foreign policy—presumably through historical learning, talking things over, and making use of simple heuristics and media-reported collective deliberation. Moreover, individual Americans' preferences concerning foreign policy tend to be embedded in *purposive belief systems,* in which policy preferences flow logically from the foreign policy goals that individuals embrace, the international threats they perceive, their feelings about particular foreign countries and foreign leaders, and (sometimes) their ideologies: liberal or conservative, internationalist or isolationist.

Yet policy makers often fail to heed the views of ordinary citizens. Actual U.S. foreign policy frequently deviates markedly from what the public wants. Year after year, decade after decade, there have been many large gaps between the foreign policies favored by officials and those favored by the public. Majorities of foreign policy decision makers have actually taken the opposite side from majorities of the public on about a quarter of the issues we studied.

The public is not always right, of course; there is a role for experts. But we have seen surprisingly little evidence that these gaps result from disparities in knowledge—citizens' ignorance versus policy makers' superior wisdom. Instead, many or most appear to reflect differences in goals and values: greater concern among ordinary citizens than among elites about jobs at home and military casualties abroad, for example. Other gaps result from principled differences concerning what kinds of foreign policy are most effective; the public clearly prefers a multilateral approach, as do many experts, while officials have often been inclined toward unilateralism.

Our detailed look at Americans' foreign policy preferences indicates that they could indeed generally serve as a useful guide to decision makers. In such cases democratic theory, as we understand it, calls for public officials to be more responsive to what their citizens say they want.

PURSUING SECURITY AND JUSTICE
THROUGH COOPERATIVE MEANS

Not surprisingly, most Americans put a very high priority on *security from attack,* whether by terrorists or by hostile nation-states. When many possible objectives are ranked according to the proportions of respondents who say each should be a "very important" goal of U.S. foreign policy, the highest rankings have, since the end of the Cold War, commonly gone to the aims of "preventing the spread of nuclear weapons" and (since 1998) "combating international terrorism." During the Cold War, too, security from attack—especially through "worldwide arms control"—was naturally a very high priority.

Every bit as important to the public, however, are less obvious foreign policy goals related to what we have called *security of domestic well-being:* especially protecting the jobs of American workers, stopping the inflow of illegal drugs, securing adequate supplies of energy, and controlling and reducing illegal immigration. Throughout the history of the CCFR surveys *job protection* has ranked at or near the top of the long list of goals; it took third place in 2002 and was number one in 2004. Securing energy supplies has often followed not far behind. Since 1990, the goals of stopping illegal drugs and of controlling and reducing illegal immigration have regularly been called very important by more Americans than have said the same about such traditional foreign policy aims as maintaining superior military power worldwide, protecting the interests of American business abroad, or defending our allies' security. This emphasis on actively pursuing economic security and social well-being within the United States, central to what the citizenry wants from American foreign policy, is one of our major findings. Some foreign policy elites seem uncomfortable with, or unaware of, the public's priorities, but a more democratic foreign policy would pay close attention to them.

Security from attack and security of domestic well-being come first, but most Americans also ascribe substantial importance to achieving *justice* for people abroad and want the United States to pursue altruistic, humanitarian aims internationally. Over the years, pluralities or majorities of the public have regularly said that, in particular, combating world hunger and strengthening the United Nations should be very important goals of U.S. foreign policy. Most also say it is at least somewhat important to protect weaker nations against foreign aggression, to help improve the standards of living of less developed nations, and to promote democracy abroad.

Public support for or opposition to concrete policy alternatives generally follows from the goals that Americans embrace. The high priority placed on domestic well-being, for example, helps explain why the public has given much greater support, in nearly every CCFR survey, to spending on domestic social programs than on military or foreign policy programs. The precise nature of Americans' concerns about security from attack helps explain the very high level of public support for measures to combat terrorism, maintain homeland security, and defend our shores, as well as the marked lack of enthusiasm for involving U.S. troops in major combat abroad that is not directly related to defending the homeland of the United States. The goals that Americans endorse help illuminate why the public's support for foreign trade is conditioned on measures to protect jobs or retrain displaced workers, why most Americans want to reduce levels of immigration, and why humanitarian foreign aid is far more popular than strategic or military aid.

Another major theme of this book is that the American public—more than some U.S. officials—generally prefers to use *cooperative* and multilateral means to pursue its foreign policy aims. The preference for multilateralism is implicit in certain of the goals that large numbers of Americans embrace—particularly worldwide arms control and strengthening the United Nations. But it is most clearly evident when we consider which specific policy measures win high levels of public support. In the realm of military and defense policy, for example, while most Americans favor a strong military and are comfortable with being the world's sole superpower, most reject the idea of the United States acting alone or serving as a "world policeman." Majorities generally oppose large-scale, potentially costly uses of force to repel hypothetical invasions of other countries, unless U.S. action is specified to be part of a joint effort with allies and the United Nations. Before the U.S. invasion of Iraq, support for such an attack was much higher when UN approval and the support of allies were postulated in survey questions than when they were not. In retrospect it is hard to deny that the public was right. The American public has also favored multilateral rather than unilateral action to deal with North Korea's emerging nuclear capability.

Even in combating terrorism the public wants diplomacy to play a prominent role. Most Americans favor using force (unilateral force if necessary) against terrorist camps and facilities, but equally large or larger majorities favor cooperative, multilateral measures to apprehend terrorist suspects, to cut off terrorists' funding, to strengthen international laws against terrorism, and to improve relations with potential adversary countries. The chief lesson of the September 11 attacks is taken to be that we need to work more closely with other countries, not that we need to act more on our own.

Americans' preference for cooperation and multilateralism is also evident in strong support for alliances like NATO and international organizations like the United Nations. Even after the end of the Cold War, majorities say they consider NATO to be essential to U.S. security. Most Americans want to maintain our commitment to the alliance and have favored expanding it eastward, even to include Russia. Most Americans also favor U.S. participation in UN peacekeeping missions, both in general and in specific locations like Bosnia and Afghanistan, and most favor building up UN military capability through joint training exercises and the establishment of a rapid deployment force with contributions from all member states.

In the more purely political realm, most Americans have warm feelings toward a number of allies, particularly Canada, Britain, Mexico, countries of continental Europe, Japan, and perhaps Russia. Most want the European Union to take an active role in world affairs, and most favor joint decision making with the EU even if the United States does not always get its own way. NATO is seen as an important political institution, not just a military alliance.

Most Americans also want to deal with adversary countries through diplomacy. Majorities or pluralities have favored maintaining diplomatic relations with several countries that U.S. officials have shunned: Cuba, Iran, North Korea, and even (before the U.S. invasion) Saddam Hussein's Iraq. Most favor diplomatic rather than military solutions to the Israeli-Palestinian conflict, directed toward establishing an independent Palestinian state, and most want the United States to play an evenhanded role, not taking either side.

The United Nations is central to the U.S. public's hopes for cooperative relationships through international organizations. Most Americans feel quite warm toward the UN. Besides seeking to strengthen the organization generally and to set up a rapid deployment force, most favor paying U.S. dues in full and allowing the UN to raise revenues through a small tax on international transactions. Even after the divisive Security Council disputes over whether or not to invade Iraq, most Americans continued to favor a leading role for the UN in Iraq's relief and reconstruction. Remarkably, most would even be willing to give up the United States' power to veto otherwise unanimous Security Council decisions. Most Americans also favor giving substantial powers to the World Health Organization and accepting the jurisdiction of the World Court. The public's enthusiasm for international organizations contrasts sharply with the views of many of our foreign policy decision makers.

Large majorities of Americans also favor U.S. participation in a broad range of international treaties and agreements, including several that U.S. policy makers have actively opposed. Majorities of the public have favored several important arms control treaties: the Comprehensive Nuclear Test Ban Treaty, the treaty to ban all use of land mines, the Anti-Ballistic Missile Treaty, and (during the Cold War) various bilateral arms control agreements with the Soviet Union. There is also a very high level of public support for the Kyoto agreement to reduce global warming and for the International Criminal Court, support that persists when counterarguments are explicitly mentioned. The U.S. renunciation of Kyoto and the ICC, and the campaign to destroy the court, have clearly flown in the face of the public's wishes.

All in all, the pattern of strong, widespread public support for international organizations, multilateral agreements and actions, and collective international decision making suggests that most Americans are—in effect, though of course not in conscious self-description—"neoliberals." Most, in fact, favor policies amounting to something like a system of global governance, to deal with a range of political, economic, and military issues. This public support does not seem to be shared, or even understood, by most U.S. foreign policy decision makers.

In the economic realm, most members of the public favor certain policies designed to protect Americans' jobs, such as putting conditions on trade (help for displaced workers, workplace and environmental standards in trade agreements, perhaps tariffs) and restricting both legal and illegal immigration. But they are not economic isolationists: they favor extensive international trade and cooperative economic relationships with foreign countries and international organizations. Substantial majorities of Americans consider globalization to be "mostly a good thing." Majorities see globalization and international trade as being good for American consumers, for American companies, and for the U.S. economy as a whole, though not for the job security of American workers. Most see major U.S. trading partners (though not China) as practicing fair trade, and most want to engage in trade with other countries, including China and Cuba, though not Iran or North Korea. Majorities of Americans say that poor countries have not been treated fairly in trade negotiations, and most oppose U.S. agricultural subsidies except for small farmers on a short-term basis. Most feel fairly warm toward the World Trade Organization, want to strengthen it, and say the United States should comply with any adverse WTO decisions.

Foreign aid does not arouse much enthusiasm from the U.S. public, at least aid that is seen as strategically oriented, as wasteful, or as going to corrupt human rights abusers. (The amount of aid actually given is also grossly overestimated.) Pluralities or majorities of Americans have said they want to cut aid to traditional recipients of strategically oriented assistance like Israel or Egypt. Contrary to conventional wisdom, however, *humanitarian* aid wins high levels of public support. Especially popular are aid to African countries, food and medical assistance, help with the prevention and treatment of AIDS, and help with economic development. Substantial majorities of Americans also favor aid to reduce population growth through women's education or birth control.

In all three policy areas covered by chapters 4 through 6, then—military, political, and economic—majorities of Americans favor a wide range of policies involving friendly relations with other countries, multilateral cooperation, and action through international organizations.

THE PUBLIC'S VIEWS ARE WORTHY OF ATTENTION

The skeptical comments on public opinion expressed by Alexander Hamilton, Walter Lippmann, Hans Morgenthau, and others get little support from our findings. Contrary to their claims, the foreign policy preferences of the American public are well founded and worthy of attention from policy makers. For one thing, Americans' collective foreign policy preferences generally fit the conception of a "rational public." They are not generally incoherent, inconsistent, vacillating, or random; instead collective preferences are mostly coherent, consistent, and—in our judgment—sensible. The public makes clear distinctions among policy alternatives. Preferences change in reasonable ways in response to events like economic downturns or the end of the Cold War but otherwise are generally stable.

Beyond confirming the "rationality" (in this sense) of *collective* public opinion, our analyses have provided new evidence about *individuals'* foreign policy preferences that helps account for the coherence of collective opinion and adds to our confidence that it is worth paying attention to. We have found that individual Americans tend to organize their foreign policy attitudes into *purposive belief systems,* in which their policy preferences reflect logically related goals for foreign policy, perceptions of international threats, feelings about foreign countries and foreign leaders, and predispositions toward international activity or isolationism. These attitudes and perceptions generally have stronger and more direct effects on policy preferences than do an individual's personal and social characteristics.

The limited role of personal and social characteristics. To be sure, we have reported a number of interesting, moderate-sized bivariate differences between groups: that is, differences in opinion when one group is simply compared with another. But seldom have these differences been very large: on most issues, majorities of Americans of all sorts, from all walks of life, hold rather similar opinions. And only in a few cases did such differences actually represent independent *effects* of personal characteristics, with statistically significant coefficients in multiple regressions that controlled for (or "held constant") fourteen demographic traits at the same time. Usually, all fourteen demographic factors together could not account for even 5 percent of the variation in individuals' opinions.

Very seldom, for example, are foreign policy opinions much affected (controlling for other factors, such as income and education) by whether people are young or old, single or married. Being Hispanic affects attitudes toward immigration and toward Mexico (though not the rest of Latin America) and leads to cooler feelings toward a few powerful countries, but not much else. Being Asian American leads to warmer feelings toward a few (not most) Asian countries. Being African American has somewhat broader, but still limited, effects: it leads to putting higher priorities on the goals of protecting Americans' jobs, helping poor countries, strengthening the UN, and promoting democracy abroad. It also leads to cooler feelings toward several powerful U.S. allies, to more support for aid to Africa (but not warmer feelings about African countries), and to increased opposition to certain uses of U.S. troops and to spending money on the military.

Gender and religion make more independent difference. Being female leads to putting higher priority on certain justice-related goals—particularly strengthening the UN and protecting the global environment—and on some goals related to domestic well-being (protecting jobs, stopping drugs). Being female also causes people to favor certain humanitarian policies, such as increasing economic aid to African countries and paying UN dues in full. Being male, on the other hand, leads people to favor using U.S. troops in case of hypothetical invasions (e.g., of South Korea, Saudi Arabia, or Israel).

We were surprised by the potent effect upon quite a few foreign policy opinions of certain religious affiliations, especially evangelical Protestantism. Being an evangelical Protestant (controlling for other personal characteristics) leads to putting higher priority on the goals of stopping drugs and combating terrorism, and lower priority on protecting the environment or strengthening the UN. It leads to warmer feelings toward Israel and some conservative world leaders but cooler feelings toward the European Union. Being evangelical Protestant also causes people to favor strengthening military capabilities and using force in a variety of ways: increasing spending on defense, homeland security, and intelligence gathering; using U.S. troops in case of hypothetical invasions of South Korea, Saudi Arabia, or Israel; using air strikes and perhaps troops against terrorist camps. Evangelical Protestantism also inclines individuals to oppose such diplomatic or multilateral activities as participating in UN peacekeeping, making joint decisions with the European Union, complying with WTO decisions, participating in the Kyoto agreement on global warming, engaging in trade or diplomacy with Cuba or Iran, and working toward an independent Palestinian state. The estimated effects of evangelical Protestantism tend to drop when basic political attitudes are taken into account, indicating that part of its impact works through ideology and partisanship: through evangelicals' tendency to be conservative and Republican. The current centrality of evangelical Protestants in Republican Party politics has important implications for the making of U.S. foreign policy when that party is in power.

Catholicism has similar but generally smaller effects: it leads people to put higher priorities on the goals of stopping drugs, defending jobs, and promoting democracy abroad, and to feel more warmly toward a few Catholic countries and conservative world leaders. It contributes to the likelihood of favoring the use of U.S. troops if South Korea were invaded and favoring increases in spending for defense, homeland security, and perhaps intelligence gathering. Catholicism also decreases support for trade or diplomatic relations with Cuba but increases support for the Comprehensive Nuclear Test Ban Treaty and for economic aid to Africa.

Being Jewish or being Muslim has strong effects on certain feelings concerning the Middle East—such strong effects that they show up as highly significant in multiple regression analyses despite the small numbers of Jewish or Muslim respondents in the CCFR surveys. Controlling as usual for other demographic characteristics, being Jewish leads to much warmer feelings toward Israel and Ariel Sharon but considerably cooler feelings toward the Palestinians, Arafat, the Muslim people, Saudi Arabia, Egypt, and Iran (though not toward more distant or more Israel-friendly Muslim countries), as well as cooler feelings toward Poland, Germany, and France. Being Jewish has little direct effect on policy preferences, however, even with respect to the Middle East. Being a Muslim American leads to putting a higher priority on the goal of promoting democracy abroad and to much warmer thermometer ratings of the Muslim people, the Palestinians, Saudi Arabia, Iran, Iraq, and Pakistan but has no significant effect on feelings about Israel or Sharon.

More complicated is the role of an individual's level of formal education. Our research indicates that formal education does have substantial effects on certain kinds of foreign policy opinions, but that those effects are much more limited and of a different nature than is often believed to be the case. In a simple bivariate sense, the opinions of highly educated individuals often differ markedly from the opinions of those with little formal education. We reported some cases in which the opinions of Americans with postgraduate educations differed by as much as 30 or 40 percentage points from those who had not finished high school. This might seem to support claims for a highly educated "attentive public" with distinctive—and presumably more enlightened—views of the world. But when other demographic factors (including income level, race, ethnicity, and employment status) are controlled for, the *independent* effects of education are much smaller and less frequently significant. It becomes clear that foreign policy opinions often differ by education levels because of variations in individuals' economic or social status (which is associated with education), not because of education itself. Moreover, the independent effects of education largely work through distinctive foreign policy goals and orientations, rather than through knowledge or exposure to the world—which usually have surprisingly little independent effect. This indicates that the effects of education largely signal the working of different values and interests based on socioeconomic status, rather than superior or inferior wisdom.

Education levels do indeed have significant—though only moderately large—independent effects on a few policy preferences: participating in UN peacekeeping, having diplomatic relations with Cuba and Iran, paying UN dues in full, and perhaps supporting the Comprehensive Nuclear Test Ban Treaty, but hardly any other issues among the many we studied. More impressively, an individual's level of education has a substantial, independent, positive impact on his or her feeling thermometer ratings of many foreign countries. Moreover, in the cases of several countries or peoples that are arguably important to U.S. interests but that are misunderstood or little known by many Americans—Afghanistan, Taiwan, Pakistan, South Korea, Cuba, the Palestinians—individuals' *information levels* about foreign affairs have unusually large independent effects on feelings and appear to account for about half of education's impact. (The other half mostly works through "active part" internationalism.) Clearly, education and the knowledge it brings helps Americans to understand and appreciate some of the diverse countries of the world.

But education levels also have substantial independent effects on the priorities that individuals assign to various foreign policy goals, effects that have virtually nothing to do with information or knowledge. Being highly educated leads, for example, to less enthusiasm for several domestic well-being goals: protecting Americans' jobs, stopping the inflow of drugs, controlling illegal immigration, and securing adequate supplies of energy. Since the highly educated are generally more affluent, better established, and more secure against such threats, this may simply reflect self-interest.

So our conclusions about the effects of formal education are mixed. We see little reason to argue that decision makers should ignore the general public and heed only an educated elite.

In any case, our main point about individuals' personal and social characteristics is that they usually do not matter much. It makes sense to talk about "the public" as a fairly uniform whole. All fourteen demographic characteristics that we studied, taken together, account for little of the variation in Americans' foreign policy preferences. A much higher proportion of the variance—often more than three or four times as much—can be accounted for by a handful of measures of individuals' basic political attitudes, perceptions of threats or vital interests, feelings about foreign countries or leaders, and foreign policy goals. These attitudinal factors have substantial (though of course not absolute) autonomy from demographic characteristics, and they tend to fit together into logically coherent purposive belief systems.

Purposive belief systems. We have seen a great deal of evidence confirming the existence of purposive belief systems of the sort outlined in chapter 1—that is, sets of attitudes, beliefs, and orientations concerning world affairs that are linked both logically and empirically with support for particular policy alternatives.

Again and again, for example, we have seen that individuals' assignment of high priority to particular *goals* of U.S. foreign policy, along with their perceptions of particular *threats* to the United States, fairly strongly and independently affect preferences for policies that can reasonably be expected to achieve those goals or deal with those threats. Controlling for many other factors, endorsement of the goal of "defending our allies" or "protecting weaker nations" contributes to support for using U.S. troops to deal with military invasions; downgrading those goals leads to opposition. Concern about terrorism or threats from nuclear, chemical, and biological weapons leads people to favor using force against terrorists or "rogue" states. Seeking to maintain superior military power worldwide contributes to support for increases in defense spending and for keeping long-term military bases abroad.

No kidding! you may say. *Of course* we found that people tend to favor participating in the Kyoto agreement on global warming if they see global warming as a critical threat to the vital interest of the United States. And that individuals who embrace the goals of strengthening international law or protecting human rights tend to favor participating in the International Criminal Court and joining UN peacekeeping operations, that those who say the United States should seek to combat world hunger or to raise the standard of living in poor countries tend to support increasing economic aid to Africa, and that those who see a vital U.S. interest in China tend to favor engaging in trade with China. It is hardly startling to learn that putting a high priority on securing adequate supplies of energy contributes to support for using U.S. military troops to "ensure the supply of oil." The logical connections are obvious.

But that is precisely the point. For years, many pundits—and some scholars—have deplored Americans' ignorance of world affairs and bemoaned their alleged tendency to make up "doorstep opinions," random expressions of "non-attitudes," to please survey interviewers. Such talk has created a widespread impression that there is no logic or structure at all to the policy preferences that individuals express. The fact that Americans do indeed tend to favor foreign policies aimed at achieving the foreign policy goals they embrace may not be startling, but it certainly contradicts a good deal of conventional wisdom.

Moreover, in many cases particular policies are related to more than a single, obvious goal. In those cases, our multivariate analyses have been useful for sorting out exactly *which* goals or concerns have the biggest independent effects on policy preferences. It is striking, for example, that desires to restrict immigration into the United States are independently affected by three different types of concerns: the aim to protect U.S. jobs, worries about terrorism, and cultural anxiety (particularly with respect to Mexican immigrants). It is noteworthy that environmental concerns as well as security objectives independently affect preferences concerning the Comprehensive Nuclear Test Ban Treaty and the treaty banning land mines. It is interesting that attitudes about NATO have a political as well as a military dimension, and that they are closely linked to attitudes about the United Nations. We would not claim that the U.S. public always engages in long-term strategic thinking, but it is striking that already at the outset of the twenty-first century, preferences for increasing spending on defense and on intelligence gathering were each independently affected by perceptions that the rise of Chinese military power is a critical threat to vital U.S. interests.

The central role of explicit foreign policy goals in affecting individuals' policy preferences helps account for why the *collective* policy preferences held by majorities of Americans tend to reflect, in a logically coherent fashion, the goals that majorities of Americans embrace.

We also found that individuals' *feelings* about specific countries and world leaders often have substantial effects on policy preferences. Independently of many other factors, feeling warmer toward a particular country tends to make people favor engaging in trade and diplomatic relations with that country, defending it from invasion, maintaining long-term military bases there, and (in certain cases) making joint decisions with that country or giving it foreign aid. Warm feelings toward "the Muslim people" or toward the Palestinians lead to support for participating in Bosnia peacekeeping and working toward a Palestinian state and to opposition to restricting immigration from Arab or Muslim countries. Especially cold feelings toward Fidel Castro, Iran, or Saddam Hussein's Iraq have contributed to support for economic sanctions—and opposition to trade—with the relevant countries. Feeling warm toward the United Nations leads to favoring a wide range of cooperative and multilateral foreign policies, from participating in UN peacekeeping operations, to strengthening NATO, the European Union, and the UN itself, to participating in the International Criminal Court.

We believe that these feelings, as measured on the CCFR surveys' thermometer scale, are not purely affective or "emotional": they probably serve as heuristics for bundles of attitudes and beliefs that are logically relevant to policy preferences. Warm feelings toward a country may, for example, sum up beliefs that that country shares our values and interests, has a competent and reasonably democratic government, will be a friendly host for the U.S. military, has virtues worth defending, or has goods or ideas of use to us. Cold feelings, on the other hand, may reflect beliefs (which we could not directly measure) that the country poses a security threat, can't be trusted, or is in need of regime change.

Here, too, not all the findings are obvious. We would not have guessed beforehand that individual Americans' feelings about three very different African countries (Egypt, Nigeria, and South Africa) would each independently affect preferences concerning economic aid to Africa. Or that, even back in 2002, feelings about North Korea would independently affect opinions about using U.S. troops against terrorist camps. It is interesting to find that feelings about Israel and Ariel Sharon, as well as feelings about Iran and Saddam Hussein's Iraq themselves, independently contributed to support for imposing economic sanctions upon, or engaging in trade with, Iran and Iraq.

The general political orientations or predispositions that we have called "basic attitudes"—individuals' liberal or conservative ideologies, their Republican or Democratic party identifications, and especially their internationalist or isolationist inclinations (as manifested in statements that the United States should take an "active part" in or "stay out" of world affairs)—play a more limited, but still important, role in our conception of how purposive belief systems work. We see such basic attitudes as representing relatively stable and enduring political beliefs and values (partly rooted in social or personal characteristics but partly autonomous) that in turn affect many of the foreign policy goals that people hold. Liberal ideology, for example, contributes to placing high importance on such justice-related, humanitarian foreign policy goals as protecting the global environment, promoting human rights, improving the standards of living of poor countries, combating hunger, and strengthening the United Nations, while conservatism contributes to the goals of maintaining military strength, controlling immigration, stopping drugs, securing energy supplies, and protecting American businesses abroad. "Active part" internationalism engenders warmer feelings toward many foreign countries and leaders and leads to putting higher priorities on the justice-related goals of combating hunger, protecting weaker countries, promoting human rights, promoting democracy abroad, improving standards of living, strengthening international law, and strengthening the UN.

For the most part these basic attitudes or orientations affect policy preferences only indirectly, through the specific goals and threat perceptions that they help shape. Only occasionally does liberal or conservative ideology (or even more rarely party affiliation) have direct effects on policy preferences independently of specific goals; this generally happens only when domestic political cleavages have been directly engaged by debates in Washington, as in the case of defense spending or a national missile defense. "Active part" internationalism somewhat more often has direct, independent effects on policy preferences. In most of our multiple regressions, however, the estimated impact even of "active part" internationalism faded away when specific foreign policy goals, perceived threats, and the like were taken into account.

We found substantial evidence of purposive belief systems in all the areas of foreign policy we studied, military, political, and economic. But we do not want to exaggerate the strength of our findings. We certainly do not claim that most Americans have their minds crammed full of perfectly logical, tightly constrained foreign policy belief systems. The attitudinal elements we have emphasized as central to belief systems—the foreign policy goals that individuals say should be important, the threats they perceive as critical, their feelings about foreign countries and leaders, and the vital interests they perceive around the world, along with their basic political orientations—even when considered all together, never come close to accounting for all of the variation in individuals' policy preferences.

Usually, in our analyses, about half a dozen of these attitudes had significant effects on opinions about any given issue. But they could generally account for only about 10 to 15 percent of the variance in preferences concerning major military issues (troop use in invasion scenarios, participation in UN peacekeeping operations, defense spending); 10 to 15 percent of the variance for most major issues of political cooperation (strengthening NATO, having diplomatic relations with Cuba or Iran, working for a Palestinian state, participating in various treaties); and only a bit more, roughly 15 to 20 percent of the variance, in preferences concerning trade with Cuba and restrictions on immigration. There were variations—they accounted for more than 15 percent of the variance in support for use of U.S. troops if Israel were invaded—but only occasionally, as in the cases of the Kyoto agreement and economic aid to African countries, could half a dozen goals, threats, and other attitudinal factors account for as much as 30 or 35 percent of the variance in policy preferences. Even given the inevitable relationship-depressing measurement errors in survey data, that is not an enormous amount of variation accounted for.

Still, this degree of constraint in individuals' belief systems is considerably greater than most observers imagine. And it seems to be enough to provide a foundation for the rationality of *collective* public opinion. Because individual Americans tend to favor concrete policies designed to realize the foreign policy goals they seek, for example, *majorities* of Americans generally favor policies that will advance the goals that *majorities* of Americans seek. When individuals' opinions are aggregated into collective public opinion, the public as a whole expresses many attitudes and opinions that are connected in a logical fashion. The existence of logically coherent, purposive belief systems in the minds of individual citizens, then, helps bolster our argument that collective public opinion on foreign policy generally makes sense and is worth paying attention to.

ARE POLICY MAKERS OUT OF TOUCH?

Nonetheless, we have seen that official U.S. foreign policy often differs markedly from the policies that most Americans want. And foreign policy decision makers often express quite different policy preferences than the American public does. As chapter 7 indicated, over a thirty-year period there have consistently been many substantial gaps between the proportions of citizens and the proportions of foreign policy decision makers that have favored particular policy alternatives. On every one of the eight pairs of CCFR surveys we analyzed, there were gaps of 10 percentage points or more on at least two-thirds of the issues. Overall, taking the eight studies together, substantial gaps existed on nearly *three-quarters* (73 percent) of all the questions that were asked at the same time of both decision makers and the public. Most of the gaps involved differences of 20 percentage points or more.

We have argued that such gaps are important even when majorities of citizens and majorities of decision makers pick the same survey response option, because they signal that the average citizen and the average official are probably taking quite different stands on underlying policy dimensions. That is, when quite different-sized majorities of citizens and decision makers say they "favor" the same dichotomous policy alternative, the *average* citizen and the average decision maker probably want (for example) to spend quite different amounts of money on a domestic or foreign program, to station quite different numbers of troops abroad, or to insist on a very different level of foreign threat before using military force.

Perhaps even more striking, however, is the finding that on about one-quarter (26 percent) of all the parallel CCFR survey questions over the years, *majorities* of decision makers have disagreed with majorities of the American citizenry. To say that officials are "out of touch" or "disconnected" may be to put the matter too strongly, but on a great many important issues the preferences of citizens and foreign policy officials have been quite different, pushing in opposite directions.

The precise nature of the gaps and opposing majorities has varied somewhat from one survey year to another. In 2002, for example, the Bush administration was unusually out of harmony with the public's wishes on diplomatic issues, including a number of international treaties and agreements (the Kyoto Protocol, the International Criminal Court, the Comprehensive Nuclear Test Ban Treaty, the land mines treaty) that the public favored but the administration spurned. In that year a majority of decision makers disagreed with a majority of citizens on nearly one-third (32 percent) of all diplomatic issues, whereas in 1978, during the Carter administration—with its strong record on human rights and multilateralism—there was majority disagreement on only 13 percent of diplomatic issues.

Over the years, however, certain patterns of citizen/decision maker disagreement have held fairly steady. Year after year, economic issues have been a focal point for disagreement, with more gaps and more opposing majorities than in other areas. Ordinary Americans, much more than decision makers, have worried about security of domestic well-being, especially job protection and its connections with trade and immigration policies. In the defense area, year after year, citizens have been less eager than decision makers to commit U.S. troops to major combat abroad, where loved ones may become casualties of some official's geopolitical calculations. In the diplomatic realm, year after year, ordinary citizens—much more than decision makers—have expressed strong support for international organizations and international agreements, especially for the United Nations and for arms control agreements.

Gaps between elites and the public are sometimes attributed to ignorance, error, or shortsightedness on the part of ordinary citizens, as contrasted with high levels of knowledge and expertise among leaders. We did find a few cases consistent with this picture, such as the public's misunderstanding of the magnitude and effects of foreign aid programs (a misunderstanding encouraged by some politicians) and the public's relative sluggishness in comprehending the end of the Cold War. Often, however, disagreements between decision makers and the citizenry have hinged on disagreements over *values, interests,* and *principles.* These include the general public's much greater concern about security of domestic well-being; jobs, health care, and drug use worry middle- and lower-income Americans a lot more than they do Washington officials or Georgetown think-tankers. The same point applies to the public's much sharper sensitivity to the costs of war: their sons and daughters more frequently get shipped off to Iraq than do senators' or representatives' offspring. And to the public's greater commitment to multilateralism and collective decision making. Some members of Congress and executive branch officials may consider it no fun at all to share power with foreigners, but the American public appears to be willing to do so, for the sake of the burden sharing, the increased legitimacy, and the reciprocal benefits that come with international cooperation.

We do not think the public is always right: poll results are not the voice of God. But it does seem quite possible that a more democratic foreign policy would also be a generally better and more sustainable foreign policy. Certainly it is hard to argue that the republic would be endangered if our leaders heeded the public's voice on such matters as supporting the United Nations, joining the International Criminal Court, avoiding major unilateral military engagements, stopping arms sales abroad, or renouncing the first use of nuclear weapons. Whatever our own wishes may be, it would not likely have devastating effects on the nation if decision makers paid more attention to the public's worries about trade and immigration. Better border enforcement, more serious workplace and environmental provisions in trade agreements, and better compensation (from the gains of trade) for job and wage losses could go a long way. The public is not clamoring for protectionism or economic and social isolation, just for some help.

As American leaders actively promote and encourage democracy around the world, a rudimentary regard for consistency would seem to call for practicing foreign policy democracy here at home. In a democracy, every citizen's values and interests are supposed to count equally. When aggregated they are supposed to shape what governments do. It is particularly hard to argue that decision makers should defy the foreign policy *goals* that most Americans seek. And to the extent that specific policy disagreements between citizens and decision makers are based on disagreements about interests, values, or principles, rather than differences in knowledge or expertise, we believe that democratic theory calls for elected officials and their appointees to pay attention to public opinion and do what the citizens want. If they did so, U.S. foreign policy might well be more humane, more effective, and more sustainable, as well as more democratic.

TOWARD A MORE DEMOCRATIC FOREIGN POLICY

How could we achieve a more democratic foreign policy? It would be nice if just getting the facts about public opinion to policy makers would lead them to change course. Then the key would be to persuade officials or staffers to look at the evidence in this book and to keep track of new surveys conducted by CCFR, PIPA, and other organizations as they come along.[1] That could well have an effect, particularly upon those who would like to respond democratically but have been unaware of, or confused about, what sort of foreign policy the American public actually wants. (Representatives would do well to recognize that the constituents in their particular districts are *not* much different from the national public. As we have seen repeatedly, demographic characteristics and party affiliations generally make little difference to foreign policy preferences.)

But the facts, alone or accompanied by exhortations, may not be sufficient. Concrete incentives may be required. The persistence over time of large gaps between policy makers and the public suggests that there have not been strong incentives for officials to close them. In fact electoral pressures (originating elsewhere than from ordinary citizens) may actually have pointed in the opposite direction. On many issues, over long periods, policy makers have been able to get away with ignoring the public's wishes while still winning elections. What could we do to ensure that it is clearly in officials' electoral self-interest to pay more heed to the public?

One time-honored strategy, which can be carried out by organized citizens' groups, by journalists, or even by committed private individuals, is to *make a fuss.* Loudly pointing out—through print or electronic media, or by protests and demonstrations—cases in which officials are blatantly defying the will of the citizenry should increase voters' awareness of the discrepancies and heighten concern about them; it should increase the likelihood that Americans will hold their officials accountable at the polls. Officials, alert to the danger of a reckoning, might then change policy to head it off. It is much harder to defy the public's will in the full glare of public attention.[2] In institutional terms, more independent, watch-dog-oriented media, devoting more attention to foreign affairs, would certainly be helpful. The media would do well to show less automatic deference to what officials say, while offering fuller and more respectful reporting of what the American public thinks and wants.

The "make a fuss" strategy has the advantage that it can increase the influence of the public upon policy making without requiring changes in laws or the political system. But it cannot solve the whole problem, because it is not feasible to fuss about everything at once. People can pay attention to only so many issues at a time. Additional approaches are needed. Drawing upon our discussions of barriers to democratic responsiveness in chapters 5 and 7, it is easy to identify targets for further action. To lower or remove these barriers, however, would require not just efforts by individuals but coordinated, sustained political activity by parties, citizens' groups, or social movements. Some useful reforms would involve minor changes in current laws or regulations; others would entail rather sweeping changes in public policy; and a few (the hardest to achieve) would involve fundamental changes in the U.S. political system.

One relatively simple move would be to *make elections more competitive*, especially for the House of Representatives, where many one-party districts blunt popular control. Efforts to have the courts declare political gerrymandering an unconstitutional violation of equal protection of the law are worthwhile; so are campaigns to persuade or force state legislatures to have nonpartisan commissions, rather than partisan politicians, draw district lines. Success would reduce the power of extremist party activists. It would help prevent extreme policies like the recent resorts to diplomatic and military unilateralism. It would also reduce disruptive policy lurches when one party replaces another in power.

Another relatively easy move would be to *expand the electorate and make it more representative*, so that voters' choices and their messages to officials would more faithfully reflect the views of all American citizens—including the low-income and minority citizens who currently tend to be underrepresented. One simple way to do this would be to make election day a national holiday, as most of the world does, so that working people have plenty of time to get to the polls. It would also be feasible to repeal (at either the state or federal level) state measures that disenfranchise ex-felons, make registration difficult, and restrict voting opportunities—especially in populous urban areas—by limiting access to polling places and voting machines. Better still would be to replace the system that requires personal registration with universal, automatic registration of all citizens by government and to institute a small fine for not voting. Such measures would increase the pressure from voters on officials to enact foreign policies aimed at domestic well-being.[3]

More difficult, but very helpful, would be to *decrease the political power of money and organized interests.* Many multinational corporations work for policies contrary to the American public's desires on such economics-related matters as trade and immigration, while other organized interests push policy in unpopular directions on such matters as population control and ethnic-related regional policies. One should have no illusions about the ease of enacting effective regulations to restrict lobbying or political money giving; business and other interest groups have repeatedly fended off legislation, co-opted regulators, and invented new legal loopholes. Still, tighter limits on campaign contributions, political advertising, and political action could help. So could requirements for fuller disclosure of lobbying and campaign contributions, which—if widely reported—could be useful in mobilizing opposition.[4]

Reduce two-party collusion. It would be very hard—and not necessarily desirable—to do away with the two-party system itself. But certain rather modest reforms, such as permitting "fusion" tickets (allowing third parties to endorse major party candidates) in all states and reducing onerous state requirements for third parties trying to get on the ballot, could increase popular pressures on the established parties. This would lead to more democratic responsiveness on issues where the two major parties have sometimes gotten together and resisted the popular will, including certain international economic issues.

The above suggestions do not confront several of the major causes of political inequality in the United States, such as the weakness of organized labor—which can no longer provide much of a counterweight to business— or the constitutional biases of the Senate.[5] Our suggestions only indirectly grapple with the most fundamental problems, high political information costs and very unequally distributed economic and other resources. More direct and thoroughgoing changes aimed at information costs and resource inequalities would certainly make a difference, and some such changes may be feasible. Energetic, politically independent public television, for example, has worked well at cutting political information costs in other countries. Reducing the extreme economic inequalities now prevalent in the United States could increase political equality (and have other benefits as well) at little or no net cost to the country.[6] But it would not be necessary to reshape American society in order to achieve a much more democratic foreign policy. The moderate steps we have emphasized would go a long way.

Appendix. How Goals Cluster

Table A1. Correlations among Goals, 2002

Goal	1 Living standards	2 World hunger	3 Human rights	4 UN	5 Int'l law	6 Environment	7 Democracy	8 Protect weak	9 Financial stability	10 Market econ.	11 U.S. business	12 Drugs	13 Immigration	14 U.S. jobs	15 Energy supplies	16 Trade deficit	17 Military power	18 Defend allies	19 Terrorism
1. Raise living standards																			
2. Combat world hunger	.45																		
3. Promote human rights	.41	.46																	
4. Strengthen UN	.26	.32	.21																
5. Strengthen int'l law	.32	.26	.23	.40															
6. Improve environment	.35	.34	.22	.34	.28														
7. Bring democracy	.35	.34	.29	.21	.31	.14													
8. Protect weaker nations	.35	.23	.49	.19	.25	.18	.33												
9. Financial stability	.30	.29	.20	.27	.41	.34	.26	.23											
10. Promote market econ.	.29	.26	.16	.13	.32	.17	.28	.21	.30										
11. Protect U.S. business	.11	.18	.08	.17	.34	.15	.22	.13	.36	.35									
12. Stop flow of drugs	.03	.08	.00	.10	.13	.07	.18	.02	.14	.13	.25								
13. Control immigration	-.04	.07	-.03	.10	.12	-.02	.15	.06	.15	.12	.27	.33							
14. Protect U.S. jobs	.02	-.02	.07	.01	.12	.21	.16	.07	.12	.13	.26	.30	.27						
15. Secure energy supplies	.07	.12	.05	.26	.18	.11	.22	.05	.20	.29	.25	.23	.25	.23					
16. Reduce trade deficit	.03	.07	.06	.11	.17	.09	.12	.11	.12	.16	.12	.13	.20	.19	.20				
17. Superior military power	.01	.05	.07	.10	.10	-.04	.28	.15	.16	.20	.26	.20	.30	.19	.27	.13			
18. Defend allies	.24	.01	.20	-.01	.23	.11	.27	.28	.21	.33	.25	.09	.17	.12	.17	.12	.27		
19. Combat terrorism	.05	.17	.13	.03	.12	.03	.15	.13	.11	.12	.17	.14	.19	.12	.18	.12	.38	.20	
20. Prevent spread of nukes	.10	.09	.05	.04	.12	.17	.06	.07	.22	.08	.12	.15	.16	.13	.18	.12	.13	.14	.19
	1	2	3	4	5	6	7	8	9	10	11	12	13	14	15	16	17	18	19

Table A2. Factor Analysis of Goals, 2002

Goal	(S) Security from attack	(J) Justice	(D) Security of domestic well-being
Superior military power	−.591	−.161	.364
Defend allies' security	−.494	.220	.125
Combat international terrorism	−.481	—	.238
Protect weaker nations	−.456	.534	−.164
Bring democracy	−.402	.352	.174
Raise living standards	−.122	.723	−.119
Combat world hunger	—	.698	—
Improve global environment	.347	.634	.220
Promote human rights	−.353	.632	−.233
Strengthen United Nations	.319	.606	.215
Strengthen international law	—	.545	.274
Ensure financial stability	—	.470	.383
Promote market economies	−.292	.302	.271
Stop flow of illegal drugs	—	—	.633
Control illegal immigration	−.204	−.230	.614
Protect U.S. jobs	.173	.112	.605
Secure energy supplies	−.148	—	.559
Protect U.S. business abroad	−.101	.140	.557
Reduce trade deficit	—	—	.398
Prevent spread of nuclear weapons	—	—	.339

Note: Entries are loadings from the pattern matrix of a factor analysis using princi-pal components extraction and an oblimin rotation with Kaiser normalization. Con-strained to three factors, cumulatively accounting for 41.2 percent of the variance. An unconstrained factor analysis of the same type produced five factors with initial eigenvalues over 1.0, cumulatively accounting for 52.0 percent of the variance. They included clear Justice and Security of domestic well-being factors, and a limited (nuclear proliferation and terrorism) Security from attack factor, but also one factor centering on global markets and finance and another centered on the environment.

Table A3. Factor Analysis of Goals, 2004

Goal	(S) Security from attack	(J) Justice	(D) Security of domestic well-being
Superior military power	.756	−.278	.194
Bring democracy	.686	.248	−.113
Protect weaker nations	.662	.328	−.135
Combat international terrorism	.617	—	.275
Protect U.S. business abroad	.527	—	.234
Prevent spread of nuclear weapons	.484	.113	.317
Combat world hunger	.195	.724	—
Raise living standards	.377	.683	−.250
Improve global environment	−.105	.680	.296
Strengthen United Nations	−.107	.670	.283
Protect U.S. jobs	—	.195	.727
Control illegal immigration	.188	−.118	.707
Stop flow of illegal drugs	.221	.119	.508
Secure energy supplies	.253	.149	.504

Note: Entries are pattern matrix loadings from a factor analysis using principal components extraction and oblimin rotation with Kaiser normalization. Cumulative proportion of variance explained: 56.6 percent. Initial eigenvalues for no other factor reached 1.0.

Notes

INTRODUCTION

This introduction owes much to an anonymous reviewer for the University of Chicago Press. For comments and suggestions we are grateful to Ian Hurd, Risa Brooks, Beth Hurd, Michael Loriaux, and Hendrik Spruyt.

1. George W. Bush, State of the Union address, January 29, 2002, http://www.whitehouse.gov/news/releases/2002/01/print/20020129-11.html.

2. George W. Bush, speech at West Point, June 1, 2002, http://www.whitehouse.gov/news/releases/2002/06/print/20020601-3.html.

3. Neoconservatives' letter to Clinton on Iraq, http://www.newamericancentury.org/iraqclintonletter.htm (the Web site of the Project for the New American Century). George W. Bush, remarks at the National Endowment for Democracy, November 6, 2003, http://www.whitehouse.gov/news/releases/2003/11/20031106-2.html; speech to Republican National Convention, *New York Times*, September 2, 2004. The president first clearly embraced neoconservative principles in a speech to the American Enterprise Institute just before the U.S. invasion of Iraq: http://www.whitehouse.gov/news/releases/2003/02/print/20030226-11.html.

4. The leading statement of "classical" realism is Morgenthau (1973); of "structural" realism, Waltz (1979). On "offensive" realism, which rests on structural imperatives but posits limitless power goals, see Mearsheimer (2001, esp. chaps. 1–2 and pp. 361, 384, 396–400).

5. On redefinitions of "national security," see Mathews (1989) and United Nations Commission on Human Security (2003).

6. Trubowitz (1998, 4, 12). Trubowitz argues that political coalitions among geographic regions with distinctive economic interests have often defined "the national interest."

7. Joseph Nye (2002, 139) suggests that "in a democracy, the national interest is simply what citizens, after proper deliberation, say it is." This can include values such as human rights and democracy abroad.

8. On Woodrow Wilson's "progressive" internationalism, see Knock (1995).

9. On the Millennium Development Goals, see Sachs (2005, esp. 86–87).

10. International Commission on Intervention and State Sovereignty (2001). The ICISS was established, with a multinational membership, by the government of Canada, and was chaired by Gareth Evans and Mohamed Sahnoun.

11. For a neoconservative argument in favor of "transformation" of tyrannical regimes, see Kristol and Kaplan (2003). Doyle (1997, chaps. 7–8) discusses the theory of democratic (or liberal) peace, but certainly does not advocate spreading democracy by force.

12. Our list of international public goods draws upon Nye (2002, 142). On global public goods generally, see Kaul, Grunberg, and Stern (1999).

13. Waltz (1979). Walt (2005) documents many contemporary efforts by other nations to "balance" against unilateral U.S. policy moves.

14. Leading realist Hans Morgenthau (1973) strongly opposed the Vietnam war. Mearsheimer and Walt, like most international relations scholars of all stripes, opposed the invasion of Iraq; see Mearsheimer and Walt (2003).

15. The pioneering neoliberal view of economic relationships is Keohane (1984). On security applications, see Ikenberry (2001).

16. On "soft power," see Nye (2004, esp. chaps. 1–2 and p. 17).

17. Speech by George W. Bush, *New York Times,* April 13, 2004.

18. N. Ferguson (2005, ix, x, xxvii–xxix).

19. On a "neo-imperial vision" and empire: Ikenberry (2002), Johnson (2004, 12–13, 285).

20. United Nations (2004, articles 2(4), 42, 51); Walzer (2000, chap. 2, esp. 76–78, 80–81, 85).

21. United States National Security Council (2002, ii, 6).

22. Johnson (2004, 290).

23. Krauthammer (2001); United States National Security Council (2002, 6); Kagan (2003, 3). Kagan did, however, write that the United States should "pay its respects to multilateralism and the rule of law, and try to build some international political capital for those moments when multilateralism is impossible and unilateral action unavoidable" (102).

24. Nye (2002). See also Ikenberry (2001).

25. On Kant's vision of "perpetual peace," see Doyle (1997, chap. 8).

26. An excellent general account of the history of U.S. foreign policy is LaFeber (1994). For a cleverly argued rosy view see Mead (2002). A useful textbook on U.S. economic history, including nineteenth-century tariff and trade policy and the role of foreign investment, is Walton and Rockoff (1998).

27. On the Monroe Doctrine, see Perkins (1966). On Manifest Destiny and Polk's annexations, see Weinberg (1935), Merk (1966), and Pletcher (1975). For an overview, see LaFeber (1994, chaps. 3–4) and, on settlement and economic development, Walton and Rockoff (1998, chaps. 8–10, 15).

28. Walton and Rockoff (1998, esp. chaps. 16–17) describe the late-nineteenth-century industrialization of the United States. LaFeber (1994, chaps. 6–8) covers the emergence of the United States as a great power. On Theodore Roosevelt, a key figure in this emergence, see Morris (1979, 2001). Trubowitz (1998, chap. 2) discusses the role of sectional politics in key decisions of the 1890s.

29. LaFeber (1994, chaps. 9–11) deals with U.S. foreign policy from World War I to 1933. Knock (1995) and Cooper (2003) discuss Woodrow Wilson, World War I, and the League of Nations.

30. LaFeber (1994, chaps. 12–13) covers the run-up to World War II and the war itself. On the American public's shift from isolationism to internationalism, see Foster (1983).

31. The Cold War period of U.S. foreign policy is well described and analyzed in LaFeber (1994, chaps. 14–19).

32. On the Korean War, see Cumings (1990) and Stueck (2002); on Vietnam, Herring (2001) and Kaiser (2000). U.S. relations with the shah's Iran are discussed in Bill (1988); with Marcos' Philippines, in Bonner (1988).

33. The lessons learned from the Cold War and subsequently are evident in Chicago Council on Foreign Relations surveys, from 1974 on, of both "foreign policy leaders" and the general public; see Rielly (1975 et seq.), Holsti (2004), and later chapters of this book. On the Powell Doctrine, see Powell (1995).

34. Cyr (2000) offers an interesting brief account of U.S. foreign policy before and after the end of the Cold War (which may, however, be a bit too rough on Bill Clinton).

CHAPTER ONE

We are grateful to Ed Greenberg, Susan Herbst, Elizabeth Hurd, Ole Holsti, and Art Cyr for comments on a draft of this chapter.

1. Hamilton, Madison, and Jay (1961, 384, 432). See also Madison's Federalist number 49, which alludes to "public passions" in arguing against allowing the people directly to amend the Constitution (315, 317); his number 62, which defends bicameralism and a small, select Senate by noting "the propensity of all single and numerous assemblies to yield to the impulse of sudden and violent passions" (379); and Hamilton's number 68, which argues for indirect election of the president (separately in each state) in order to avoid "tumult and disorder," "extraordinary or violent movements" that would convulse the community, or "heats and ferments" that direct or unified election would bring (412).

2. On democracy as entailing responsiveness to citizens' policy preferences, as vs. "trusteeship" or procedural views of democracy, contrast Dahl (1989) with Burke (1949), Schumpeter (1947), and Sartori (1987).

3. Morgenthau (1973, 135, 146–48).

4. Kennan (1951, 93–100); Lippmann (1955, 20, 26–27). See also Lippmann (1965, 1925).

5. Kull and Destler (1999) document foreign policy elites' widespread misperceptions of public opinion about foreign policy (especially erroneous perceptions of isolationism) and their insistence that real or "effective" opinion differs from that revealed by polls. Jacobs and Shapiro (2000) note that responsiveness to public opinion is often dismissed by politicians and pundits as "pandering." Cook, Barabas, and Page (2002a, 2002b) and Paden and Page (2003) document the infrequent, vague, and sometimes erroneous invocations of public opinion in officials' statements and policy debates.

6. For early survey evidence of an inattentive or erratic public, see Lazarsfeld, Berelson, and Gaudet (1968); Berelson, Lazarsfeld, and McPhee (1954); Campbell et al. (1960); Almond (1960); and Rosenau (1961, 39–40).

7. On opinion instability and "non-attitudes" among individuals, see Converse (1964, 1970).

8. For qualifications about the early evidence, see Achen (1975), along with Erikson (1979) and Feldman (1989); Caspary (1970); Pomper (1972); Page (1978); Aldrich, Sullivan, and Borgida (1989); Popkin (1991).

9. The extent of political knowledge or ignorance among the U.S. public is documented in Delli Carpini and Keeter (1996, esp. 69–89, 269–70).

10. On stability in collective public opinion, see Page and Shapiro (1992, 45–47, 54–55, 58). William Mayer (1991, 155) found changes of twenty percentage points or more on fully 42 percent of the questions he analyzed, a much higher proportion, but this figure was

based on only 166 survey questions (less than a sixth of the number studied by Page and Shapiro), selected because they were repeated over periods of ten years or more. These are precisely the cases in which one would expect to find substantial (though mostly gradual) opinion changes, especially since survey organizations tend to keep repeating questions for which they can report interesting changes.

11. Examples of distinctions made by collective public opinion are given in Page and Shapiro (1992, 64, 70, 97, 241, 267, 276).

12. On collective deliberation through the mass media and conversations among citizens, see Page (1996), Just et al. (1996), and Gamson (1993). On individuals' use of simple cues and heuristics to form sensible opinions without detailed policy information, see Sniderman, Brody, and Tetlock (1991); Lupia and McCubbins (1998), and Lupia, McCubbins, and Popkin (2000).

13. The logic of how individuals' unstable survey responses can be aggregated into stable measures of "rational" collective public opinion is discussed in Page and Shapiro (1992, 15–27). This logic is consistent with various probabilistic theories of the survey response (e.g., the averaging of accessible "considerations" postulated in Zaller 1992, 28–52; see also Zaller and Feldman 1992) as well as models of independent random measurement errors in surveys (Achen 1975; Erikson 1979; Feldman 1989).

14. On the general "wisdom of crowds," see Surowiecki (2004).

15. A classic text on survey sampling is Kish (1995).

16. On views and interests that tend to be neglected in survey-based measures of collective public opinion due to "don't know" or poorly informed responses (especially those of relatively low-income and less educated people), see Brehm (1993), Bartels (1996), Althaus (1998, 2003), and Berinsky (2002, 2004). These biases generally tend to be fairly small.

17. When asked by survey interviewers about an unfamiliar policy (e.g., the very obscure Agricultural Trade Act of 1978 or Monetary Control Bill of 1979), some people apparently use key words in the policy's name as cues about how that policy relates to their basic beliefs and values, and offer a pro or con response—especially if "don't know" responses are discouraged. We agree with Schuman and Presser (1981, 147–60) that such responses do not constitute evidence of non-attitudes: they are not random, they show some stability over time, and they relate empirically to other attitudes. This can be true even of responses concerning fictitious policies made up by researchers.

18. See Page and Shapiro (1992, 215–16).

19. On balance and tone in question wording, see Schuman and Presser (1981, chaps. 7, 11). But Schuman and Presser point out that invocations of authority can boomerang (presumably when the authority is less popular than the policy at issue) and also argue that the most blatant biases in question wording may actually have the least impact (295–96).

20. Evidence on media effects includes Iyengar and Kinder (1987); Page, Shapiro, and Dempsey (1987). See also Page and Shapiro (1992, 339–54).

21. Evidence of the predominance in the media of official news sources and official viewpoints on foreign policy includes Sigal (1973), Gans (1979), Hallin (1986), Bennett (1990), and Bennett and Paletz (1994). Herman and Chomsky (1988) outline a "propaganda model" and present numerous examples of misleading media content reflecting official U.S. foreign policy.

22. A lively critique of the George W. Bush administration's rhetoric about Saddam Hussein's Iraq is Rampton and Stauber (2003). A still-interesting account of past U.S. government

secrecy and misinformation concerning various foreign policies, including Vietnam, is Wise (1973). See also Page and Shapiro (1992, 366–82) and Alterman (2004).

23. A similar position on the generally authentic and well-informed nature of poll-measured collective public opinion is articulated in Page and Shapiro (1992, chap. 10). A particularly forceful opposing view is T. Ferguson (1995, including the appendix).

24. We use the term "belief system," as Converse (1964) and a number of subsequent scholars have done, despite the way it highlights the cognitive to the apparent exclusion of the affective. Like Converse we are interested in "constraints," or empirical linkages, among a variety of political values, attitudes, beliefs, and perceptions. But we are also concerned with the *effects* of some attitudes on others, and we emphasize *logical* rather than social or psychological sources of constraint.

25. Dukhong Kim, in his dissertation research at Northwestern University, is working on some complex theoretical and empirical issues related to purposive foreign policy belief systems, using the CCFR data.

26. The "J. Q. Public" interview appears in Kull (2001b).

27. On values and preferences, see Feldman (1988), Feldman and Steenbergen (2001), and Kinder (1983). On the dimensional structure of foreign policy goals and attitudes, see Bardes and Oldendick (1978); Mandelbaum and Schneider (1979); Wittkopf and Maggiotto (1983); Wittkopf (1986, 1990); Chittick, Billingsley, and Travis (1995); and Richman, Malone, and Nolle (1997). As we will see in chapter 2, these scholars differ somewhat over the number, nature, and labeling of dimensions, but they agree that internationalism has at least two or three distinct faces. Hurwitz and Peffley (1987) postulate a three-level hierarchical belief system involving values, "postures" or beliefs (including an "enemies" heuristic concerning the Soviet Union), and policy preferences, testing it on a local sample from Lexington, Kentucky. Hermann, Tetlock, and Visser (1999) argue that ordinary Americans engage in at least some strategic calculations concerning foreign policy. An excellent general treatment of U.S. public and elite opinion on foreign policy is Holsti (2004).

28. One way to judge the tightness or looseness of purposive belief systems (the degree of "constraint") is to examine statistical measures—such as the adjusted R-squared in regression equations—of how well various attitudes and perceptions can account for individuals' policy preferences. If a perfect, totally constrained belief system with common structure were shared by every single individual in the population, then 100 percent of the variance in policy preferences could be accounted for: R-squared would reach 1.00. Our analyses never come close to such perfect predictive power. In some cases the relationships are quite substantial, but in others we will be satisfied to report modest adjusted R-squared values and coefficients that (according to statistical tests) are significantly greater than zero. Again, only a *tendency* for individuals to have purposive belief systems is required in order to account for the coherence of collective public opinion.

29. In principle, one-way causal paths could be identified, and simultaneity bias could be avoided, through simultaneous equation analysis. But we have not been able to find sufficiently plausible exogenous identifying variables to do this.

30. The 1978 through 1998 surveys were conducted by the Gallup organization. The 1974 survey was fielded by Louis Harris Associates, the 2002 survey by its successor organization, Harris Interactive, and the 2004 survey by Knowledge Networks (KN). For 1974 through 1998 all interviews were conducted in person, with sample sizes of 1,513, 1,546, 1,546, 1,585, 1,662, 1,492, and 1,507, respectively. Interview dates were December 6–14, 1974;

November 17–26, 1978; October 29–November 6, 1982; October 30–November 12, 1986 (with a supplemental survey January 14–18, 1987; $N = 1,000$); October 23–November 15, 1990; October 7–25, 1994; and October 15–November 10, 1998. The 2002 and 2004 survey modes, interview dates, and sample designs are described below. "House effects" caused by switches in survey organizations chiefly affect proportions of "don't know" responses; in our data they appear to be small. But some substantial "mode effects" are discussed below.

31. Small deviations from demographic representativeness in the public samples were corrected by weighting respondents. The marginal frequencies and cross-tabulations we report are based on weighted data. Correlations and regressions are generally based on *unweighted* data, in order to ensure that statistical tests are valid. In principle this means that the correlations and regressions apply to slightly different populations than the marginal frequencies do, but in practice the differences between weighted and unweighted relationships are quite small.

32. The leader surveys were carried out by the same organizations that did the general public surveys, except that Ipsos-Public Affairs did the leader survey in 2004. Sample sizes from 1974 through 2004 were 328, 366, 341, 343, 377, 383, 370, 397, and 450. These surveys were carried out in the late autumn through 1998 (early summer in 2002 and 2004), generally over somewhat longer intervals than those for the general public. Interview dates were December 10–29, 1974; November 20, 1978–January 12, 1979; early November to mid-December, 1982; mid-September to mid-November, 1986; October 19–November 16, 1990; October 26–December 7, 1994; November 2–December 21, 1998; May 17–July 15, 2002; and June 23–July 20, 2004.

33. The 2002 general public survey involved a random-digit-dialing (RDD) telephone sample of 2,862 respondents, plus an in-person sample of 400 respondents. Many questions (particularly those posed for the first time in 2002) were asked only of randomly selected subsamples of about 700 telephone respondents. "Core" questions, nearly all repeated from earlier CCFR surveys, were asked of similar RDD subsamples and also the 400 in-person respondents. Some especially important questions, including all demographic characteristics as well as "active part" internationalism, liberal-conservative self-ratings, and party identification, were asked of all 3,262 respondents. Certain information or knowledge questions were asked of all telephone respondents but not the in-person respondents.

34. Data from telephone surveys tend to differ somewhat from in-person data both in the kinds of people who are reached and who complete interviews (those with little interest in politics may be harder to line up for personal interviews, for example) and in the type of responses they give (e.g., it may be easier to give flip, top-of-the-head answers on the telephone than when looking an interviewer in the eye; see Holbrook, Green, and Krosnick 2003). In the 2002 CCFR study, telephone interviewees tended to give fewer "don't know" responses and to offer more "positive" or first-option responses, including more perceptions of a U.S. "vital interest" in countries around the world, and more judgments that various foreign policy goals should be "very important."

In our view, neither survey mode is inferior or incorrect. Both meet professional standards and accurately reflect the responses of the populations from which they sample. In-person interviews may be somewhat superior for accurately ascertaining the thinking of individuals, but telephone surveys have become a near-universal standard in the United States for describing collective public opinion. Telephone random digit dialing techniques also produce a more truly random sampling of respondents scattered around the country than is feasible with in-person interviewing; this is particularly helpful when analyzing the views of small population subgroups like American Jews or Muslims (see chapter 3).

Except when otherwise noted, all analyses of the 2002 data in this book are based on a *combined* in-person and telephone data set. For "core" questions asked in both modes, this has the effect of muting mode differences, with an approximately 7:4 weighting of telephone and in-person respondents. This compromise generally allows for reasonable comparisons with the 1998 purely in-person data (but no inferences about change are drawn except after examining 2002 in-person-only data for confirmation), while at the same time permitting comparison with the results of standard RDD surveys done by media outlets and commercial polling firms. For "RDD-only" items, use of the combined data set means simply reporting telephone-only results comparable to those in most other national surveys. Most multivariate analyses with the combined data set necessarily turn out to rely heavily on the four hundred in-person interviews, in which respondents were all asked the same questions (see below).

35. The 2004 Web-based survey was conducted between July 6 and July 12, with 1,195 completed questionnaires (of 1,831 solicited) from a representative sample from KN's continuing panel. Responses were weighted. A monetary incentive was given for the short completion period. The order of items on batteries was fully randomized. For evidence that such computerized, self-administered interviewing techniques are "viable"—with somewhat less sampling representativeness but more accurate responses than telephone interviews—see Chang and Krosnick (2003).

36. As we will see in chapter 3, KN's Web-based respondents tended to give foreign countries "feeling thermometer" ratings about 6 or 7 degrees cooler on the 100-point scale than did telephone or in-person respondents.

37. The short 2002 Web-based pilot survey, fielded between July 19 and August 7, elicited 1,091 "qualified complete" responses from 1,429 individuals randomly drawn from KN's representative panel, who had been given WebTV hardware and free Internet access. Questions involved fourteen country "feeling thermometers," twenty foreign policy goals, four international treaties, six policies to "combat terrorism," and several other matters. The very small 2004 CCI telephone survey involved 505 respondents, who were asked about six government programs, twelve international threats, and a few other matters.

38. The "essential" demographic and attitudinal questions that were asked in 2002 of all 3,262 respondents can of course be included in all bivariate and multivariate analyses. An "RDD-only" question, asked only of roughly 700 telephone respondents (about one quarter of the 2,800 total phone respondents), generally shares about 175 respondents (one quarter of the 700) with any other RDD-only question asked of an independent, similarly sized random subsample, which is sufficient for reasonably reliable estimates of bivariate relationships. But some telephone-interview questions (long "thermometer" batteries, for example) were asked exclusively of others, in order to avoid fatigue effects or the contamination of responses by related questions; in such cases it is not possible to explore even bivariate relationships. Bivariate relationships among "core," RDD plus in-person, variables can generally be estimated with a considerably more satisfactory N of about 575 (400 in-person plus roughly 175 telephone respondents).

For multivariate analyses, the number of common respondents to questions asked of independent random RDD subsamples quickly diminishes, to roughly 44 for three variables and a useless 11 for four variables. A further complication is that not all RDD subsamples were in fact independently random; some questions fully shared the same respondents and others were asked entirely exclusively of each other. Of course no pairs of variables asked exclusively of each other can be included at all in the same data analyses. In practice, most of our multivariate analyses had to rely heavily upon the 400 in-person respondents who were asked all the "essential" and "core" questions; noncore variables could not generally be included. These in-person interview data probably have the advantage of higher individual-level reliability than the telephone responses.

CHAPTER TWO

For comments and suggestions on this chapter we are grateful to Larry Jacobs, Ed Greenberg, Bob Shapiro, Art Cyr, Tom Ferguson, Andrew Martin, William Chittick, Ole Holsti, and Eugene Wittkopf, who provided a particular detailed and helpful analysis.

1. Arguments for trusteeship and accountability rather than immediate responsiveness to citizens' wishes include Burke (1949), Schumpeter (1947), and Sartori (1987). Contrast Dahl (1989), and cf. Pitkin (1967).

2. For convenience we will sometimes speak of CCFR surveys as including the 2002 survey, which was jointly sponsored by the Chicago Council on Foreign Relations and the German Marshall Fund of the United States, as well as the 1974, 1978, 1982, 1986, 1990, 1994, 1998, and 2004 surveys, which were sponsored by the Chicago Council alone. As noted in chapter 1, the surveys were carried out by the Harris organization (1974), Gallup (1978–1998), Harris Interactive (2002), and Knowledge Networks (2004). The 1974 through 1998 surveys were implemented exclusively through in-person interviews, with sample sizes of approximately 1,500. The 2002 survey had a total N of 3,262, with 2,862 telephone (random digit dialing) and 400 in-person interviews; many questions were asked only of random subsamples of about 700 telephone interviewees, either exclusively or in combination with the 400 in-person interviewees. Issues related to sample sizes and mode differences will be discussed below. The 2004 survey was Web-based, bringing a new set of mode effects and complicating over-time comparisons in ways we will discuss; the sample size was 1,195.

3. The percentage of people calling a given goal "very important" is only an imperfect indicator of exactly how important the average American considers it to be. In theory, for example, even if 80 percent call goal A "very important" while only 70 percent say the same about goal B, all of those 70 percent might be much more enthusiastic about goal B than goal A. If so, the average American might be said to judge goal B as more important than A. But we believe this is unlikely to happen in many cases. We consider our rankings based on percentages of "very important" responses to be generally sound reflections of collective priorities.

4. Trubowitz (1998) emphasizes the contested nature of concepts of "national interest." A more traditional approach to national interests in the economic realm is Krasner (1978).

5. One reason the correlation coefficients are higher among altruistic and humanitarian goals than within other goal clusters is that there was less unanimity (hence more meaningful variation) concerning their importance than was generally true of security against attack or security of domestic well-being.

6. The labeling of dimensions is inherently subjective; different scholars' labels for identical factors tend to vary according to their own theoretical orientations. Further, the basic dimensional models are statistically underidentified. Somewhat arbitrary decisions about

rotations, eigenvalue cutoffs, and the like inevitably affect the number and nature of factors discovered.

7. Chittick, Billingsley, and Travis (1995, 325). In replicating Chittick and his colleagues' factor analyses for the four CCFR surveys between 1974 and 1986, Dukhong Kim found what appear to be errors in the "prosperity" factor loadings they reported for 1986. He found the jobs goal to load at .758 rather than .008, securing energy to load at .560 rather than .165, and reducing the trade deficit (apparently confused with the old "value of the dollar" goal) to load at .675 rather than .145. If these changes are made, the 1986 findings look less anomalous and their study's general argument is strengthened. The absence of 1990 findings in their analysis may reflect the tabulation errors in the original 1990 data that are discussed below, which presumably rendered factor-analytic results meaningless.

The reasoning given by Chittick et al. for associating their factors with the theoretical dimensions of "multilateralism," "militarism," and "internationalism" are plausible: that people who want to help other countries generally also want to consult and work with them, that people concerned about security are likely to favor the use of force in response, and (perhaps less compellingly) that those who stress the importance of domestic prosperity are prone to be optimistic about it and hence to favor more international involvement (1995, 319–20). But we believe that multilateralism, militarism, and international activism instead characterize broad *means* of attaining foreign policy goals and do not constitute goals in themselves. Our labels for clusters of goals emphasize results sought rather than methods favored to attain them, although we recognize that means and ends often blend together.

The 1995 Chittick, Billingsley, and Travis findings generally confirm results based on earlier data reported by Bardes and Oldendick (1978, 1980) and Mandelbaum and Schneider (1979). Their results improve upon the two-factor model of Maggiotto and Wittkopf (1981) and Wittkopf (1990), which nonetheless represented pioneering work that spurred a great deal of subsequent research. Two-dimensional factor solutions continue to account for a large portion of the variation in foreign policy attitudes.

8. Richman, Malone, and Nolle (1997, 945) labeled the dimensions much as we do, except that they called the second (primarily domestic) factor a "U.S. global interest" dimension (GINT). They labeled the first factor "global altruism" (GALT), the third "domestic," and the fourth "U.S. military security" (MILSEC). A strength of their approach, evident in the CCFR factor loadings and the factor intercorrelations based on Times-Mirror data that they report (945, 951), is that when goals factors were permitted to be intercorrelated, several were found to do so at moderate levels.

9. For the 2002 goals data, a Chittick-style, principal-components factor analysis with orthogonal, Varimax rotation (constraining the solution to four factors), produced less clear results, including some mingling of security from attack and security of domestic well-being. But we know of no strong theoretical reason why the factors should be forced to be wholly independent of one another in this way.

Dukhong Kim applied the same Chittick-style factor analytic methods to the 1998 goals data and found that only two factors satisfied the usual criterion (eigenvalue > 1.0) for acceptance as valid; five factors did so in the initial 2002 analysis. One 1998 factor clearly emphasized justice or altruistic goals; the other combined security from attack with security of domestic well-being.

10. The crucial timing of the 1990 survey, right at the end of the Cold War, makes it particularly unfortunate that the Gallup Organization in that year made a tabulation error

(incorrectly combining data from two questionnaire forms that reversed the order of goals questions) that led to erroneous—in fact meaningless—goals rankings that have been published in Rielly (1991, 15) and elsewhere. Apparently this error went undetected for many years until Dukhong Kim, Ann Janda, and the staff of the Inter-University Consortium for Political and Social Research discovered it in 2002. In this book all 1990 figures on goals (and on troop use, which suffered from the same problem) are corrected.

11. Certain goals asked about only in 1974 are omitted from table 2.2: "Fostering international cooperation to solve common problems, such as food, inflation and energy" (called "very important" by 67 percent of respondents); "Helping solve world inflation" (64 percent); "Maintaining a balance of power among nations" (48 percent); "Strengthening countries who are friendly toward us" (37 percent); and "Promoting the development of capitalism abroad" (16 percent).

12. The telephone respondents in 2002 apparently more often gave facile, "first box" responses to certain long batteries of questions than in-person interviewees did, including more "very important" ratings of the lower-priority goals. If only the in-person 2002 responses are compared with the purely in-person 1998 data, "very important" ratings for superior military power appear to have risen significantly, but those for defending allies and protecting weaker nations do not. Contrary to the impression given by table 2.3, the importance to the public of combating world hunger and improving the standard of living of less developed nations appears to have *dropped* significantly between 1998 and 2002, while reactions to other altruistic goals stayed about the same; the importance attributed to improving the global environment did not increase significantly.

Percentage point changes between 1998 and 2002 in "very important" responses, based solely on in-person data, are as follows: preventing proliferation +6, combating terrorism +11, protecting jobs +5, stopping drugs +1, securing energy +16, controlling immigration +15, improving the environment +1, combating hunger −10, reducing the trade deficit −5, maintaining military power +7, strengthening the UN +6, defending allies +1, promoting human rights 0, promoting market economies −3, protecting weaker nations −1, improving standards of living −8, bringing democracy −2. There had been no question about protecting American business interests abroad in 1998. "Safeguarding against financial instability (not shown in table 2.3) dropped by a hefty 37 percentage points.

Note that the 2002 *ranking* of goals stayed very similar to that of 1998, according to in-person-only data. For consistency with table 2.1, we have kept the combined-data (mostly telephone-interview) results in the 2002 column of table 2.3. Throughout the book we report 2002 combined-data percentages in the text and tables. But we base assertions about change only on same-mode surveys, discussing mode effects in endnotes.

13. Based on comparisons of the 2004 Web-based survey with the 2002 Web-based pilot, percentage-point changes in the proportions of Americans calling various goals "very important" were as follows: preventing proliferation −13, combating terrorism −12, protecting jobs −3, stopping drugs −9, securing energy −1, controlling immigration −10, improving the global environment −8, combating hunger −11, maintaining military power −17, strengthening the UN −17, protecting American business −19, protecting weaker nations −17, improving standards of living −10, and bringing democracy −10.

14. Of the fourteen goals asked about in both surveys, the "very important" ratings for securing energy and protecting jobs dropped the least, by one and three percentage points,

respectively. For changes in other goal ratings between 2002 and 2004, based on comparable, Web-based surveys, see the previous note.

15. Unfortunately the key "combating world hunger" goal question was not asked in 1994.

16. The difference between means and ends is a relative matter. In purposive belief systems we see various elements as forming a hierarchy, with each end (except the most basic and fundamental of values) constituting a means toward attaining some higher end, and with each means (except the most concrete and detailed means possible) constituting an end that some more specific means is designed to attain. The boundaries between basic values, goals, and policies of varying specificity are therefore inherently fuzzy. Examination of the CCFR questions suggests that some of the possible goals are closer to basic values ("keeping peace in the world," "combating world hunger"), while others are closer to specific policies ("controlling and reducing illegal immigration," "reducing our trade deficit").

17. Only the first question was asked in 1974. Then and in 1978 the wording was different from that of later years, referring to problems "that you would like to see the Federal government do something about." Neither "biggest problems" question was asked in 2004.

18. On Americans' weariness with Vietnam in 1974, and the paucity of foreign policy matters cited as important problems, see Rielly (1975, esp. 10). This and subsequent quadrennial reports edited by Rielly provide valuable information on trends in perceived problems and other foreign policy attitudes and perceptions.

19. As with the goals rankings, the percentage of Americans calling a particular threat "critical" is an imperfect indicator of how important the average American considered that threat to be. But we believe it is generally a good indicator. It would go badly astray only if the frequency distribution between "important but not critical" and "not important" responses, or the meaning attached to those responses, varied markedly from one issue to another. We have seen no evidence of such phenomena.

20. Percentages calling each threat "critical" in the small CCI 2004 telephone survey (which is more comparable to the 2002 data in table 2.4 than the main 2004 Web-based survey was), with percentage-point changes from 2002 in parentheses: international terrorism 81 percent (−10), chemical and biological weapons 70 percent (−17), unfriendly nuclear powers 66 percent (−19), AIDs and Ebola 55 percent (−13), Israel/Arab conflict 43 percent (−24), Islamic fundamentalism 40 percent (−21), large numbers of immigrants 51 percent (−9), China as a world power 40 percent (−16), tensions between India and Pakistan 27 percent (−27), global warming 37 percent (−9), economic competition from low-wage countries 35 percent (+4, one of only two rises), economic competition from Europe 20 percent (+7, the other rise).

21. Considering only data from the in-person 2002 interviews, perceptions of Islamic fundamentalism as a critical threat rose from 1998 by 20 percentage points, very similar to the 23 point combined-data figure cited in the text. In general, the in-person "critical threat" percentages (unlike "very important" goal percentages) did not differ much from the combined-data percentages, with some a bit higher and some a bit lower. Most significantly different were the six-point-higher proportion of in-person interviewees seeing "economic competition from low-wage countries" as a critical threat and the five-point-lower percentage seeing civil wars in Africa or military conflict between Israel and its Arab neighbors as critical threats.

22. See note 20.

23. Pearson coefficients *(r)* for the correlations between the goal of combating international terrorism and the threats of terrorism, chemical and biological weapons, Iraqi WMDs, and nuclear proliferation were .36, .24, .27, and .26, respectively. Given the random-subsample design of the CCFR study, the sample sizes available for cross-tabulations and correlations are often small (in this case, just under 400), but each of these coefficients is significantly different from zero (by two-tailed test) at better than the $p = .001$ level.

Pearson's *r* can be misleading when the distributions of responses for two variables are markedly different. In such cases, *r* cannot reach its theoretical maximum value of 1.00 even if there is a perfect relationship between two variables in the sense that a particular response to one is either a necessary or a sufficient condition for a particular response to the other. Pearson's *r* can also be misleadingly low (as, arguably, in the correlations involving terrorism and nuclear weapons) when responses are highly skewed and measurement error constitutes a substantial portion of the observed variation. Still, Pearson's *r* (and its square) have strong intuitive meanings in connection with the proportion of variance accounted for. It is particularly appropriate when dealing with multiple-option variables like thermometer scores, goals, and threats, where the distances between response categories arguably carry some interval-level information.

24. Pearson's coefficients for the correlations between the goal of preventing nuclear proliferation and the threats of terrorism, CBWs, Iraqi WMDs, and nuclear proliferation were .20, .19, .27, and a puzzlingly low .13, respectively. All are significant at better than $p = .001$ except the last ($p = .008$). This and other correlations involving terrorism and nuclear weapons are probably depressed by the fact that very large majorities agreed that these were critical threats and very important goals; much of the meager variance in responses probably represents measurement noise that one would not expect to correlate highly across variables.

25. The correlation between seeing immigration control as a goal and immigrants as a threat was $r = .56$. The goal of improving the environment correlated $r = .42$ with the threat of global warming and $r = .29$ with the threat of population growth. The goal of job protection correlated $r = .25$ with the threat of immigrants.

26. The 2002 in-person-only data indicate that the proportion of Americans rating competition from low-wage countries as a critical threat dipped only from 40 percent in 1998 to 37 percent in 2002, though the combined 2002 data misleadingly seem to show a bigger drop, to 31 percent.

27. The highest adjusted *R*-squared values in regressions of goals on demographic characteristics were for protecting jobs (.09), stopping drugs (.08), strengthening the UN (.08), and protecting the global environment (.05). The lowest were for protecting weaker nations (−.003), defending allies (−.001), preventing the spread of nuclear weapons (.004), improving the standard of living of less developed countries (.005), promoting market economies (.006), reducing the trade deficit (.007), securing energy supplies (.008), and combating terrorism (.009).

28. Parallel regressions of *threats* on demographic, attitudinal, and informational factors—not discussed in the text—produced results very similar to those for the goals regressions, including the very low predictive power of demographic factors. As later chapters will indicate, the same was true of thermometer-measured feeling about countries and of most specific policy preferences.

29. These demographic goals regressions were based on all 400 in-person respondents and a random subsample of 706 telephone respondents. Because of missing values for some demographic variables, in most cases N was in the low 900s. Significance was assessed at the $p < .05$ level by two-tailed tests.

30. Standardized regression coefficients from demographic regressions that were statistically significant ($p < .05$) were as follows. For the goal of job protection: education −.21, gender .10, African American .09, income −.08, Catholic .07. For the goal of stopping drugs: evangelical .15, age .13, Catholic .12, gender .10, education −.14. For strengthening the UN: gender .17, income −.11, African American .08, evangelical −.08. For improving the environment: gender .13, income −.08. For bringing democracy: income .10, Catholic .07, African American .07, Muslim .06, education −.12. We report standardized coefficients here in order to allow comparability across independent variables and to keep the focus on proportions of variance explained in the whole U.S. population. Below, however, we note some distinctive effects of membership in certain small ethnic and religious groups that are better measured by *unstandardized* coefficients.

31. Rosenau (1961, 39–40). See also Almond (1960, chap. 6).

32. In fourteen-independent-variable demographic regressions standardized coefficients for the effect of education were significant in relation to the goals of job protection (−.21), stopping drugs (−.14), controlling immigration (−.12), securing energy supplies (−.13), maintaining military power (−.17), combating terrorism (−.09), and bringing democracy (−.12). Coefficients for other goals were not significant.

33. Standardized coefficients for the effects of income in comprehensive demographic regressions were significant vis-à-vis the goals of job protection (−.08), strengthening the UN (−.11), strengthening international law (−.09), and improving the global environment (−.08). Having a higher income made people *more* likely to attribute high importance to the goals of promoting democracy abroad (.10) and maintaining superior military power (.10). These cases are unusual in that income and education had opposite effects. Thus these particular effects of education apparently did not result from income or status; still, it is not easy to argue that they reflected superior enlightenment. Because education is generally better measured than income in surveys (incomes are sometimes misrepresented or mistakenly reported, partly because of definitional ambiguities), and because education has class or status implications distinct from income, income effects probably tend to be underestimated; thus, statistical controls for measured income do not wholly eliminate the class- or status-related aspects of estimated education effects.

34. In regressions with a full set of demographic, ideological, and informational variables, knowledge of the euro had a significantly ($p < .05$) negative coefficient for seven of the twenty foreign policy goals: strengthening the UN (−.17), military power (−.13), protecting jobs (−.15), promoting democracy (−.10), protecting the environment (−.11), protecting American business (−.13), and strengthening international law (−.16). Relatively correct perceptions of the foreign aid budget had significant effects only on four goals: combating world hunger (−.10), military power (−.12), protecting jobs (−.11), and stopping drugs (−.12). Travel abroad (including Mexico and Canada) affected just two goals: protecting jobs (+.10) and stopping illegal drugs (−.09).

35. On gender differences, see Shapiro and Mahajan (1986). A good summary of bivariate gender and age (or "generation") differences on foreign policy is Holsti (2004, 196–224).

36. In demographic multiple regressions, standardized coefficients for the effects of gender on goals were significant in relation to the goals of strengthening the UN (.17), improving the environment (.13), strengthening international law (.09), combating world hunger (.10), promoting human rights (.07), protecting jobs (.10), protecting business (.07), and stopping drugs (.10). The standardized coefficient for the effect of being married upon viewing the promotion of human rights as very important was −.08.

37. McManus (1996) documents many substantial bivariate age differences in the 1990s over domestic policy, and some concerning foreign policy, especially the global environment and the use of U.S. forces (see pp. 215–18, 232–33).

38. Standardized coefficients for the effects of age were significant for the goals of maintaining military power (.09), stopping drugs (.13), and controlling immigration (.12).

39. The survey's race question read, "Do you consider yourself White, Black or African American, Asian or Pacific Islander, Native American or Alaskan native, or some other race?"; 6.1% of respondents said "Black" and another 6.1% "African American." We combine the two under the label "African American." Standardized coefficients for the effect of being African American were significant for the goals of protecting jobs (.09), improving foreign standards of living (.09), strengthening the UN (.08), and bringing democracy abroad (.07).

40. All respondents were asked, "Are you of Spanish, Hispanic, or Latino origin or descent?"; 10 percent of the sample (322 people) said yes. In demographic regressions, standardized coefficients for the effects of being Hispanic were significant for the goals of controlling immigration (−.10; *unstandardized* coefficient, −.25) and improving the environment (.10). Standardized coefficients give a sense for how well variation in a characteristic like race or ethnicity accounts for opinion variation in the population as a whole. For small population subgroups, unstandardized coefficients are superior for indicating the *effect of membership in that group*. The −.25 unstandardized coefficient for Hispanics, for example, indicates that, controlling for other demographic characteristics, being Hispanic led to a drop of about one-quarter of the distance between calling immigration restrictions a "very important" goal and calling them only "somewhat important."

41. In the 2002 survey, 2 percent of respondents (64 individuals) said they considered themselves "Asian or Pacific Islander." The only significant coefficients for effects of being Asian on foreign policy goals involved the goal of protecting weaker nations: standardized, −.08; unstandardized, a substantial −.33.

42. Standardized coefficients for the effects of being evangelical were significant for the goals of stopping drugs (.15), combating terrorism (.10), improving the environment (−.14), and strengthening the UN (−.08). We label as "evangelical" the 39 percent of Protestant respondents who called themselves "fundamentalist, evangelical, charismatic, [or] Pentecostal," as opposed to "moderate to liberal." Regular church attendance (unfortunately not measured in the CCFR surveys) undoubtedly leads to still stronger effects of religious affiliations.

43. Standardized coefficients for the effects of being Catholic were significant for the goals of stopping drugs (.12), protecting jobs (.07), and bringing democracy (.07).

44. The only significant coefficient for the effect of being Jewish on foreign policy goals was for safeguarding against global financial instability (standardized, .08; unstandardized, a substantial .33). Just forty-three Jews (1.3 percent of the sample) were included in the 2002 survey. As we will see in the next chapter, however, this number—like the even

smaller number of Muslims—was sufficient for multiple regressions to reveal some very distinctive, independent effects on feelings about Middle Eastern countries.

45. The only significant standardized coefficient for effects of being Muslim on foreign policy goals was for helping bring democracy to other nations (.06; unstandardized, a remarkable .62). American Muslims clearly want to democratize the Middle East. Only fifteen Muslims were included in the 2002 survey, but the geographically scattered sample produced by random-digit dialing and the statistical significance of these coefficients give us confidence that this finding is real.

46. On regional conflicts over foreign policy, see Trubowitz (1998).

47. Hero (1965); Markusen et al. (1991).

48. To be sure, the four-region breakdown is rather crude. Finer distinctions might reveal more geographically based differences. The thinly populated Rocky Mountain states, for example, may retain some of the cowboy characteristics that are no longer applicable to the West as a whole.

49. Experiments are the most reliable source of information about causal connections among individuals' attitudes and beliefs. Cross-sectional data can be causally ambiguous, absent plausible specifications of exogenous variables for simultaneous equation analysis, and convincing specifications are rare. Even time series data rarely provide much leverage, since cognitive processes tend to be nearly instantaneous: too quick to be untangled by data lags of days or weeks, let alone years.

50. When the three ideological or partisan basic attitude variables were added to the fourteen variables used in demographic regressions, the adjusted R-squared values increased particularly strongly for improving the global environment (from .053 to .141), promoting human rights (.013 to .094), combating world hunger (.012 to .082), strengthening the UN (.075 to .138), and improving standards of living (.005 to .064). In sixteen of the twenty cases (compared to only three for knowledge and international exposure), the adjusted R-squared rose by .010 or more. Only in the cases of reducing our trade deficit (little connected with any of our variables) and protecting the jobs of American workers and stopping the flow of illegal drugs (both already well accounted for by demographics) did basic attitudes add no appreciable explanatory power.

51. Liberal/conservative self-ratings correlated fairly highly ($r = .45$) with the seven-point party identification scale.

52. These and subsequent percentage figures combine "very" and "fairly" liberal people, for contrast with those who were "very" or "fairly" conservative. The opinions of very conservative and very liberal people diverged even more.

53. In regressions combining demographic and basic attitudinal variables, coefficients for the effects of liberalism were significant for the goals of improving the environment (.18), promoting human rights (.15), improving standards of living (.15), combating hunger (.15), strengthening the UN (.12), military superiority ($-.17$), controlling immigration ($-.16$), stopping drugs ($-.11$); securing energy ($-.13$), and protecting business ($-.09$). A useful review of bivariate evidence on ideological and partisan differences concerning foreign policy, among both the public and elites, is Holsti (2004, 165–96).

54. In demographic plus basic attitudes regressions, the only significant coefficients for Democratic party identification were for improving the environment (.18), strengthening the UN (.18), and combating hunger (.12). For bivariate evidence of increased partisan polarization between 1998 and 2004, especially at the elite level, see Shapiro and Bloch-Elkon (2005).

55. On the distinction between hawkish and dovish internationalism among Americans, see Wittkopf (1990). See also the discussion of factor analyses of goals, above.

56. For a line graph of proportions of "active part" internationalists in CCFR surveys between 1974 and 2002, see Bouton and Page (2002, 13). The inference of a substantial increase in international activism after 1998 is complicated by the mode change in the 2002 survey. Among 2002 in-person respondents (those most comparable to the wholly in-person survey of 1998), there were only 63 percent "active part" responses, not significantly different from the 61 percent of 1998. Collateral evidence from other surveys, however, indicates that a real change occurred. In the not strictly comparable Web-based survey of 2004, 67 percent said we should "take an active part" in world affairs and 30 percent said "stay out."

Here and elsewhere in the text we present 2002 combined-data results, which we consider to provide the best information about contemporary opinion and to be most comparable with the predominantly telephone results of other survey organizations.

57. In demographic plus basic attitudes regressions, coefficients for the effect of "active part" internationalism were significant for the goals of combating hunger (.21), protecting weaker nations (.24), promoting human rights (.24), bringing democracy (.18), improving standards of living (.19), strengthening international law (.11), strengthening the UN (.10), defending allies (.16), nonproliferation (.12), military power (.13), combating terrorism (.10), financial instability (.15), and controlling immigration (−.07).

CHAPTER THREE

For research assistance on this chapter we are particularly grateful to Julia Rabinovich, who has also conducted independent research on feelings toward countries and leaders. We are grateful for comments and suggestions from Ole Holsti, Steve Kull, Art Cyr, Eugene Wittkopf, and John Tadayeski.

1. Concern about "passions" among ordinary citizens was prominent in the thinking of the founders of the United States (see, e.g., Hamilton, Madison, and Jay 1961) and remains a theme in "realist" theories of international relations (see chaps. 1 and 7). Contrary arguments, upholding the relevance and usefulness of emotions to political thinking, are given in Marcus (2002), Marcus, Neuman, and MacKuen (2000), and Sniderman, Brody, and Tetlock (1991). But see Sullivan and Masters (1988).

2. In 2002, all in-person respondents ($N = 400$) and a random subsample of telephone interviewees ($N = 699$) were asked to give thermometer ratings for fourteen countries: Italy, Russia, North Korea, Germany, Iran, Japan, Mexico, Israel, Iraq, India, Canada, Brazil, Great Britain, and China. An entirely separate, telephone-only subsample ($N = 737$) was asked to rate another fourteen countries: Saudi Arabia, France, Taiwan, South Korea, Poland, South Africa, Cuba, Argentina, Pakistan, Nigeria, Turkey, Colombia, Egypt, and Afghanistan. For some control of order effects and for consistency with past in-person surveys, the order of countries on both lists was randomly reversed for different respondents.

As in past CCFR surveys, in-person respondents were shown a printed card with a labeled picture of a thermometer and told, "Next I'd like you to rate several countries on this feeling thermometer. If you feel neutral toward a country, give it a temperature of 50 degrees. If you have a warm feeling toward a country, give it a temperature higher than 50 degrees. If you have a cool feeling toward a country, give it a temperature lower than 50 degrees. First what temperature would you give to . . . ?" Telephone respondents, who could not be shown a printed thermometer, were given a slightly different introduction designed to convey the full range of the 100-point scale: "I'd like you to rate your feelings toward some countries, with 100 meaning a very warm, favorable feeling, zero meaning a very cold, unfavorable feeling, and fifty meaning not particularly warm or cold. You can use any number from zero to one hundred, the higher the number the more favorable your feelings are toward that country. If you have no opinion or have never heard of that country, please say so."

A second telephone-only subsample ($N = 703$) was given the same scale description as the other telephone interviewees and asked to "rate your feelings toward some people and organizations." Respondents were asked to rate several international organizations and groups, including the European Union, "the Muslim people," and "the Palestinians." We believe that these ratings are comparable to those of countries despite the difference in context.

Telephone/in-person mode differences in average 2002 thermometer scores were slight, with mean ratings by in-person respondents tending to be a degree or two lower for countries with warm average ratings, and a degree or two higher for those with cool average ratings. (One exception: Israel had a mean rating of 58 degrees by telephone but only 49 degrees in-person. Parallel differences occurred on several other questions related to Israel, for reasons that remain unclear.) We therefore feel comfortable combining the in-person and telephone data for the first fourteen countries and considering the results comparable to those for the telephone-only fourteen. The mode differences in means probably resulted from more in-person respondents giving exactly 50-degree ratings, because the in-person question wording and visual thermometer display made the 50-degree point more prominent.

3. In the 2004 Web-based survey conducted for the CCFR by Knowledge Networks, 1,195 respondents were shown a thermometer graphic and asked, with essentially the same instructions as in the 2002 Harris telephone survey, to rate their feelings about "some countries and peoples": North Korea, Germany, Mexico, Israel, Great Britain, China, Saudi Arabia, France, South Korea, Cuba, and "the Muslim people."

4. In 2002, a telephone-only random subsample ($N = 709$) was asked to "rate your feelings toward some American and foreign leaders" on the previously described telephone thermometer scale. Respondents were asked about sixteen leaders, each identified by country and position.

Using median rather than mean thermometer scores generally sharpens distinctions among countries and leaders somewhat by reducing the impact of extremely out-of-step ratings. We report means here both because they have been used in previous reports of CCFR survey findings and because they are more easily subject to statistical tests. *Rankings* of countries or leaders by both measures are highly similar.

5. A short, pilot Web-based survey conducted by Knowledge Networks for the CCFR in 2002 produced average ratings that were substantially lower, by roughly 6 degrees, than those given by telephone or in-person respondents to the main CCFR survey conducted by Harris at the same time. This mode effect may have resulted from the somewhat different thermometer display on the Web-based survey and/or from respondents' being more frank and deliberative in the absence of interviewers or time pressure. In any case, the 2004 Web-based ratings, which look relatively low (see Bouton 2004, 16–17), should not be directly compared to the ratings from the main 2002 study, displayed in table 3.1. Comparisons between

the 2002 and 2004 Web-based surveys, which used identical methods, show little change (perhaps a slight rise) in the ratings of countries that were included both times. Changes (in degrees) were: Britain 0; Germany +2; Mexico +1; Israel +4; China +4; North Korea 0.

6. Sniderman, Brody, and Tetlock (1991) argue that a "likeability heuristic" is useful to individuals for inferring whether or not particular social groups agree with their own issue positions (23, 94, 114). Similarly, we believe that affect toward a country or leader may act as a useful summary of, or guide to, beliefs about how well that actor's characteristics and behavior in the international arena match the respondent's wishes.

7. In 2002 all in-person interviewees ($N = 400$) and a random subsample of telephone interviewees ($N = 790$) were asked: "Many people believe that the United States has a vital interest in certain areas of the world and not in other areas. That is, certain countries of the world are important to the U.S. for political, economic or security reasons. I am going to read a list of countries. For each, tell me whether you feel the U.S. does or does not have a vital interest in that country." The countries (percentage "yes, has vital interest" in parentheses): Japan (83 percent), Saudi Arabia (83), Russia (81), Israel (79), Great Britain (78), Canada (76), Afghanistan (73), Mexico (72), Germany (68), Egypt (53), Bosnia (43), Brazil (36), and Indonesia (33). Using the same "vital interest" question, an entirely separate, telephone-only subsample ($N = 723$) was asked about the following countries (percentage "yes, vital interest" in parentheses): China (83 percent), Pakistan (76), Iraq (76), Iran (75), South Korea (69), India (65), Taiwan (65), Philippines (62), Colombia (62), North Korea (62), Cuba (60), France (53), Turkey (52), Sudan (52), South Africa (49), Argentina (39), and Nigeria (31).

For all mixed-mode countries but one (Canada), telephone respondents gave more "yes, vital interest" responses than in-person interviewees did, sometimes by substantial amounts (11, 13, 15, 15, and 17 percentage points more for Afghanistan, Germany, Brazil, Russia, and Bosnia respectively).This mode difference—which, like that for the goals questions, probably resulted from more facile, "first box" responses by telephone respondents to long question batteries—makes it problematic to compare purely in-person or mixed-mode percentages with figures for countries that were asked about only by telephone. China, for example, with an exclusively telephone 83 percent "vital interest" rating, should probably not be seen as equal in rank to mixed-mode Japan and Saudi Arabia, each of which had combined-data ratings of 83 percent but a telephone-only 86 percent, or to Russia, with combined 81 percent and telephone-only 86 percent. Similarly, Germany should probably be seen as ranked slightly above rather than slightly below South Korea as a vital interest. The relatively small size of the in-person sample in 2002, however, reduces the magnitude of this problem for within-year comparisons; very few relative rankings are affected. Comparisons with the wholly in-person data from 1998 and previous years are trickier. Following our usual practice, we report 2002 combined-data percentages in the text, treating across-mode comparisons with caution and footnoting important mode differences.

In CCFR reports over the years, percentages of "vital interest" responses have been used by Nora Dell, Catherine Hug, and others to produce shaded world maps that indicate the level of the American public's attention to different countries. In every survey the northern hemisphere has elicited considerably greater concern than the southern, though South Africa has sometimes stood out as relatively salient. See Bouton and Page (2002, 47), Rielly (1999, 13), Rielly (1995, 20), Rielly (1991, 18), Rielly (1987, 18), Rielly (1983, 17), and Rielly (1979, 18 [no map]).

8. Canada's mean thermometer ratings in the CCFR surveys from 1978 to 2002 were 72, 74, 77, 76, 73, 72, and 77 degrees.

9. Great Britain's mean thermometer ratings in the seven CCFR surveys starting in 1978 were 67, 68, 73, 74, 69, 69, and 76 degrees. In the 2004 Web-based survey it was 70, identical to the figure in the comparable 2002 Web-based pilot.

10. British prime minister Margaret Thatcher's average thermometer ratings were 61, 68, and 66 degrees in 1982, 1986, and 1990. The latter two years also saw Britain's highest pre-2002 ratings.

11. According to the combined 2002 data set, thermometer scores for Canada, Britain, Germany, and Japan rose by 5, 7, 5, and 5 degrees, respectively, from 1998. Part, but only part, of these apparent rises may be due to the switch in survey modes. In-person-only data for 2002 still show significant rises, of 3, 5, 3, and 3 degrees. The in-person data indicate a slightly *greater* increase for Mexico, of 4 degrees rather than 3. Comparing Web-based results in 2002 and 2004, the average thermometer ratings of Britain, Germany, and Mexico changed by 0, +2, and +1 degrees, respectively.

12. In 2002, a subsample of telephone interviewees ($N = 688$) was asked, "Thinking about the war on terrorism, do you believe that the following countries have been very reliable partners of the U.S., somewhat reliable, somewhat unreliable or very unreliable?" Percentages of "very reliable" plus "somewhat reliable" responses (with "very reliable" percentages in parentheses) were: "The countries of the European Union," 77 percent (29 percent); Russia 74 percent (15 percent); Japan 69 percent (14 percent); Israel 67 percent (25 percent); Pakistan 43 percent (10 percent); China 41 percent (5 percent); Saudi Arabia 31 percent (3 percent).

Between 1998 and 2002, according to comparable (in-person-only) 2002 data, the percentage of respondents seeing a U.S. "vital interest" in a particular country rose by 9 points for Britain, 7 for Canada, and 4 for Mexico. It remained unchanged for Germany, however, and *fell* by 9 points for Japan, perhaps because of perceptions of a weakened Japanese economy. Italy was not asked about.

13. In CCFR surveys from 1978 to 2002, the mean thermometer ratings of Italy were 56, 55, 58, 59, 58, 62, and 65 degrees; of Germany (before 1990, "West Germany"), 57, 59, 62, 62, 57, 56, and 61 degrees; of Mexico, 58, 60, 59, 56, 57, 57, and 60 degrees; and of Japan, 56, 53, 61, 52, 53, 55, and 60 degrees.

14. The average thermometer ratings of Japanese prime ministers Yashuhiro Nakasone, Toshiki Kaifu, and Junichiro Koizumi were just 50, 46, and 50 degrees in 1986, 1990, and 2002, respectively. German chancellor Helmut Kohl was rated at only 52, 53, and 51 degrees in 1986, 1990, and 1994; Gerhard Schroeder, at just 49 and 52 degrees in 1998 and 2002.

The most frequent "not familiar/no opinion" or "not sure/decline to say" thermometer responses in 2002 were for Annan (41 percent), Koizumi (40 percent), Schroeder (37 percent), Zemin (31 percent), and Chirac (29 percent). Nonratings for Putin were 20 percent, for Blair 16 percent, for Sharon 14 percent, for Arafat 6 percent, for John Paul II 4 percent, for Hussein 3 percent, and for Castro 2 percent. Fewer respondents failed to rate most American leaders: Rumsfeld (11 percent), Powell (4 percent), Bush (1 percent), Clinton (0 percent). For countries, thermometer nonratings were all well under 10 percent except for Nigeria (13 percent), Argentina (10 percent), Turkey (9 percent), and Brazil (9 percent).

15. Israel's average rating in the 2004 Web-based survey was a relatively warm 53 degrees, up 4 degrees from the figure in the 2002 Web-based pilot.

16. 2002 combined-data "vital interest" ratings: Russia 81 percent, Israel 79 percent, France 53 percent, Brazil 36 percent. The figure for France, derived exclusively from telephone interviews, should really be compared with telephone-only figures for the others (86, 82, and 42), which would make it look even a bit lower in relative terms. But the sharp 16-point rise for France from in-person 1998 to telephone-only 2002 is too large to be entirely an artifact of the change in survey mode; it fits the "huddling together" hypothesis.

17. France's average thermometer scores from 1978 to 2002 were 62, 60, 58, 56, 55, 55, and 55 degrees. Mitterand averaged 50 and 48 degrees in 1990 and 1994; Chirac, 47 and 51 degrees in 1998 and 2002.

18. "World's View of U.S. Sours after Iraq War, Poll Finds," *New York Times*, June 4, 2003, A19; "Views of a Changing World 2003: War with Iraq Further Divides Global Publics," Pew Research Center Web site, June 3, 2003. The 47-degree average rating of France in the 2004 Web-based survey (with its thermometer ratings generally lower than in other modes by 6 or 7 degrees) suggests that feelings toward France may have warmed somewhat. Lacking 2002 Web-based data, we cannot be sure.

19. Brazil's average thermometer scores for 1978 through 2002 were 52, 54, 54, 54, 54, 56, and 55 degrees; Argentina's, first assessed in 1994, were 47, 49, and 47 degrees; Colombia's (2002 only) was 36 degrees. The 2002 telephone-only vital-interest figure for Brazil, 42 percent, is more comparable to the telephone-based figures given in the text, but substantially similar to the combined-data figure.

20. Israel's average thermometer ratings starting in 1978 were 61, 55, 59, 54, 54, 55, and 55 degrees. In 2002, curiously, the average rating by in-person interviewees was only 49 degrees, but by telephone interviewees, 58 degrees. Americans' feelings toward Israel have been more polarized, with more extremely positive and extremely negative ratings, than for other countries. Average ratings of Israeli Prime Ministers include Menachem Begin, 45 degrees in 1982 (down from 57 degrees in 1978, when he was seen as a peacemaker; see Rielly [1983, 19]); Yitzhak Shamir, 44 (1990); Yitzhak Rabin, 51 (1994); Benjamin Netanyahu, 48 (1998); and Ariel Sharon 51 (2002). For a detailed review of Americans' past opinions about Israel, see Gilboa (1987).

21. The average thermometer ratings of the Soviet Union from 1978 through 1990 were 34, 26, 31, and 59 degrees, respectively, with the low point in the "new Cold War" year 1982. Russia was rated at 54, 49, and 55 degrees in the 1994, 1998, and 2002 surveys. Cold warrior Leonid Brezhnev was rated at a chilly 31 degrees in 1982; reformer Mikhail Gorbachev, at 42 degrees in 1986 but a markedly higher 64 degrees in post–Cold War 1990; Boris Yeltsin, at 53 and 49 degrees in 1994 and 1998; and Vladimir Putin, at 56 degrees in 2002.

Even more than "rogue" or hostile states, certain individual world leaders have been disdained by the American public. Idi Amin, the brutal dictator of Uganda, received a very cold 22-degree average thermometer rating in 1978. Erratic Libyan ruler Muammar Gadhafi (associated with terrorism in western Europe and the target of an airborne Reagan-administration assassination attempt) was rated at a frigid 11 degrees in 1986. On Castro, Khomeini, and Hussein, see the discussions of Cuba, Iran, and Iraq, below.

22. Cuba's average thermometer rating was 32 degrees in 1978, 27 in 1982, not ascertained in 1986 or 1990, and 38, 38, and 35 degrees from 1994 to 2002. Premier Fidel Castro was rated at an even colder 20, 18, 20, 23, and 22 degrees in the five surveys from 1986 to 2002.

23. North Korea's average thermometer ratings, beginning only in 1994, were 34, 36, and 34 degrees. Comparison of 2002 and 2004 Web-based surveys indicates there was no change in 2004.

24. Average thermometer ratings of the People's Republic of China (or, in 2002, just "China") starting in 1978 were 44, 47, 53, 45, 46, 47, and 48 degrees, with the Tienanmen Square crackdown probably accounting for the 8-degree drop between 1986 and 1990. China's average rating in the 2004 Web-based survey was up 4 degrees from the 2002 Web-based pilot. Chinese party chairman Deng Xiaoping, though a Westernizer, was rated at just 46 degrees in 1986; President Jiang Zemin at only 43, 37, and 38 degrees in 1994–2002. In 1994, when the question was first asked, 68 percent perceived a vital U.S. interest in China; 74 percent did so in 1998 and 83 percent in 2002. Part of the increase from in-person 1998 to telephone-only 2002 is probably due to the change in survey mode, but the trend over the decade is clear. For data on Americans' views of China in earlier periods, see Steele (1966) and Kusnitz (1984).

25. Poland's average thermometer ratings starting in 1978 were 50, 52, 54, 57, 52, 50, and 50 degrees. Nicaragua's, in 1986 and 1990, were 46 and 44 degrees; Daniel Ortega's in 1986 was just 29 degrees.

26. India's average thermometer scores starting in 1978 were 49, 48, 48, 48, 48, 46, and 46 degrees. Proportions of Americans seeing a vital U.S. interest in India were 37 percent, 30 percent, and 36 percent in 1978–1986, and 31 percent, 36 percent, and 65 percent in 1994–2002; the question was not asked in 1990. The jump from 1998's in-person rating to 2002's telephone-only rating is much too large to have resulted from the survey mode change. Recall from chapter 2 that perceptions of a "critical threat" from tensions between India and Pakistan were high (54 percent) in 2002 but dropped markedly by 2004.

27. Average thermometer ratings of South Korea starting in 1978 were 48, 44, 51, 47, 48, 50, and 46 degrees (its 49-degree rating in the 2004 Web-based survey is almost certainly a significant rise from 2002, since Web-based ratings have generally been 6 or 7 degrees cooler than those based on telephone interviews). For more on South Korea, see Page, Rabinovich, and Tully (2005). Ratings of Taiwan were 51, 49, 52, 48, 48, 50, and 50 degrees; of the Philippines, 59 and 53 degrees in 1986 and 1990. The high 1986 rating of the Philippines coincided with early enthusiasm for reformist president Corazon Aquino, herself rated at a very warm 62 degrees.

28. For South Africa, Nigeria, and Egypt in 2002, the thermometer question was asked only of telephone interviewees, who tended to give *fewer* exactly 50-degree responses than did in-person interviewees. Several other countries of relatively low visibility that were asked about only in telephone interviews also had high proportions of exactly 50-degree thermometer ratings: Poland, Argentina, Turkey, and South Korea were in the 31–35 percent range, most other countries in the 16–20 percent range.

Among countries for which thermometer questions were asked in both in-person and telephone interviews, the combined data show that a few (Brazil, India, and—oddly—Italy and China) received 30–34 percent exactly 50-degree responses; most other countries received such ratings from little more than 20 percent of respondents, though some very popular or very unpopular countries (Britain, Canada, Iran, and Iraq) drew only 10 percent or so exactly 50-degree responses. But such ratings tended to be more common among in-person than telephone respondents, especially for certain countries with high average thermometer scores: there was a 14-percentage-point mode difference for Italy, 11 for Germany, 10 for Japan, and 7 for Brazil, with differences for most other countries in the 2–4-percentage-point range. This mode difference probably occurred because the wording of the in-person question and the visual thermometer display directed more attention to the 50-degree point. Considering only telephone interviewees for mixed-mode countries (as one should, for comparability), only India and Brazil, with 33 percent and 32 percent exactly 50-degree ratings, approached the levels of South Africa, Nigeria, Egypt, and the other relatively low visibility telephone-only countries.

29. Average thermometer scores for South Africa, starting in 1978, were 46, 45, 48, 51, 52, 54, and 50 degrees. Tutu's rating in 1986 was 53 degrees, as compared to De Klerk's 39; Mandela received ratings of 53, 58, and 60 degrees in 1990, 1994, and 1998.

30. Nigeria's average thermometer scores were 47, 44, 46, and 47 degrees for 1978–1990 and 46 and 42 degrees for 1998 and 2002, with no rating for 1994. Egypt's were 53, 52, 49, and 52 degrees for 1978–1990 and 45 degrees for 2002, with no rating in 1994 or 1998.

31. Saudi Arabia's mean thermometer ratings from 1978 on were 48, 52, 50, 53, 48, 46, and, in 2002, just 33 degrees.

32. Iran's average thermometer ratings starting in 1978 were 50, 28, 23, 27, 28, 28, and 28 degrees. Ayatollah Khomeini was rated at a frigid 11 degrees in 1982.

33. Iraq's average thermometer ratings beginning in 1990 were 20, 24, 25, and 23 degrees. Hussein's 9- and 8-degree ratings in 1990 and 2002 were all-time lows for any world leader.

34. Saudi Arabia's telephone-based average thermometer rating of 33 degrees in 2002 was followed by an average rating of 37 degrees in the Web-based survey of 2004, despite the fact that Web-based ratings are usually *lower*. Similar reasoning underlies our earlier inference of a 2004 rebound for France.

35. Arafat's average thermometer scores were 28 degrees in 1982, 36 in 1994, 38 in 1998, and 22 in 2002.

36. The average thermometer rating of "the Muslim people" in the 2004 Web-based survey was just 39 degrees, lower than the 2002 telephone-based survey's 49-degree rating by a bit more than mode differences alone would predict.

37. Between 1998 and 2002 the proportion of Americans perceiving a vital interest in Afghanistan rose from 45 percent to 73 percent; in Turkey, from 33 percent to 52 percent; in Iran, from 61 percent to 75 percent. The survey mode change is likely to have contributed only moderately to these rises. Among comparable in-person 2002 interviewees the vital-interest figure for Afghanistan was 66 percent, 21 points higher than in 1998. Over the same interval the comparable figures for Bosnia, a major trouble spot in the 1990s, dropped by 19 points, from 51 percent to just 32 percent.

38. OLS regression is particularly appropriate here because thermometer ratings convey substantial interval-level information and are distributed in a more or less normal fashion over many categories. As we have noted earlier, attitudinal and informational "independent" variables may not be purely independent; they may sometimes be affected by the variables (e.g., feelings about countries) that they are being used to account for, producing simultaneity bias in coefficient estimates. This does not appear to be a serious problem, however, in these analyses.

39. The highest adjusted R-squared values for regressions of thermometer ratings for countries or peoples with fourteen demographic independent variables were for Great Britain and Poland (.11), Israel, North Korea, and the Muslim people (.09), and Nigeria (.08); the lowest were for Brazil and China (less than .01); the average was .053. The highest adjusted R-squared values for leaders' ratings and the demographic variables were for Clinton (.13), Bush (.12), Rumsfeld (.10), Sharon (.09), and John Paul II (.08); the lowest were for Koizumi, Annan, Chirac, Hussein, and Powell (all less than .01), with an average of just .036.

40. For country rating regressions with both demographic and basic attitudinal independent variables, the highest adjusted R-squared values were for the EU (.14), Israel and Britain (.13), Muslims (.12), Poland (.11), Taiwan (.10), and North Korea, Japan, Canada, and Nigeria (.09). The lowest were for Brazil (.01) and China and South Africa (.03); the average was .072. For ratings of leaders, adjusted R-squared values rose markedly from demographics-only levels for Clinton (to .34), Bush (.31), Rumsfeld (.23), Sharon (.16), and Annan (.09), but others stayed about the same. The high adjusted R-squared values for Clinton and Bush indicate that respondents are able to use the thermometer scale in meaningful and predictable ways; the low values for most world leaders represent a substantive finding of little demographic impact on feelings, rather than a methodological artifact of the measurement technique.

When information and exposure variables were added, adjusted R-squared values rose by a percentage point or two for Poland (to .13), Taiwan (.12), Afghanistan (.11), Turkey (.09), and Mexico (.08), but all others stayed about the same or dropped slightly. The drops resulted mainly from decreases in N (from more than nine hundred to something over six hundred) for the fourteen mixed-mode-survey countries. (Since questions about knowledge of and exposure to world affairs were asked only of telephone respondents, no in-person interviewees could be included in the third set of regressions.) Among leaders' ratings, the only substantial rise in adjusted R-squared values was for Putin's—which increased by two percentage points, to .09.

41. Unstandardized OLS coefficients for gender (male = 1, female = 0) in demographics-only thermometer regressions (with full-control coefficients in parentheses) were for Putin 9.0** (6.7**), for Schroeder 5.3** (n.s.), for Taiwan 5.3** (n.s.), for Turkey 4.2* (n.s.), for Japan 3.2* (n.s.), for Russia 2.8* (n.s.), for North Korea −7.2** (−5.5**), for Italy −4.0** (−5.1**), for Nigeria −4.2* (−4.5), and for France −4.1* (n.s.); all others not significant at $p < .05$. For marital status (married = 1, not married = 0): Clinton −10.1** (−8.1**), Nigeria −4.3* (−4.0*), Germany 3.0* (n.s.); all others n.s. at $p < .05$. (In this and subsequent notes and tables, ** denotes significance at $p < .01$, * denotes $p < .05$, and + is sometimes used to denote $p < .10$, all by two-tailed test. We will generally refer to $p < .10$ (and sometimes to $p < .05$) results as only "possibly" significant, since a number of such results would be expected to occur by chance in our many regressions with multiple independent variables.

42. In these regressions, employed = 1, nonemployed = 0. Since "unemployed" but seeking work was also included as a dummy variable, the comparison group for both is retirees, students, and homemakers. Coefficients in demographic thermometer regressions (with full-control coefficients in parentheses) for employed: Iran −5.7** (−6.0**), North Korea −4.9** (−5.2*), Iraq −4.0* (−4.3*), Saudi Arabia −4.3* (−4.5*), India −4.0* (−4.3*), China −3.8* (n.s.), Poland −3.7* (−3.9*), Afghanistan n.s. (−4.5*); all others n.s. For unemployed: Poland −9.5** (−9.4**), Argentina −7.7* (−7.7*), John Paul II −10.5* (n.s.); all others n.s. For income level (eleven-point scale): Taiwan 1.0* (n.s.), Turkey 1.0* (n.s.), Russia n.s. (−1.1*), Bush 1.2* (n.s.), Rumsfeld 1.3* (n.s.), all others n.s.

43. Coefficients for age (in years) in demographics-only thermometer regressions (full-control coefficients in parentheses): Nigeria −.26** (−.29**), South Africa −.24** (−.25**), Colombia −.27** (−.28**), Argentina −.22** (−.26**), Cuba −.20** (−.21**), Brazil −.10* (−.12*), North Korea −.21** (−.19**), Taiwan −.15** (−.18**), China −.14** (−.15*), Japan −.11* (−.14*), South Korea n.s. (−.12*), Afghanistan .13* (n.s.), Egypt −.20** (−.23**), Muslims

−.15* (−.18*), Israel .11* (n.s.), France −.27** (−.29**), Poland −.17** (−.19**), Italy −.10* (n.s.), Britain .12** (n.s.), Putin .13* (n.s.); all others n.s.

44. In demographics-only thermometer regressions, the coefficients for education level (measured on a six-point scale: 1 = eighth grade or less, 6 = postgraduate study) were significantly different from zero at the $p < .01$ level for twenty of the thirty-one countries or peoples; they were significant only at the $p < .05$ level for six additional countries. Among world leaders, only the coefficients for Bush (−2.8**) and possibly Annan (2.5*) and Castro (1.8*) were significant. These coefficients must be multiplied by five to estimate the effect of moving from the bottom to the top of the education scale.

45. In thermometer regressions with full attitudinal and informational as well as demographic controls, the education coefficients remained clearly significant ($p < .01$) for only four countries or peoples, and possibly significant for a few others (in addition to those shown in table 3.3, Colombia had a coefficient of 1.8*). For leaders, only the education coefficient for Bush (−2.0*) remained possibly significant, and those for Sharon (−2.1*) and Blair (−1.9*) rose to possible significance.

46. On the "attentive public," see Rosenau (1961) and Almond (1960); see also Delli Carpini and Keeter (1996). In full-controls thermometer regressions, the only clearly significant coefficients not shown in the third column of table 3.3 for knowledge of the euro (1 = a correct open-ended response, 0 = an incorrect response or confession of lack of knowledge) were for Turkey (8.1**), Poland (6.7**), Argentina (5.9**), China (4.9**), and Putin (7.3**); possibly significant were the coefficients for Israel (5.3*), North Korea (−5.3*), Iraq (−4.5*), Saudi Arabia (4.4*), Sharon (6.4*), Castro (4.8*), and Powell (−4.7*). Coefficients for knowledge of the foreign aid budget were clearly significant only for Mexico (3.8**) and Italy (2.4**), and possibly significant for Pakistan (1.9*) and the pope (−2.6*). Controlling for these and other factors, foreign travel (1 = traveled outside the U.S., 0 = no such travel) was never clearly significant; it was possibly significant only for Japan (4.9*), Clinton (6.8*), and Bush (−5.0*). But multicollinearity undoubtedly depressed these significance levels.

47. For more detail on the effects of religion and ethnicity on Americans' feelings about foreign countries and leaders, see Page and Rabinovich (2005).

48. Coefficients for effects of Catholicism in thermometer regressions with full statistical controls (those with controls for demographics only were quite similar): the pope 20.7**, Poland 4.9*, Colombia 4.3*, Italy 3.6+, Argentina 3.7+, France 2.6, Cuba 2.6, Mexico 2.4, Brazil −0.5, Rumsfeld 7.5**, Bush 5.8*, Blair 5.4*. The last three suggest differential esteem for conservative and religiously inclined leaders.

49. Coefficients for effects of being Hispanic in thermometer regressions with full controls (those with more limited controls yielded virtually the same results): Mexico 14.3*, Argentina 2.0, Brazil 4.2, Colombia 1.8, Cuba 5.2, Canada −8.0*, EU −10.3*, Blair −9.1*, Britain −4.3, Arafat 9.6*, Iran 6.6+, Iraq 4.6+, Hussein 4.8+.

50. Coefficients for effects of being Asian or a Pacific islander in demographic thermometer regressions (with full-control coefficients in parentheses): North Korea 13.1* (13.2*), Japan 9.4+ (10.6+; 10.9* in the demographics plus attitudes regression), Koizumi 12.8+ (14.3+), Taiwan 7.0 (8.4), South Korea 4.0 (4.8), China −0.2 (0.3), Zemin 11.5 (12.0). The fact that coefficients did not drop when informational variables were included argues against the hypothesis that effects resulted from special knowledge of Asia among Asian Americans. But it does not conclusively refute it, since the CCFR information measures

centered on Europe (the euro), the U.S. budget (foreign aid), and travel by Americans, which mostly involved Canada or Mexico.

51. Coefficients for the effects of being African American in purely demographic thermometer regressions (full-control coefficients in parentheses): Egypt 3.9 (3.2), Nigeria 3.2 (2.3), South Africa 3.2 (2.3), Annan −1.4 (−0.2), Powell −0.03 (1.7) (all nonsignificant even at the $p < .10$ level); Britain −15.6** (−13.1**), Poland −13.8** (−12.8**), Russia −13.6** (−11.0**), Germany −12.9** (−11.0**), Canada −11.7** (−10.6**), South Korea −7.8* (−6.2*), Mexico −0.6 (0.1), Clinton 26.4** (16.2**), Bush −17.4** (−9.4**). The last two reflect African Americans' distinctly Democratic and liberal orientation.

52. Significant coefficients for the effects of being Jewish not included in table 3.4 are, for Germany, −14.4** with controls only for demographics (−14.0* with full controls); for France, −10.6+ (−13.3*); for Poland, −16.9** (−17.6**); for the EU, −8.7 (−10.8, $p = .137$); for Bill Clinton, 24.8** (15.4*); and for George W. Bush 6.6 (14.9*).

53. All religious affiliations were measured as dummy variables (e.g., evangelical = 1, not evangelical = 0); the comparison group for all of them is nonevangelical Protestants and the nonreligious. Clearly significant coefficients for the effect of being evangelical in thermometer regressions with demographic controls only (full controls in parentheses) were, for Israel, 11.3** (7.5**); for Sharon, 19.5** (13.9**); for the EU, −10.5** (−7.1*); for Bush, 19.5** (10.0**); and for Rumsfeld, 16.3** (9.7**). Possibly significant was Taiwan, n.s. (−4.6*).

54. Coefficients for effects of party identification (1 = strong Republican, 7 = strong Democrat) from full-control thermometer regressions: France 1.6**, Saudi Arabia 1.5**, Argentina 1.5**, South Africa 1.0*, Cuba 1.0*, Turkey 1.0*, Clinton 6.1**, Bush −4.5**, Rumsfeld −3.2**, Sharon −2.0**, Powell −1.1*, Putin −1.0*; all others n.s. In order to calculate the effects, in thermometer degrees, of changing from strong Republican (1) to strong Democrat (7), one must multiply these coefficients by six.

55. Coefficients for effects of liberal versus conservative ideology (measured on a five-point scale: 1 = very conservative, 5 = very liberal) in full-control thermometer regressions: Israel −3.1**, Muslims 3.2**, EU 3.4*, Italy 2.2*, France 2.1*, Taiwan −2.0*, Clinton 5.5**, Bush −5.9**, Rumsfeld −3.7**, Powell −2.0*, Sharon −4.3**, Castro 3.8**, the pope −3.5**, Arafat 3.1**, Annan 4.3*; all others nonsignificant. To estimate the effect of changing from very conservative (1) to very liberal (5) these coefficients should be multiplied by four.

56. Coefficients for the effects of internationalism (1 = "active part," 0 = "stay out") in full-control thermometer regressions: EU 12.2**, India 10.5**, Japan 10.2**, Muslims 9.7**, Israel 8.5**, Russia 8.3**, Mexico 7.8**, Afghanistan 7.8**, Iraq 7.7**, Saudi Arabia 7.2**, Taiwan 7.0**, Iran 6.7**, Germany 6.6**, Britain 6.5**, China 6.5**, Canada 5.7**, the Palestinians 3.9*, Pakistan 5.6*, South Korea 5.3*, Brazil 4.9*, Poland 4.3*, Argentina 4.2*, Annan 12.8**, Clinton 9.1**, Zemin 8.1**, Powell 7.7**, Koizumi 7.7**, Rumsfeld 7.3**, the pope 7.0*, Arafat 6.9**, Chirac 6.6**, Bush 6.4**, Schroeder 5.3*, Blair 4.9*; others n.s. These estimates of the direct impact of internationalism include the indirect effects that formal education has *through* internationalism.

57. The correlation of "active part" internationalism with liberal/conservative ideology was just $r = −.003$ (n.s.), and with party identification only −.065** (Republicans tended to be a bit more activist). In a fourteen-variable demographic regression, the only significant standardized coefficients were for education level, .19** (unstandardized .064**, amounting to a large, .32 increase in the linear probability of saying "active part" as one moves from one end to the other of the six-point education scale); for age, .10**; for income, .09**; for

being African American, −.07**; and possibly for being Asian (−.04+) and evangelical (.03+). Rather little variance was accounted for (adjusted *R*-squared = .080, df = 2612).

58. In addition to our three basic attitudes, feelings about foreign countries (as well as other foreign policy attitudes) may well be affected by a generalized "international trust" or distrust; see Brewer, Gross, Aday, and Wilnat (2004). Unfortunately no good measures of international trust have been included in the CCFR surveys, so we cannot analyze its role. We suspect that individuals' trust or distrust toward a particular country is one of a number of beliefs and attitudes summed up by that country's thermometer scores, and that an individual's *generalized* international trust or distrust is closely related to his or her average thermometer scores across many countries.

59. The collective public's capacities to make sharp distinctions, to hold stable attitudes, and to react reasonably to new information are discussed in Page and Shapiro (1992). For a theoretical account of how this is possible, see Lupia and McCubbins (1998). We must, however, note a problem in taking the public's feelings toward foreign countries—and especially foreign leaders—as guides to policy makers: they (more than specific policy preferences) may be subject to manipulation through media campaigns by officials and elites. The transformation at the end of the 1980s of Saddam Hussein from quiet U.S. ally to demonized enemy—while his thuggish and aggressive behavior remained fairly constant— tells a cautionary tale.

CHAPTER FOUR

We are grateful to Tom Ferguson, Ed Greenberg, Arthur Cyr, Ole Holsti, and William Chittick for comments on earlier drafts of this chapter.

1. Classic critiques of the quality of U.S. public opinion on foreign policy include Lippman (1925, 1955, 1965), Almond (1960), and Rosenau (1961). See Holsti (2004, chaps. 2–3) on the "post–World War II consensus" critical of the public, as well as later refutations of it. Kull and Destler (1999) offer numerous quotes from contemporary foreign policy practitioners on the public's supposed disengagement from foreign affairs, low support for multilateralism, absolute aversion to U.S. casualties, and the like (e.g., 36–42, 82–92), and proceed to show that those perceptions are incorrect.

2. Jentleson (1992) and Jentleson and Britton (1998) make a strong case for "prudent" public opinion concerning U.S. military interventions, both before and after the end of the Cold War and the 1991 Persian Gulf War. They do not contradict Mueller's (1973) important demonstration, based on the Korean and Vietnam wars, that the cumulative magnitude of U.S. casualties tends to have a major negative impact on Americans' support for "limited" wars. Rather they point out that the public takes into account perceived benefits as well as costs of interventions and that the "principal policy objective" (e.g., humanitarian relief or peacekeeping, as versus helping one side in a civil war) can be crucial in relatively low-level engagements.

3. In the 2004 Web-based survey, 52 percent said the United States should "make active efforts to ensure that no other country becomes a superpower," 41 percent that it should not. This probably does not mean, however, that most Americans would favor using military force for this purpose, as might be inferred from the Bush administration's 2002 "National Security Strategy" (United States National Security Council 2002).

4. In the 2004 Web-based survey, 76 percent said "no" to the world policeman role, and 80 percent agreed that the United States is playing the role of world policemen more than

it should be. The apparent rises of 14 and 15 percentage points since 2002 are probably larger than any mode effects would produce.

5. In the 2004-web-based survey, 78 percent said "the U.S. should do its share" and only 8 percent thought it should be the "preeminent world leader," nearly identical to the 79 percent and 7 percent figures in the 2002 Web-based pilot survey.

6. In 2002, a telephone-only subsample (N = 706) was asked, "For each of the following reasons, would you approve or disapprove of the use of U.S. military troops?" Respondents were then asked about six possible reasons to use troops (the percentage who approved in each case is shown in parentheses): to ensure the supply of oil (65 percent), to destroy a terrorist camp (92 percent), to help bring peace to a region where there is civil war (48 percent), to liberate hostages (77 percent), to assist a population struck by famine (81 percent), and to uphold international law (76 percent). Troop uses not connected with terrorism are discussed later in this chapter.

7. All 2002 in-person respondents (N = 400) and a telephone subsample (N = 722) were asked a battery of questions, repeated from 1998, with the prologue "In order to combat international terrorism, please say whether you favor or oppose each of the following measures" (percentages in favor shown in parentheses): "U.S. air strikes against terrorist training camps and other facilities" (87 percent favored in 2002; 74 percent in 1998; "attacks by U.S. ground troops against terrorist training camps and other facilities" (84 percent; up markedly from 57 percent in 1998); "assassination of individual terrorist leaders" (66 percent; 54 percent in 1998): "trial of suspected terrorists in an International Criminal Court" (83 percent; 84 percent in 1998); "diplomatic efforts to apprehend terrorist suspects and dismantle terrorist training camps" (89 percent; 84 percent in 1998); and "diplomatic efforts to improve relations with potential adversary countries" (80 percent; 79 percent in 1998). The nonmilitary actions will be discussed in the next chapter. These data indicate that most Americans favored using force (especially air strikes) against terrorist camps, and favored assassination of terrorist leaders, well before September 11, 2001. After 9/11, support for diplomatic antiterrorist measures stayed steady. But support for air strikes and assassinations rose significantly, and support for troop use jumped quite sharply, by 27 percentage points. In-person and telephone responses in 2002 did not significantly differ, indicating that none of these changes were artifacts of the switch in survey modes.

In 2002 an entirely separate, telephone-only subsample (N = 687) was read the same prologue and then asked about eight measures, mostly diplomatic, to combat terrorism (percentages in favor in parentheses): "helping poor countries develop their economies" (78 percent); "working through the UN to strengthen international laws against terrorism and make sure UN members enforce them" (88 percent); "making a major effort to be even-handed in the Israeli-Palestinian conflict" (66 percent); "setting up an international system to cut off funding for terrorism" (89 percent); "toppling unfriendly regimes that support terrorist groups threatening the U.S." (73 percent); "restricting immigration into the U.S." (77 percent); "using racial profiling in airport security checks" (54 percent); and "sharing intelligence information with other countries" (58 percent). The diplomatic measures will be discussed in the next chapter.

8. In 2002 a subsample of telephone respondents entirely distinct from those asked about the invasion scenarios discussed below (N = 684) was asked, "There has been some discussion about the circumstances that might justify using U.S. troops in other parts of the world. I'd like to ask your opinion about some situations. First, would you favor or oppose

the use of U.S. troops: if the government of Pakistan requested our help against a radical Islamic revolution [61 percent favored]; in order to overthrow Saddam Hussein's government in Iraq [75 percent]; to be part of an international peacekeeping force in Afghanistan [76 percent]; if the government of Saudi Arabia requested our help against an attempt to overthrow it [54 percent]; to fight drug lords in Colombia [66 percent]; to assist the Philippine government to fight terrorism [78 percent]; to be part of an international peacekeeping force to enforce a peace agreement between Israel and the Palestinians [65 percent]; to stop a government from committing genocide and killing large numbers of its own people [77 percent]." Only the items concerning the Philippines, Pakistan, and Saudi Arabia are discussed here; the others are discussed below. In contrast to the Pakistan case, only a significantly lower 54 percent favored the use of U.S. troops if the government of Saudi Arabia requested our help against an attempt to overthrow it, perhaps because the nature of the insurgent group (Islamic radicals? prodemocracy demonstrators?) was not specified.

In the 2004 Web-based survey, 76 percent of respondents favored ground troops, 83 percent air strikes, 67 percent toppling unfriendly regimes, 68 percent assassinating terrorist leaders, and just 51 percent helping Pakistan. Compared to the 2002 Web-based pilot survey, support for use of ground troops was down by 6 percentage points, for air strikes down by 7, and for assassinations down by 9; the other questions were not asked in the pilot survey.

9. In the 2004 Web-based survey, 75 percent favored troop use to stop genocide, and 72 percent favored it "to deal with humanitarian crises." See also the discussion below on unilateral versus multilateral force.

10. In the 2004 Web-based survey, 60 percent favored (36 percent opposed) being part of an international peacekeeping force in Afghanistan; 52 percent (versus 43 percent) favored enforcing peace between Israel and the Palestinians; and 51 percent (versus 44 percent) favored being part of "a UN-sponsored force to help keep peace between India and Pakistan." No comparable 2002 Web-based data are available, but the apparent drops in support seem too big to be accounted for by mode effects, especially since the Web mode may have elicited *more* support for UN peacekeeping. In 2004, fully 78 percent said the U.S. should be part of "a United Nations international peacekeeping force in a troubled part of the world"—exactly the same figure as in the 2002 Web-based pilot (and much higher than the 64 percent support in the main 2002 survey). A wording change (the phrase "or should we leave this job to other countries" was deleted) probably increased pro-peacekeeping responses in 2004, however, making our inference of drops in support for the specific items stronger than the inference of steadiness in the general one.

11. See Sobel (2001, chaps. 11–13) on the Bosnia case.

12. In the 2004 Web-based survey, 54 percent favored (42 percent opposed) using troops to ensure the oil supply, and 51 percent (versus 45 percent) favored using troops to fight drug lords in Colombia.

13. See Rielly (1975, 18).

14. In the 1978 survey respondents were asked, "would you favor or oppose the use of U.S. troops if . . . ," "Russians" was changed to "Soviets," "attack" was changed to "invade," and several scenarios were changed from passive voice to active, with (in some cases) "the Soviets" supplied as the actor. These changes, which coincided with the shift from Harris to Gallup as the fielder of CCFR surveys, probably contributed something to the increase in responses favoring the use of U.S. troops. Subsequent surveys generally retained wording

identical to that of 1978 whenever items were repeated, except for a shift back to "Russia" after the disintegration of the Soviet Union.

15. See Rielly (1979, 26).

16. See Rielly (1983, 29, 37; 1987, 32). Here, and for most other past CCFR surveys, our figures are drawn from the original Gallup "topline" reports of weighted marginal frequencies.

17. The 1990 data on troop use previously reported in Rielly (1991, 34) and elsewhere are incorrect, due to a tabulation error (a failure to distinguish between form A and reversed-order form B questionnaires) that was discovered in 2002 by Dukhong Kim, Ann Janda, and the staff of the Inter-university Consortium for Political and Social Research. The percentages given here are corrected.

18. An outstanding, highly detailed study of public opinion before, during, and after the Gulf War is Mueller (1994). Sina Foroohar, while a student at Northwestern University, carried out a systematic regression analysis of the level of public support in 1990–91 for military action against Iraq as measured by 108 repetitions of fifty distinct survey questions asked between the invasion of Kuwait and the beginning of the war. Foroohar (2003, 6–7) found a "baseline" of 74 percent support for multilateral military action, with no appreciable change over time, but with large drops in support when questions mentioned major war (-31 percentage points), the aim of obtaining cheap oil (-40 points), protecting oil supplies (-21), U.S. casualties (-19), diplomatic alternatives (-17), and/or restoring the Kuwaiti government (-14); adjusted R-squared $= .74$. UN approval and multinational involvement (including backing by most major Arab countries) were taken as a given by respondents, since multilateral support had already been secured when most of the survey questions were asked.

19. Use of U.S. troops against "Arab forces" invading Israel was favored by only 22 percent of Americans in 1978, 33 percent in 1986, 45 percent in 1990, 42 percent in 1994, 38 percent in 1998, and 48 percent in 2002. Most of the apparent rise from 1998 to 2002 appears to be an artifact of the change in survey modes: only 41 percent of 2002 in-person respondents favored troop use, while 52 percent of telephone respondents did. Similarly, 51 percent of telephone respondents but only 42 percent of in-person respondents favored U.S. troop use if Iraq invaded Saudi Arabia.

20. In 1998 there was, however, slight plurality support for using troops to defend Saudi Arabia against a hypothetical Iraqi invasion. Percentages for and against troop use: Saudi Arabia 46 percent versus 43 percent; Israel 38 percent versus 49 percent; Cuba 38 percent versus 51 percent; Kosovo 36 percent versus 47 percent; South Korea 30 percent versus 58 percent; Poland 28 percent versus 55 percent; Taiwan 37 percent versus 58 percent.

21. In 2002, all in-person respondents ($N = 400$) and a subsample of telephone respondents ($N = 709$) were asked, "There has been some discussion about the circumstances that might justify using U.S. troops in other parts of the world. I'd like to ask your opinion about some situations. First, would you favor or oppose the use of U.S. troops . . . if North Korea invaded South Korea . . . if Iraq invaded Saudi Arabia . . . if Arab forces invaded Israel . . . if China invaded Taiwan."

22. The apparent rise after 1998 in general willingness to use troops in invasion scenarios was almost certainly an artifact of including telephone interviews in the combined 2002 data set. Using only the more comparable 2002 in-person data, none of the rises was statistically significant, and there was actually a significant increase in *opposition* to using

U.S. troops to defend Saudi Arabia, with 49 percent opposed instead of the combined data's 46 percent.

23. In the 2004 Web-based survey, just 43 percent favored (52 percent opposed) using U.S. troops to defend Israel, 43 percent (versus 51 percent) to defend South Korea, and 33 percent (versus 61 percent) to defend Taiwan. The invasion of Iraq and new alarms about North Korea may have increased support for defending South Korea relative to Israel, but no comparable 2002 data are available to gauge absolute changes.

24. Telephone-only subsamples in 2002 were asked the explicitly multilateral questions about hypothetical invasions of Saudi Arabia ($N = 758$) and South Korea ($N = 713$). The precise wording of the questions is given in table 4.3. Support for troop use is probably slightly inflated relative to the nonmultilateral combined-data results, which include some (fewer than 400) in-person respondents, but that could not account for much of the difference.

25. In the 2004 Web-based survey, support for defending South Korea in the explicitly multilateral, "UN-sponsored" context was 64 percent; support for use of U.S. troops in the standard invasion scenario was only 43 percent.

26. The Bush administration's rhetorical offensive against Iraq and its early plans to invade are chronicled in Woodward (2004). See also Mann (2004) and Daalder and Lindsay (2003).

27. In addition to the Gulf War analysis noted above, Foroohar (2003, 10–11) did a multiple regression analysis of aggregate responses to 143 repetitions of thirty-two distinct questions about military action against Iraq (not necessarily an invasion) that were asked between September 11, 2001, and March 12, 2003. Baseline support for military action—indicated by the intercept—was 71 percent; this tended to rise by 13 percentage points when UN support was explicitly postulated but to drop by 14 points when lack of UN support was mentioned and/or by another 14 points when the U.S. was specified as acting alone. After August 2002, changes in support over time were slight. Mention of reliance on airstrikes increased support a bit (by 5 points), whereas mention of war, U.S. casualties, or using ground troops decreased it by 11, 9, and/or 6 points, respectively (adjusted R-squared = .86).

28. On or around September 4, 2002, the present authors and others briefed officials at the U.S. Department of State, the Pentagon, the Senate, and the House of Representatives on the results of the U.S. survey and the parallel surveys in six European countries (Germany, France, Britain, Italy, the Netherlands, and Poland) cosponsored by CCFR and the German Marshall Fund. Majorities in every European country said that the U.S. should invade Iraq only with UN approval and the support of its allies, rather than invading unilaterally or not at all. Experimental manipulation of survey questions among random subsamples also indicated that in all scenarios tested (varying reasons for invasion and levels of casualties), UN approval led modest majorities of Europeans to favor *their own governments* taking part in an invasion, whereas in no scenario without UN approval did a majority in any country favor taking part (Grand et al. 2002, 22; see also Kennedy and Bouton, 2002).

29. On events leading up to the U.S. invasion of Iraq, see Daalder and Lindsay (2003, chaps. 9–10) and Woodward (2004).

30. A meticulously detailed analysis of contrasts between Bush administration rhetoric on Iraq and the (already excessively alarmist) intelligence information available at the time is Prados (2004). For a lively popular account of "weapons of mass deception," see Rampton and Stauber (2003). See also Daalder and Lindsay (2003, chaps. 9–10) and Woodward (2004).

Wilson (2004) discusses President Bush's State of the Union allegation (partly based on forged documents) that Iraq tried to purchase uranium from Niger, and describes the apparent vendetta against Wilson and his wife after his public critique of the allegation. Blix (2004) indicates that UN weapons inspections and disarmament efforts in Iraq were working well but were obstructed and denigrated by U.S. officials.

31. The *New York Times,* June 20, 2004, sec. 4, p. 4, summarized a series of CBS/NYT polls showing that more than 50 percent of Americans erroneously believed, in September 2002 and in March and April 2003, that Saddam Hussein was "personally involved" in the 9/11 attacks against the World Trade Center and the Pentagon. (That figure dipped temporarily just before the war and dropped below 40 percent by April 2004.) The *Times* also summarized many allegations by members of the Bush administration of "links," "ties," "interactions," "connections," "contacts," and the like between al Qaeda and Iraq. The administration did not explicitly claim any Iraqi role in 9/11 or any history of Iraq and al Qaeda collaborating in plots against the United States but encouraged inferences of that sort. For evidence that citizens' partisanship affected their misperceptions, see Kull, Ramsay, and Lewis (2003–4) and Bloch-Elkon and Shapiro (2005).

32. On the proposition that even a rational public can sometimes be fooled (especially in the realm of foreign affairs), when information is tightly controlled by the executive branch and the two political parties collude, see Page and Shapiro (1992, chaps. 9–10). An extensive literature documents the tendency of U.S. media to reflect, or "index," what U.S. officials in Washington say about foreign affairs: see Sigal (1973), Gans (1979), Hallin (1986), and Bennett (1990). When administrations choose to mislead, this can arguably cause media to perform a "propaganda" function (Herman and Chomsky 1988). For an emphasis on the role of business in manipulation of public opinion, see Ferguson and Rogers (1986) and T. Ferguson (1995; on the failure of information markets, see the appendix).

33. In the 2004 Web-based survey, 63 percent opposed (only 30 percent favored) using U.S. troops "to install democratic governments in states where dictators rule." The foreign policy goal of "helping to bring a democratic form of government to other nations" was called "very important" by a lower proportion of the public—just 24 percent—than was any other of the fourteen goals included in that survey.

34. In the 2004 Web-based survey, the level of support for a UN Security Council right to authorize military force was, to prevent genocide, 85 percent; to stop support of terrorist groups, 81 percent; to defend a country that has been attacked, 77 percent; to prevent a country from acquiring nuclear weapons, 70 percent; and to restore a democratic government, 60 percent.

35. In the 2004 Web-based survey, the level of support for the right of "a country" without UN approval to use military force was, to prevent genocide, 70 percent; to stop support of terrorist groups, 61 percent; to defend a country that has been attacked, 59 percent; to prevent a country from acquiring nuclear weapons, 50 percent; and to restore a democratic government, just 40 percent.

36. By contrasting the four scenarios in which a given actor was postulated to approve the U.S. using force to destroy North Korea's nuclear capability with the four scenarios in which it was postulated to oppose (or "not approve") the use of force, we can estimate the *independent* impact upon opinion of each actor's approval. Average support for using force with UN approval was 66 percent, without it only 48.5 percent; thus the average impact of UN approval was 18.5 percentage points. Support with allies' approval was 62 percent, without it

51.5 percent (a 10.5-point impact); with South Korea's approval 58 percent, without it 55.5 percent (a 2.5-point impact). See Bouton (2004, 23–26). Of course, the UN and most allies would be quite unlikely to approve such action without approval by South Korea.

37. The Nuclear Non-Proliferation Treaty forbids nonnuclear signatories from developing nuclear weapons. North Korea may have violated that treaty while party to it but later exercised its legal right to withdraw from the treaty. Recent rhetoric from the United States and others concerning North Korea and Iran implies a shift from a voluntary to a compulsory nonproliferation regime.

38. Proportions of the public saying that "worldwide arms control" should be a very important foreign policy goal were 64 percent in 1974, 1978, and 1982; 69 percent in 1986, and 68 percent in 1990. Proportions saying the same about "matching Soviet military power" were just 49 percent in 1982, 53 percent in 1986, and 40 percent in 1990 (the question was not asked in earlier years). The 1990 figures are corrected for the tabulation error that affected both goals and invasion/use of force figures that year.

39. Answering a different question, only a small minority (26 percent in 1982, 23 percent in 1986) said that "the U.S. should continue to build nuclear weapons regardless of what the Soviets do." A plurality or majority (49 percent in 1982, 58 percent in 1986) said "the U.S. should stop building nuclear weapons only if the Soviet Union agrees to do so," with an additional number (19 percent in 1982, 14 percent in 1986) saying that "the U.S. should stop building nuclear weapons even if the Soviet Union does not."

40. The 2002 question on U.S. first use of nuclear weapons was asked of a telephone-only subsample ($N = 708$). In the Web-based 2004 survey, 22 percent said "never use" nuclear weapons, 57 percent said use them only in response to nuclear attack, and just 19 percent said first use should be permissible in certain circumstances.

41. U.S. National Security Council (2002).

42. The "government program" questions, mostly repeated from past CCFR surveys, were asked of all 400 in-person interviewees plus a subsample of 684 telephone interviewees. There were some mode differences: in-person respondents said "not sure" a bit more often than telephone respondents did; were significantly more supportive of expanding education, Social Security, health, and homeland security programs (by a margin of 77 percent compared to 58 percent in the case of homeland security); but were more likely than telephone interviewees to favor *cutting* military aid (51 percent versus 43 percent). On defense, in-person interviewees were significantly less likely to say that spending should be "kept about the same" (33 percent, compared to 41 percent), but the overall balance of opinion was quite similar in both modes.

43. In the 2004 Web-based survey, just 51 percent said homeland security should be expanded (11 percent wanted it cut back); only 43 percent said intelligence gathering should be expanded (11 percent cut back). Mode effects were large, however. In the small 2004 CCI telephone survey, support for expanding intelligence dropped just 10 percentage points from 2002, and support for expanding homeland security dropped only 5 points. Rankings of domestic and foreign programs stayed essentially the same in 2004 as in 2002, according to both modes.

44. Page and Shapiro (1992, 264–72) discuss surveys by various organizations showing the sharp rise in support for expanding defense spending before 1980–81 and the subsequent sharp decline. In CCFR surveys, the proportions of Americans saying that defense spending should be "expanded" (versus those that said it should be "cut back"), were,

in 1974, 14 percent (42 percent); 1978, 34 percent (24 percent); 1982, 24 percent (34 percent); 1986, 22 percent (34 percent); 1990, 14 percent (43 percent); 1994, 21 percent (34 percent); 1998, 30 percent (28 percent); and 2002, 44 percent (15 percent).

45. The inference that most Americans probably favored at least some increase in defense spending in 2002 proceeds from a particular understanding of preferences and survey responses. If we assume that individuals each had a most preferred amount of spending that was subject to uncertainty but centered at a specific dollar value along a continuum of possible spending levels (e.g., at $250 billion or $350 billion per year for defense), and that each of the CCFR's three response alternatives grouped together respondents whose most preferred points were scattered across a substantial segment of that continuum (substantially above, substantially below, or about equal to current spending), then those who said "kept about the same" presumably included some people who wanted a small increase and some who wanted a small decrease. It seems reasonable to suppose that the 38 percent who said "kept about the same" included at least 7 percent (probably more) who wanted a small increase. Seven percent, when added to the 44 percent who picked "expand," would constitute a 51 percent majority favoring some increase in spending.

This logic, like our reference to a "tilt" in the "balance of opinion" around a status quo point, seems to baffle or annoy some students of public opinion. But we believe that such language is useful for understanding items in which multiple, discrete response options each summarize a range of opinions in relation to a status-quo point. Similar logic will be used to interpret responses to other questions for which "increase," "decrease," and "keep the same" were the options given, such as those concerning troop levels abroad, commitment to NATO, and economic aid to specific countries.

46. "Americans on Defense Spending and the War on Terrorism," press release on a survey by PIPA (the Program on International Policy Attitudes) and Knowledge Network, August 2, 2002.

47. Actual federal budget outlays for national defense, in millions of dollars: fiscal year 2001, $304,882; 2002, 348,555; 2003, 404,920; 2004, 455,908. United States Office of Management and Budget (2005b, 57–58).

48. In the 2004 Web-based survey, only 29 percent said defense spending should be expanded; 25 percent said cut back, and 44 percent said kept about the same. According to the more comparable 2004 CCI telephone survey (in which 37 percent said expand, 13 percent cut back, and 46 percent keep about the same), support for expansion had dropped by 7 percentage points and support for "kept about the same" had risen 8 points since 2002.

49. On U.S. withdrawal from the ABM treaty, see Daalder and Lindsay (2003, 62–64, 81).

50. On the expensive history of Reagan's "Star Wars" missile defense, see Fitzgerald (2000).

51. Johnson (2004, 151–85). Johnson notes that the official sources for these figures, the Department of Defense "Base Structure Report" and "Worldwide Manpower Distribution," are not inclusive. Many U.S. bases (e.g., six sites in Israel where US. forces appear to be "prepositioned"), are cloaked in secrecy (153).

52. The 2002 questions about ten possible locations for long-term U.S. military bases were asked of a subsample of telephone interviewees only (N = 705).

53. In the 2004 Web-based survey, only 11 percent said we should have more bases overseas; 31 percent said fewer, and 54 percent said about as many as now. Proportions favoring bases in specific locations: South Korea 62 percent (30 percent opposed),

Guantanamo 58 percent (34 percent), Germany 57 percent (35 percent), Japan 52 percent (39 percent), Saudi Arabia 50 percent (42 percent), Afghanistan 47 percent (45 percent), Turkey 46 percent (45 percent), Iraq 42 percent (50 percent), Pakistan 39 percent (52 percent), Uzbekistan 30 percent (59 percent). "If a majority of people in the Middle East want the U.S. to remove its military presence there," 59 percent said the U.S. should do so and 37 percent said it should not. Told that "the United States currently has about 37,000 troops in South Korea," 52 percent said that was "too many"; only 7 percent said "too few," and 34 percent said "about right." Told that Washington officials had proposed a one-third reduction, only 29 percent said that would be somewhat bad or very bad for South Korea's security; 53 percent said no significant effect, and 11 percent said good or very good.

54. In the eight CCFR surveys between 1974 and 2002, the proportions of Americans wanting to keep our commitment to NATO the same were 50 percent, 58 percent, 58 percent, 62 percent, 56 percent, 56 percent, 59 percent, and 65 percent. The proportions favoring an increased commitment were 4 percent, 9 percent, 9 percent, 8 percent, 4 percent, 5 percent, 9 percent, and 11 percent.

55. In 1998, 59 percent wanted to keep the U.S. commitment to NATO the same; 9 percent favored an increase, 16 percent a decrease, and 5 percent withdrawal. These figures, very close to those in surveys from 1978 on, indicated a slight tilt toward decreasing the U.S. commitment. The increased support for NATO in 2002 is confirmed by data from in-person-only interviews. In the 2004 Web-based survey, 58 percent said keep our commitment what it is now, 14 percent said increase it, 14 percent said decrease it, and 6 percent said withdraw entirely. But this represented a significant rise from the 2002 Web-based pilot survey in support for a decrease (up 6 percentage points) and withdrawal from NATO (up 3 points), at the expense of support for the status quo (down 10 points).

56. The "specific steps . . . to strengthen the UN" questions were asked in 2002 of a telephone-only subsample of respondents ($N = 701$). In the same context in the 2004 Web-based survey, 74 percent favored a standing UN peacekeeping force (only 20 percent opposed) and 57 percent favored UN regulation of the international arms trade (36 percent opposed). Separately, a solid 66 percent agreed (29 percent disagreed) that the United States should be more willing to make decisions within the UN.

57. On the greater than expected willingness of the American public to support the United Nations and UN peacekeeping efforts (even putting U.S. troops under foreign UN commanders), see Kull and Destler (1999, chaps. 3–4).

58. Starting with the 1974 CCFR survey, the proportions saying military aid should be cut back were 70 percent, 64 percent, 65 percent, 62 percent, 73 percent, 68 percent, 56 percent, and 46 percent. The apparent drop between 1998 and 2002 appears to be partly an artifact of the change in survey modes: among in-person-only 2002 interviewees, 51 percent said "cut back." In the 2004 Web-based survey, 65 percent said "cut back" military aid; just 5 percent said expand and 28 percent said keep it the same.

59. In CCFR surveys from 1974 through 1990, the proportions of the public saying they favored giving military aid to other nations were 22 percent, 29 percent, 28 percent, 33 percent, and 28 percent.

60. In 1990, only 8 percent wanted to increase military aid to Israel, while 50 percent wanted to decrease or stop it. The figures for Egypt were 5 percent and 47 percent; for South Korea, 2 percent and 55 percent; for Turkey, 4 percent and 46 percent; for the Philippines, 6 percent and 51 percent; and for El Salvador, 5 percent and 55 percent.

61. From "Fast Facts" on U.S. arms sales at the Web site of the Federation of American Scientists (http://www.fas.org/asmp/fast_facts.htm), based partly on Richard Grimmett's detailed 1994–2001 study for the Congressional Research Service. For up-to-date figures from a non-U.S. source, see http://www.sipri.org, the Web site of the Stockholm International Peace Research Institute.

62. In CCFR surveys the proportions of the public favoring (and opposing) arms sales were, in 1974, 35 percent (53 percent); 1978, 33 percent (54 percent); 1982, 39 percent (53 percent); 1986, 37 percent (53 percent); 1990, 32 percent (59 percent); 1994, 15 percent (78 percent); 1998, 14 percent (79 percent); and 2002, 18 percent (77 percent). The small apparent rise in support for arms sales from 1998 to 2002 is almost certainly an artifact of the change in survey modes: among in-person respondents only, the 2002 figures were 15 percent in favor, 79 percent opposed, virtually identical to those of 1998.

63. The apparent paradox that highly educated people tend to support concrete uses of military force but are *less* likely to call maintaining superior military power a "very important" goal may result from the tendency of people with little education to call many goals of all sorts "very important" (see chapter 2).

64. In a set of regressions for each of fifteen different military-policy dependent variables with our fourteen demographic independent variables, adjusted R-squared values neared the .10 level (where 10 percent of the variance would be accounted for) only four times: for whether or not the United States should be the "sole superpower" (adjusted R-squared = .08); whether U.S. troops should be used if North Korea invaded South Korea (.08); whether the U.S. should contribute troops together with other countries to reverse North Korean aggression against South Korea (.07); and whether the United States should exert strong leadership in world affairs (.07). Several military policy items were almost entirely unrelated to demographic factors, including whether the U.S. should participate in a multilateral force to resist an Iraqi invasion of Saudi Arabia (adjusted R-squared = .01); whether the U.S. should "continue to be the preeminent world leader" or do its share together with other countries (.01); whether U.S. troops should be used if China invaded Taiwan (.02); and whether economic or military strength is more important in determining a country's overall power and influence in the world (.02).

65. In the 2002 survey, in bivariate terms, use of U.S. troops if North Korea invaded South Korea was supported by many more men than women (46 percent versus 26 percent); more people with postgraduate education than with high school or less (46 percent, compared to 33 percent); more older people than young (41 percent to 29 percent); and a few more high-income than very-low-income people (42 percent to 32 percent). Bivariate demographic relationships were even larger—among the largest in the 2002 data—for the multilateral item: the United States' "contributing military forces, together with other countries, to a UN sponsored effort to reverse the aggression" was supported by 70 percent of men but only 47 percent of women; 70 percent of older people and 47 percent of younger; 80 percent of postgraduates and 49 percent of those with less than high school education; and 63 percent of high-income and 47 percent of low-income people. "Active part" internationalists supported involvement by an still bigger margin: 68 percent to just 31 percent for "stay out" isolationists (r = .37**). Our multivariate analyses deal with the item that refers simply to "using U.S. troops," because the multilateral item was asked only by telephone and had too few respondents who were also asked the questions on goals, threats, thermometer feelings, and vital interests to allow a satisfactory multivariate regression.

66. Thermometer ratings and vital interest perceptions for South Korea were asked only of subsamples of telephone respondents, who did not overlap sufficiently with respondents to the goals questions to be included in these regression analyses.

Here and in the remainder of the book most regressions that include goals as independent variables rely heavily upon the CCFR survey's four hundred in-person respondents, who were asked all twenty questions concerning goals and many about threats, feelings, and vital interests. Demographic questions and the three basic attitudinal questions were asked of all respondents, including all who were asked the dependent variable question. Hence the substantial drop in degrees of freedom between columns two and three in this and most subsequent tables, and the need to select particular variables for inclusion in column-three and column-four regressions. Variables involving goals, threats, feelings, and vital interests were selected both for theoretical reasons and for reasons of practicality (sufficient overlap of respondents, existence of substantial empirical relationships, avoidance of excessive multicollinearity). In our attitudinal analyses, as in much social science research generally, the final regressions displayed in tables often represent end products of experimentation. One implication of this is that significance levels in our third and fourth columns should be treated with more caution than those in the first and second columns, which always include the same fixed sets of variables.

67. Feeling thermometer ratings of Saudi Arabia could not be included in the Saudi invasion regressions because they were asked only of a random subsample of telephone respondents, but a significant bivariate relationship indicates that they may have been important as well. Thermometer-measured feelings about foreign countries probably tend to reflect, among other things, judgments about the importance of a given country to the United States and the utility of helping to assist or defend it.

68. Adjusted R-squared values for OLS regressions with dichotomous dependent variables (as in the invasion cases) usually understate predictive power. Our logit and probit regressions, with more appropriate (nonlinear) functional forms, generally yielded pseudo-R-squared values that indicated even stronger relationships. Here and in most of the book (except chapter 3) we generally present standardized OLS coefficients, chiefly because they are more easily interpretable and more comparable in terms of variance accounted for by different independent variables. For all their limitations, standardized coefficients generally give a reasonable picture of which factors are more or less important in accounting for observed variations in responses.

69. For the use of U.S. troops to defend Israel against an invasion by Arab forces, bivariate correlations were $r = .39^{**}$ with thermometer ratings of Israel, $.23^{**}$ with perceptions of a vital U.S. interest in Israel, and $.24^{**}$ with assessments of Arab-Israeli conflict as a critical threat to the United States. Significant coefficients in our demographics-only OLS regression were for male $(.12^{**})$, evangelical Protestant $(.14^{**})$, African American $(-.08^{*})$, and perhaps education $(.07+)$ and Jewish $(.06+)$; adjusted R-squared $= .041$. With basic attitudes added, only male $(.10^{**})$, evangelical $(.09^{**})$, Jewish $(.07^{*})$, "active part" $(.20^{**})$, and Republican $(.11^{**})$ had clearly significant coefficients. When goals, feelings, etc. were also added, the only clearly significant relationships involved the goals of protecting weaker nations $(.16^{**})$ and defending allies $(.18^{**})$, feelings toward Israel $(.27^{**})$, and perceptions of a vital interest in Israel $(.10^{*})$; adjusted R-squared rose to .244. In the purely attitudinal regression those same attitudes (except perception of a vital interest) were significant, with coefficients of $.16^{**}$, $.18^{**}$, $.28^{**}$, and n.s., respectively; adjusted R-squared rose slightly more, to .252.

70. The bivariate correlation between preferences for using U.S. troops if China invaded Taiwan and a perception of vital U.S. interest in Taiwan was $r = .25$**. In an attitudes-only regression, significant coefficients were for "active part" internationalism, .16**; the goal of protecting weaker nations, .15**; the goal of defending allies' security, .16**; conservatism, .12*; and perception of a threat from India-Pakistan tensions, .11*; adjusted R-squared = .13.

71. In alternative attitudinal regressions for ground attacks against terrorist training camps, the threat of nuclear weapons could be substituted for the threat of chemical and biological weapons, but it had a slightly smaller coefficient.

72. The bivariate correlation between favoring use of troops "to destroy a terrorist camp" and the goal of combating terrorism was $r = .37$**. Because of barely overlapping random subsamples of telephone respondents, the $r = .38$** correlation between favoring "toppling unfriendly regimes that support terrorist groups" and perceiving Iraqi WMDs as a "critical threat" to the U.S. was based on very few cases ($N = 54$), yet it was highly significant ($p < .005$). In this and many other cases, the non-overlap problem made it impossible to include in multiple regressions some key independent variables that had substantial bivariate relationships with the dependent variables. In general, we mention only bivariate relationships that were significant at the $p < .01$ level.

73. In a demographic regression for air strikes on terrorist camps, only evangelical Protestantism had a clearly significant ($p < .05$) coefficient (.08*; adjusted R-squared = just .009). When goals and other attitudes were added, the only clearly significant coefficients were for the goal of superior military power (.15**), the goal of preventing the spread of nuclear weapons (.15**), the goal of defending allies (.12*), and the threat of unfriendly nuclear weapons (.13*). When the demographic variables were dropped these coefficients remained essentially the same but conservatism became significant (.12*) and the adjusted R-squared rose a bit, from .100 to .123.

74. No respondents to the drug lords question were asked goals questions. Bivariate correlations with favoring troop use to ensure oil supplies: goal of ensuring adequate supplies of energy, $r = .36$**; goal of combating terrorism, .34**; goal of maintaining superior military power, .31**; goal of defending allies, .25**.

75. In an attitudes-only regression for Afghan peacekeeping, OLS coefficients were "active part," .24**; liberalism, n.s.; Afghan thermometer rating, .12+; and human rights goal, .12+; adjusted R-squared = .11, df = 233. In logit and probit regressions, rating of Afghanistan on the feeling thermometer but not liberalism was significant at the $p < .05$ level.

U.S. participation in peacekeeping in Bosnia was particularly supported (in bivariate terms) by women, liberals, and strong Democrats; by those who embraced the goals of strengthening the UN ($r = .24$**), strengthening international law and institutions (.22**), and promoting human rights; and especially by those who felt relatively warm toward Muslims (.37**) and Palestinians (.36**).

76. In the famine case, no bivariate demographic differences were significant except for a puzzling tendency for a few more Protestants than Catholics to favor troop use (85 percent compared to 74 percent). But support for troop use was substantially higher among those who called the goals of combating world hunger and promoting and defending human rights "very important" (89 percent in each case) than among those who considered these goals just "somewhat important" (58 percent and 68 percent, respectively).

77. Most statistical relationships involving the perceived threat of terrorism or the goal of combating terrorism, however, are depressed by skewed marginal frequencies. Since

nearly all Americans consider the threat of terrorism to be critical and the goal of combating it to be very important, variations in those attitudes (a substantial part of which is probably just measurement error) cannot account for much variation in specific policy preferences or predict big differences in preferences.

78. As in many other cases, our defense spending regressions could not include some relevant variables (e.g., thermometer ratings of Muslims or the UN, $r = -.28^{**}$ and $-.24^{**}$, respectively) because of non-overlap of respondents. Likewise the number of threats and goals that could be included was limited by multicollinearity and low degrees of freedom. Experimentation with seven threats and goals indicated that those displayed in table 4.10 had the biggest independent effects and that the "restrict . . . immigration" goal better captured domestic priorities than did desires to expand Social Security or the goal of reducing trade deficits.

79. Bivariate correlations for support of expanding homeland security programs included $r = .26^{**}$ with the goal of combating terrorism, $.23^{**}$ with the threat of international terrorism, $.12^{**}$ with the threat of Islamic fundamentalism, and $.29^{**}$ with thermometer ratings of Donald Rumsfeld. Significant coefficients in a demographics-only regression were for Catholic, $.14^{**}$; evangelical, $.10^{**}$; education, $-.09^*$; woman, $.08^*$; Asian, $.08^*$; and unemployed, $-.06+$ (adjusted R-squared $= .032$). In a comprehensive regression including demographics along with the three basic attitudes and seven threats and goals, the only significant coefficients were for Catholic $(.12^*)$, perceived threat of international terrorism $(.14^*)$, and the goal of combating terrorism $(.19^{**};$ adjusted R-squared $= .081,$ df $= 360)$. The terrorism threat $(b = .15^{**})$ and goal $(.19^{**})$ had the only significant coefficients in an attitudinal-only regression (adjusted R-squared $= .083,$ df $= 360$).

80. Bivariate correlations with preferences for expanding intelligence gathering tended to be relatively weak: e.g., $r = .18^{**}$ with the threat of nuclear proliferation, $.17^{**}$ with the threat of international terrorism, and a barely significant $.13^*$ with the goal of combating terrorism (but $.28^{**}$ with Rumsfeld thermometer ratings). In a demographics-only regression, the only significant coefficients were for evangelical $(.13^{**})$ and perhaps Catholic $(.07+)$; adjusted R-squared was only $.011$. The evangelical and Catholic coefficients (and one for "active part" internationalism) became nonsignificant when seven threats and goals were added to the regression, but so did those for all the threats and goals. In an attitudes-only regression, only conservatism $(b = .10+)$ met even the loose $p < .10$ criterion for significance, though perceptions of the threat of international terrorism $(b = .09,$ $p = .102)$ and the threat of China as a power $(b = .08,$ $p = .127)$ came close; adjusted R-squared $= .057$.

81. We cannot be sure about individuals' motivations regarding European defense spending because no respondents were asked both about European spending and about foreign policy goals. But perceptions of Islamic fundamentalism as a threat to U.S. vital interests correlated rather highly $(r = .29^{**})$ with desires to have European governments expand defense spending.

82. U.S. bases in Turkey were favored substantially more by high-income people than low (68 percent to 33 percent), by people with postgraduate education than those with less than high school (72 percent to 42 percent), by whites than blacks (63 percent to 41 percent), by internationalists than isolationists (66 percent to 31 percent), by strong Republicans than strong Democrats (69 percent to 50 percent), and by conservatives than liberals (70 percent to 52 percent). But the goal of superior military power worldwide did not so

strongly differentiate opinions, with 62 percent of respondents who deemed it "very important" and 50 percent of those who called it "somewhat important" favoring U.S. military bases in Turkey.

83. Bivariate correlations between embracing the goal of defending allies and favoring bases in various countries were $r = .07^*$ for Germany, $.15^{**}$ for Cuba, $.15^{**}$ for Uzbekistan, $.16^{**}$ for Saudi Arabia, $.15^{**}$ for Pakistan, $.14^{**}$ for Afghanistan, and only $-.0009$ (n.s.) for South Korea. The Philippines ($r = .20^{**}$) was highest.

84. In a comprehensive regression (factoring in demographics, basic attitudes, and selected goals and threats) for increased or decreased commitment to NATO, only the coefficient for the goal of strengthening the UN was significant ($b = .18^{**}$; adjusted R-squared $= .03$, df $= 344$). When the demographic variables were dropped, only "active part" internationalism ($b = .11^*$) and strengthening the UN ($b = .18^{**}$) were significant (adjusted R-squared $= .05$, df $= 344$). The bivariate correlation between increasing commitment to NATO and warm feelings toward the UN was a striking $r = .41^{**}$.

85. We cannot be sure of motivations, because the goals questions were not asked of any respondents who answered the UN joint training or rapid deployment force questions.

CHAPTER FIVE

For comments and suggestions on earlier drafts we are grateful to Edward Greenberg, Arthur Cyr, Elly Page, Karen Alter, Ian Hurd, Michael Loriaux, Elizabeth Hurd, Steven Kull, Paul Sniderman, and Richard Sobel. For helpful comments on this chapter as well as on the broader project we thank a number of scholars at a spring 2003 University of Michigan seminar, including Kenneth Kollman, Donald Kinder, Gregory Markus, Arthur Lupia, Nancy Burns, and Christopher Achen. Also Dennis Chong, Jeffrey Jenkins, Kenneth Janda, and other participants in Northwestern University's American Politics Workshop; those who commented at an Institute for Policy Research seminar; and Thomas Walker, Peter Trubowitz, and John Ikenberry, who commented at an APSA panel.

1. For an early description and critique of Bush administration unilateralism, see Daalder and Lindsay (2003). A prominent neoconservative critic of European multilateralism and advocate of U.S. unilateral use of force is Kagan (2003); see also Hanson (2002).

2. On global governance, see Kaul, Grunberg, and Stern (1999); United Nations Commission on Global Governance (1995). It is unlikely that many citizens are familiar with this terminology, but the "neoliberal" and "global governance" labels do fit empirical patterns in citizens' policy preferences. To a remarkable extent, Americans' preferences parallel the neoliberal prescriptions of Nye (2002, 2004).

3. In the 2004 Web-based survey, only 8 percent said that the United States should continue to be the "preeminent world leader"; 78 percent said it should "do its share . . . together with other countries." These figures were nearly identical to the 7 percent and 79 percent figures in the comparable 2002 Web-based pilot survey. The "take action alone" question was not asked in 2004.

4. The Pew Research Center for the People and the Press found negative feelings about France, June 3, 2003, http://people-press.org. In the 2004 CCFR Web-based survey, France received an apparently cool, 47-degree average thermometer rating, but that was actually rather warm by Web-based standards (nearly all Web-based ratings have been 6 or 7 degrees lower than ratings based on contemporaneous telephone surveys). No definite trend can be established because France was not included in the 2002 Web-based thermometer battery.

In 2004 the mean thermometer rating of Germany (58 degrees) remained as high or higher than it had been in the 2002 Web-based survey (56 degrees).

5. In the 2004 Internet survey, a majority (52 percent to 41 percent) said the U.S. should make "active efforts" to ensure that no other country becomes a superpower. The EU's thermometer rating of 49 degrees remained only in the lukewarm range (lacking Internet data from 2002, we cannot compare that year) and remained substantially below those of Germany (58 degrees) or Britain (70 degrees).

6. For this and most other policy preference questions discussed in this chapter we performed four sets of multiple regression analyses: with fourteen demographic independent variables only; with the demographics plus three basic political attitudes (internationalism/isolationism, liberal/conservative ideological self-ratings, and party identification); with the demographics and basic attitudes plus a selected set of goals, threats, and other attitudinal variables; and with those goals and attitudes only. For reasons discussed previously (easy comprehensibility and comparability in terms of observed variation accounted for) we primarily report standardized OLS coefficients. Goals and other attitudinal factors were selected for inclusion on the basis of theoretical relevance, the existence of sufficient overlapping observations (given the CCFR's subsample design), empirical power, and the avoidance of excessive multicollinearity.

7. In regressions for support for or opposition to strengthening the EU, no demographic or basic attitudinal factors were significant except for Democratic party identification ($b = .14^{**}$), which became nonsignificant when goals were included. The regressions with only demographics and/or basic attitudes accounted for only tiny proportions of the variance (adjusted R-squared $= -.003, .010$). In the comprehensive demographics + attitudes + goals regression, the adjusted R-squared rose sharply to .073. Only goals had significant coefficients: strengthening the UN ($.15^{**}$), safeguarding against global financial insecurity ($.16^{**}$), and combating world hunger ($.12^{**}$). Results for the regression including goals and attitudes only were quite similar, with adjusted R-squared rising further to .087.

8. Bivariate correlations with desires to strengthen NATO: goal of strengthening UN, $r = .25^{**}$; goal of financial stability, $.24^{**}$; goal of promoting democracy abroad, $.20^{**}$; goal of superior military power, $.23^{**}$. According to a comprehensive multiple regression, being female led to support for strengthening NATO ($b = .12^{**}$), as did emphasizing the goals of strengthening the UN ($.17^{**}$), maintaining superior military power ($.18^{**}$), and safeguarding against global financial instability ($.12^{*}$); the goal of promoting democracy was not quite significant (adjusted R-squared $= .135$; df $= 443$).

9. Bivariate correlations with favoring an increase in our "commitment to NATO": UN thermometer rating, $r = .35^{**}$; goal of strengthening the UN, $.20^{**}$; goal of promoting democracy, $.13^{*}$; threat of global warming, $.16^{**}$; threat of AIDS, $.16^{**}$; threat of chemical and biological weapons, $.13^{**}$; threat of civil wars in Africa, $.12^{**}$. Similar relationships appear in various multiple regressions as well. But non-overlap of respondents prevented including all relevant factors in a single regression, and (compared with the "strengthen NATO" item) only a moderate amount of variance was accounted for; the adjusted R-squared hovered around .07.

10. Ian Hurd has pointed out to us the apparent public support for a system of global governance, involving multilateralism across a number of policy areas and support for several different international organizations as part of a single system. He notes that this has conservative implications; it suggests opposition to any radical (e.g., hegemonic) revision of a broad distribution of power (personal communication, June 19, 2003).

11. In 2002, a telephone-only random subsample of respondents ($N = 686$) was asked, "Do you favor or oppose having diplomatic relations with the following countries?"; the list included Cuba, Iraq, Iran, North Korea, and China. In the 2004 Web-based survey, majorities again favored diplomatic relations with all the countries asked about: Iran (59 percent), North Korea (56 percent), Cuba (62 percent), and China (75 percent).

12. Unfortunately no correlations or regressions with any goals could be computed for the diplomatic relations items because of complete non-overlap of respondents. In multiple regressions for support of diplomatic relations with Cuba that included only demographic factors and the three basic attitudes, the significant standardized coefficients were for education level (.20**), being male (.15**), being Catholic (−.12**), being evangelical (−.09*), and being an "active part" internationalist (.11**). In a carefully pieced-together attitudinal regression, significant coefficients were for thermometer rating of Castro (.22**), seeing a vital interest in Brazil (.15*), support for assassinations (−.18*), travel abroad (.16*), and knowledge of the euro (.14+; $p = .052$); adjusted R-squared = .18, df = 177.

It was particularly difficult to do multiple regression analyses with questions such as this that were asked only of random subsamples of telephone respondents, because few or none of those respondents also fell into the random subsamples that were asked questions about various relevant independent variables. Degrees of freedom vanished quickly if too many (or poorly chosen) independent variables were included. For example, the apparently innocuous substitution of Brazil thermometer scores for perceptions of a vital interests in Brazil dropped the degrees of freedom in the above regression to 93. That, together with the inclusion of all three basic attitudes, left only the Castro thermometer with a significant coefficient (.22*), though other coefficient estimates stayed similar in magnitude.

13. In a demographics + basic attitudes regression for diplomatic relations with Iran, significant coefficients were for education level (.17**), "active part" internationalism (.15**), being male (.09*), identifying oneself as liberal (.09+), being Catholic (−.11**), being evangelical (−.09*), and being Asian (−.07+); adjusted. R-squared = .086, df = 587. In a regression with selected attitudes only, standardized coefficients were for rating of Jiang Zemin (.29**), rating of Ariel Sharon (−.16*), support for assassinating terrorists (−.17*), knowledge of the euro (.16*), and "active part" internationalism (.12; n.s.); adjusted R-squared = .143, df = 135. When the assassination variable was excluded the df rose to 389 and significance levels rose markedly, but the magnitudes of coefficients stayed nearly the same. Feelings about the EU, Palestinians, Muslims, and Iran itself could not be included in these regressions but were substantially correlated ($r = .39**, .33**, .30**,$ and .22* respectively) with favoring diplomatic relations with Iran.

14. Unfortunately the CCFR surveys have not included questions directly probing trade-offs or temporal priorities between diplomatic and military measures. We infer a general preference for diplomatic measures from the very high levels of support they receive, their relatively low cost, and empirical patterns discussed below.

15. The two questions about attacking terrorist training camps, along with questions about the assassination of individual terrorist leaders, the trial of suspected terrorists by an International Criminal Court, diplomatic efforts to apprehend terrorist suspects, and diplomatic efforts to improve U.S. relations with potential adversary countries, were asked of all in-person respondents ($N = 400$) plus a telephone subsample ($N = 722$), in a battery introduced as follows: "In order to combat terrorism, please say whether you favor or oppose each of the following measures." See chapter 4.

16. A telephone-only subsample ($N = 687$), entirely exclusive of those asked the battery of terrorism questions described above, was given the same prologue ("In order to combat international terrorism, please say whether you favor or oppose each of the following measures") and asked about eight measures: helping poor countries develop, working through the UN to strengthen international laws against terrorism, being evenhanded in the Israeli-Palestinian conflict, setting up an international system to cut off funding for terrorists, toppling regimes that support terrorist groups, restricting immigration into the U.S., using racial profiling in airport security checks, and sharing intelligence information with other countries.

17. The Rome Statute of the International Criminal Court, Article 5(1)b, provides for jurisdiction over "crimes against humanity," which are defined in Article 7(1) as "any of the following acts [later specified to include 'murder' and 'extermination'] when committed as part of a widespread or systematic attack directed against any civilian population" (http://www.un.org/law/icc/statute/romefra.htm). See also http://www.iccnow.org. For information on many complex aspects of international law and U.S. criminal laws concerning terrorism, see the American Society for International Law Web site, http://www.asil.org.

18. Proportions favoring various measures "to combat terrorism" in the single battery asked in the 2004 Web-based survey: working through the UN to strengthen international laws against terrorism, 87 percent; U.S. air strikes against terrorist camps, 83 percent; trial of suspected terrorists in the ICC, 82 percent; attacks by U.S. ground troops against terrorist camps, 76 percent; restricting immigration, 76 percent; assassination of individual terrorist leaders, 68 percent; toppling regimes that support terrorists, 67 percent; helping poor countries develop, 64 percent; making a major effort to be evenhanded in the Israeli-Palestinian conflict, 64 percent; racial profiling at airports, 44 percent; and (a new item) "using torture to extract information from suspected terrorists," only 29 percent.

Inferences about opinion changes between 2002 and 2004 are complicated by possible mode effects; for example, more Web-based than telephone respondents in 2002 (by 11 percentage points) said they favored assassinations. Compared with the available 2002 Web-based data, support in 2004 clearly dropped for assassinations (down 9 percentage points), air strikes (-7), and use of ground troops (-6), while holding steady on trial in the ICC. Contrasts with 2002 telephone data were sufficiently large on helping poor countries develop (-14 points) and racial profiling (-10) to suggest that there were drops in support for them as well, while most diplomatic items stayed within 1 or 2 percentage points of the 2002 telephone results.

19. Among the nonmilitary approaches to terrorism, only the ICC trial, "apprehend suspects," and "improve relations" items could be correlated with Goals questions; the others had no respondents in common.

20. Correlations with support for improving relations with adversaries: favor diplomatic relations with Iran ($r = .28^{**}$), with Iraq ($.26^{**}$), with Cuba ($.20^{**}$); favor Palestinian state ($.21^{**}$); favor participation in ICC ($.26^{**}$); favor participation in UN peacekeeping ($.21^{**}$). The "improve U.S. relations with adversary countries" question was a particularly frustrating subject for multiple regression analysis because very few individuals who responded to it were asked more than one or two of the other questions with the strongest bivariate relationships to it. In one attitudes-only regression the standardized coefficients were, for support of participation in UN peacekeeping, $.14^{*}$; for the goal of securing energy supplies, $.13^{*}$; for the goal of promoting markets, $.11^{*}$; for the goal of improving the global

environment, .11+; for "active part" internationalism, .11*; for self-identification as a lib-eral, .11+; and for party identification, n.s. (adjusted R-squared = .102, df = 359). Regres-sions with other subsets of independent variables indicated independent positive effects of support for the ICC and for UN peacekeeping as well as desires for strong U.S. leadership, and a negative impact of warm feelings toward Defense Secretary Donald Rumsfeld.

21. Bivariate correlations for trying terrorists in an ICC: with goal of strengthening in-ternational law, r = .30**; with Annan thermometer, .32**; with goal of improving the global environment, .28**; with goal of combating world hunger, .24**; with goal of protecting U.S. jobs, .29**; with goal of safeguarding against financial instability, .23**. In an attitudinal multiple regression, standardized coefficients for various goals were, for protecting jobs, .23**; strengthening international law and institutions, .17**; improving the global envi-ronment, .10+; and combating world hunger, .10+. Coefficients for "active part" interna-tionalism, party affiliation, and the goal of safeguarding against financial instability were not significant (adjusted R-squared = .188, df = 360).

22. In 1994 39 percent favored a Palestinian state, with only 20 percent opposed; in 1998 the margin was 36 percent to 26 percent. The 2002 in-person interviewees favored a Pales-tinian state by a margin of just 38 percent to 32 percent, indicating that there was a real change between 1998 and 2002. For earlier data on Americans' attitudes about Israel and the Arab-Israeli conflict, see Gilboa (1987).

23. The question about establishment of a Palestinian state was asked in 2002 of all in-person interviewees (N = 400) plus a random subsample of telephone respondents (N = 689); telephone-only subsamples were asked the questions about active U.S. involvement (N = 698) and Bush's endorsement of such a state (N = 718), with the Bush question coming last so as not to prejudice those respondents who were asked one or both of the others.

24. According to a PIPA/KN poll released May 30, 2003, if Israel failed to take steps called for in the road map, 65 percent of Americans favored withholding military aid, 63 percent favored withholding economic aid, and 60 percent favored withholding military spare parts. In case of noncompliance by the Palestinians, 74 percent favored withholding eco-nomic aid, 62 percent favored encouraging other countries to withhold aid, and 53 percent favored refusing to deal with the Palestinian leadership. See the PIPA Study Archive at http://www.pipa.org.

25. The small 2004 CCFR telephone survey by CCI found just 43 percent calling Israeli-Arab conflict a "critical threat" to the U.S., down markedly from 67 percent in 2002; in the 2004 Web-based survey an even lower 39 percent deemed it a critical threat. In the Web-based survey's single troop-use battery, only 52 percent favored using U.S. troops to help en-force a peace agreement between Israel and the Palestinians (43% opposed). In the 2004 Web-based survey the mean thermometer rating of Israel was 53 degrees (up 4 degrees from the 2002 Web-based pilot survey); support for taking Israel's side in the conflict, however, was just 17 percent (down 7 points) and for taking neither side, 74 percent (up 4 points).

26. There was a slightly *positive* bivariate relationship between seeing Israel as a "vital interest" and favoring a Palestinian state (r = .08*) and a stronger positive relationship with favoring use of U.S. troops to enforce a peace agreement (.16*) but no significant relation-ship with favoring or opposing active U.S. efforts to establish such a state or telling Israel not to use U.S. weapons in disapproved operations. (Non-overlap of respondents prevented checking the other three policy items.) Thermometer ratings of Israel were unrelated to at-titudes about the Palestinian state itself but *positively* related to favoring the United States'

actively working for it ($r = .17^{**}$) and favoring U.S. troops as a peacekeeping force ($.10^{*}$). Warm feelings toward Israel were, however, negatively related to forbidding Israeli use of U.S. weapons ($r = -.24^{**}$). No respondents to the thermometer question overlapped with the other three Middle East policy items.

Fully 83 percent of the small number of Jews interviewed ($N = 43$), compared with just 30 percent of Protestants and only 12 percent of Catholics, said that the United States should "take Israel's side" in the Middle East conflict, yet large majorities of Jews favored an independent Palestinian state.

27. Thermometer ratings of "the Palestinians" and "the Muslim people" correlated at $r = .38^{**}$ and $.29^{**}$, respectively, with favoring an independent Palestinian state, and at $r = .33^{**}$ and $.28^{**}$ with wanting the United States to work actively toward the creation of such a state.

28. In an attitudinal regression for support for actively working for a Palestinian state standardized OLS coefficients were, for thermometer rating of the Palestinians, $.27^{**}$; for "active part" internationalism, $.16^{*}$; for Democratic party affiliation, $.14+$; for the goal of securing adequate energy supplies, $.14+$; for liberal/conservative self-rating and the goals of promoting human rights, improving standards of living, and combating terrorism, n.s. (adjusted R-squared $= .163$; df $= 163$).

29. On long-term trends in public opinion about the UN, see Page and Shapiro (1992, 215–20) and Hero (1966); for more recent data, see Kull and Destler (1999, chaps. 3–4.)

30. Among face-to-face respondents in 2002 only 51 percent said strengthening the UN should be a very important goal, indicating that about half of the apparent rise from 45 percent in 1998 may have been an artifact of the change in survey mode.

31. A telephone-only subsample ($N = 703$) was asked (with the usual prologue describing the thermometer scale) to "rate your feelings toward some people and organizations"—the ten groups or organizations shown in table 5.4 plus "the Muslim people" (mean rating 49 degrees) and "the Palestinians" (mean rating 35 degrees). See chapter 3.

32. The "needs to be strengthened" questions concerning the eight international institutions listed in table 5.5 were asked of a telephone-only subsample ($N = 752$).

33. On the complex 1999 deal in which the United States promised to pay some of its back dues in return for anti-family planning provisions insisted upon by conservatives, see BBC news releases of November 15 and November 16, 1999, available at http://news.bbc .co.uk. The U.S. has continued to withhold dues and push for various changes at the UN.

34. Long ago Clark and Sohn (1966, esp. 349–58) set forth major proposals for revision of the UN Charter, including a revenue system based on direct collection of UN taxes by member nations from their own populations. Recent proposals for UN taxing authority, including a Tobin tax, are discussed in United Nations Commission on Global Governance (1995); see also the Web site of the Global Policy Forum, http://www.globalpolicy.org/ socecon/glotax/index.htm.

35. Pew Research Center for the People and the Press, "Views of a Changing World 2003," June 3, 2003, http://people-press.org.

36. Program on International Policy Attitudes, "New PIPA/KN Poll on US Role after Iraq War," April 29, 2003; "Americans on Iraq: WMD, Links to al-Qaeda, Reconstruction," July 1, 2003. Both at http://www.pipa.org under Study Archive.

37. Glennon (2003), among others, argued after the invasion of Iraq that hopes for establishing binding international law on the use of force through the UN Security Council had "failed." For a critique see Hurd (2003).

38. In the 2004 Web-based survey, only 38 percent said that strengthening the UN should be a very important goal of U.S. foreign policy, down 17 points from the pilot Web-based survey in 2002. But comparable declines occurred for the goals of protecting American business abroad (down 19 points), maintaining superior military power (down 17), protecting weaker nations against aggression (down 17), and even preventing the spread of nuclear weapons (down 13) and combating international terrorism (down 12). Only securing adequate energy supplies and protecting the jobs of American workers showed no significant drops. The 57-degree mean thermometer rating of the UN in the 2004 Web-based survey was lower than the 64-degree mean in the 2002 telephone survey, but Web-based ratings of most countries in 2002 were a similar 6 or 7 percentage points lower than telephone-measured ratings of those same countries that year; hence the apparent change was probably an artifact of mode effects. In terms of rankings, only the WHO, Britain, and Germany—out of eight other international organizations and eleven countries—evoked warmer feelings in 2004 than the UN did.

Also in the 2004 Web-based survey, 74 percent favored a standing UN peacekeeping force (20 percent opposed), 57 percent favored empowering the UN to regulate the international arms trade (36 percent opposed), and 49 percent favored the small UN tax (45 percent opposed); 71 percent favored giving the UN a stronger role than the U.S. in democratizing Iraq (25 percent favored a stronger U.S. role); 78 percent favored giving the WHO intervention power (only 18 percent opposed); and 66 percent agreed with the idea of making more decisions within the UN even if it meant going along with nonpreferred policies (29 percent disagreed). In response to a long question about whether countries should "give the World Court more power" by "making a general commitment to accept the decisions of the World Court" or "restrict the power of the Court" by "deciding on a case-by-case basis whether they will accept the Court's decisions," 57 percent said the U.S. should "make a general commitment"; 35 percent said it should not. In response to a question that explained the veto power of the five permanent members of the UN Security Council and then declared that "some people have proposed that this should be changed so that if a decision was supported by *all* the other members [emphasis added], no member, not even the United States, could veto the decision," a total of 59 percent said they would "strongly" (15 percent) or "somewhat" (44 percent) favor this change; a total of just 36 percent said they would "somewhat" (23 percent) or "strongly" (13 percent) oppose it.

39. In 2002 the goal of "strengthening the United Nations" correlated $r = .48^{**}$ with the UN thermometer and $.63^{**}$ with the opinion that the UN "needs to be strengthened." It may seem altogether obvious that those who say that strengthening the United Nations should be a very important goal of U.S. foreign policy would also say that the UN "needs to be strengthened," while those who regard the goal as not at all important would say it does not. But these questions were separated in time and differed significantly in context: for example, the "needs to be strengthened" item mentioned the possibility of creating "unwieldy bureaucracies." Those who consider survey-measured policy preferences to be essentially random would expect the correlation between these two items to be close to zero, not the observed $.63^{**}$.

40. In a comprehensive (demographics + basic attitudes + goals) regression for the question about strengthening the UN, significant coefficients were, for the goal of strengthening the UN, $.55^{**}$; for the goal of improving the global environment, $.17^{**}$; for the goal of controlling illegal immigration, $-.11^{**}$; for the goal of protecting weaker nations from

aggression, (puzzlingly) −.08*; for the goal of combating hunger, −.02 (n.s.); for being female, .10**; and for Democratic party identification ..12**. (Adjusted R-squared was an unusually high .456; df = 469.) Information variables (unfortunately asked only of telephone interviewees) could not be included in this or most of our other attitudinal regressions, which had to rely heavily upon the in-person respondents who were asked all "core" questions.

41. From an attitudinal probit regression for paying UN dues (corresponding to the fourth column of table 5.6), "first difference" estimates were, for "active part" internationalism, .15*; for the goal of strengthening the UN, .31**; for the goal of improving the global environment, .21*; for the goal of maintaining superior military power, −.17*; for support of U.S. peacekeeping in Bosnia, .26**; and for opposition to tightening Muslim immigration, .19**, with no other variables significant. We consider probit "first differences" to be based on a metric no less arbitrary than our standardized OLS coefficients (namely the effect of a hypothetical movement from the lowest to the highest response alternative, no matter how many or few people actually chose those alternatives). As in this example, the probit first differences we calculated for various regressions with dichotomous dependent variables tended to be larger than OLS coefficients but conveyed very similar qualitative findings. Only rarely did they differ markedly in statistical significance. This supports our decision to report standardized OLS coefficients in our tables.

42. On global public goods, see Kaul, Grunberg, and Stern (1999).

43. On public opinion and arms control, including the Baruch Plan episode, see Graham (1989).

44. The Cold War arms control questions discussed in the text were introduced using this prologue: "Relations between the Soviet Union and the United States have been the subject of disagreement for some time. Please tell me if you would favor or oppose the following types of relationship with the Soviet Union." See the 1986 Gallup Topline Report to CCFR, pp. 94–95.

45. On public support for arms control agreements during the 1980s, see Rielly (1987) and Gallup's 1986 Topline Report to the CCFR, p. 86.

46. All 2002 in-person respondents (N = 400) plus a random subsample of telephone respondents (N = 713) were asked, "Based on what you know, do you think the U.S. should or should not participate in the following treaties and agreements": the Kyoto agreement on global warming, the land mines treaty, the comprehensive test ban treaty, and the agreement to establish the International Criminal Court (exact wordings are given in the text and table 5.7).

47. A list of signatories to the CNTBT can be found at http://www.ctbto.org. As of December 11, 2005, 176 of the world's 194 countries had signed and 126 had ratified.

48. See Cameron et al. (1998) and the Web sites of the International Campaign to Ban Landmines (http://www.icbl.org, which listed 147 states party to the treaty as of September 5, 2005), the Center for International Rehabilitation (http://www.cirnetwork.org), the U.S. Campaign to Ban Landmines (http://www.banminesusa.org), Physicians for Human Rights (http://www.phrusa.org), and the Landmines Survivors Network (http://www.landminesurvivors.org).

49. In the 2004 Web-based survey, 87 percent favored U.S. participation in the CNTBT (with only 9 percent opposed), and 80 percent favored participating in the land mines treaty (with 16 percent opposed), rises in support of 3 and 4 percentage points, respectively, compared with the 2002 pilot Web-based survey.

50. In a demographics + basic attitudes regression predicting support for U.S. participation in the treaty banning land mines, the only significant coefficients were for age (.12**), education level (.09*), being female (.07*), Democratic party affiliation (.12**), and liberalism (.08*); adjusted R-squared = .048, df = 911. When selected goals and threats were added to the regression, the coefficients for gender, party affiliation, and ideology lost statistical significance, but the proportion of variance accounted for rose markedly. Significant coefficients were .20** for the goal of preventing the spread of nuclear weapons; .13* for the goal of improving the global environment; .13* for the threat of unfriendly countries becoming nuclear powers; .13* for age; and .11+ for education level (adjusted R-squared = .097, df = 349). In a similar logit regression, coefficients for the nuclear threat and the environmental goal were less significant, apparently because that analysis had to rely on listwise rather than our usual pairwise deletion of missing values, thus reducing the effective degrees of freedom.

51. On public opinion concerning energy and environmental agreements in the 1970s, see Rielly (1979, 24) and Gallup's 1986 Topline Report to the CCFR, p. 95.

52. Texts and ratification data for the UN Framework Convention on Climate Change and the Kyoto Protocol can be found at http://www.unfccc.int, which, as of November 18, 2005, listed 157 ratifiers of the Kyoto Protocol (notably including major polluter Russia). The protocol went into force February 16, 2005. On the science and politics of global warming, see the Web sites of the Union of Concerned Scientists (http://www.ucsusa.org), the Natural Resources Defense Council (http://www.nrdc.org), and Environmental Defense (http://www.environmentaldefense.org).

53. Proportions of the public in 2002 saying that the Bush administration handling of various matters was "excellent" or "good" were as follows: "overall foreign policy," 53 percent; "relations with Russia," 61 percent; "relations with Europe," 60 percent; "the war in Afghanistan," 55 percent; "international terrorism," 55 percent; "relations with Japan," 51 percent; "overall trade policy," 45 percent; "the Anti-Ballistic Missile Treaty," 41 percent (43 percent "fair" or "poor"); "relations with China," 39 percent; "nuclear proliferation," 39 percent; "the Arab/Israeli peace process," 33 percent; "the situation in Iraq," 32 percent; "immigration policy," 27 percent; and "global warming," 25 percent.

54. A random subsample of telephone respondents (N = 700) who had not been asked the four-part question about international treaties and agreements were asked the longer global warming treaty question.

55. In the 2004 Web-based survey, 71 percent said the United States should participate in the "Kyoto agreement to reduce global warming" (19 percent were opposed); this was up 2 percentage points from the 2002 Web-based pilot survey.

56. In bivariate terms, perceptions of global warming as a threat correlated .55** with the short Kyoto agreement question and .43** with the long; the goal of improving the global environment correlated .40** with the short Kyoto question but was not asked of respondents to the long question.

57. See Barbara Crossette, "War Crimes Tribunal Becomes Reality, without U.S. Role," *New York Times,* April 12, 2002, A3.

58. On the struggles over the ICC, see the Web sites of the Coalition for the International Criminal Court (http://www.iccnow.org) and Amnesty International (http://web.amnesty .org/pages/icc=index.eng).

59. A random subsample of telephone respondents ($N = 700$) who had not been asked the four-part general question about international treaties and agreements was asked the longer ICC question.

60. To judge the merits of the ICC and the flimsiness of U.S. government arguments against it, see the text of the Rome Statute of the International Criminal Court (available at http://www.un.org/law/icc/statute/romefra.htm), the legal arguments at http://www.asil .org, and Sewall and Kaysen (2000).

61. In the 2004 Web-based survey, 76 percent said the United States should participate in the ICC, with 19 percent opposed; these results were statistically indistinguishable from the 77 percent support and 20 percent opposition in the 2002 Web-based pilot survey.

62. In a demographics + basic attitudes regression predicting support for the ICC (using the short question) the only significant coefficients were for "active part" internationalism (.15**), liberalism (.08*), Democratic party affiliation (.08+), and being Asian (.07*); adjusted R-squared = .037, df = 915. When selected goals were added, all those factors lost statistical significance, but the proportion of variance accounted for rose sharply. The only significant coefficients were for the goals of strengthening international law and institutions (.24**) and strengthening the United Nations (.16**); controlling for those factors, the goal of promoting human rights was not quite significant (.08, p = .134); adjusted R-squared = .124, df = 344.

63. On the theory of "democratic peace" (or liberal peace), see Doyle (1997, chaps. 7–8). In a demographics + basic attitudes OLS regression predicting support for "assistance to promote democracy abroad," the only significant coefficients were for "active part" internationalism (.20**) and income level (.08+); adjusted R-squared = .045, df = 875. Those factors dropped in statistical significance when selected goals and threats were added to the regression, but the proportion of variance accounted for rose sharply. Significant coefficients were .27** for the goal of bringing democratic government to other nations; .13* for the threat of military conflict between Israel and Arabs; .12* for the goal of protecting weaker nations against foreign aggression; and .10+ for "active part" internationalism (adjusted R-squared = .149, df = 336). Probit estimates produced nearly identical results but some significance levels were lower, apparently because of listwise deletion.

64. On the daunting past history of military-based U.S. efforts at democratic nation building, see Pei and Kasper (2003, esp. table 1, p. 4).

65. Program on International Policy Attitudes, "New PIPA/KN Poll on US Role after Iraq War," press release, April 29, 2003, p. 2 (see Study Archive at http://www.pipa.org).

66. "Security Council Almost Unanimously Approves Broad Mandate for Allies in Iraq," *New York Times*, May 23, 2003, A12. The *Times* printed excerpts from Security Council Resolution 1483; the full text is available from http://www.un.org/Docs/sc. Parliamentary elections at the end of January 2005 and in December 2005 shifted control still further to Iraqis, but they did not have an easy time forming a government or writing a constitution that could win support from Sunnis as well as Shia and Kurds.

67. In the 2004 Web-based survey, only 14 percent of the public said that "helping to bring a democratic form of government to other nations" should be a very important goal of U.S. foreign policy, putting it dead last in priority among fourteen goals. The drop of 10 percentage points from the 2002 Web-based pilot survey was just average among goals in terms of absolute magnitude, but very large proportionally: there was not much room for support to fall any further. Only 53 percent favored "assistance to promote democracy

abroad," down 16 points from the 2002 pilot survey, while support for most other types of humanitarian aid dropped by only 1 or 2 percentage points. Only 35 percent said the United States should "put greater pressure on countries in the Middle East, like Saudi Arabia and Egypt, to become more democratic"; 57 percent said it should not.

68. On features of the Constitution that impede democracy in the United States, see Dahl (2003).

69. American Political Science Association Task Force on Inequality (2004) provides a brief summary of available evidence on political inequality in the United States. A much more thorough review of the evidence, with many useful citations, is Jacobs and Skocpol (2005).

70. Downs (1957, chap. 6) gives a lucid account of how costly information and uncertainty lead to the transformation of economic inequality into political inequality.

CHAPTER SIX

For comments on this chapter we are grateful to Steven Kull, Karen Alter, Edward Greenberg, and Arthur Cyr.

1. On benefits and costs of globalization see, among others, Friedman (2000), Rifkin (1995), Longworth (1998), Barber (1996, e.g., 295, 297, 299), Mander and Goldsmith (1996), and Rodrik (1997, 2003).

2. The proportions of the public calling economic competition from Japan a "critical threat" in CCFR surveys were, in 1990, 60 percent; 1994, 62 percent; 1998, 45 percent; and 2002, 29 percent (the question was not asked in 2004). The figures for Europe in those years were 30 percent, 27 percent, 24 percent, and 13 percent; opinion stayed about the same in 2004 according to the Web-based survey (14 percent) but rose by 7 points according to the more comparable CCI telephone survey (20 percent). Competition from low-wage countries was not asked about before 1998, when 40 percent called it a critical threat; in 2002 the figure was just 31 percent based on the combined data from Harris Interactive, but 37 percent among in-person interviewees, suggesting that there might not have been a real drop since 1998. (The 2002 figures for competition from Japan and Europe were only 3 and 4 percentage points higher for in-person interviewees than for the combined data.) In 2004 the Knowledge Networks Web-based survey and the small CCI telephone survey both found 35 percent saying that economic competition from low-wage countries posed a critical threat, suggesting a slight rise from the 31 percent combined in-person and telephone figure of 2002. Despite the jumble of changes in survey modes, it is clear that concerns about economic competition from Japan and Europe dropped markedly between the early 1990s and the early 2000s, and that worry about low-wage countries stayed at a moderate and fairly constant level from the late 1990s to 2004.

3. Figures for perceptions of fairness in trade with the United States in 2002: Canada, 79 percent "fair" versus 10 percent "unfair"; EU, 60 percent fair, 20 percent unfair; Mexico, 50 percent fair, 36 percent unfair; Japan, 47 percent fair, 41 percent unfair; China 32 percent fair, 53 percent unfair. In the 2004 Web-based survey: Canada 74 percent fair, 15 percent unfair; EU, 60 percent fair, 26 percent unfair; Japan, 52 percent fair, 35 percent unfair; Mexico, 50 percent fair, 38 percent unfair; South Korea, 49 percent fair, 35 percent unfair; China, 36 percent fair, 51 percent unfair. We should be wary of comparisons across these survey modes, but the results suggest a slight rise in concern about Europe and Canada and a continued drop in worry about Japan, corresponding to changes in those countries'

relative competitive strength. Americans may tend to see vigorous trade competition as "unfair" competition.

4. In the 2004 Web-based survey, 64 percent (up slightly from 61 percent in the 2002 Web-based pilot) said globalization is "mostly good" for the United States; 31 percent said "mostly bad."

5. A random subsample of 700 telephone respondents in 2002 was asked, "Overall, do you think globalization is good or bad for" each of ten objects. A relatively high proportion of respondents (generally around 15 percent) said "not sure" or declined to answer each of these questions; an additional 1 or 2 percent volunteered "equally good or bad" or "neither good nor bad." A partly overlapping random subsample of 810 telephone respondents had been asked, immediately before this battery of questions, "Do you believe that globalization, especially the increasing connections of our economy with others around the world, is mostly good or mostly bad for the United States?"

6. In an OLS regression for the general question about whether globalization was good or bad for the United States with the ten more specific good/bad questions, only "consumers like you" (standardized $b = .24^{**}$), "the U.S. economy" ($.22^{**}$), and "your own standard of living" ($.19^{**}$) had coefficients significant at the $p < .01$ level; no other coefficient was significant at even $p < .10$. (Adjusted R-squared $= .35$; df $= 372$.)

7. In an OLS regression of responses to the question of whether the United States should "actively promote globalization" with responses to the ten "good/ bad for" questions, the strongest predictors were judgments concerning "your own standard of living" ($b = .19^{**}$), "democracy and human rights abroad" ($.19^{**}$), "creating jobs in the U.S." ($.18^{**}$), and "maintaining cultural diversity in the world" ($.08+$). (Adjusted R-squared $= .35$; df $= 382$.) But multicollinearity made these estimates unstable. When only the top seven independent variables were included, the best predictors were "your own standard of living" ($.23^{**}$), "creating jobs" ($.20^{**}$), "consumers like you" ($.16^{**}$), and "providing jobs and strengthening the economy in poor countries" ($.10^{*}$); "democracy and human rights abroad" then had a significantly *negative* coefficient ($-.11^{*}$). Still more parsimonious regressions likewise highlighted factors of economic self-interest.

8. Stolper and Samuelson (1941); Samuelson (1948). Many theoretical complexities are explored in Wong (1995). For an introductory treatment see, e.g., Ethier (1995) and Krugman and Obstfeld (2003).

9. Leamer (1995, 4–5). See also Page (1997). Page and Simmons (2000) is more optimistic about the fate of workers in rich countries, perhaps because it was written at the height of the Clinton economic boom.

10. In the 2004 Web-based survey 73 percent said international trade was good for consumers; 65 percent said it was good for their own standard of living, 59 percent for American companies, and 57 percent for the U.S. economy. But only 45 percent said trade was good (46 percent said bad) for the environment, 38 percent for creating U.S. jobs, and 31 percent for U.S. job security. Asked about outsourcing, 72 percent deemed it "mostly a bad thing because American workers lose their jobs to people in other countries"; just 22 percent said it is "mostly a good thing because it results in lower prices . . . helps stimulate the economy and create new jobs." In 2004 these questions about trade replaced the "globalization" battery of 2002.

11. Proportions saying they sympathized with eliminating tariffs in CCFR surveys were 22 percent (in 1978 and 1982), 28 percent (1986), 25 percent (1990), 32 percent (1994 and

1998), and 38 percent (2002). The apparent rise between 1998 and 2002 is probably an artifact of the change in survey mode: the in-person figure for 2002 was just 30 percent. Proportions saying "tariffs are necessary" varied between a high of 57 percent in 1978 and a low of 48 percent in 1994.

12. There are reasons to suspect, however, that the three-alternative "free trade and help workers" question may have confused some respondents. Two rather long and complex response options differed only by the single word "not," which interviewers may not have emphasized. (On the other hand, the response frequencies suggest that many respondents did distinguish sharply between the two.) Responses did not correlate strongly with other variables, not even with responses to logically related questions about eliminating tariffs (r = .06; n.s.) or requiring parties to trade agreements "to maintain minimum standards for working conditions" (r = −.09*; barely significant at p < .05). The dichotomous and wordy "eliminate tariffs" question is not without similar problems. It correlated only weakly with other variables: not significantly with any foreign policy goals, for example. Its relationship with the feeling that the U.S. should "promote globalization" (r = .15**) was one of its largest, along with perceptions that globalization is good for creating jobs (.25**) and for job security (.21**).

13. In the 2004 Web-based survey, 48 percent favored lowering trade barriers provided there were job programs; only 10 percent favored lowering barriers but opposed job programs; and 34 percent opposed agreements to lower trade barriers altogether.

14. Support in 2002 for standards on working conditions in trade agreements correlated positively with perceptions of threats from economic competition from Japan (r = .12**) or Europe (.12**), as well as threats from global warming (.14**) and from the development of China as a world power (.10*). When all these factors were included in a multiple regression, however, only global warming had a significant (not very large) coefficient (b = .11**), and the regression as a whole was quite unimpressive (adjusted R-squared = .03, df = 646). Unfortunately, the goals questions were not asked of any interviewees who responded to the questions about working or environmental standards.

15. On Clinton administration policies that deemphasized worker protection, see Reich (1997). On U.S. and Mexican attitudes toward NAFTA, see Bouton (2004, 46–47) and Gonzalez, Minushkin, and Shapiro (2004, 36–38).

16. Favoring environmental standards in trade agreements correlated with seeing global warming as a critical threat (r = .21**) and with liberalism (.12**).

17. In the 2004 Web-based survey, just 51 percent said the U.S. practices fair trade with poor countries; 36 percent said unfair. Fully 65 percent disagreed (either "strongly" or "somewhat") with the statement that "rich countries are playing fair in trade negotiations with poor countries." On farm subsidies, 71 percent said they favored giving subsidies to small farmers with less than five hundred acres, but more than half of those said "only in bad years" rather than "on a regular annual basis"—an arrangement favored by just 31 percent of the total sample. Only 27 percent said they favored giving subsidies to "large farming businesses," and two-thirds of those said "only in bad years." Thus only 9 percent of the total sample favored regular annual subsidies to large farms. See Bouton (2004, 41–44).

18. In the 2004 Web-based survey the mean thermometer rating of the WTO was only 48 degrees (median 50 degrees), but the apparent drop from 2002 appears to be mostly or entirely due to mode differences. As we have noted, Web-based thermometer ratings have generally been lower than telephone-based ratings by 6 or 7 degrees. In the 2004 Web-based

survey, mean ratings of the WTO continued to be higher than those of the World Bank (46 degrees) and especially the International Monetary Fund (44 degrees).

19. In the 2004 Web-based survey, 69 percent said the United States should comply with WTO rulings against it (24 percent said no), and 68 percent said international economic decisions should always be made by majority rule; only 27 percent said the U.S. should be able to veto a majority decision.

20. In a demographics-only OLS regression predicting whether or not respondents favored compliance with WTO rulings, the only significant standardized coefficients were for being an evangelical (−.15**), education level (.11*), and age (−.08+; adjusted R-squared=.037, df=575). When our three basic attitudes were added to the regression, all three had significant coefficients (for being an internationalist, .09*; a liberal, .13**; a Democrat,.10*). The coefficient for being an evangelical then dropped to −.09* (indicating, as usual, that some of the effect of being evangelical works through ideological conservatism), the age and education coefficients stayed about the same, and the coefficient for being African American became marginally significant (−.07+; adjusted R-squared = .075, df = 575). In a full demographics + attitudes + goals regression all the demographic factors faded away; only liberal self-ratings (.13*) and perceptions of fair trade by Europeans (.17**) had significant coefficients (adjusted R-squared = .085, df = 370). For goals + attitudes only, the significant coefficients were for "active part" internationalism (.10*), liberal self-rating (.15**), and fair trade by Europe (.19**; adjusted R-squared = .084, df = 370).

21. In 2002, all 400 in-person interviewees plus a random subsample of telephone respondents (N = 686) were asked, "On another issue, do you favor or oppose the use of economic sanctions against each of the following countries": Cuba, Iraq, Iran, North Korea, and China. The same respondents were subsequently asked whether they favored or opposed "having diplomatic relations with" and "engaging in trade with" each of the same five countries. See Bouton and Page (2002, p. 36, figs. 4–8).

22. Among in-person interviewees, opposition to economic sanctions against Cuba was 9 percentage points higher in 2002 than in 1998 . The purely in-person data do not confirm any changes between those years for the other four countries.

23. In a small-N attitudinal OLS regression predicting support for economic sanctions against Cuba, significant standardized coefficients were −.36** for thermometer ratings of Castro and −.31** for the perception that globalization creates U.S. jobs (adjusted R-squared = .21, df = 90).

24. In an OLS regression predicting support for economic sanctions against Iraq (probably complicated by the fact that some opponents of sanctions favored war rather than trade), hot-button concerns with nuclear proliferation, international terrorism, and Iraqi weapons of mass destruction, support for assassinating terrorist leaders, and even thermometer ratings of Saddam Hussein all yielded completely nonsignificant coefficients. But controlling for all these factors, the significant standardized coefficients were −.23** for general thermometer ratings of Iraq and .22** for thermometer ratings of Ariel Sharon (adjusted R-squared = .11, df = 165).

25. In a demographics-only OLS regression predicting support for economic sanctions against Iran, the only even marginally significant standardized coefficients were for income level (.07+) and being Muslim (−.06+), evangelical (.06+), or African American (−.06+); the coefficient for being Jewish was not significant, and little variance was accounted for (adjusted R-squared = .014, df = 874). When our three basic attitudes were

added to a regression, all the above coefficients became nonsignificant except for being Muslim (−.06+); "active part" internationalism (.11**) and liberalism (−.13**) had significant effects, but party identification did not (adjusted R-squared = .037, df = 874). In a full demographics + attitudes + goals regression the only significant coefficients were for "active part" internationalism (.12*), thermometer ratings of Iran (−.28**), thermometer ratings of Israel (.19**), and support for combating terrorism by assassinating individual terrorist leaders (.13*; adjusted R-squared = .119, df = 343). Results were essentially the same in a goals + attitudes only regression, with coefficients of .14**, −.28**, .19**, and .12*, respectively, and a fairly substantial portion of variance was accounted for (adjusted R-squared = .148, df = 343). Attitudes toward assassination of individual terrorist leaders constitute our best measure of intense feelings about terrorism; when the highly skewed perceptions of threat from unfriendly countries becoming nuclear powers and from international terrorism were also included in regressions, neither one had a coefficient significant at the $p < .10$ level.

26. See Rielly (1987, 27).

27. In 2002, trade with Iran was favored by 37 percent and opposed by 60 percent; trade with North Korea was favored by 44 percent and opposed by 50 percent. In the 2004 Web-based survey, proportions favoring engaging in trade with various countries were, for Mexico, 76 percent; China, 63 percent; Cuba, 48 percent (46 percent opposed); Iran, 40 percent; and North Korea, 31 percent. The apparent drops from 2002 of 8 points for China and 13 points for North Korea probably exceed any mode effects.

28. Pearson correlations in 2002 between thermometer ratings of particular leaders or countries and favoring trade with those countries were all in the range of $r = .34**$ to .39**. Correlations between favoring trade with a particular country and favoring diplomatic relations with that country were $r = .50**$ for Cuba, .46** for Iran, .39** for North Korea, .37** for Iraq, and .34** for China.

29. In a demographics-only OLS regression for support for engaging in trade with Cuba, significant coefficients were for education level (.14**) and being male (.14**), evangelical (−.20**), or Catholic (−.12**; adjusted R-squared = .080, df = 597). When our three basic attitudes were added the above coefficients stayed about the same and liberalism was independently related (.18**, adjusted R-squared = .108, df = 597). In a full regression including demographics and attitudes, only thermometer ratings of Castro (.31**) and reactions to combating terrorism by "improving U.S. relations with adversary countries" (.21**) had clearly significant coefficients (being male and evangelical had marginally significant coefficients of .14+ and −.14+, respectively), which stayed about the same and accounted for a substantial portion of the variance in an attitudes-only regression (adjusted R-squared = .197, df = 177).

30. For engaging in trade with China, in a demographics-only regression the significant coefficients were for education level (.13**) and being Hispanic (−.08*), unemployed (.08+), or evangelical (−.08+); being Asian was not significant (adjusted R-squared = .022, df = 590). When basic attitudes were added the demographic coefficients stayed about the same; liberalism (.13**) and "active part" internationalism (.09*) had significant coefficients (adjusted R-squared = .039, df = 590). In a full regression the above factors were not significant, except being unemployed (.10+) and liberalism (.12+), while perceptions of a vital U.S. interest in China (.16**) and perhaps of a threat from the development of China as a world power (−.10+) emerged as significant (adjusted R-squared = .045, df = 332). In a

purely attitudinal regression the significant coefficients were for "active part" internationalism" (.09+), liberalism (.14*), and perception of a vital interest in China (.15**) or of threats from China as a world power (−.09+) or from economic competition from low-wage countries (−.10+; adjusted R-squared = .053, df = 332). With alternative specifications, thermometer ratings of China or of Jiang Zemin played a role similar to, though slightly weaker than, perceptions of a vital U.S. interest in China.

31. In an attitudinal regression for support for engaging in trade with Iran, the standardized OLS coefficient for thermometer ratings of Iran was .35**; for thermometer ratings of Israel, −.33**. In a similar regression for trade with Iraq, the coefficient for thermometer ratings of Iraq was .46** and for ratings of Israel, −.32**.

32. On the history of immigration into the United States, see Jones (1992), Daniels (1990), Zolberg (2006).

33. The 2004 Web-based survey found 59 percent saying that controlling and reducing illegal immigration should be a "very important" goal of U.S. foreign policy, down ten points from 69 percent in the comparable 2002 KN survey. Similarly, in 2004 immigrants were seen as a "critical threat" by 52 percent of KN online respondents and 51 percent of CCI telephone interviewees, down 8 or 9 points since 2002. And in the 2004 survey 54 percent said legal immigration should be decreased, down from 61 percent in the comparable 2002 Web-based survey.

34. The proportions saying that controlling immigration should be a very important goal were 72 percent in 1994, 55 percent in 1998, and 70 percent in 2002 (69 percent for in-person interviewees). Those saying that large numbers of immigrants were a critical threat were 72 percent in 1994, 55 percent in 1998, and 60 percent in 2002 (63 percent for in-person interviewees).

35. Bivariate correlations of desires to *increase* the number of legal immigrants were $r = -.15^{**}$ with emphasis on the goal of protecting the jobs of American workers, .09* with income level, and .21** with education level. In harmony with the idea of purposive belief systems, preferences for increasing the number of legal immigrants had rather strong (though far from perfect) negative correlations with perceptions that large numbers of immigrants are a threat ($r = -.34^{**}$) and with the goal of controlling illegal immigration (−.28**).

36. Borjas (2004, table 1 and fig. 3). See also Borjas (2003) and Smith and Edmonston (1997).

37. Desires to increase the number of legal immigrants were correlated at $r = .15^{**}$ with thermometer ratings of Mexico, and $r = .30^{**}$ with thermometer ratings of "the Muslim people."

38. Bivariate correlations of support for restricting the number of immigrants from Arab or Muslim countries: with thermometer ratings of "the Muslim people," $r = -.41^{**}$; with beliefs that the 9/11 attacks represented the "true teachings of Islam," .29**; with beliefs that Muslim ways are incompatible with Western ways and violent conflict inevitable, .17**; with the goal of protecting jobs of American workers, .28**; with education level, −.25**.

39. In the 2004 Web-based survey, "the Muslim people" got an average thermometer rating of just 39 degrees. But average ratings of countries and peoples in the 2002 KN Web-based pilot study had generally been 6 or 7 degrees lower than those in that year's main CCFR study; the apparent 10-degree drop in regard to Muslims only slightly exceeds this mode difference.

40. The following discussion is based on regressions in which opinion about the goal of "controlling and reducing illegal immigration" is the dependent variable. Unlike most of the goals questions, this one measures rather specific policy preferences. The word "illegal" does not appear to be very important. Results were quite similar when the dependent variable was ratings of the threat of "large numbers of immigrants and refugees coming into the U.S.," except that in this case the perceived threat of "economic competition from low-wage countries" was significant and the goal of reducing trade deficits (which gets at similar economic concerns) was not. Regressions using preferences about increasing or decreasing the level of legal immigration were considerably less robust, with only the goal of job protection having a significant coefficient.

41. Thermometer ratings of "the Muslim people" could not be included in the immigration regressions because they were not obtained from the same respondents who answered the other relevant questions. This is a particularly vexing example of how the CCFR's balkanized subsample research design for 2002, which maximized the number of questions for which marginal frequencies of responses could be obtained, at the same time made it difficult to analyze relationships among variables.

42. Statistics are from United Nations Development Programme (2004). Dollar figures given in the text are Purchasing Power Parity equivalents.

43. "Ranking the Rich 2004," a report by the Center for Global Development and *Foreign Policy* magazine, printed in *Foreign Policy,* May/June 2004; see http://www.cgdev.org and http://www.foreignpolicy.com. The United States did considerably better on the Commitment to Development Index as a whole, ranking seventh of twenty-one countries when investment, trade, technology, peacekeeping, and especially migration and remittances were taken into account. A lucid analysis of U.S. foreign aid and its shortfalls with respect to the UN Millennium Development Goals is Sachs (2005).

44. For similar points about U.S. public opinion concerning foreign aid, based on extensive PIPA data, see Kull and Destler (1999, chap. 5).

45. The proportions favoring economic aid in CCFR surveys were 52 percent (1974), 46 percent (1978), 50 percent (1982), 53 percent (1986), 45 percent (1990 and 1994), 47 percent (1998), and 54 percent (2002). The 2002 figure for in-person interviewees only was just 47 percent, identical to the figure for the 1998 in-person survey. This suggests that the apparent rise from 1998 to 2002 may be entirely an artifact of the change in survey mode. Although CCFR reports (e.g., Rielly, 1999, 21) have graphed these response frequencies as a time series, there was a wording change in 1994. Through 1990 the question read, "On the whole, do you favor or oppose our giving economic aid to other nations for purposes of economic development and technical assistance?" In 1994 both this and a shorter version ("On the whole, do you favor or oppose our giving economic aid to other nations?") were asked, with similar results. In subsequent years only the short version was asked. The 1994 splicing and the flatness of the trend line just before and afterwards indicate that the wording change made little difference.

46. The inference that the balance of opinion has always favored a reduction in aid is based on the assumption that few people who say aid should be "kept about the same" mean *exactly* the same, and that roughly as many of the "about the same" people favor a small decrease as favor a small increase. In the 2004 Web-based survey 64 percent said aid should be cut back, apparently up dramatically from the 48 percent of 2002. But the 2004 CCI telephone survey found only 49 percent saying "cut back," indicating that most or all of the apparent change was due to the difference in survey mode.

47. To be sure, the country-specific economic aid questions are oddly unbalanced. The two options representing reductions—"decreased" and "stopped altogether"—may tend to encourage a cut-oriented response, as opposed to choice of the single option "increased"; no "greatly increased" option was offered.

48. Again, this inference assumes that few respondents who said aid should be "kept about the same" meant *exactly* the same, and that roughly the same number of them favored a small decrease as favored a small increase. The proportions favoring increases in aid were, for the Palestinians, 12 percent; Pakistan, 12 percent; Afghanistan, 22 percent; Israel, 18 percent; Egypt, 7 percent; India, 11 percent; and Russia, 16 percent. These questions (and the "African countries" question discussed below) were asked of all 400 in-person interviewees and a random subsample of 726 telephone interviewees. Responses did not differ substantially by mode.

49. Kull and Destler (1999, 123–8).

50. Actual outlays in fiscal year 2002 for subfunction 151, "international development and humanitarian assistance," were $7.8 billion, amounting to just 0.39 percent of total federal outlays or 0.075 percent of GDP. Calculated from United States Office of Management and Budget (2005b, 57, 52, 24). The *mean* 2002 survey estimate was that 22.4 percent of the federal budget goes to foreign aid. Because of data entry errors by the survey organization (some "don't know" or NA responses were entered as 99.8 or 99.9 percent instead of 998 or 999, the codes for missing values), the mean originally appeared to be a startling 31 percent, and the median figure was erroneously reported as 25 percent instead of 20 percent in Bouton and Page (2002, 43).

51. The mean response as to what percentage of the federal budget should go to foreign aid was 12.4 percent. Data entry errors originally made the *mean* figure appear to be 17 percent; the median stayed the same at 10 percent.

52. Kull and Destler (1999, 125–8). See also Kull (1995, 2001a).

53. Rielly (1975, 27; 1983, 25); Kull (2001a, 20).

54. See Kull and Destler (1999, 128–33).

55. Rielly (1975, 26–27; 1979, 22–24; 1983, 24–26).

56. Rielly (1979, 24; 1983, 25).

57. In the 2004 Web-based survey, only 43 percent said combating world hunger should be a "very important" goal of U.S. foreign policy, down 11 points from the comparable KN survey in 2002, but 47 percent (up 7 points) said "somewhat important." Similarly, in 2004 only 18 percent said improving standards of living should be a very important goal (down 10 points from the previous KN survey), but 59 percent (the same as in KN 2002) said somewhat important.

58. In 2002 the battery of questions about six types of humanitarian aid was asked of all 400 in-person respondents plus 707 telephone respondents. The in-person-only percentages were lower than those for the combined data set by 3 points in the cases of food aid and development aid, 6 points on women's education, 7 points on AIDS, 9 points on promoting democracy, and 11 points on birth control. These mode differences are statistically significant. But in every case a substantial majority of in-person-only respondents favored the program, and the ranking of programs was virtually the same as in the combined data.

59. In the 2004 Web-based survey, support for food and medical assistance was 82 percent; for helping needy countries develop, 70 percent; and for assistance with AIDS, 80 percent—down by only 5, 4, and 1 point(s), respectively, from comparable KN data in 2002.

60. See "The Millennium Challenge Account," White House Web site, accessed January 28, 2003; Sperling and Hart (2003); United States Office of Management and Budget (2005a, 224–25); and critiques at http://www.cgdev.org. Outlays for international development and humanitarian assistance rose from 0.39 percent of the federal budget (0.075 percent of GDP) in 2002, to 0.48 percent (0.095 percent) in 2003, to 0.60 percent (0.12 percent) in 2004, and were estimated as staying at the same level in 2005. Figures calculated from United States Office of Management and Budget (2005b, 57–58, 24, 52).

61. In the 2004 Web-based survey, proportions favoring aid for women's education and for birth control were 76 percent and 70 percent, respectively, statistically indistinguishable from the 77 percent and 71 percent in the 2002 Web-based pilot study.

62. Differently specified probit regressions produced similar results but also indicated that domestic concerns, including the goal of U.S. job protection, have negative effects on support for aid to Africa.

63. On the "rational public," see Page and Shapiro (1992). Our findings probably understate the strength of connections among relevant attitudes and beliefs because measurement errors of various sorts have attenuated the relationships. For one thing, we believe that individuals' low information and uncertainty about foreign affairs generally creates a dispersion of an individual's opinions around their central tendency (arguably the "real" opinion) and that this weakens observed relationships involving measured policy preferences.

64. The federal budget for FY 2006 proposed $1.34 billion for these and other multilateral development banks. United States Office of Management and Budget (2005a, 225).

65. In 2002, the IMF received higher thermometer ratings than only two of ten other international groups or organizations: "protesters against globalization" (45 degrees) and "the Palestinians" (35 degrees). In the 2004 Web-based survey the IMF fell below seven groups or organizations on a slightly different list, barely edging out "multinational corporations" to avoid the bottom ranking. The 2004 average thermometer ratings of the World Bank (46 degrees) and IMF (44 degrees) look lower than in 2002 but this is probably an artifact of the mode difference; no comparable 2002 data are available.

66. A particularly trenchant critique of IMF policies as harming both economic growth and equity in developing countries is Stiglitz (2002). Econometric evidence on growth and equity effects of World Bank as well as IMF "structural adjustment" loans and privatization measures is given in Easterly (2002) and Birdsall and Nellis (2002). The IMF has subsequently changed course somewhat. For critiques of the World Bank, see also Pincus and Winters (2002).

67. On business corporations' power to influence U.S. foreign policy in opposition to the public, see Ferguson and Rogers (1986), T. Ferguson (1995), and Jacobs and Page (2005).

CHAPTER SEVEN

For comments and suggestions on this chapter we are grateful to Arthur Cyr, Ron Krebs, Richard Price, Kathryn Sikkink, Karen Alter, and Tom Ferguson. For research assistance we thank Dukhong Kim and Martin Kifer.

1. Morgenthau (1973, 135, 146–48).

2. Lippmann (1955, 24–25, 20, 26–27).

3. Kennan (1951, 93–100).

4. For refutations of mood theory, see Caspary (1970), Russett (1990), Page and Shapiro (1992, chap. 2), and Holsti (2004, 42–49). Gabriel Almond set forth the mood theory in 1950

but subsequently shifted his views somewhat, speaking of a "maturation" of mass opinion and increases in attention and opinion stability (1960, xx–xxvi).

5. On heuristics, see Sniderman, Brody, and Tetlock (1991) and Popkin (1991). Page and Shapiro (1992) make a case that collective public opinion achieves properties of rationality through individuals' use of heuristics, collective deliberative processes, and offsetting errors by individuals. But concerning systematic errors and biases in collective opinion (some examples of which we have noted in previous chapters), see Kuklinski and Quirk (2000) and Althaus (2003).

6. Contrast Burke (1949), Schumpeter (1947), and Sartori (1987) with Dahl (1989). On latent opinion, see Key (1961), Zaller (2003). On different types of representation, see Mansbridge (2003).

7. On "democratic peace," see Russett (1996); Russett and Oneal (2001); Doyle (1983).

8. E.g., George (2002).

9. In-depth case studies of the impact of public opinion on particular foreign policies are reported in Graham (1989), Russett (1990), Risse-Kappen (1991), Peterson (1995), Foyle (1999), and Sobel (2001). Many case studies are compactly summarized in Holsti (2004, chap. 3). Generalizability is of course always a troubling issue with case studies. Most existing quantitative, aggregate-data studies, which also find substantial public influence— e.g., Monroe (1979, 1998), Page and Shapiro (1983), Ostrom and Job (1986), Hartley and Russett (1992)—suffer from ambiguities in causal inference. Often they do not test for other influences (e.g., from organized interest groups) at the same time they investigate the impact of public opinion. See the further discussion below.

10. Morgenthau (1973, 146–48).

11. Most previous analyses of CCFR data have combined the entire set of "foreign policy leaders" that were surveyed—including not only government officials but also media figures, foreign policy experts, and leaders of business, labor, and religious organizations (Rielly 1975 et seq.; Holsti 2004; Page and Barabas 2000; Bouton and Page 2002, chap. 8). Here we examine the views of government officials only.

12. The number of officials interviewed each year averaged about 19 from the Senate, 36 from the House, and 23 from the administration, for a total of 78 decision makers. The larger surveys of "foreign policy leaders" that included these officials averaged 365 respondents in each of the eight years.

Data on large numbers of key policy makers are very difficult to obtain, especially comparable data over multiple years. An important additional source of data on foreign policy leaders (though without parallel surveys of the public) is the set of large-sample surveys conducted every four years between 1976 and 1996 by the Foreign Policy Leadership Project (FPLP) directed by Ole Holsti and James Rosenau. The FPLP sample includes high military officers, who are unfortunately excluded from the Chicago Council surveys. Holsti (2004, esp. chap. 4) reports extensive results over the years from the FPLP, CCFR, and other leadership surveys, along with some contrasting opinions of the public. See also Holsti and Rosenau (1984) and numerous other publications by those authors, many of them cited in Holsti (2004).

13. In some cases (involving, for example, various international treaties and certain uses of force) the preferences expressed by foreign policy decision makers in our data appear to be closer to the public's views than actual foreign policy was at the time. To the extent that this is true, our measures of gaps may *understate* differences between citizens' views and actual policy.

14. The number of questions common to both leader and public surveys varied from a high of 246 in 1974 to a low of 93 in 1986. To avoid distortions due to this variation, we have calculated the frequencies of opinion-policy agreement or disagreement in terms of proportions of the total number of common questions that were asked in a given year.

15. Questions about diplomatic policies were asked most frequently, averaging 73 common items per year, followed by defense policies (38 items) and economic policies (28 items).

16. "Don't know" responses are generally more common among the general public than among policy makers; it is necessary to exclude them in order to compare the views of those with opinions in each group. This exclusion, as well as the dichotomization of all items, is also necessary in order to obtain unique measures of the "gaps" between citizens and policy makers.

There is inevitably some arbitrariness in defining a minimum percentage point difference as indicative of a "disagreement." We selected a difference of 10 percentage points, partly because it would approximate a statistically significant level of difference if decision makers were treated as a random sample (the precise level would depend on marginal frequencies and on the varying number of decision makers surveyed), but more importantly because a difference of this magnitude seems to us to be real, notable, and substantively significant. We examined the effects of increasing the threshold by a few percentage points and found that it did not much alter our basic results. As table 7.2 indicates, most public/policy maker disagreements were substantially larger than 10 points: 80 percent of them involved 15 percentage points or more, and 58 percent involved 20 points or more.

17. Our argument that percentage point gaps generally matter even when majorities agree raises some complex technical issues. For one thing, it rests on the assumption that policy alternatives usually fall along a continuum of possibilities (e.g., spending some exact amount of money between zero and a hundred billion dollars), rather than being simple yes/no dichotomies. It also assumes that the citizens who pick a general survey response (e.g., those who say they favor "increasing" foreign economic aid) tend to prefer, on the dollar continuum, some particular amount of aid. But to translate precisely from the percentage of Americans who favor increasing aid to a dollar figure specifying how big an increase would be extremely difficult. It would require considerably more knowledge about survey responses and underlying preferences than we have. To translate a percentage point gap between two groups into a difference in average preferred spending levels would require such knowledge about both groups.

18. Jacobs and Page (2005, 118) found indications of *greater* public influence on decision makers' preferences in the economic realm than for other kinds of policies. But the same data reveal unusually sharp preference differences between business leaders and the public on economic issues, so that moderate business influence on policy could translate into unusually big gaps.

19. It is suggestive (though based on a small number of cases) that the sharpest observed divergence between policy makers and the public on economic foreign policy issues occurred in 1994, when Democrats controlled both Congress and the presidency and Robert Rubin served as secretary of the treasury. Ferguson and Rogers (1986) and Ferguson (1995) argue that the Democratic Party, dependent on at least a modicum of corporate financial contributions, has come to favor probusiness international economic policies opposed by most working-class Americans. Jacobs and Page (2005) offer quantitative evidence of generally greater influence by business than the public on U.S. foreign policy.

20. It was apparently common for staffers, rather than decision makers themselves, to be interviewed for some or all of the CCFR surveys. We believe that staffers' responses generally reflect the views of those who hire, promote, and supervise them.

21. The idea of democratic control through policy makers' "anticipated reactions" of voters' retrospective judgments or "electoral punishment" is an important one, with threads (mostly underdeveloped threads) woven through many studies of democratic theory and/or public opinion: e.g., Key (1961) and Zaller (2003) on "latent opinion"; Page (1978, chap. 7); Fiorina (1981); Mansbridge (2003).

22. On electoral impacts of foreign policy, see Aldrich, Sullivan, and Borgida (1989).

23. Concerning the ability of legislators to dodge policy accountability to their constituents see Fenno (1978, 136, 240–41), Mayhew (1974), Kingdon (1989), Jacobs and Shapiro (2000, chap. 1), and Arnold (1990).

24. On the foreign policy primacy of the U.S. president, see Wildavsky (1991) and Silverstein (1997).

25. The international relations literature related to a "bias in representation" or power of business includes Moravcsik (1997, 530); Milner (1997); Gourevitch (1986); Rogowski (1989); Snyder (1991); Frieden (1991); Grossman and Helpman (1994, 1995); Keohane and Milner (1996). See also Ferguson (1995).

26. Kull and Destler (1999).

27. Bouton (2004, 49–53) discusses the 2004 CCFR data on foreign policy leaders' misperceptions of public opinion.

28. Jacobs and Page (2005) indicates that business leaders and experts have had much more influence on foreign policy decision makers than public opinion has.

29. On the stability of collective opinion, see Page and Shapiro (1992, chap. 2).

30. On barriers against persuasion by presidents, see Jacobs (2002) and Edwards (2003). But see the telling examples of effective deception in Alterman (2004).

31. An influential argument that public opinion is mainly shaped by elites is given in Zaller (1992).

32. George (2002).

33. Results from White House polling can be found at the Lyndon Johnson Presidential Library in the files of Bill Moyers, Marvin Watson, and Fred Panzer. See Jacobs and Shapiro (1999).

34. Records from the Lyndon Johnson Presidential Library: LBJ, Ex FG165, Memo to LBJ from J. Gardner, December 19, 1966; LBJ, Kinter Papers, Box 7, Memo to LBJ from Robert Kinter, May 30, 1966.

35. Records from the Lyndon Johnson Presidential Library: LBJ, Panzer, Box 395, Memo to Redmon from Tad Cantril, August 11, 1966, and Moyers, Box 12, Memo to Charles Roche from Redmon, July 26, 1966; LBJ, Moyers, Box 12, Memo to Moyers from Redmon, August 4, 1966; LBJ, Moyers, Box 12, Memo to Moyers from Redmon, September 27, 1966.

CHAPTER EIGHT

For comments and suggestions that contributed to this chapter, we are very grateful to Larry Jacobs, Tom Ferguson, Ed Greenberg, and an anonymous reviewer for the University of Chicago Press.

1. The most efficient way to keep track of the latest in-depth data on the public's foreign policy preferences is to visit the websites http://www.americans-world.org, http://

www.pipa.org, and http://www.ccfr.org. Also useful, though focusing more on imagery and judgments of performance than on policy preferences, are the periodic Pew surveys and Yankelovich "Public Agenda" polls; see Yankelovich (2005).Various media and commercial poll results are reported at individual media and pollster Web sites. Many are brought together at http://people-press.org and http://www.pollingreport.com.

2. As a concrete example of highlighting gaps between officials and the public, journalists could routinely contrast roll-call votes by senators and representatives, legislation they pass, and actions by the executive branch with survey evidence on what the public wants. A classic argument for the efficacy of raising issue salience, or "expanding the scope of conflict," in order to increase the political power of ordinary citizens is Schattschneider (1960, esp. chap. 2). Some empirical evidence that increased salience does in fact lead to a greater impact of public opinion on foreign policy is given in Page and Shapiro (1983, table 5, p. 181) and, less strongly, in Jacobs and Page (2005, p. 118, n. 16).

3. Some of these recommendations are shared by the Carter-Baker Federal Commission on Election Reform, whose 2005 final report is at http://www.american.edu/ia/cfer or http://www.american.edu/carter-baker. Unfortunately the commission also endorsed compulsory photo identification for voting, which—unless great care is taken—could disenfranchise those without drivers licenses.

4. A particularly useful source of information on corporate and other sources of political money, with the names of politician recipients, is the Center for Responsive Politics, at http://www.opensecrets.org.

5. The small-state bias of the Senate and other constitutionally embedded sources of U.S. political inequality are carefully and insightfully analyzed by Dahl (2003), who expresses "measured pessimism" (154) about the possibility of reform. Organized labor, always weaker and more divided in the United States than in most advanced industrial countries, now faces the devastating implications of competition among workers in a low-wage, global labor market. This competitive pressure should eventually be reduced by economic growth abroad and perhaps by a worldwide workers movement, but substantial improvement may be decades away. Still, energetic efforts might well win some political battles even in the short run.

6. For suggestions on a number of ways by which extreme economic inequalities could be reduced with little or no net cost to the aggregate U.S. economy, see Page and Simmons (2000).

References

Achen, Christopher H. 1975. "Mass Political Attitudes and the Survey Response." *American Political Science Review* 69:1218–31.

Aldrich, John H., John L. Sullivan, and Eugene Borgida. 1989. "Foreign Affairs and Issue Voting: Do Presidential Candidates Waltz before a Blind Audience?" *American Political Science Review* 63:123–41.

Almond, Gabriel. 1960. *The American People and Foreign Policy.* New York: Praeger. (Orig. pub. 1950.)

Alterman, Eric. 2004. *When Presidents Lie: A History of Official Deception and Its Consequences.* New York: Viking.

Althaus, Scott L. 1998. "Information Effects in Collective Preferences." *American Political Science Review* 92: 545–58.

———. 2003. *Collective Preferences in Democratic Politics: Opinion Surveys and the Will of the People.* New York: Cambridge University Press.

American Political Science Association Task Force on Inequality. 2004. "American Democracy in an Age of Rising Inequality." *Perspectives on Politics* 2(4):651–66.

Arnold, R. Douglas. 1990. *The Logic of Congressional Action.* New Haven: Yale University Press.

Barber, Benjamin R. 1996. *Jihad* vs. *McWorld.* New York: Ballantine.

Bardes, Barbara, and Robert Oldendick. 1978. "Beyond Internationalism: A Case for Multiple Dimensions in the Structure of Foreign Policy Attitudes." *Social Science Quarterly* 59:496–508.

———. 1980. "The Dimensions of Mass Opinion in Foreign Policy: A Trend Analysis." Presented at the annual meeting of the Southwestern Political Science Association, Houston.

Bartels, Larry. 1991. "Constituency Opinion and Congressional Policy Making: The Reagan Defense Buildup." *American Political Science Review* 85:457–74.

———. 1996. "Uninformed Votes: Information Effects in Presidential Elections." *American Journal of Political Science* 40:194–230.

Bennett, W. Lance. 1990. "Toward a Theory of Press-State Relations in the United States." *Journal of Communication* 40(2):103–25.

Bennett, W. Lance, and David L. Paletz, eds. 1994. *Taken by Storm: The Media, Public Opinion, and U.S. Foreign Policy in the Gulf War.* Chicago: University of Chicago Press.

Berelson, Bernard R., Paul F. Lazarsfeld, and William N. McPhee. 1954. *Voting: A Study of Opinion Formation in a Presidential Campaign*. Chicago: University of Chicago Press.

Berinsky, Adam J. 2002. "Silent Voices: Social Welfare Policy Opinions and Political Equality in America." *American Journal of Political Science* 46:276–87.

———. 2004. *Silent Voices: Public Opinion and Political Participation in America*. Princeton: Princeton University Press.

Bill, James A. 1988. *The Eagle and the Lion: The Tragedy of American-Iranian Relations*. New Haven: Yale University Press.

Birdsall, Nancy, and John Nellis. 2002. "Winners and Losers: Assessing the Distributional Impact of Privatization." Working Paper 6. Washington, D.C.: Center for Global Development.

Blix, Hans. 2004. *Disarming Iraq*. New York: Pantheon.

Bloch-Elkon, Yaeli, and Robert Y. Shapiro. 2005. "Deep Suspicion: Iraq, Misperception, and Partisanship." *Public Opinion Pros*. http://www.publicopinionpros.com.

Bonner, Raymond. 1988. *Waltzing with a Dictator: The Marcoses and the Making of American Policy*. New York: Vintage.

Borjas, George J. 2003. "The Labor Demand Curve *Is* Downward Sloping: Reexamining the Impact of Immigration on the Labor Market." *Quarterly Journal of Economics* (November): 1335–74.

———. 2004. "Increasing the Supply of Labor through Immigration: Measuring the Impact on Native-born Workers." Center for Immigration Studies, Backgrounder (May). http://www.cis.org/articles/2004/back504.html.

Bouton, Marshall M., ed. 2004. *Global Views 2004: American Public Opinion and Foreign Policy*. Chicago: Chicago Council on Foreign Relations.

Bouton, Marshall M., and Benjamin I. Page, eds. 2002. *Worldviews 2002: American Public Opinion and Foreign Policy*. Chicago: Chicago Council on Foreign Relations.

Brehm, John. 1993. *The Phantom Respondents*. Ann Arbor: University of Michigan Press.

Brewer, Paul R., Kimberly Gross, Sean Aday, and Lars Wilnat. 2004. "International Trust and Public Opinion about World Affairs." *American Journal of Political Science* 48 (1):93–109.

Burke, Edmund. 1949. "Speech to the Electors of Bristol." In *Burke's Politics, Selected Writings and Speeches*. Ed. R. Hoffmann and P. Levack. New York: Alfred Knopf.

Cameron, Max, Robert Lawson, and Brian Tomlin, eds. 1998. *To Walk without Fear*. New York: Oxford University Press.

Campbell, Angus, Phillip E. Converse, Warren E. Miller, and Donald E. Stokes. 1960. *The American Voter*. New York: Wiley.

Caspary, William R. 1970. "The 'Mood Theory': A Study of Public Opinion and Foreign Policy." *American Political Science Review* 64:536–47.

Chang, LinChiat, and Jon A. Krosnick. 2003. "Comparing Oral Interviewing with Self-Administered Computerized Questionnaires: An Experiment." Unpublished paper, Ohio State University.

Chittick, William O., Keith R. Billingsley, and Rick Travis. 1995. "A Three-Dimensional Model of American Foreign Policy Beliefs." *International Studies Quarterly* 39(3):313–31.

Clark, Grenville, and Louis B. Sohn. 1966. *World Peace through World Law: Two Alternative Plans*. 3rd exp. ed. Cambridge, Mass.: Harvard University Press.

Converse, Philip E. 1964. "The Nature of Belief Systems in Mass Publics." In *Ideology and Discontent*, ed. David E. Apter, 206–61. New York: Free Press.

———. 1970. "Attitudes and Non-Attitudes: Continuation of a Dialogue." In *The Quantitative Analysis of Social Problems,* ed. Edward R. Tufte, 168–89. Reading, Mass.: Addison-Wesley.

Cook, Fay Lomax, Jason Barabas, and Benjamin I. Page. 2002a. "Invoking Public Opinion: Polls, Policy Debates, and the Future of Social Security." *Public Opinion Quarterly* 66(2):235–64.

———. 2002b. "Policy Elites Invoke Public Opinion: Polls, Policy Debates, and the Future of Social Security." In *Navigating Public Opinion: Polls, Policy, and the Future of American Democracy,* ed. Jeff Manza, Fay Lomax Cook, and Benjamin I. Page, 141–70. New York: Oxford University Press.

Cooper, John Milton. 2003. *Breaking the Heart of the World: Woodrow Wilson and the Fight for the League of Nations.* New York: Cambridge University Press.

Crossette, Barbara. 2002. "War Crimes Tribunal Becomes Reality, without U.S. Role." *New York Times,* April 12, A3.

Cumings, Bruce. 1990. *The Origins of the Korean War.* Vol. 2, *The Roaring of the Cataract 1947–1950.* Princeton: Princeton University Press.

Cyr, Arthur. 2000. *After the Cold War: American Foreign Policy, Europe, and Asia.* Rev. ed. New York: New York University Press. (Orig. pub. 1997.)

Daalder, Ivo H., and James M. Lindsay. 2003. *America Unbound: The Bush Revolution in Foreign Policy.* Washington, D.C.: Brookings.

Dahl, Robert A. 1989. *Democracy and Its Critics.* New Haven: Yale University Press.

———. 2003. *How Democratic Is the American Constitution?* 2nd ed. New Haven: Yale University Press.

Daniels, Roger. 1990. *Coming to America: A History of Immigration and Ethnicity in American Life.* New York: Harper Collins.

Delli Carpini, Michael X., and Scott Keeter. 1996. *What Americans Know about Politics and Why It Matters.* New Haven: Yale University Press.

Downs, Anthony. 1957. *An Economic Theory of Democracy.* New York: Harper & Row.

Doyle, Michael W. 1983. "Kant, Liberal Legacies, and Foreign Affairs." *Philosophy and Public Affairs* 12, no. 3 (summer): 205–35; 12, no. 4 (fall): 323–53.

———. 1997. *Ways of War and Peace.* New York: W. W. Norton.

Easterly, William. 2002. "What Did Structural Adjustment Adjust? The Association of Policies and Growth with Repeated IMF and World Bank Adjustment Loans." Working Paper 11. Washington, D.C.: Center for Global Development.

Edwards, George C., III. 2003. *On Deaf Ears: The Limits of the Bully Pulpit.* New Haven: Yale University Press.

Erikson, Robert. 1979. "The SRC Panel Data and Mass Political Attitudes." *British Journal of Political Science* 9:89–114.

Ethier, Wilfred J. 1995. *Modern International Economics.* 3rd ed. New York: W. W. Norton.

Feldman, Stanley. 1988. "Structure and Consistency in Public Opinion: The Role of Core Beliefs and Values." *American Journal of Political Science* 32:416–40.

———. 1989. "Reliability and Stability of Policy Positions: Evidence from a Five-wave Panel." *Political Analysis* 1:25–60.

Feldman, Stanley, and Marco R. Steenbergen. 2001. "The Humanitarian Foundation of Public Support for Social Welfare." *American Journal of Political Science* 45:658–77.

Fenno, Richard. 1978. *Homestyle: House Members in Their Districts.* Boston: Little, Brown.

Ferejohn, John A., and James H. Kuklinski, eds. 1990. *Information and Democratic Processes.* Urbana: University of Illinois Press.

Ferguson, Niall. 2005. *Colossus: The Rise and Fall of the American Empire.* Paperback ed. with new preface. New York: Penguin. (Orig. pub. 2004.)

Ferguson, Thomas. 1995. *Golden Rule: The Investment Theory of Party Competition and the Logic of Money-Driven Political Systems.* Chicago: University of Chicago Press.

Ferguson, Thomas, and Joel Rogers. 1986. *Right Turn: The Decline of the Democrats and the Future of American Politics.* New York: Hill and Wang.

Fiorina, Morris P. 1981. *Retrospective Voting in American National Elections.* New Haven: Yale University Press.

Fitzgerald, Frances. 2000. *Way Out There in the Blue: Reagan, Star Wars, and the End of the Cold War.* New York: Simon & Schuster.

Foroohar, Sina. 2003. "Question Wording and Public Support for Military Action against Iraq." Unpublished paper, Northwestern University.

Foster, H. Schuyler. 1983. *Activism Replaces Isolationism: U.S. Public Attitudes 1940–1975.* Washington, D.C.: Foxhall Press.

Foyle, Douglas. 1999. *Counting the Public In: Presidents, Public Opinion, and Foreign Policy.* New York: Columbia University Press.

Frieden, Jeffry. 1991. "Invested Interests: The Politics of National Economic Policies in a World of Global Finance." *International Organization* 45:425–51.

Friedman, Thomas L. 2000. *The Lexus and the Olive Tree.* New York: Random House.

Gamson, William. 1993. *Talking Politics.* New York: Cambridge University Press.

Gans, Herbert J. 1979. *Deciding What's News.* New York: Random House.

George, Alexander. 2002. "Domestic Constraints on Regime Change in U.S. Foreign Policy: The Need for Policy Legitimacy." In *American Foreign Policy: Theoretical Essays,* 4th ed, 320–44. Ed. G. John Ikenberry. New York: Longman.

Gilboa, Eytan. 1987. *American Public Opinion toward Israel and the Arab-Israeli Conflict.* Lexington, Mass.: D. C. Heath.

Glennon, Michael J. 2003. "Why the Security Council Failed." *Foreign Affairs* 82, no. 3 (May/June): 16–35.

Gonzalez, Guadeloupe, Susan Minushkin, and Robert Y. Shapiro, eds. 2004. *Global Views 2004: Mexican Public Opinion and Foreign Policy.* Mexico City: Centro de Investigacion y Docencia Economica, and Consejo Mexicano de Asuntos Internacionales.

Gourevitch, Peter. 1986. *Politics in Hard Times.* Ithaca, N.Y.: Cornell University Press.

Graham, Thomas W. 1989. "The Politics of Failure: Strategic Nuclear Arms Control, Public Opinion, and Domestic Politics in the United States, 1945–1985." PhD diss., Massachusetts Institute of Technology.

Grand, Stephen, Natalie La Balme, Julianne Smith, Pierangelo Isernia, and Philip Everts. 2002. *Worldviews 2002: European Public Opinion on Foreign Policy.* Washington, D.C.: German Marshall Fund.

Grossman, Gene, and Ehhanan Helpman. 1994. "Protection for Sale." *American Economic Review* 84 (September): 833–50.

———. 1995. "Trade Wars and Trade Talks." *Journal of Political Economy* 103 (August): 675–708.

Hallin, Daniel C. 1986. *The "Uncensored War": The Media and Vietnam.* New York: Oxford University Press.

Hamilton, Alexander, James Madison, and John Jay. 1961. *The Federalist Papers.* Ed. Clinton Rossiter. New York: New American Library. (Orig. pub. 1787–88.)

Hanson, Victor Davis. 2002. *An Autumn of War: What America Learned from September 11 and the War on Terrorism.* New York: Random House.

Hartley, Thomas, and Bruce Russett. 1992. "Public Opinion and the Common Defense: Who Governs Military Spending in the United States?" *American Political Science Review* 86:905–15.

Herman, Edward S., and Noam Chomsky. 1988. *Manufacturing Consent: The Political Economy of the Mass Media.* New York: Pantheon.

Hermann, Richard K., Philip E. Tetlock, and Penny S. Visser. 1999. "Mass Public Decisions to Go to War: A Cognitive-Interactionist Framework." *American Political Science Review* 93:553–73.

Hero, Alfred O., Jr. 1965. *The Southerner and World Affairs.* Baton Rouge: Louisiana State University Press.

———. 1966. "The American Public and the U.N., 1954–1966." *Journal of Conflict Resolution* 10:436–75.

Herring, George. 2001. *America's Longest War: The United States and Vietnam 1950–1975.* 4th ed. New York: McGraw-Hill.

Holbrook, A. L., M. C. Green, and J. A. Krosnick. 2003. "Telephone vs. Face-to-Face Interviewing of National Probability Samples with Long Questionnaires: Comparisons of Respondent Satisficing and Social Desirability." *Public Opinion Quarterly* 67:79–125.

Holsti, Ole R. 2004. *Public Opinion and American Foreign Policy.* Rev. ed. Ann Arbor: University of Michigan Press. (Orig. pub. 1996.)

Holsti, Ole R., and James N. Rosenau. 1984. *American Leadership in World Affairs: Vietnam and the Breakdown of Consensus.* London: Allen and Unwin.

Hurd, Ian. 2003. "Stayin' Alive: The Rumors of the UN's Death Have Been Greatly Exaggerated." *Foreign Affairs* 82, no. 4 (July/August).

Hurwitz, Jon, and Mark Peffley. 1987. "How Are Foreign Policy Attitudes Structured?" *American Political Science Review* 81:1099–1120.

Ikenberry, G. John. 2001. "Getting Hegemony Right." *National Interest,* spring, 17–24.

———. 2002. "America's Imperial Ambition." *Foreign Affairs,* September/October.

International Commission on Intervention and State Sovereignty. 2001. *The Responsibility to Protect.* Ottawa, Canada: International Development Research Center.

Iyengar, Shanto, and Donald R. Kinder. 1987. *News That Matters.* Chicago: University of Chicago Press.

Jacobs, Lawrence R. 2002. "The Presidency and the Press: The Paradox of the White House Communications War." In *The Presidency and the Political System,* 7th ed. Ed. Michael Nelson. Washington, D.C.: Congressional Quarterly Press.

Jacobs, Lawrence R., and Benjamin I. Page. 2005. "Who Influences U.S. Foreign Policy?" *American Political Science Review* 99:107–23.

Jacobs, Lawrence R.. and Robert Y. Shapiro. 1999. "Lyndon Johnson, Vietnam, and Public Opinion: Rethinking Realists' Theory of Leadership." *Presidential Studies Quarterly* 29 (September): 592–616.

———. 2000. *Politicians Don't Pander: Political Manipulation and the Loss of Democratic Responsiveness.* Chicago: University of Chicago Press.

Jacobs, Lawrence R., and Theda Skocpol, eds. 2005. *Inequality and American Democracy.* New York: Russell Sage.

Jentleson, Bruce W. 1992. "The Pretty Prudent Public: Post-Vietnam American Opinion on the Use of Military Force." *International Studies Quarterly* 36(1):49–74.

Jentleson, Bruce W., and Rebecca L. Britton. 1998. "Still Pretty Prudent: Post–Cold War American Public Opinion on the Use of Military Force." *Journal of Conflict Resolution* 42 (August): 395–487.

Johnson, Chalmers. 2004. *The Sorrows of Empire: Militarism, Secrecy, and the End of the Republic.* New York: Henry Holt.

Jones, Maldwn. 1992. *American Immigration.* Chicago: University of Chicago Press.

Just, Marion R., Ann N. Crigler, Dean E. Alger, Timothy E. Cook, Montague Kern, and Darrell E. West. 1996. *Crosstalk: Citizens, Candidates, and the Media in a Presidential Campaign.* Chicago: University of Chicago Press.

Kagan, Robert. 2003. *Of Paradise and Power: America and Europe in the New World Order.* New York: Knopf.

Kaiser, David. 2000. *American Tragedy: Kennedy, Johnson, and the Origins of the Vietnam War.* Cambridge: Harvard University Press.

Kaul, Inge, Isabelle Grunberg, and Marc A. Stern, eds. 1999. *Global Public Goods: International Cooperation in the 21st Century.* New York: Oxford University Press.

Kennan, George. 1951. *American Diplomacy, 1900–1950.* Chicago: University of Chicago Press.

Kennedy, Craig, and Marshall M. Bouton. 2002. "The Real Trans-Atlantic Gap." *Foreign Policy,* November/December, 66–74.

Keohane, Robert O. 1984. *After Hegemony: Cooperation and Discord in the World Political Economy.* Princeton: Princeton University Press.

Keohane, Robert O., and Helen Milner, eds. 1996. *Internationalization and Domestic Politics.* Cambridge: Cambridge University Press.

Key, V. O., Jr. 1961. *Public Opinion and American Democracy.* New York: Knopf.

Kinder, Donald R. 1983. "Diversity and Complexity in American Public Opinion." In *Political Science: The State of the Discipline,* ed. Ada W. Finifter. Washington, D.C.: American Political Science Association.

Kingdon, John. 1989. *Congressmen's Voting Decisions.* 3rd ed. Ann Arbor: University of Michigan Press.

Kish, Leslie. 1995. *Survey Sampling.* New York: Wiley. (Orig. pub. 1965.)

Knock, Thomas J. 1995. *To End All Wars: Woodrow Wilson and the Quest for a New World Order.* Princeton: Princeton University Press.

Krasner, Stephen. 1978. *In Defense of the National Interest: Raw Materials, Investments, and U.S. Foreign Policy.* Princeton: Princeton University Press.

Krauthammer, Charles. 2001. "The New Unilateralism." *Washington Post,* June 8, A29.

Kristol, William, and Lawrence Kaplan. 2003. *The War over Iraq: Saddam's Tyranny and America's Mission.* San Francisco: Encounter Books.

Krugman, Paul R., and Maurice Obstfeld. 2003. *International Economics.* 6th ed. New York: Addison-Wesley.

Kuklinski, James H., and Paul J. Quirk. 2000. "Reconsidering the Rational Public: Cognition, Heuristics, and Mass Opinion." In *Elements of Reason: Cognition, Choice, and the Bounds of Rationality,* ed. Arthur Lupia, Mathew D. McCubbins and Samuel L. Popkin, 153–82. New York: Cambridge University Press.

Kull, Steven. 1995. *Americans and Foreign Aid: A Study of American Public Attitudes.* Washington, D.C.: Program on International Policy Attitudes.

———. 2001a. *Americans on Foreign Aid and World Hunger: A Study of U.S. Public Attitudes.* Washington, D.C.: Program on International Policy Attitudes.

———. 2001b. "Vox Americani." *Foreign Policy,* September/October, 29–38.

Kull, Steven, and I. M. Destler. 1999. *Misreading the Public: The Myth of a New Isolationism.* Washington, D.C.: Brookings.

Kull, Steven, Clay Ramsay, and Evan Lewis. 2003–4. "Misperceptions, the Media, and the Iraq War." *Political Science Quarterly* 118(4):569–98.

Kusnitz, Leonard A. 1984. *Public Opinion and Foreign Policy: America's China Policy, 1949–1979.* Westport, CT: Greenwood.

LaFeber, Walter. 1994. *The American Age: U.S. Foreign Policy at Home and Abroad.* 2nd ed. New York: W. W. Norton.

Lazarsfeld, Paul F., Bernard Berelson, and Hazel Gaudet. 1968. *The People's Choice: How the Voter Makes Up His Mind in a Presidential Campaign.* 3rd ed. New York: Columbia University Press. (Orig. pub. 1944.)

Leamer, Edward E. 1995. "U.S. Wages, Technological Change, and Globalization." *Jobs and Capital,* Milken Institute for Job and Capital Formation (summer), 4–10.

Lippmann, Walter. 1925. *The Phantom Public.* New York: Macmillan.

———. 1955. *Essays in the Public Philosophy.* Boston: Little, Brown.

———. 1965. *Public Opinion.* New York: Macmillan. (Orig. pub. 1922.)

Longworth, Richard C. 1998. *Global Squeeze: The Coming Crisis for First-World Nations.* Chicago: Contemporary Books.

Lupia, Arthur, and Mathew D. McCubbins. 1998. *The Democratic Dilemma: Can Citizens Learn What They Need to Know?* New York: Cambridge University Press.

Lupia, Arthur, Mathew D. McCubbins, and Samuel L. Popkin, eds. 2000. *Elements of Reason: Cognition, Choice, and the Bounds of Rationality.* New York: Cambridge University Press.

Maggiotto, M. A., and E. R. Wittkopf. 1981. "American Public Attitudes toward Foreign Policy." *International Studies Quarterly* 25:601–31.

Mandelbaum, M., and W. Schneider. 1979. "The New Internationalisms." In *Eagle Entangled: U.S. Foreign Policy in a Complex World,* ed. K. A. Oye, D. Rothchild, and R. J. Lieber, 34–88. New York: Longman.

Mander, Jerry, and Edward Goldsmith, eds. 1996. *The Case against the Global Economy and for a Turn toward the Local.* Berkeley, Calif.: Sierra Club Books.

Mann, James. 2004. *The Rise of the Vulcans: The History of Bush's War Cabinet.* New York: Viking.

Mansbridge, Jane. 2003. "Rethinking Representation." *American Political Science Review* 97:515–28.

Marcus, George E. 2002. *The Sentimental Citizen: Emotion in Democratic Politics.* State College: Pennsylvania State University Press.

Marcus, George E., W. Russell Neuman, and Michael MacKuen. 2000. *Affective Intelligence and Political Judgment.* Chicago: University of Chicago Press.

Markusen, Ann R., Peter Hall, Sabrina Deitrich, and Scott Campbell. 1991. *The Rise of the Gunbelt: The Military Remapping of Industrial America.* New York: Oxford University Press.

Mathews, Jessica. 1989. "Redefining Security." *Foreign Affairs,* spring.

Mayer, William G. 1992. *The Changing American Mind: How and Why American Public Opinion Changed between 1960 and 1988.* Ann Arbor: University of Michigan Press.

Mayhew, David R. 1974. *Congress: The Electoral Connection.* New Haven: Yale University Press.

McManus, Susan A., with Patricia A. Turner. 1996. *Young v. Old: Generational Combat in the 21st Century.* Boulder, CO: Westview.

Mead, Walter Russell. 2002. *Special Providence: American Foreign Policy and How It Changed the World.* New York: Routledge.

Mearsheimer, John J. 2001. *The Tragedy of Great Power Politics.* New York: W. W. Norton.

Mearsheimer, John J., and Stephen Walt. 2003. "An Unnecessary War." *Foreign Policy,* January/February.

Merk, Frederick. 1966. *The Monroe Doctrine and American Expansionism, 1843–1849.* New York: Knopf.

Milner, Helen. 1988. *Resisting Protectionism.* Princeton: Princeton University Press.

———. 1997. *Interests, Institutions, and Information: Domestic Politics and International Relations.* Princeton: Princeton University Press.

Monroe, Alan D. 1979. "Consistency between Public Preferences and National Policy Decisions." *American Politics Quarterly* 7:3–19.

———. 1998. "Public Opinion and Public Policy 1980–1993." *Public Opinion Quarterly* 62:6–28.

Moravcsik, Andy. 1997. "Taking Preferences Seriously: A Liberal Theory of International Politics." *International Organization* 51 (autumn): 513–53.

Morgenthau, Hans. 1973. *Politics among Nations: The Struggle for Power and Peace.* 5th ed. New York: Knopf. (Orig. pub. 1948.)

Morris, Edmund. 1979. *The Rise of Theodore Roosevelt.* New York: Random House.

———. 2001. *Theodore Rex.* New York: Random House.

Mueller, John. 1973. *War, Presidents and Public Opinion.* New York: Wiley.

———. 1994. *Policy and Opinion in the Gulf War.* Chicago: University of Chicago Press.

Nye, Joseph S., Jr. 2002. *The Paradox of American Power: Why the World's Only Superpower Can't Go It Alone.* New York: Oxford University Press.

———. 2004. *Soft Power: The Means to Success in World Politics.* New York: Public Affairs.

Ostrom, Charles, and Brian Job. 1986. "The President and the Political Use of Force." *American Political Science Review* 80:541–66.

Paden, Catherine, and Benjamin I. Page. 2003. "Congress Invokes Public Opinion on Welfare Reform." *American Politics Research* 31(6):670–79.

Page, Benjamin I. 1978. *Choices and Echoes in Presidential Elections: Rational Man and Electoral Democracy.* Chicago: University of Chicago Press.

———. 1996. *Who Deliberates? Mass Media in Modern Democracy.* Chicago: University of Chicago Press.

———. 1997. "Trouble for Workers and the Poor: Economic Globalization and the Reshaping of American Politics." Paper presented at the annual meeting of the Midwest Political Science Association, Chicago. April 10–12.

Page, Benjamin I., and Jason Barabas. 2000. "Foreign Policy Gaps between Citizens and Leaders." *International Studies Quarterly* 44:339–64.

Page, Benjamin I., and Julia Rabinovich. 2005. "Twisting the Lion's Tail? Effects of Religion and Ethnicity on Americans' Feelings toward Foreign Countries." Unpublished paper, Northwestern University.

Page, Benjamin I., Julia Rabinovich, and David G. Tully. 2005. "How Americans Feel about South Korea, and Why." Paper presented at the conference on Living under U.S. Leadership. Seoul, Korea: East Asia Institute. August 19–20.

Page, Benjamin I., and Robert Y. Shapiro. 1983. "Effects of Public Opinion on Policy." *American Political Science Review* 77:175–90.

———. 1992. *The Rational Public: Fifty Years of Trends in Americans' Policy Preferences.* Chicago: University of Chicago Press.

Page, Benjamin I., Robert Y. Shapiro, and Glenn R. Dempsey. 1987. "What Moves Public Opinion?" *American Political Science Review* 81:23–43.

Page, Benjamin I., and James R. Simmons. 2000. *What Government Can Do: Dealing with Poverty and Inequality.* Chicago: University of Chicago Press.

Peffley, Mark, and Jon Hurwitz. 1992. "International Events and Foreign Policy Beliefs: Public Response to Changing U.S.-Soviet Relations." *American Journal of Political Science* 36 (May): 431–61.

Pei, Minxin, and Sara Kasper. 2003."Lessons from the Past: The American Record on Nation Building." Policy Brief 24 (May). Washington, D.C.: Carnegie Endowment for International Peace.

Perkins, Dexter. 1966. *The Monroe Doctrine, 1823–1826.* Gloucester, Mass.: P. Smith.

Peterson, Susan. 1995. "How Democracies Differ: Public Opinion, State Structure, and the Lessons of the Fashoda Crisis." *Security Studies* 5 (autumn): 3–37.

Pincus, Jonathan R., and Jeffrey A. Winters, eds. 2002. *Reinventing the World Bank.* Ithaca, N.Y.: Cornell University Press.

Pitkin, Hannah Fenichel. 1967. *The Concept of Representation.* Berkeley: University of California Press.

Pletcher, David M. 1975. *The Diplomacy of Annexation: Texas, Oregon and the Mexican War.* 2nd ed. Columbia: University of Missouri Press.

Pomper, Gerald M. 1972. "From Confusion to Clarity: Issues and American Voters 1956–1968." *American Political Science Review* 66:415–28.

Popkin, Samuel L. 1991. *The Reasoning Voter: Communication and Persuasion in Presidential Campaigns.* Chicago: University of Chicago Press.

Powell, Colin L. 1995. *My American Journey.* With Joseph E. Persico. New York: Random House.

Powlick, Philip J. 1991. "The Attitudinal Bases for Responsiveness to Public Opinion among American Foreign Policy Officials." *Journal of Conflict Resolution* 35:611–41.

———. 1995. "The Sources of Public Opinion for American Foreign Policy Officials." *International Studies Quarterly* 39:427–52.

Prados, John. 2004. *Hoodwinked: The Documents That Reveal How Bush Sold Us a War.* New York: New Press.

Rampton, Sheldon, and John Stauber. 2003. *Weapons of Mass Deception: The Uses of Propaganda in Bush's War on Iraq.* New York: Penguin.

Reich, Robert B. 1997. *Locked in the Cabinet.* New York: Knopf.

Richman, Alvin, Eloise Malone, and David B. Nolle. 1997. "Testing Foreign Policy Belief Structures of the American Public in the Post–Cold War Period: Cross Validations from Two National Surveys." *Political Research Quarterly* 50(4):939–55.

Rielly, John E., ed. 1975. *American Public Opinion and U.S. Foreign Policy 1975.* Chicago: Chicago Council on Foreign Relations. Parallel studies published in 1979, 1983, 1987, 1991, 1995, and 1999.

Rifkin, Jeremy. 1995. *The End of Work: The Decline of the Global Labor Force and the Dawn of the Post-Market Era.* New York: G. P. Putnam's Sons.

Risse-Kappen, Thomas. 1991. "Public Opinion, Domestic Structure, and Foreign Policy." *World Politics* 43:479–512.

Rodrik, Dani. 1997. *Has Globalization Gone Too Far?* Washington, D.C.: Institute for International Economics.

———, ed. 2003. *In Search of Prosperity: Analytic Narratives on Economic Growth.* Princeton: Princeton University Press.

Rogowski, Ronald. 1989. *Commerce and Coalitions.* Princeton: Princeton University Press.

Rosenau, James N. 1961. *Public Opinion and Foreign Policy.* New York: Random House.

Russett, Bruce. 1990. *Controlling the Sword: The Democratic Governance of National Security.* Cambridge, MA: Harvard University Press.

———. 1996. "Why Democratic Peace?" In *Debating the Democratic Peace,* ed. M. Brown, S. Lynn-Jones, and S. Miller, 82–115. Cambridge, MA: MIT Press.

Russett, Bruce, and John Oneal. 2001. *Triangulating Peace: Democracy, Interdependence, and International Organizations.* New York: W. W. Norton.

Sachs, Jeffrey D. 2005. "The Development Challenge." *Foreign Affairs* 84, no. 2 (March/April): 78–90.

Samuelson, Paul A. 1948. "International Trade and the Equalization of Factor Prices." *Economic Journal* 58:181–97.

Sartori, Giovanni. 1987. *The Theory of Democracy Revisited.* Chatham, NJ: Chatham House.

Schattschneider, E. E. 1960. *The Semi-sovereign People: A Realist's View of Democracy in America.* New York: Holt, Rinehart and Winston.

Schuman, Howard, and Stanley Presser. 1981. *Questions and Answers in Attitude Surveys: Experiments on Question Form, Wording, and Context.* New York: Academic Press.

Schumpeter, Joseph. 1947. *Capitalism, Socialism and Democracy.* 2nd ed. New York: Harper.

Sewall, Sarah B., and Carl Kaysen, eds. 2000. *The United States and the International Criminal Court: National Security and International Law.* New York: Rowman & Littlefield.

Shapiro, Robert Y., and Yaeli Bloch-Elkon. 2005. "Partisan Conflict in the United States and Prospects for an International Security Order." Paper presented at the conference on Living under U.S. Leadership. Seoul, Korea: East Asian Institute. August 19–20.

Shapiro, Robert Y., and Harpreet Mahajan. 1986. "Gender Differences in Policy Preferences: A Summary of Trends from the 1960s to the 1980s." *Public Opinion Quarterly* 50:42–61.

Sigal, Leon V. 1973. *Reporters and Officials: The Organization and Politics of Newsmaking.* Lexington, Mass.: D. C. Heath.

Silverstein, Gordon. 1997. *Imbalance of Powers: Constitutional Interpretation and the Making of American Foreign Policy.* New York: Oxford University Press.

Smith, James P., and Barry Edmonston. 1997. *The New Americans: Economic, Demographic and Fiscal Effects of Immigration.* Washington, D.C.: National Academy Press.

Sniderman, Paul M., Richard A. Brody, and Philip E. Tetlock. 1991. *Reasoning and Choice: Explorations in Political Psychology.* New York: Cambridge University Press, 1991.

Snyder, Jack. 1991. *Myths of Empire: Domestic Politics and International Ambition.* Ithaca: Cornell University Press.

Sobel, Richard. 2001. *The Impact of Public Opinion on U.S. Foreign Policy since Vietnam.* New York: Oxford University Press.

Sperling, Gene, and Tom Hart. 2003. "A Better Way to Fight Global Poverty: Broadening the Millennium Challenge Account." *Foreign Affairs* 82(2):9–14.

Steele, A. J. 1966. *The American People and China.* New York: McGraw-Hill.

Stiglitz, Joseph. 2002. *Globalization and Its Discontents.* New York: Norton.

Stolper, Wolfgang F., and Paul A. Samuelson. 1941. "Protection and Real Wages." *Review of Economic Studies* 9(1):58–73.

Stueck, William. 2002. *Rethinking the Korean War: A New Diplomatic and Strategic History.* Princeton: Princeton University Press.

Sullivan, Denis, and Roger D. Masters. 1988. "'Happy Warriors': Leaders' Facial Displays, Viewers' Emotions, and Political Support." *American Journal of Political Science* 32:345–68.

Surowiecki, James. 2004. *The Wisdom of Crowds.* New York: Doubleday.

Trubowitz, Peter. 1998. *Defining the National Interest: Conflict and Change in American Foreign Policy.* Chicago: University of Chicago Press.

United Nations. 2004. *Charter of the United Nations and Statute of the International Court of Justice.* New York: United Nations Department of Public Information.

United Nations Commission on Global Governance. 1995. *Our Global Neighborhood.* New York: United Nations.

United Nations Commission on Human Security. 2003. *Human Security Now.* New York: United Nations. http://www.humansecurity-chs.org/finalreport.

United Nations Development Programme. 2004. *United Nations Human Development Report 2004.* New York: United Nations. http://hdr.undp.org.

United States National Security Council. 2002. *The National Security Strategy of the United States of America.* Washington, D.C.: National Security Council. September.

United States Office of Management and Budget. 2005a. *Budget of the United States, Fiscal Year 2006.* Washington, D.C.: U.S. Government Printing Office.

United States Office of Management and Budget. 2005b. *Budget of the United States, Fiscal Year 2006: Historical Tables.* Washington, D.C.: U.S. Government Printing Office.

Walt, Stephen M. 2005. *Taming American Power: The Global Response to U.S. Primacy.* New York: W. W. Norton.

Walton, Gary, and Hugh Rockoff. 1998. *History of the American Economy.* 8th ed. Mason, OH: Thomson-Southwestern.

Waltz, Kenneth. 1979. *Theory of International Politics.* Reading, MA: Addison-Wesley.

Walzer, Michael. 2000. *Just and Unjust Wars: A Moral Argument with Historical Illustrations.* 3rd ed. New York: Basic. (Orig. pub. 1977.)

Weinberg, Albert K. 1935. *Manifest Destiny: A Study of Nationalist Expansionism in American History.* Baltimore: Johns Hopkins University Press.

Wildavsky, Aaron. 1991. "The Two Presidencies." In *The Two Presidencies: A Quarter Century Assessment,* ed. Steven Shull, 11–25. Chicago: Nelson-Hall Publishers.

Wilson, Joseph. 2004. *The Politics of Truth: Inside the Lies That Led to War and Betrayed My Wife's CIA Identity.* New York: Carroll & Graf.

Wise, David. 1973. *The Politics of Lying.* New York: Random House.

Wittkopf, Eugene R. 1986. "On the Foreign Policy Beliefs of the American People: A Critique and Some Evidence." *International Studies Quarterly* 30 (December): 425–45.

——. 1990. *Faces of Internationalism: Public Opinion and American Foreign Policy.* Durham, N.C.: Duke University Press.

Wittkopf, Eugene R., and M. A. Maggiotto. 1983. "Elites and Masses: A Comparative Analysis of Attitudes toward America's World Role." *Journal of Politics* 45:303–34.

Wong, Kar-yiu. 1995. *International Trade in Goods and Factor Mobility.* Cambridge, Mass.: MIT Press.

Woodward, Bob. 2004. *Plan of Attack.* New York: Simon & Schuster.

Yankelovich, Daniel. 2005. "Poll Positions." *Foreign Affairs* 84, no. 5 (September/October): 2–16.

Zaller, John R. 1992. *The Nature and Origins of Mass Opinion.* New York: Cambridge University Press.

———. 2003. "Coming to Grips with V. O. Key's Concept of Latent Opinion." In *Electoral Democracy,* ed. Michael MacKuen and George Rabinovitz. Ann Arbor: University of Michigan Press.

Zaller, John R., and Stanley Feldman. 1992. "A Simple Model of the Survey Response: Answering Questions versus Revealing Preferences." *American Journal of Political Science* 36:579–616.

Zolberg, Aristide. 2006. *A Nation by Design: Immigration Policy in the Making of America.* Cambridge: Harvard University Press.

Index